A GUIDE
AMERICAN
SILVER EAGLES

Joshua McMorrow-Hernandez

Foreword by
Q. David Bowers

Whitman
Publishing, LLC
PUBLISHING SINCE 1934
Whitman.com

A GUIDE BOOK OF
AMERICAN SILVER EAGLES

© 2023 Whitman Publishing, LLC
1974 Chandalar Drive, Suite D, Pelham, AL 35124

Correspondence concerning this book may be directed to
Whitman Publishing, Attn: American Silver Eagles, at the address above.

ISBN: 0794849792
Printed in China

Disclaimer: Expert opinion should be sought in any significant numismatic purchase. This book is presented as a guide only. No warranty or representation of any kind is made concerning the completeness of the information presented. The author, a professional numismatist, regularly buys, sells, and holds certain of the items discussed in this book.

Caveat: The value estimates given are subject to variation and differences of opinion. Before making decisions to buy or sell, consult the latest information. Past performance of the rare-coin market or any coin or series within that market is not necessarily an indication of future performance, as the future is unknown. Such factors as changing demand, popularity, grading interpretations, strength of the overall coin market, and economic conditions will continue to be influences.

Other books in the Bowers Series include: *A Guide Book of Morgan Silver Dollars; A Guide Book of Double Eagle Gold Coins; A Guide Book of United States Type Coins; A Guide Book of Modern United States Proof Coin Sets; A Guide Book of Shield and Liberty Head Nickels; A Guide Book of Flying Eagle and Indian Head Cents; A Guide Book of Washington Quarters; A Guide Book of Buffalo and Jefferson Nickels; A Guide Book of Lincoln Cents; A Guide Book of United States Commemorative Coins; A Guide Book of United States Tokens and Medals; A Guide Book of Gold Dollars; A Guide Book of Peace Dollars; A Guide Book of the Official Red Book of United States Coins; A Guide Book of Franklin and Kennedy Half Dollars; A Guide Book of Civil War Tokens; A Guide Book of Hard Times Tokens; A Guide Book of Mercury Dimes, Standing Liberty Quarters, and Liberty Walking Half Dollars; A Guide Book of Half Cents and Large Cents; A Guide Book of Barber Silver Coins; A Guide Book of Liberty Seated Silver Coins; A Guide Book of Modern United States Dollar Coins; A Guide Book of the United States Mint; A Guide Book of Gold Eagles; A Guide Book of Continental Currency and Coins;* and *A Guide Book of Quarter Eagle Gold Coins.*

Whitman Publishing is a leading publisher of numismatic reference books, supplies, and storage and display products that help you build, appreciate, and share great collections. To browse our complete catalog, visit Whitman Publishing online at www.Whitman.com.

If you enjoy this book, we invite you to learn more about America's history by starting a new coin collection and reading as much as possible.

You can join the American Numismatic Association (ANA), the nation's largest hobby group for coin collectors. Collect coins and other currency, learn about numismatics, and make new friends in the hobby. Explore the ANA at Money.org.

Whitman®

CONTENTS

Foreword *by Q. David Bowers* iv

Publisher's Preface vi

Introduction. viii

Chapter 1: Before the American Silver Eagle. 1

Chapter 2: There's Something About Silver Dollars. 19

Chapter 3: A Modern Silver Dollar for Modern Times. 35

Chapter 4: Minting a Legendary Coin 62

Chapter 5: The American Silver Eagle: Collecting and Investing. 112

Chapter 6: Key Dates, Varieties, and Errors 162

Chapter 7: A New Generation of American Silver Eagles. 174

Chapter 8: Analysis and Market Guide to American Silver Eagles 208

Appendix A: Can You Retire on Your Coins? 341

Appendix B: Protecting Your Coins from the Elements 348

Appendix C: Keeping Track of Your Coins Can Be Taxing 353

Bibliography 361

About the Author. 368

Credits and Acknowledgements 368

Image Credits 368

Index 370

FOREWORD

Welcome to the first edition of the *Guide Book of American Silver Eagles*—and I say "first edition" because I'm certain many more will follow! The bullion coin series covered in this volume has been with us for more than 35 years, and it shows no sign of slowing down.

There's something to be said for longevity in the hobby of coin collecting. The Bowers Series of reference books— of which this is volume 28—will soon celebrate its 20th anniversary, and I myself have been in numismatics as a hobbyist and a professional for 70 years.

Maybe you're new to the hobby yourself, and American Silver Eagles are your gateway to the fun and excitement. Or you might be a longtime collector, and these coins are a series you've collected for decades, or one you're just beginning to explore. Whatever your experience level, you have a talented guide in Joshua McMorrow-Hernandez, who shares insight to help you understand and appreciate American Silver Eagles. Read and learn from Josh's book, and you can build a beautiful and valuable collection of your own.

Josh himself is no newcomer to the hobby. He's written about coins for many years, as a freelance journalist, a market reporter, and a book author. His enthusiasm for American Silver Eagles is contagious!

In 1986, the year the American Eagle bullion program was launched, Florence M. Schook was president of the American Numismatic Association. My own term as president had just ended. Florence emphasized, as I always have, the importance of *knowledge* in the hobby, more than just buying and selling, and she dedicated her energy to educating collectors, especially young collectors. She would be pleased to see the growth in the number of coin-related books published since then, certainly in the past 20 years.

American Silver Eagles deserve their own books among the hobby's literature. They're popular—any program that sells 600 million or more coins is an unqualified barnburner! And they appeal to a variety of interests. Maybe you're an investor or speculator, looking to build a reserve of precious metal. American Silver Eagles fill the bill nicely. You could be a hobbyist who collects from pocket change and has never bought a "rare" coin before, and be drawn in by the American Silver Eagle's attractive designs. If you like challenging and interesting series, American Silver Eagles boast Proof coins of flawless quality, rarities that make the 1909-S V.D.B. cent look common, and many innovative new finishes and formats to collect. And if you're a history buff, as I am, the American Silver Eagles beckon. They were born in a fascinating numismatic era and they connect to many points of national and international historical interest.

I remember in 1985 I was introduced at a symposium as "one of the leading figures in the coin industry." This prompted me to reply that I don't consider myself an *industrialist*—someone who presides over factories and loading docks and railroad connections. Instead, I consider myself to be a *professional numismatist*. I might be industrious, but I'm not an industrialist! In the same era of 1985, 1986, 1987, as the American Eagle program was in planning and then got underway, more and more newcomers to coin collecting were expressing interest in *investment* and *price appreciation*. A senior numismatist at my firm, Bowers and Merena Galleries, shared with me typical questions he was hearing from people just entering the hobby: "What kind of profits will I see next year on coins I buy today? What newsletters should I subscribe to if I want to maximize my investment? What coin series is the hottest now? What will be hot tomorrow?"

In the *Guide Book of American Silver Eagles*, Josh explores the almost unique collector/investor energy that these coins enjoy—part of what sells them in the millions. Not only do they capture the eyes and imaginations of hobbyists, but they also appeal to investors and speculators, the "silver bugs" and "stackers" attracted to their precious-metal content. This two-audiences-in-one appeal isn't entirely unique: There's another coin series that shares the same high level of popularity among both collectors and investors. That coin is the classic Morgan silver dollar of 1878 to 1921, a personal favorite of mine. Inside this delightful book, Josh shows us why many collectors and dealers consider the American Silver Eagle "the Morgan dollar of today."

Get ready to immerse yourself in one of the biggest and most important coinage programs of modern times. There's a lot to learn in the *Guide Book of American Silver Eagles*, and fun to be had while collecting. Enjoy!

Q. David Bowers
Wolfeboro, New Hampshire

David Bowers has been in the rare-coin business since he was a teenager in 1953, including in later times as a founder of Stack's Bowers Galleries. He has served as president of the American Numismatic Association (1983–1985) and president of the Professional Numismatists Guild (1977–1979); he is a recipient of the highest honor bestowed by the ANA (the Farran Zerbe Award); he was the first ANA member to be named Numismatist of the Year (1995); and he is one of only a few living people enshrined in the Numismatic Hall of Fame. Bowers is a recipient of the highest honor given by the Professional Numismatists Guild and has received more Book of the Year Awards and Best Columnist honors given by the Numismatic Literary Guild than any other writer. For Whitman Publishing, he has been the numismatic director since 2003. In Wolfeboro, New Hampshire, he previously served on the Board of Selectmen and as the town historian.

Publisher's Preface

The American Silver Eagle is one of the most popularly collected U.S. coins today—and it has some of the most passionate collectors. At Whitman Publishing headquarters we witnessed this in no uncertain terms in 2018.

That year, under pressure to fit more and more America the Beautiful quarters, commemoratives, and other content into the *Red Book*, which was already bursting at the seams, we made a radical change to our coverage of bullion coins: We condensed the book's silver, gold, and platinum bullion from 21 pages into 8 pages. Instead of the usual highly detailed charts with mintages and pricing for each coin, we summarized each bullion program with a bit of historical information, a narrative giving typical price ranges for various formats (Proof, bullion strike, etc.), and brief descriptions and pricing for the key dates. The American Silver Eagles were trimmed down from two pages to one.

In hindsight, I can firmly say—*the page savings were not worth it!*

Almost immediately after the 72nd edition of the *Red Book* hit the shelves, we started getting phone calls and emails from alarmed collectors. "What happened to the Silver Eagles?" "The *Red Book* is where I always go for mintages." "You've made a big mistake!"

It was the most vociferous, widespread, grassroots wave of feedback we've received on any *Red Book* subject in the nearly 20 years I've been Whitman's publisher.

Determined to make things right, we quickly laid out the American Silver Eagles in their previous highly detailed format and created a PDF to email or mail to anyone who contacted us with a complaint. You can rest assured that in 2019, in the 73rd edition of the *Red Book*, the American Silver Eagles were back to their two full pages of complete coverage!

Today as I write this preface, these popular (and staunchly defended) coins occupy about two and a half pages in the 76th edition of the *Red Book*, and we're planning an expansion to four pages in the 77th edition, with pricing in more grades.

Joshua McMorrow-Hernandez's new *Guide Book of American Silver Eagles* is the latest in-depth reference on these coins. It joins John M. Mercanti's *American Silver Eagles: A Guide to the U.S. Bullion Coin Program*, which has been a Whitman best-seller since its first edition debuted. Before Mercanti's book was published in 2012, collectors had only hobby newspapers and magazines, online forums, and coin-shop and coin-show conversations to guide them in their collecting, along with the *Red Book*'s annual coverage of the latest coins and sets. There was no comprehensive book-length study.

Mercanti, working with professional numismatist Michael "Miles" Standish, brought personal insight to the study of American Silver Eagles—he was, after all, the designer and sculptor of the coin's original reverse. Now Joshua McMorrow-Hernandez, in the *Guide Book of American Silver Eagles*, expands the theme with even more historical information and interviews with Mint officials, silver-mine suppliers, CCAC committee members, active dealers, experienced collectors, investment advisors, and others involved in the nation's best-selling bullion coin program. He brings a journalist's hunger for answers and a market analyst's focus on numbers, to show readers how to wisely build a valuable numismatic collection (or, if they prefer, how to spend intelligently as a bullion investor).

In the summer of 2022, I informally polled 114 hobbyists for their opinions on American Silver Eagles. The results were interesting:

- 41 percent identify themselves as either a collector or an investor (or both) in American Silver Eagles (4 percent active collector; 1 percent active investor; 9 percent active collector and investor; 12 percent casual collector; 4 percent casual investor; and 11 percent casual collector and investor).
- 39 percent own some of the coins, but don't consider them a carefully assembled collection or a significant investment.
- 20 percent don't collect or invest in them at all, and don't own any.

Within these numbers we see a coin with broad presence in the hobby community. The data also show a population of casual buyers who might jump to more active collecting and investing.

It's anecdotally informative to look beyond the numbers and learn collectors' and investors' opinions and the feelings inspired by the American Silver Eagle.

One collector of Liberty Walking half dollars said, "The ASE is a great way to see a fully struck, larger-sized Walker." Another called them "one of the most beautiful coins of the 1900s, if not the most beautiful."

One hobbyist buys "two every year to keep the set current. I'll pass them to my two kids someday." On a similar note: "Mainly I buy them every year to give out as Christmas presents to some relatives and to people at work."

For some, buying comes down to price: "When I have extra cash, I get a few as bullion, but it depends on the premium." "Highly recommend for investment. I go where the deal is. Both slabbed and raw. They are a really super deal vs. generic silver dollars, plus have more silver in them. I will not buy classic dollars at current prices." And "They are fun to own, and I salt some away when silver is low."

Of course, not every hobbyist is a fan of the American Silver Eagle. One young collector who favors Barber silver coinage said, "A coin has to be older than me to attract my attention." A skeptic who doesn't own any dismissed American Silver Eagles as "just more hunks of silver."

Many, though, describe the coins as "fun," and those lucky enough to own the series' rarities love to talk about them. "Yes, I have the 1995-W . . . had it since 1996!" bragged one collector. Another reminisced, "I got the home-run from the Mint, the 2019 Enhanced Reverse Proof—which I traded for 13 Silver Eagles and an ounce of gold!"

Joshua McMorrow-Hernandez explores these angles of the American Silver Eagle and many more in his new book. This is a guide for the active buyer, a history for the numismatist, and an inspiration for those yet to join the field. Whether you're new to silver bullion or a longtime collector or investor, you'll find much to learn and profit from in the *Guide Book of American Silver Eagles*.

Dennis Tucker
Publisher, Whitman Publishing

INTRODUCTION

My introduction to American Silver Eagles came about in a most interesting way. My cousin, who also collected coins at the time, had visited from out of town for a short summer vacation during 1993. So, there we were—along with my sister, herself a collector back then—three kids talking about coins as a shared interest during much of our cousin's visit. My mom and dad, who encouraged my numismatic pursuits by purchasing books and magazines on the hobby, had heard about a fairly large local coin show that was happening during the week of my cousin's visit. It was to occur over the course of four days, ending on a Sunday. My family and I had never been to a coin show before, but Sunday was our best day to attend for a couple hours in the afternoon—and the advertisement in that Sunday's newspaper declared it was running from 10 a.m. to 6 p.m. that day.

The show was held in the event hall of a ritzy shoreside hotel in Sand Key, Florida. My dad had driven us over and my mom, wanting to make sure we were at the right place, hopped out of the van to scope out the event before getting all of us kids. She walked into the hotel lobby and was back out before too long, visibly upset. The show manager had apparently told her they were already closing up shop—that it was the last day and most of the dealers were heading home. My mom, armed with the newspaper advertisement touting the four-day show and the published hours, reasoned it was still at least two hours before the advertised closing time.

She went back inside to talk with one of the club's top brass and see if there was any way they could let us at least check out the bourse floor, if even for a short bit. She must've been inside the lobby talking with the club's leaders for at least five or ten minutes. Soon, she returned to the van holding three silver coins in plastic flips and announced that the show manager had apologized for the situation. They wanted us to come in and visit with the few coin dealers who were still there—they'd stick around for us for the next half an hour or so.

As she announced to us kids this news, she started passing around the three coins she had been given. She said they were called "Silver Eagles" and that they were brand new—dated for that year, 1993—and that we should save them. I had never seen such a large, heavy, or shiny silver coin; not even the cull Morgan dollar I had spent $5.50 to purchase a few months earlier, for my first twentieth-century type set, could compare.

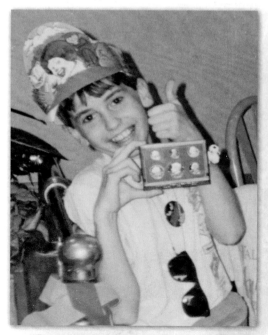

The author, then 12 years old, holding the 1981 United States Proof set he received as a birthday gift from his family in May 1993.

Mom, Dad, and we three kids sprang out of the van and ventured onto the largely deserted bourse floor. I was after a handful of Lincoln cents for my 1909–1940 Whitman folder. Sis wanted a Peace dollar, and my cousin was looking for foreign coins. We visited two dealers. One gave us back in change a rag-condition 1957 $1 Silver Certificate, which was something I had never seen before. Another gave each of us kids a free vintage cull nickel. Mine was a corroded 1882 Shield nickel.

Mom introduced us to the officials who gave us the three American Silver Eagles, and we thanked them for the coins and for keeping the show open for us. I remember them being very kind to us and encouraging us to stay interested in the hobby. And that we did, at least through our teen years. I ended up sticking with the hobby as an active collector the longest, though my cousin's interest in foreign coins later parlayed into a globe-trekking career in journalism and the visual arts, while Sis still has her coin collection and is herself an artist.

Some years went by, and I was in college and trying to keep the debt at bay by selling off some of my belongings, including a swath of my coin collection. "Don't sell that silver coin I got for you at that coin show!" my mom jokingly warned. "I worked hard for that!"

My dear mom passed away in 2009 from cancer, and I thankfully hung onto that American Silver Eagle—something I now view as a memento of how much she supported my ambitions, including numismatics. As my foray into the hobby morphed from collecting to writing, editing, and journalism, I have enjoyed researching American Silver Eagles, which hold a unique place in numismatics given their crossover appeal to both investors and collectors.

That's something that many numismatists may not immediately realize about the American Silver Eagle. It's not "just" a bullion coin. Even in 1986, when the first American Silver Eagles were struck, the coin was offered in Proof format and marketed to collectors. Over the years since, the U.S. Mint has produced the American Silver Eagle in myriad finishes and collectible variations suitable for numismatic tastes. But even the

The author's coin collection in 1993, about a year after he began building it.

bullion issues (which were originally marketed as "Uncircu-lated") draw countless hobbyists into building date sets.

The American Silver Eagle is a legitimate collectible on every front, including rarity, value, and numismatic challenge. The bullion strikes boast several relatively scarce issues, including the key-date 1996 American Silver Eagle and several earlier semi-key dates that have lower mintages and conditional rarity in the higher grades. There are also some significant varieties, with the 2008-W Burnished, Reverse of 2007, a decidedly scarce entry. The undisputed "king" of American Silver Eagles is the 1995-W Proof, which has a mintage of just 30,125 pieces. But contending for that spot is the 2019-S, Enhanced Reverse Proof, which saw an output of merely 29,909.

The author's 1993 American Silver Eagle that he was gifted at his first coin show. The coin shows evidence of mishandling due to some juvenile numismatic indiscretions.

The American Silver Eagle series boasts numerous expensive keys, semi-keys, and varieties, yet the series is financially accessible, too. A handsome set of bullion strikes can be completed for an outlay fairly close to the prevailing spot price of the coins. Meanwhile, more intrepid collectors can work on a comprehensive set encompassing the myriad finishes and varieties. And collectors anywhere within that spectrum may choose to complete the set with coins in the middle Uncirculated or Proof grades, or go all-out on a competitive registry set incorporating certified coins boasting a "perfect" 70 on the numerical grading scale.

No matter the depth of one's American Silver Eagle collection, sets like these represent an optimal merging of the bullion and numismatic spheres. The precious metals investor who wants to dabble in collectibles can build a decent set of Silver Eagles for prices close to their metal value. Meanwhile, the collector who wants to speculate in precious metals has a built-in silver portfolio by completing a set of American Silver Eagles.

Sweetening the pot even further is the outstanding liquidity of a set of American Silver Eagles. Not only are these popular silver bullion coins in high demand among United States collectors and dealers, but they also have global appeal and are quite sought after around the world.

Sealing the deal for many collectors is their colorful legacy. The American Silver Eagle incorporates one of the most beloved designs of all time, Adolph A. Weinman's Liberty Walking motif. This graceful, patriotic design first appeared on the half dollar in 1916 and continued for the duration of that series until 1947. The Liberty Walking half dollar has become a favorite collectible and enjoys incredible demand among collectors of all ages.

Weinman's design became a top choice for the nation's first one-ounce silver bullion coin after President Ronald Reagan signed the Liberty Coin Act into law on July 9, 1985, authorizing production of the American Silver Eagle. The classic design was paired on the Silver Eagle with sculptor-engraver John Mercanti's heraldic eagle reverse, which was retired in 2021 to make way for artist Emily S. Damstra's soaring flying eagle design. Still, the timeless Liberty Walking design continues marching well into the twenty-first century.

1
Before the
American Silver Eagle

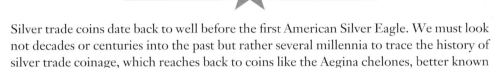

Silver trade coins date back to well before the first American Silver Eagle. We must look not decades or centuries into the past but rather several millennia to trace the history of silver trade coinage, which reaches back to coins like the Aegina chelones, better known as the "silver turtle" stater.

First minted around 550–525 B.C., the silver turtle staters were struck by the maritime stronghold of Aegina and remained popular throughout the Mediterranean for more than a century. They weigh about 12.2 grams and were produced with great precision to ensure that each was struck at its full weight and with quality silver. Silver turtles were also minted in fractional denominations and went on to see widespread use on an international scale.

Aegina silver turtle staters
were minted circa 550–525 B.C.

After Athens overtook Aegina in 458 B.C., the Athenian silver tetradrachm soon supplanted the silver turtles from their position of prominence in international trade. These are among the most widely familiar of all ancient coinage, their obverse portrait of the goddess Athena and reverse motif of an owl appearing in countless popular references to primeval Greek culture. They were produced in fractional formats and trusted far and wide beyond the confines of ancient Athens.

The silver tetradrachm of Athens was a widely used silver coin that dates back to 460–450 B.C. and was struck for 300 years.

The rise of the Roman Empire brought with it the silver denarius. This coin sported many designs and was used throughout Italy and eventually migrated throughout western Europe. Medieval Europe spawned a variety of silver coinage, including those of the Byzantine Empire, Sicily, France, and England. Meanwhile, other

The Roman denarius is enshrined as one of the most famous early silver trade coins, perhaps in part because it is mentioned in the New Testament of the Bible.

regions of the world produced their own widely circulating silver coins, with the silver dirhems of the Arab and Persian regions seeing extensive use as far away as the Viking-dominated regions of Europe during between the tenth and twelfth centuries.

In 1486 Austria struck a large silver coin known as the guldengroschen, which later inspired the creation of the talers of central Europe and the 8 reales (also known as the Spanish milled dollar or "pieces of eight") of the Spanish Empire. Both the talers and 8-reales coins sparked a new era in world coinage, setting a standard of silver coins weighing roughly one ounce and approximating 40 millimeters in diameter.

The taler, an abbreviated form of the word *joachimsthaler*, was first coined in Joachimsthal, Bohemia, in 1518. It spawned a plethora of German silver coins of approximately the same size that incorporated a form of the word *taler* in the name, including the reichsthaler, silbertaler, and kronenthaler. Meanwhile, large Dutch silver coinage of similar physical specifications to the German taler became known as the daalder. In England the fledgling crown had first been issued as a gold coin under Henry VIII in 1544 and would be regularly struck in silver in 1662 under the reign of Charles II.

The first British silver crowns were struck in 1551 under Edward VI alongside gold crowns, but they wouldn't be regularly struck until 1662.

The taler evolved as the German states and their interests saw the redrawing of boundaries, consolidation of powers, and eventual replacement by the German unit of currency known as the mark. But the legacy of the taler lived on in the physical form of the Maria Theresa thaler, a silver trade coin that has been struck since 1741 and bears the portrait of Maria Theresa, the empress of Austria, Hungary, and Bohemia from 1740 until 1780. The year of her death is permanently emblazoned on the obverse of these large coins. Maria Theresa thalers

The Maria Theresa thaler became one of the most widely known silver trade coins of the eighteenth and nineteenth centuries.

Hailing from Austria, this Schlick joachimsthaler from 1526 features Stephan I and his three brothers.

have since circulated widely throughout the Arab countries, Ethiopia, and India, and in other parts of the world and are still struck by the Austrian Mint.

Seeing wider use in international trade was the Spanish milled (machine-made) dollar, which arose in the Spanish Empire in the years following monetary reforms in 1497. These milled dollars were struck well into the millions through the nineteenth century at mints in Spain and in the New World. The coin was hailed around the world, due in large part to its uniform standards, and saw wide use in Europe, southeast Asia, and North America, including the 13 British colonies that later conjoined to become the United States.

The Spanish pieces of eight took on a life of its own well beyond the Spanish Empire and essentially became a global currency. It directly influenced the creation of several world currencies, including the Chinese yuan, Japanese yen, Korean won, Philippine peso, and French Indochinese piastre. Furthermore, the Spanish milled dollar's popularity in the American colonies inspired the United States dollar, which was adopted as the official unit of currency in 1792.

The Spanish pieces of eight was the direct inspiration of the United States dollar.

The United States dollar was conceived during a flurry of monetary-system proposals pitched during the nation's early days. Among the matters that were addressed in the 1780s and early 1790s, alongside the Constitution and the Bill of Rights, was determining a national monetary system.

Myriad proposals for the new United States monetary system were based on a decimal formula. Thomas Jefferson and Alexander Hamilton largely drove the proposal that ultimately proved successful. Serving as George Washington's Treasury secretary, Hamilton proposed a monetary system to Congress in 1791 that was built around much of Jefferson's research. It pitched a unitary denomination to be known as a dollar, with fractions amounting to one-hundredth of a dollar to be known as cents.

George Washington, Thomas Jefferson, and Alexander Hamilton were all central figures in building the foundation of the monetary system for a young United States in the 1780s and early 1790s.

The first United States silver dollars were struck in 1794 and within a few short years were being shipped to Asia, as the young nation was building its prominence as a significant player on the international trade scene. As trade with Asia continued expanding during the nineteenth century, the government eventually passed a law for the creation of a large silver coin patently designed for use in Asia and capable of competing alongside the silver trade coinage from other nations. In 1873 the United States trade dollar was first coined and saw use throughout southeast Asia during the years that followed.

In 1878 the United States Mint began coining the Liberty Head dollar, a coin more commonly known as the "Morgan dollar" for its designer, George T. Morgan. While Morgan dollars failed to see widespread use on the bustling Eastern Seaboard, they were embraced in the West, where most people distrusted the value of paper currency and culturally favored hard money made from silver and gold. The Morgan dollar was succeeded by the Peace dollar in 1921, the latter lasting into the depths of the Great Depression, to 1935.

The first United States silver dollar was struck in 1794.

"Inspecting the First United States Coinage" is a famous painting by John W. Dunsmore that imagines the scene where Martha Washington is inspecting a tray of silver half dismes presented by first United States Mint Chief Coiner Henry Voigt in 1792. In the scene are President George Washington, Treasury secretary Alexander Hamilton and Elizabeth Schuyler Hamilton, Thomas Jefferson, and the first director of the United States Mint, David Rittenhouse, who is gesturing toward the new batch of silver coins.

While the United States wouldn't produce another dollar coin until 1971, other nations were churning out larger silver pieces during the mid-twentieth century, including Australia, Canada, and Mexico. Rising silver prices in the mid-1960s brought an end to circulating silver coinage in the United States and other nations, but this wouldn't spell the end of silver coins. The precious-metal bullion-coin revolution was coming over the next two decades.

In 1967 South Africa launched what became the first modern bullion-coin program with its produc-

The Liberty Head silver dollar, more commonly known as the "Morgan dollar" for its designer George T. Morgan, is on the top, while the Peace dollar is on the bottom.

tion of the one-ounce gold Krugerrand, a coin that in the early 1980s represented some 90 percent of the gold bullion being traded on an international level. Around the time that the South African Krugerrand hit its crescendo on the world markets, other nations were launching their own bullion programs.

Mexico unveiled its silver Libertad in 1982, a year after the nation premiered gold bullion coins under the same name. China issued its first silver Panda in 1983, also one

The South African gold Krugerrand became the first modern bullion coin and sparked other countries around the world to issue similar precious-metal coins, including Mexico's Libertad and China's Panda.

year after the similarly branded Panda gold coins hit the market. Canada began issuing gold Maple Leaf coins in 1979 and wouldn't produce its first silver Maple Leaf until 1988, by which time the American Silver Eagle was already soaring to popularity in its native United States and on the global scene. Over the next decades other nations unveiled their own bullion-coin programs, yielding seemingly endless exciting possibilities for both collectors and investors of these precious-metal coins.

THE LOWDOWN ON SILVER: IT'S ALL AN ACT!

When the Coinage Act of 1792 established both the United States Mint and the nation's coinage system, the value of the dollar was originally pegged to silver rather than gold. The U.S. Constitution called for a bimetallic monetary system utilizing both silver and gold, and this worked perfectly well for the next few decades. However, things began changing as the nineteenth century moved along. A significant gold rush in northern Georgia and western North Carolina during the 1820s and the California Gold Rush that began in 1848 changed the nation's bullion dynamics.

Silver prices rose in response to the new influx of domestic gold, and soon spot values of silver coinage began rising above their respective face values. A coin shortage ensued, leading to the Coinage Act of 1853, which was signed into law by President Millard Fillmore and mandated a reduction in the weight of the half dime, dime, quarter, and half dollar by approximately 7 percent to help reduce silver usage. Other provisions of the act limited the legal-tender status of silver to not more than five dollars per transaction and banned private deposits of silver bullion from being converted to half dimes, dimes, quarters, or half dollars.

The Coinage Act of 1853 reduced the amount of silver content in the half dime, dime, quarter, and half dollar, a change demarcated by the presence of arrows around the dates of those coins during the mid-1850s.

A gold mining camp in El Dorado, California, during the California Gold Rush, circa 1848 to 1853.

The Coinage Act of 1873 was a game-changer for the United States, simultaneously thrusting the country onto the gold standard while demonetizing silver. Before the passage of this act, signed into law by President Ulysses S. Grant, anybody could deposit raw silver bullion at the U.S. Mint to be assayed and converted into silver coinage of equivalent value. That was prohibited under the new law. Many called the new law the "Crime of '73." The other significant changes brought about by the Coinage Act of 1873 were the elimination of the two-cent, three-cent silver, half dime, and silver dollar coins and the increase in weight of the dime, quarter, and half dollar. It also created a new, heavier "trade dollar," a silver coin intended for commercial use in Asia, to compete with the popular Mexican silver dollar.

The Panic of 1873 spurred great economic distress, causing bank runs like this one at the Fourth National Bank in New York City, as depicted in the October 4, 1873, edition of *Frank Leslie's Illustrated Newspaper*.

Demonetization of silver along with inflation, major fires in Boston and Chicago, and other trying events led to a long-lasting period of economic malaise known as the Panic of 1873. Despite the economic troubles affecting much of the United States, fortunes were brighter on the horizons of the Western frontier, where massive silver discoveries, including the famous Comstock Lode, were occurring. As more silver discoveries racked up in the American West and other nations like Germany, oversupplies of the precious metal led to tumbling prices.

Some opportunists in the silver industry and their political bigwig friends touted expansionary monetary policy based on "free silver" as one way to allay the economic misfortunes of the day. The Free Silver movement, vaunted by so-called Silverites, proposed the unlimited conversion of silver into money and loosening of the rigid monetary policies set forth under the gold standard.

Among the proponents was Senator Richard P. Bland, a Democratic lawmaker from Missouri who was sympathetic to the concerns of the silver miners' lobby. Jumping aboard a bill that supported the government purchase of domestic silver was Iowa Republican Senator William Boyd Allison. Bland drummed up enough support in Congress to override the veto of President Rutherford B. Hayes, and the Bland-Allison Act became law on February 28, 1878.

Ushering in a de facto return to a semblance of bimetallism, the new law required the United States Treasury to purchase between $2 million and $4 million of domestic silver each month for the production of silver dollars. It was a move that United States Mint director Henry Linderman had seen coming before the Bland-Allison Act became official law and had prompted him to work with Mint assistant engraver George T. Morgan to create a new design for the silver dollar that would result from passage of the bill.

The Free Silver movement was built on the idea that by minting all the silver it could, the U.S. government could augment national prosperity by creating more money. But the plan had its detractors, as seen in this 1896 political cartoon drawn by Charles J. Taylor.

The legislated demand for silver encouraged even greater oversupply of the metal, pushing prices downward to the brink of making it unprofitable for mining activity to continue. Meanwhile, deflation was making it harder for farmers to repay their debts, causing many in the agricultural communities to support a bill that became known as the Sherman Silver Purchase Act. This law, brokered on Capitol Hill by Ohio Republican senator John Sherman, required the monthly acquisition of 4.5 million ounces in domestic silver and repealed the Bland-Allison Act.

Banking reforms prompted the Gold Standard Act of 1900, which was signed by President William McKinley and officially implemented the gold standard in the United States. The price of gold was fixed to the tune of $20.67 per troy ounce, where it remained until the Great Depression some three decades later. The gold standard would continue until August 15, 1971, with President Richard Nixon halting conversion of dollars to gold at a fixed value.

International affairs flared up in 1914 with the assassination of Austria's Archduke Franz Ferdinand and his wife, Sophie, throwing Europe into the Great War. Great Britain, in the thick of the war, faced a potential revolution in its colony of India. British nemesis Germany began spreading rumors that Great Britain lacked adequate bullion supplies to back its Silver Certificates, sending India into economic chaos.

With aims of preventing socioeconomic turmoil in the United States' ally during the height of the Great War, Democratic senator Key Pittman of Nevada pitched a bill addressing the delicate considerations at hand. The Pittman Act, going into effect on April 23, 1918, authorized the melting of up to 350 million silver dollars into bullion, with a major portion to be sold overseas at the rate of $1 per ounce (which was above the market rate). The law additionally required the United States Mint to buy an equal amount of silver bullion from domestic sources to produce the same number of dollar coins that were melted—a provision that mollified Western politicians and mining interests. All told, the Pittman Act sent 270,232,722 (mostly Morgan) silver dollars to the smelting pot. Bullion from 259,121,554 of these silver dollars was sold to Great Britain, which in turn sent it to India. The balance of the melted silver, amounting to 11,111,168 silver dollars, was converted into United States dimes, quarters, and half dollars.

After World War I ended in 1918, the Mint geared up to satisfy the other portion of the Pittman Act: replacing all the silver dollars that were melted. Following a 17-year hiatus, the Morgan dollar was resurrected in 1921 and saw production at the Mint facilities in Philadelphia, Denver, and San Francisco. A total of 86,730,000 Morgan dollars were minted in 1921 alone. Minting of the Peace dollar, carrying an ebullient design by Anthony de Francisci symbolizing the end of the Great War, began in late 1921 and provided the remainder of silver dollars necessary for meeting the terms of the Pittman Act.

The U.S. Mint struck tens of millions of Morgan dollars in 1921 to help fulfill the obligations of the Pittman Act.

Landmark bullion changes came along during the Great Depression. The most significant was the far-reaching Executive Order 6102, issued by President Franklin Delano Roosevelt on April 5, 1933, "forbidding the hoarding of gold coin, gold bullion, and gold certificates within the continental United States." The ban required "all persons" to "deliver on or before May 1, 1933, all gold coin, gold bullion, and Gold Certificates now owned by them to a Federal Reserve Bank, branch, or agency, or to any member bank of the Federal Reserve System." This gold was exchanged for $20.67 in federal paper currency per troy ounce.

President Franklin Delano Roosevelt signed Executive Order 6102, "forbidding the hoarding of gold coin, gold bullion, and gold certificates within the continental United States."

Stiff criminal penalties of up to $10,000 or 10 years of imprisonment could meet anybody who didn't comply, though there were exceptions for coin collectors owning rare gold coins, dentists who used gold for fillings, and those in other pursuits wherein gold served a critical function. Furthermore, individuals were allowed to own up to $100 face value in gold. Later, the price of gold would be raised to $35 per ounce to stimulate healthy inflation and help farmers, who were hammered by decreasing revenues during the depths of the Great Depression.

SILVER'S '60S SWAN SONG

By the early 1960s, world demand for silver soared to highs never before seen, outpacing mine output. From 1960 through 1964, annual demand for silver averaged 410 million ounces, while new output was just 210 million ounces. Many consumers turned to the large reserves of silver held by the U.S. Treasury, putting its 1.7 billion ounces at risk of depletion. The fixed price for silver set by the U.S. Treasury was 91.62 cents in 1961, and the U.S. government was selling more silver bullion than it was acquiring. It was an unsustainable situation that, if continued, would imperil its reserves held as backing for Silver Certificates. To resolve this, the Treasury temporarily suspended the sale of silver bullion and recalled $5 and $10 Silver Certificates from circulation.

The Treasury's withdrawal of silver bullion sales to the public only caused continued spikes in the price of silver, which rose to $1.29 by 1963. This caused yet another untenable situation—$1 Silver Certificates could be turned in for silver that was more valuable than the face value of the currency. In March 1964 the United States government stopped redeeming Silver Certificates for silver dollars, which the public were taking home by the wheelbarrow-full, in some cases. The Treasury had more than 270 million on hand in 1964 but fewer than 3 million by March 1965.

Aiming to keep silver prices low while silver was removed from the currency system, the Treasury reinstituted bullion sales to the public to ensure a steady supply of the precious metal to the marketplace. This didn't dissuade investors from hoarding circulating silver coins, exacerbating a national coin shortage that only got worse as commerce needs grew

Silver Certificates were printed from 1878 through 1964.

and bullion prices rose. If silver reached $1.38 per ounce, it would become profitable for 90 percent silver coins to be melted for their precious metal content.

Further compounding the issue was the release of the 1964 Kennedy half dollar, honoring the late President John F. Kennedy after his assassination. The coin was so popular that it was hoarded by the millions. The half dollar all but disappeared from circulation from that point forward. Meanwhile, rising silver prices increasingly tempted silver stackers to remove dimes and quarters from circulation, too. The U.S. government placed some of the blame for the coin shortage on coin collectors, who in the early 1960s had developed an inclination to speculate in roll quantities of new coinage.

What would be the best solution for getting coins back into circulation at a reasonable cost? The U.S. Treasury researched the situation and determined that base-metal dimes and quarters and half dollars of reduced silver content would be the panacea.

President Lyndon B. Johnson advocated for Congress to take up the issue over the summer of 1965. With some pushback by legislators from states where silver mining was big business, Congress approved the measures and President Johnson signed the bill into law on July 23, 1965. Production of copper-nickel clad coinage began with quarters on August 23, 1965. Copper-nickel clad

After President John F. Kennedy's assassination at the age of 46 on November 22, 1963, his likeness was swiftly placed on the circulating half dollar beginning in 1964.

President Lyndon B. Johnson signed a coinage act into law in 1965 that required debasing the 90 percent silver dime and quarter, which were made with a less-expensive copper-nickel clad alloy beginning that year. The Kennedy half dollar was demoted from a 90 percent silver content profile to a 40 percent copper-silver clad format, which was eventually scrapped in 1971 for a copper-nickel clad composition.

dimes and 40 percent silver half dollars soon followed in big numbers, gradually miti-gating the coin shortage.

The last of the 40 percent silver Kennedy half dollars were made for circulation in 1969, with a final run coming in 1970—the latter made for numismatic sale only. It was the end of the line for the 176-year tradition of circulating silver coinage in the United States.

SILVER'S STAR RISES IN THE '70S

While the 1970-D Kennedy half dollar marked the curtain call for circulating silver coins in the United States, many more silver coins would be struck at the U.S. Mint. On March 28, 1969, former President Dwight D. Eisenhower passed away at the age of 78, leading many Republicans in Congress to call for a numismatic tribute to "Ike" on an upcoming dollar coin. The effort saw bipartisan support, as even Democratic Missouri representative Leonor Sullivan said honoring Eisenhower in such a fashion likened to a form of "equal time" to Democratic President John F. Kennedy's portrait on the half dollar.

However, there were disagreements about whether the new dollar coin should have been made from a silver composition or the newfangled copper-nickel clad format. The latter was made of an inner core of pure copper sandwiched between outer layers of copper-nickel. A bill calling for the new Eisenhower dollar coin was filed by Demo-cratic Connecticut congressperson Robert Giaimo and proposed a copper-nickel piece that would appeal to both Nevada casinos and the vending industry. But Republican Iowa congressperson H.R. Gross objected to the notion of placing Ike's likeness on a copper-nickel coin: "You would be doing the memory of President Eisenhower no favor to mint a dollar made of perhaps scrap metal."

Various versions of legislation for the Eisenhower dollar were kicked around Capi-tol Hill throughout the rest of 1969, with a compromise made restricting 40 percent silver dollars to numismatic strikes and requiring all circulating issues to be made in

The Eisenhower dollar was released in 1971 as a circulating clad coin and was also offered in a 40 percent silver format for collectors.

copper-nickel clad format. The bill stalled in Congress for much of 1970, blocked by the chairman of the House Banking Committee, Representative Wright Patman, a Democrat from Texas, because he opposed the creation of any more silver coins.

But fortunes soon changed for the Coinage Act of 1969. It was tacked on as an amendment to the Bank Holding Act of 1970, which Patman had spent a decade trying to pass and which had finally reached the floor for a vote. President Richard Nixon signed the Eisenhower dollar into law on December 31, 1970, just a few minutes before midnight, when the bill would have expired by pocket veto.

The Philadelphia and Denver Mints churned out circulation strikes while the San Francisco Mint produced 40 percent silver Eisenhower dollars for sale as individual numismatic collectibles. The 40 percent silver Ike dollars were offered in two product formats: an Uncirculated coin packaged in a cellophane holder with a plastic token declaring the coin's identity, sold in a blue outer envelope (also known as a "Blue Ike"), and a Proof 40 percent silver dollar in a large rigid plastic holder and distributed in a simulated woodgrain cardboard box (a "Brown Ike").

The 40 percent silver Blue and Brown Ikes were sold as individual product offerings until 1975, the year the Mint began striking Bicentennial quarters, half dollars, and dollar coins to honor the 200th anniversary of the signing of the Declaration of Independence. The Mint was authorized to strike 45 million of the three Bicentennial coins in a 40 percent silver-clad composition, and all were made at the San Francisco Mint and went into special three-piece Proof and Uncirculated collector sets.

The Mint wouldn't produce another silver coin until 1982, with the minting of a George Washington commemorative half dollar. In 1979 the Eisenhower dollar was replaced by the unpopular Susan B. Anthony dollar, which was never minted in silver and which came to a nearly two-decade pause in 1981.

However, the big news in the silver world during the late 1970s and early 1980s wasn't coming from the U.S. Mint. It was being made by brothers Nelson Bunker Hunt and William Herbert Hunt, the sons of late billionaire and Texas oil tycoon H.L. Hunt. Nelson and William began building a massive silver bullion portfolio in the early 1970s. After the passing of their father in 1974, a $5 billion inheritance was passed down to the surviving Hunt family. Flush with capital, the Hunt brothers ramped up their bullion holdings with physical silver and silver futures contracts amounting to some 200 million ounces of silver. They were trying to shelter their inheritance from tax collectors and inflation but wound up cornering the silver market.

The Susan B. Anthony dollar was not a big hit with the public.

With about one-third of the globe's private supply of silver in their hands, prices started going up. In 1977 silver averaged $4.64 an ounce, and by 1978 it edged up to $5.42. By December 1979, silver had climbed to more than $20 an ounce, closing the 1970s at $32.20. By this point, people were selling off their silver coins, silver heirlooms—anything they could sell to the smelter with the hopes of making untold sums of money.

Burglaries involving silver were up around the country, and industries wherein silver was an important commodity, including photography and medical operations, felt the painful pinch. So, too, did jewelers, such as New York's famous Tiffany's & Co, whose chairman, Walter Hoving, ran an advertisement in the *New York Times*: "We think it is unconscionable for anyone to hoard several billion, yes billion, dollars' worth of silver and thus drive the price up so high that others must pay artificially high prices for articles made of silver."

The price of silver reached its peak on January 18, 1980, when the precious metal hit $49.45. The gains didn't stick. The silver bubble burst just as it reached for $50 and then quickly began falling. On March 27, 1980, a day notoriously known as Silver Thursday, prices dropped by more than half, from $21.62 to $10.80. Just as quickly as the Hunts made money, they lost much of it, too. The billionaire silver moguls were unable to meet their financial obligations, sending ripples throughout various sectors of the economy.

Crisis was averted when a group of banks lent the Hunts more than $1 billion, enabling them to repay their debts to major financial institutions. However, the Hunts didn't survive the ordeal unscathed. They faced years of criminal and civil litigation and were ordered to pay fines and fees amounting to more than $130 million to cover losses caused by their scheme. When all was said and done, the Hunts saw their cumulative wealth fall from $5 billion to less than $1 billion by the end of the 1980s. They ended up declaring bankruptcy.

MICHAEL GAROFALO REMEMBERS DEALING IN THE BULLION MARKET BEFORE THE AMERICAN EAGLE

My start in the coin business had its earliest roots in collecting coins as a child in the 1960s. But the fascination with filling up my blue Whitman folders waned and, while I loved coins, I wanted something more. I started to attend a few local coin shows in New England. Buying coins from the dealers there was the real fun. But I also learned that selling the coins and making money on the sale allowed me to buy more and better coins. I eventually got the courage to go to a show and actually set up as a dealer. As dealers befriended me, I learned about other, bigger coin shows that the more experienced dealers attended, and I dreamt of doing this on a full-time basis. I achieved that goal in 1979. In those days the American Numismatic Association Certification Service (ANACS) was the only grading service, and neither Professional Coin Grading Service nor Numismatic Guaranty Company existed.

In 1979 the rare-coin market was pretty strong, but the bullion market was even stronger. You see, there were these two brothers in Texas—Nelson Bunker Hunt and William Herbert Hunt—who in 1973 had begun to buy physical silver on the open market for less than $2 per troy ounce, and they amassed the largest amount of silver that had ever been gathered. At one point the Hunt brothers owned more than a third of the world's physical silver supply. The focus was on silver because when they started to purchase the physical metal in 1973, United States citizens were prohibited from buying and holding gold.

Now, back in the late 1970s most coin dealers didn't like buying bullion. Silver was less than $10 a troy ounce and it normally traded in a small and tight range of prices. It left little money for profit, so why buy it when a rare coin could provide the dealer with a bigger profit margin? Well, that all changed while the Hunt brothers were operating.

During 1979, silver began the year at $6.07 per ounce but it peaked at $32.20 on December 31. It quintupled in price during the year. Now everyone was buying and selling silver coins, silver bars, and silver rounds. Most dealers bought and sold it very quickly and you couldn't help but make a profit. How easy it was to make money in a bull market!

As 1979 closed and silver looked like it was impossible to stop, dealers began competing and paying ever-stronger premiums. The sky seemed to be the limit.

While nothing would stop that Silver Bull in 1979, the year 1980 was a different story altogether. Remember, as much as the Hunt Brothers drove the prices upward, there were economic crises also driving silver. The problems compounding it were:

- High inflation rates
- High interest rates
- High housing prices
- High oil and gasoline prices
- The United States hostage crisis in Iran
- The Soviet invasion of Afghanistan

In January 1980 silver reached a record high of $50 per ounce. The COMEX, the major commodities exchange, changed their rules under government pressure to do so. At that point, trading in silver would be limited to liquidation orders, meaning you could sell silver, but you couldn't buy any. Without any buy orders, the price of silver could only go down—and it did.

In 1979 I gave up my job and became a full-time professional numismatist. The overwhelming majority of us went back to buying bullion from customers who needed money to pay bills and selling rare coins to those customers who wanted to invest their silver profits.

At this point, the dominant silver coins on the market were pre-1965 U.S. coins and Canadian silver coins. On December 31, 1974, President Gerald Ford once again made it legal for U.S. citizens to own gold coins and bars. Only the South African Krugerrand, first minted in 1967, was available as a gold bullion coin, but there were also privately minted gold bars. In 1979 the Royal Canadian Mint jumped into the foray and began making their Canadian Gold Maple Leaf bullion coins.

Unbeknownst to most coin dealers, the U.S. government was watching these gold and silver price developments worldwide very carefully, and they were watching the success of both South Africa and Canada in monetizing their gold deposits.

SILVER IN THE SPOTLIGHT

By the early 1980s, silver took center stage in a way perhaps not seen since the demonetization of the precious metal in 1873. By the time silver prices rose under the sway of the Hunt brothers, government top brass were already planning to sell off most of the silver from the Defense National Stockpile Center. The rationale for liquidating the nation's silver holdings stems from the huge supply of domestic silver, ensuring plenty for strategic purposes should the United States ever need the bullion. Another factor contributing to a selloff plan was the increasing federal deficit, mounting to astronomical heights during the late 1970s and early 1980s.

Many lawmakers and others in the political arena decried liquidating silver from the national stockpile. Military officials expressed concerns that revenue from the sales of stockpiled silver would go toward paying down the federal deficit and would not be reciprocated with purchases of other resources to supplement the nation's defense stockpile. Those with mining interests were also dismayed by the selloffs, which began in the 1970s and helped drive silver prices down. It was a phenomenon noted in 1976 by the *Wall Street Journal*, which stated, "When the U.S. government makes noise about selling silver from the federal stockpile, futures traders start unloading futures contracts in speculation that such a sale would depress prices."

Regardless of the controversy, President Ronald Reagan ordered the sale of the silver holdings beginning in fiscal year 1982 to help balance the federal budget. On June 10, 1981, the House Armed Services Committee acquiesced to Reagan's request. By July 1981 both the House and Senate approved selling up to 75 percent of the silver in the nation's stockpile over the course of three years, meaning 105.1 million troy ounces from the defense reserves could be sold to the public. Silver prices fell by 11 percent by September in response to the planned selloff.

Senator James McClure of Idaho worked for much of his political career to shore up the strength of his state's robust silver mining industry.

President Ronald Reagan's first term, which began in 1981, saw tough economic times, federal budget cutbacks, and fights on Capitol Hill over what to do with millions of ounces of surplus silver bullion.

The silver sale was to begin in October 1981. However, a cadre of politicians from Idaho, where silver mining represents a large economic sector, suggested the selloff would impart a "disastrous effect" on silver mines in Idaho and the nation's silver mining industry at large. Adding bite to the bark, Idaho Republican senator James A. McClure successfully pitched an amendment to the Department of Defense appropriation bill, calling for the government to cease the silver sale "until the President, not later than July 1, 1982, redetermines that the silver authorized for disposal is excess to the requirements of the stockpile."

Over the course of the next several months, talk continued about a silver selloff. The more profitable concept of selling it in the form of bullion coins, rather than raw metal, began garnering support. On May 27, 1982, McClure and Representative Larry Craig, also an Idaho Republican, brought identical bills to their respective chamber floors "to provide for the disposal of silver from the National Defense Stockpile through the issuance of silver coins."

In addition to limiting the amount of silver sold from the national stockpile, the bills also called for the selloff to occur during the calendar years of 1983, 1984, and 1985. The objective as noted in the bills was to "redirect the sale of silver from our national defense stockpile in an effort to minimize its [effect] on the already depressed price of silver," something that could be achieved if the silver was dispersed to a wider spectrum of the public in smaller chunks, such as in the form of silver coins, as opposed to larger bulk quantities to a smaller pool of buyers in the wholesale or investment arenas.

Neither McClure's nor Craig's 1982 silver bills made it farther than committee circles. But that didn't stop McClure from introducing another bill on January 27, 1983, similar to his unsuccessful 1982 proposal. Posed McClure, "if we are forced to accept a sale, why use the method guaranteed to depress the price and dispose of the silver with the lowest possible return to the taxpayers[?] Why not instead, if we must sell, at least get as much for it as we can?" This meant silver *coins*. Hearings were held

Some See $1.4 Billion Budget Ploy

Reagan Would Tap Defense Silver Stockpile

By ROBERT WATERS
Courant Staff Writer

WASHINGTON — It takes 5,366 pounds of titanium, 5,204 pounds of nickel, 1,656 pounds of chromium and 910 pounds of cobalt to build the Pratt & Whitney F-100 jet — the engine which powers the two most modern Air Force fighters, the F-15 Eagle and the F-16 Fighting Falcon.

The U.S. has been attempting, without much success, to build up its national defense stockpile of these and other metals because the nation is dangerously dependent on imports for most of its supplies.

The Reagan Administration supports a stockpile buildup, but many defense-minded members of Congress don't like the price Congress is being asked to pay: 139.5 million ounces of silver, currently valued at more than $1.4 billion.

Specifically, influential members of the House Armed Services Committee raised strong objections Tuesday to an administration-supported bill which would sell off the 139.5 million ounces of silver — the entire U.S. stockpile of that metal — as a vehicle to obtain funds to buy cobalt, titanium and other strategic metals.

The lawmakers are disturbed on two counts.

Some of them suspect a budget ploy in the proposed silver sale. They are openly skeptical that the funds may not be used to buy other metals for the stockpile but, instead, will go toward reducing the budget deficit.

Others believe the U. S. needs its 139.5 million ounces of silver in the defense stockpile because silver is also vital to many weapons and defense systems and the U.S. is now importing 50 percent of its silver.

"In the Vietnam era, we used about 1.5 billion ounces of silver," said Rep. Larry McDonald, D-Ga., one of the committee's silver bugs. "If we had a major conflict, we certainly would have a greater need than that used during the Vietnam era."

McDonald believes the chief U. S. silver sources, Peru, Mexico and Canada, could all become vulnerable to growing anti-Americanism arising out of charges that the U. S. is exploiting the natural resources of those countries. "In short, we could be facing an OPEC style silver cartel in a few years," he said.

Rep. Charles E. Bennett, D-Fla., chairman of an Armed Services subcommittee hearing on the silver proposals, is another member of the panel who is suspicious of the stockpile sale.

Bennett noted that legislation dealing with existing defense stockpile sales originally required that all proceeds be used to buy other materials for the stockpile. But under pressure from the Carter Administration, he said, the legislation was amended to permit transfer of the stockpile funds to the treasury if they were not appropriated for new purchases within three years.

Bennett said he suspected the three-year "escape clause" would be exploit-ed. "Our concern and apprehension was well-founded," he said. This year, he said, the administration has proposed sales from the stockpile which would total $2.14 billion but has requested purchases that total "only $120 million."

"It appears that despite the legislative efforts of this committee and congress to keep the stockpile from being bled for the purpose of making the budget look good, this practice is being continued," said Bennett.

Rep. Dan Marriott, R-Utah, one of the most vocal stockpile advocates in Congress, told the subcommittee that he is opposed to selling off all 139.5 million ounces of silver in the stockpile but would favor sale of "a significant amount of silver" to finance purchases of other exotic metals.

Marriott said he is especially disturbed because so many sources of U. S. imports in strategic and critical metals are unstable or hostile to America.

See Silver, Page B7

Silver was making headlines in 1981 as Ronald Reagan sought to sell up to three-quarters of the nation's silver reserves.

on April 15, 1983, in the Committee on Banking, Housing, and Urban Affairs, where the bill yet again failed to be enacted. The silver selloff was shelved for two years, its long-term fate hanging in the balance.

A determined McClure set out yet again to monetize the national stockpile of silver, the sale of which still had not begun by June 1985. His third attempt proved to be the charm. No longer was McClure's Senate proposal pitching nebulous coins made from government silver. This latest effort, titled the "Liberty Coin Act" and amended to the "Statue of Liberty-Ellis Island Commemorative Coin Act," authorizing a trio of commemoratives honoring the iconic national monuments, was a solid sell. It also created a new bullion coin, to be minted "in quantities sufficient to meet public demand."

The Liberty Coin Act presented a definitive set of specifications and requirements for the new silver bullion coin, including its diameter, silver purity, design, inscriptions, and other production specifications.

Proposed on June 21, 1985, McClure's amendment received approval by a Senate voice vote that day and was quickly passed and formally added to H.R. 47, the Statue of Liberty-Ellis Island Commemorative Coin Act. The House approved the bill and off it went for President Reagan's signature on July 9, 1985. Authorized under Title II of Public Law 99-61, widely known as the Liberty Coin Act, the American Silver Eagle was born.

President Ronald Reagan signed the Liberty Coin Act into law on July 9, 1985, and with the stroke of a pen gave life to the American Silver Eagle.

2
There's Something About Silver Dollars

★

The American Silver Eagle may be classified as a bullion coin by many, but it's ultimately a silver dollar. In fact, many numismatists correctly dub the Silver Eagle as the "silver dollar of today." There really is no better way to put it. The American Silver Eagle is just the latest chapter of the denomination, which was authorized by the Coinage Act of April 2, 1792, and first struck in 1794. Silver dollars have a long and colorful history in the United States, dating back to a time when the nation was still very young and the American people had grown accustomed to using foreign coins, such as Spanish milled dollars, in everyday commerce.

While early U.S. dollars circulated extensively during the late 1790s and early 1800s, attracting little numismatic attention during that time, they were sought by the small but active fraternity of coin collectors who were building collections of these silver coins during the 1840s, 1850s, and 1860s. A century later it was the so-called "cartwheels" known as Morgan and Peace dollars that led the collecting craze of the 1950s and 1960s.

By the 1970s, silver had been removed from circulating dollar coinage. However, base-metal dollar coins marched into the twenty-first century despite as-yet unrealized hopes of modern dollars finding a place in American commerce more significant than mere novelty. Joining a parade of small-size dollar coins and commemorative silver dollars still in production are the American Silver Eagles, which premiered in 1986. To better understand the Silver Eagle's place within the broader series of U.S. silver dollars, it helps to take a step back and review the other dollar coins the United States Mint has produced since 1794.

FLOWING HAIR DOLLARS, 1794–1795

The Flowing Hair dollar represents the first silver dollars struck by the United States Mint. They were designed by first U.S. Mint chief engraver Robert Scot and feature a bust of a young Miss Liberty with flowing locks on the obverse and a small eagle on the reverse. The U.S. Mint made limited quantities of Flowing Hair dollars, with just 1,758 recorded in 1794 and 160,295 in 1795. Most saw extensive circulation up and down the

Eastern Seaboard of the fledgling nation and competed in commerce alongside Spanish milled dollars and other foreign coins, which remained legal tender in the United States until 1857.

Stories behind the striking of these earliest United States silver dollars are many, and they're often teeming with whiffs of legend and dashes of conjecture.

The exact mintage figure of 1,758 examples of 1794 dollars is likely the number of acceptable strikes created from a total of perhaps 2,000 coined on October 15, 1794. The balance unaccounted for in Mint records were probably struck too weakly, most likely a result of an inadequately built press and die-misalignment issues. After their striking on that historic October day, the 1,758 silver dollars were transferred

David Rittenhouse served as the first director of the United States Mint from 1792 through 1795.

from Chief Coiner Henry Voigt to Mint director David Rittenhouse. Some of these 1794 silver dollars were then bestowed to notable figures of the time. The 1795 production saw a much larger mintage, made possible by the availability of more working dies.

Flowing Hair dollars are popular among the more advanced collectors and those who enjoy early Americana, yet they are extremely scarce, as most examples were lost to time through wear, burial, melting, or acts of God. Most estimates suggest 150 survivors for the 1794 dollar, with the more numerous 1795 dollar probably yielding 10,500 to 12,500 coins. Uncirculated examples of either date are rare.

Base prices for even the most common Flowing Hair dollars usually start in the range of $2,000 to $4,000 and quickly rise in higher grades. Many examples have traded for high six-figure prices, while two of the most famous first-year examples have hammer prices well beyond $1 million.

The Flowing Hair dollar.

The most valuable Flowing Hair dollar to ever trade hands was a coin from 1794 that, as theorized by many of the hobby's leading experts, most plausibly was the first silver dollar ever struck by the United States Mint. Graded by PCGS as SP-66, this extraordinary coin is widely considered the finest of all 1794 Flowing Hair dollars. In January 2013 Stack's Bowers Galleries sold the immaculate example for $10,016,875—a price that stood for nearly a decade as the all-time highest price paid for any coin sold in a public auction.

DRAPED BUST DOLLARS, 1795–1804

The Draped Bust dollar, designed by Robert Scot, may be one of the most widely recognizable early United States coins, though it's not because the coin ranks as a common collectible. Rather, the series is famous for its poster child, the world-renowned 1804 dollar. An extremely rare coin with just 15 known examples, the 1804 dollar has fetched seven figures in recent decades when it has crossed the auction block. Fortunately for coin collectors who aren't multimillionaires, there are more affordable Draped Bust dollars available in the marketplace.

Mintages for various issues within the Draped Bust dollar series range from as few as 7,776 pieces dated 1797 to the high-water mark of 423,515 struck in 1799—excluding the 15 Proofs and restrikes dated 1804 and a handful of Proof restrikes dated 1801, 1802, and 1803.

As should be mentioned in any discussion of early American coinage, mintage figures are effectively more anecdotal than practical in describing the "common" issues available today for this series. While the 1798, 1799, and 1800 Draped Bust dollars saw low six-figure mintages, any single one of these dates will yield approximately 10,000 to 15,000 survivors.

The most common Draped Bust dollars, namely Heraldic Eagle coins dated from 1798 through 1800, can be had for around $1,000 in G-4. Meanwhile, those wanting a Draped Bust, Small Eagle, dollar will need to shell out closer to $2,000 and up for examples grading G-4 and better. Uncirculated coins command well into the five figures or higher.

The all-time record for the Draped Bust dollar type expectedly goes to an 1804-dated example. This particular example, presented in a Proof set as a diplomatic gift to the Sultan of Muscat, is the finest known and graded Proof-68 by PCGS. It hammered for $7,680,000 in an August 2021 Stack's Bowers Galleries offering.

The 1804 Draped Bust dollar,
"King of American Coins."

The Draped Bust dollar saw two reverse motifs, the earlier being a Small
Eagle device (1795–1798) and the latter a Heraldic Eagle (1798–1804).

Gobrecht Dollars, 1836–1839

Production of the silver dollar was officially placed on pause in 1806, two years after the last circulating 1803-dated coins rolled off the presses in March 1804. Some 25 years elapsed before the silver dollar was resurrected in 1831.

By then, the United States Mint was relocating from its original, quaint digs, housed in three small wooden buildings clustered in a compound near Seventh and Filbert Streets in Philadelphia, to a grandiose Greek-Revival edifice some blocks away. The coin shortages of yesteryear were but a fading memory. Tens of millions of coins rolled off the U.S. Mint's newfangled and highly efficient steam presses every year; it was a far cry from the flywheel presses that arduously churned out coinage three decades earlier.

In 1835 chief engraver William Kneass suffered a stroke and was succeeded by second engraver Christian Gobrecht. Late that year Gobrecht was instructed by Mint director Robert Maskell Patterson to create pattern designs for a new dollar coin, based on designs by American portraitist Thomas Sully and scientific illustrator Titian Peale.

The Gobrecht dollar.

Off to work Gobrecht went, producing obverse designs depicting Miss Liberty in a flowing gown and sitting upon a rock. The reverse features a flying eagle, with some variations of this design incorporating 26 stars to represent the number of states then admitted to the Union or anticipated to be (with Michigan joining as the 26th state in 1837).

Several varieties were made of various die alignments, edge finishes (plain and reeded), and other design modifications. While Gobrecht dollars have long been classified by several authorities as pattern coins—and many were presented to government officials and other VIPs—documents show several hundred were officially distributed

William Kneass designed the "Classic Head," as seen on the quarter eagle and half eagle gold coins minted from 1834 through 1839.

Christian Gobrecht.

into circulation. Proof restrikes were produced from the late 1850s through early 1870s, including two types dated 1836 and one each bearing the 1838 and 1839 dates.

The Gobrecht dollar is an elusive collectible, with the least pricey realizing anywhere from $12,000 to $15,000 in circulated Proof grades. Proof restrikes often fetch $30,000 to $85,000 or more, depending on variety.

Gobrecht dollars represent a unique chapter in United States silver dollar history. They bridge the era of early American dollars that dawned during the U.S. Mint's youth and predicated a century-long parade of colorful dollar coinage that concluded in 1935 with the last Peace dollar.

LIBERTY SEATED DOLLARS, 1840–1873

Christian Gobrecht's Liberty Seated motif reigned on the nation's silver dollar from 1840 through 1873. Remarkably, this 34-year span is barely two-thirds the duration that the design was seen across the broader gamut of U.S. coinage. Not counting the Gobrecht dollars, the earliest striking of a Liberty Seated coin came in 1837 while the last occurred in 1891, when the dime, quarter, and half dollar were preparing for their transition to the Liberty Head types of Charles E. Barber.

At 34 years old, the Liberty Seated dollar wasn't all that long in the tooth when it retired in 1873. However, we might better characterize the coin's demise a layoff, for the end of the series was prompted by changes in coinage law (mentioned in greater detail in chapter one) that demonetized silver in the United States.

The Liberty Seated dollar's run offered collectors no lack of challenging opportunities, thanks to a sizable number of semi-keys, key dates, and conditional rarities. The series also spawned two subtypes concerning the inscription

The Liberty Seated dollar.

tion IN GOD WE TRUST on the coin's reverse, including the Without Motto (1840–1866) and With Motto (1866–1873) types. Proofs were struck in Philadelphia and exist in varying small quantities for every year of the series. Most collectors avoid these due to cost (about $4,000 and up), though they do enjoy a dedicated collector base.

Even in well-worn circulated grades of G-4 or VG-8, building an entire set of regular-issue Liberty Seated coinage would hit the intrepid collector's pocketbook north of $60,000, and that's not counting inclusion of the ultra-rare 1866 Without Motto or 1870-S. Prices for either exceed $1 million.

The Philadelphia strikes of the 1850s are categorically scarce, as is the 1859-S and all Civil War dates (1861–1865), which were struck only in Philadelphia. Meanwhile, all four Carson City issues from 1870 through 1873 are rare. The most common of dates can be had for around $400 in G-4, while the collector seeking no less than Uncirculated grades should allocate a minimum of about $2,500 for each.

TRADE DOLLARS, 1873–1885

Struck primarily for circulation in Asia, trade dollars debuted in 1873 with the stated purpose of giving the United States an edge against competing large-size silver coinage from other nations. Chinese merchants of the mid-nineteenth century preferred Mexican silver pesos, which were larger than standard U.S. silver dollars and proved both difficult and costly for United States importers to procure as necessary. By the early 1870s, some of these American importers were lobbying legislators to approve a measure allowing the production of special large-size silver coins that could gain favor among Chinese exporters.

Proposals called for 90 percent silver coins that weigh 420 grains, or 27.22 grams—about 1.8 percent heavier than the typical U.S. silver dollar and equivalent to the silver content of a Mexican dollar.

While the coin was authorized to better facilitate trade opportunities with China, the trade dollar was given legal-tender status in the United States up to $5. Falling silver prices led the coin's domestic legal-tender standing to be repealed in 1876, two years before production of circulating issues came to an end in 1878. Numismatic coins in the form of Proofs were produced as late as 1885. The later Coinage Act of 1965 returned full legal-tender status to the trade dollar, though by that time the obsolete coin was already worth far more than its bullion value to collectors.

Chief engraver William Barber designed the trade dollar, taking cues from the prevailing Liberty Seated motif of the day, while the Heraldic Eagle reverse is similar to the design Barber later offered for the short-lived twenty-cent coin of 1875 through 1878. Many trade dollars are found counterstamped with designs from Asian merchants and bankers, who emblazoned these pieces with proprietary logos and trademarks, or symbols indicating they were acceptable. Pieces with these counterstamps, widely dubbed "chopmarks," have seen growing interest among some collectors.

The series is roundly considered scarce, with even the most "common" of dates yielding relatively small numbers of truly problem-free examples. The 1875-S, 1876-S, 1877, 1877-S, and 1878-S trade dollars are among the most common and thus attract budget-conscious type set collectors. The six Carson City issues of the series are categorically the rarest circulation strikes and generally command the highest prices.

The collector can expect to spend around $200 for a common-date example graded F-12, while the least expensive of the Carson City pieces dates fetch around $400 in

William Barber.

The obverse design of the trade dollar echoes the prevailing Seated Liberty motif of other U.S. silver coins of the period and borrows the style of Great Britain's patriotic Britannia figure.

that same grade. Those wanting an Uncirculated example must pony up $1,000 or more, while Proofs dated from 1873 through 1883 generally come in around $3,000 and higher. The most valuable entries in the trade dollar series aren't necessarily to be found among the circulation strikes. The rarest pieces are the 1884 and 1885 Proofs, which saw mintages of just ten and five pieces, respectively, and have each sold in recent years for well over $1 million apiece.

MORGAN DOLLARS, 1878–1921

There are few coins that compare to the legendary popularity of the Morgan dollar. It is formally called the Liberty Head dollar, but the far more common name nods to the coin's designer, George T. Morgan. The Morgan dollar was conceived amid the passage of the Bland-Allison Act on February 28, 1878, requiring the Treasury to purchase between $2 million and $4 million in silver from Western mines each month.

Production of Morgan dollars fluctuated from year to year, with decent output during most years but uneven distributions in terms of which mints produced the largest numbers.

Mintages of silver dollars bottomed out during the mid-1890s amid recessionary concerns, giving rise to such notable Morgan dollar key dates as the 1893-S, 1894, 1895, 1895-O, and 1895-S. Ultimately, the economy recovered, and Morgan dollars mintages recovered likewise. Striking ceased in 1904 when government allocations for silver dollars ran dry. Terms of the Pittman Act of

The Morgan dollar.

April 23, 1918, brought more than 270 million Morgan dollars to the smelter, all to be recoined with newly purchased silver bought from Western mining companies. Following a 16-year pause, the Morgan dollar was reprised for one last flourish in 1921, when 86,730,000 coins were pumped out between the Philadelphia, Denver, and San Francisco Mints.

The Morgan dollar is an expansive series even without counting Proofs and the many cataloged die varieties, the latter group numbering well into the several hundreds. A collector wanting just one common example of a Morgan dollar for a type set can buy a circulated example for a small premium over its silver spot price. However, the Morgan enthusiast who intends to build an entire date-and-mintmark set in top grades can easily spend hundreds of thousands of dollars and their entire collecting lifetime doing so.

Competition among collectors to complete the best Morgan dollar sets compels many to build lavish registry sets. The series is among the most active in the registries of both PCGS and NGC, and the distance some collectors will go to achieve top grades is extraordinary. Prices for Uncirculated Carson City coins start in the mid-hundreds, while the major keys fetch four- and five-figure prices in the better grades. One outstanding example of the 1893-S, graded MS-67 by PCGS, hammered for a whopping $2,086,875 (with 12 percent buyer's fee) in August 2021.

PEACE DOLLARS, 1921–1935

The end of World War I was cause for great celebration. In 1920 at the annual American Numismatic Association (ANA) convention, the organization's notable historian, Farran Zerbe, presented a paper titled "Commemorate the Peace with a Coin for Circulation." The reception to Zerbe's proposal was incredible, leading to the formation of a committee that soon pitched a related Congressional bill.

On November 23, 1921, the federal Commission of Fine Arts called for a design competition for eight of the nation's foremost sculptors to submit designs for a new silver dollar. Anthony de Francisci won with a design of Miss Liberty modeled mostly upon the likeness of his young wife, Teresa. The head of this Miss Liberty was crowned with rays similar in appearance to those crowning the Statue of Liberty in New York Harbor, while the reverse model of de Francisci's proposed dollar depicted an eagle upon a rock breaking a sword to symbolize peace. The sketches were preliminarily approved by the Commission of Fine Arts but were met with scorn, with several officials believing the broken sword suggested defeat.

The Peace dollar.

It was in the hands of chief engraver George T. Morgan, whose dollar was being usurped with the creation of the Peace dollar, to make necessary changes to the design. Among the revisions was the removal of the sword. The design was rushed into production on December 28, 1921, with 1,006,473 all produced with a 1921 date and high-relief format. The relief was significantly lowered going into 1922 production to help ease extreme die wear, though a few rare matte Proofs dated 1922 were struck with the 1921 high-relief profile.

Peace dollar designer Anthony de Francisci's wife, Teresa, was the model for the young Miss Liberty on the coin.

Mintages soared going into the next two years of production, with the Philadelphia, Denver, and San Francisco Mints striking a cumulative 84,275,000 Peace dollars in 1922 and 56,631,000 in 1923. Production output significantly declined going into the next two years as commerce demands necessitated a greater number of smaller-denomination coins. Moreover, mandates of the Pittman Act were met in 1928, when the total output of silver dollars minted since 1921 had replenished the stockpile of coins converted into pure silver bullion.

Production of Peace dollars came to a temporary end after 1928, but production resumed after silver mining interests helped devise various legal constructs, including the Silver Purchase Act of 1934, which compelled the U.S. Mint to strike 7,074,557 more dollars over the course of 1934 and 1935. The latter date represents the original collectible bookend for this relatively short series but did not signal the end for the Peace dollar. Legislation passed on August 3, 1964, provided for the coinage of 45 million silver dollars, and 316,076 were minted the following year in Denver with a 1964 date. However, this project was deserted, largely over concerns the coins would be collected rather than spent as intended. All 1964-D Peace dollars were melted under tight security. None are known to have been saved, but any that may remain are illegal to own.

The 1921 Peace dollar is a highly sought-after first-year coin also serving as a single-year subtype in its high-relief profile, selling for $125 in EF-40 and $425 in MS-63. However, the series key is the 1928 Philadelphia issue, and with its mintage of only 360,649 it trades for $300 in EF-40 and $600 in MS-63. Meanwhile, the 1934-S—a tough semi-key date and conditional rarity—saw a mintage of just 1,011,000 struck and fetches $200 in EF-40 and $2,300 in MS-60.

EISENHOWER DOLLARS, 1971–1978

The Eisenhower dollar was the last of the circulating large-size dollar coins like those of yore, yet it was by no means a silver dollar—at least not in the traditional sense of the term. The Eisenhower dollars that were being issued for circulation, mostly for the Nevada slot-machine circuit, were base-metal coins. President Dwight D. Eisenhower's death on March 28, 1969, hastened talk in U.S. Mint circles of reviving the dollar coin, as would've been legally permitted five years after the passage of the Coinage Act of 1965.

President Richard M. Nixon signed the Eisenhower dollar into law on December 31, 1970, with Mint chief engraver Frank Gasparro already having gone to work on preparing models for the new dollar coin.

The obverse is anchored by a left-facing profile of "Ike," while the reverse carries a design virtually identical to the Apollo 11 insignia. The first working dies were ready to go on January 2, 1971. Trials and later Proofs were struck in the following months, with circulation strikes hitting banks November 1, 1971.

The Eisenhower dollar became the first U.S. coin series ever produced for circulation only in copper-nickel clad and the largest U.S. coin struck in that metallic composition. The Philadelphia and Denver Mints struck circulation coins. Meanwhile, collector versions were produced in a 40 percent silver clad format at the San Francisco Mint.

The Eisenhower dollar.

The Apollo 11 insignia, used to symbolize the famous 1969 space flight that took the first men to the Moon.

In 1971 and 1972 even the clad Ike dollars had to be obtained by collectors individually—they were not included in regular annual Uncirculated sets and Proof sets. Both sets came to include the Eisenhower dollar as standard entries beginning in 1973 and continuing through the end of the series in 1978.

The entire series of regular circulation strikes and Proofs encompasses 32 issues, and a complete collection can be assembled in run-of-the-mill grades for only a few hundred dollars. While such a collection may satisfy many collectors, there are several notable and scarce varieties, including three varieties of 1972 Philadelphia strikes exhibiting clearly different geographical boundaries on the miniature rendition of Earth behind the Moon.

Furthermore, clad circulation-strike Ikes are tough to locate in MS-65 and frequently considered conditional rarities in grades of MS-66 or higher. This is primarily a result of the large, heavy coins being jangled in mint bags during transit to bank vaults. Premiums run extremely high on some of the rarest of these Superb Gem clad Ikes. For example, an MS-67 Denver example of the 1776–1976 dollar—one of the most common dates in the series—hammered an astounding $11,162.50 in 2015.

SUSAN B. ANTHONY DOLLARS, 1979–1981, 1999

As much as Americans may have liked Ike, they weren't too fond of spending the hefty coins minted in his honor. By late 1976, many officials were talking abolishment of the dollar coin, but fancy financial footwork showed the U.S. Treasury could save tens of millions of dollars by replacing the dollar bill with a small-size dollar coin. The fiscal rationale is based on the lifespan of a circulating coin averaging 30 years, while a typical dollar bill might last just 18 to 24 months. Figure this in with the late-1970s estimate that it cost 1.8 cents to print each $1 bill and 3 cents, only slightly more, to produce each small-size dollar, and the long-term savings to taxpayers became tantalizing.

The Susan B. Anthony dollar.

Chief engraver Frank Gasparro was tasked to begin producing models showing what a new small-size dollar coin might look like. His original concept art graced the obverse of the new coin with a radiant image of a young Miss Liberty sporting flowing locks and a Phrygian cap on a pole, while the reverse soared with an eagle flying before a rising sun. However, prevailing sociopolitical sensibilities then preempted Gasparro's classicist vision with calls for the coin to instead carry the likeness of a historical woman. Suffragist Susan B. Anthony soon became the favorite subject for the new dollar coin's obverse design.

Basing his design of Anthony from the few surviving images of the women's rights leader, Gasparro depicted her around the age of 50—at the height of her social influence during the early 1870s. Gasparro believed that his flying eagle reverse would be paired with the Anthony obverse, but a late amendment to the authorizing legislation retained the Apollo 11 motif seen on the Eisenhower dollar. Many numismatists still question the incongruous pairing of the two designs.

President Jimmy Carter signed the coin into law on October 10, 1978, and the first test strikings occurred over the next months. During the coin's original 1979–1981 run, the Philadelphia, Denver, and San Francisco Mints all produced circulation strikes. Interestingly, the striking of the Philadelphia coins marked the first time since 1945 that a "P" mintmark symbolizing the Philadelphia Mint appeared on United States coins, and this foreshadowed the regular inclusion of the "P" mintmark on all U.S. coins of a face value greater than one cent beginning in 1980.

The Susan B. Anthony dollar was officially released into circulation with great fanfare on July 2, 1979, but it didn't take long for the public to rebuke the new coin. Many confused it with the quarter, citing the mini dollar's similar size, color, and edge. The coin was panned, some critics calling the stagflation-era coin the "Carter Quarter." In short order, the U.S. Mint flooded banks and merchants with information pamphlets touting the many benefits of the new coin, but apparently few minds were changed. Circulating mintages plunged from 757,813,744 in 1979 to only 89,660,708 in 1980. Just 9,742,000 circulation strikes—all for numismatic purposes—were made in 1981, the year the coin was scrapped.

Increasing use of the Susie B. in municipal mass transit circuits and in postage-stamp vending machines during the 1980s

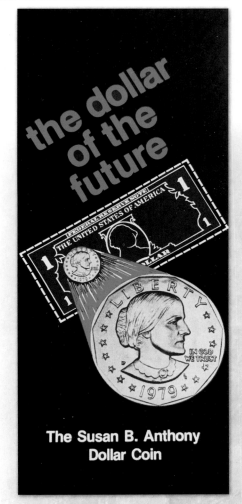

The Susan B. Anthony Dollar Coin

The Susan B. Anthony dollar failed despite a massive marketing campaign touting its benefits, including its cheaper overall cost of production to taxpayers and smaller size than previous dollar coins.

and 1990s depleted once-massive Treasury reserves of the coin. This prompted a make-do run of a little more than 41 million 1999-dated Susan B. Anthony dollars, ahead of an entirely new dollar coin program to begin in 2000.

All told, the Susan B. Anthony dollar was one of the nation's shortest-lived and most derided of coins. Yet, this compact modern series yielded a remarkable number of tough-to-find varieties, including the 1979 Near Date, and 1979-S and 1981-S Type II Proofs. A nice 18-piece set incorporating these varieties, the regular-issue circulation strikes, and Proofs can run some $300. No slouch on auction blocks are super-grade representatives, such as the MS-68 example of a 1980-P, encapsulated by PCGS, selling for $4,600 in a 2008 Heritage Auctions event. It's one of several high-grading SBA dollars to hammer for four figures.

"Golden" Dollars, 2000 to Present

The dawning of a new millennium brought with it a U.S. dollar coin promising to correct any technical and aesthetic mistakes that may have plagued the unsuccessful Susan B. Anthony dollar of yesteryear. The new dollar was authorized under the United States Dollar Coin Act of 1997 and signed into law by President Bill Clinton on December 1 of that year. Discussion surrounding what the new coin would look like swirled over the following months, with United States Treasury secretary Robert Rubin and director of the United States Mint Philip Diehl seeking public discourse on the matter. Ultimately, it was decided that a young Shoshone woman named Sacagawea, who guided explorers Meriwether Lewis and William Clark on their Pacific-bound journey, would anchor the obverse with her infant son Jean Baptiste.

The obverse was designed by sculptor-engraver Glenna Goodacre, while the reverse motif of a flying eagle was the brainchild of Thomas D. Rogers Sr. The coin's release was trumpeted across the land, with many major retailers, including Walmart, promoting the coin. It was even incorporated in a special promotion with ubiquitous breakfast cereal Cheerios, which distributed some 5,500 of the Sacagawea dollars among 10 million boxes, all of which included a 2000 Lincoln cent encased on a special commemorative card.

The public clearly found the coins to be a special novelty, and many even believed the new "golden" dollars (as they were widely promoted) were made from real gold. However, none of the circulating Sacagawea dollars contain the pricey precious metal, though a few 22-karat gold numismatic prototypes exist. Rather, the dollar's goldish hue derives from a manganese-brass composition involving an outer clad layer of 77 percent copper, 12 percent zinc, 7 percent manganese, and 4 percent nickel bonded to a pure copper core.

Widespread promotions couldn't spare the Sacagawea dollars from the same fate as their failed disco-era predecessor. By 2001, the "golden dollars" were already being condemned to the depths of Treasury vaults. Mintages fell from the cumulative 1.29 billion Philadelphia and Denver circulation strikes in 2000 to barely more than 133 million in 2001. Few wanted to spend the new Sacagawea dollar.

The U.S. government tried shaking things up for the dollar coin a few years later with the start of the Presidential dollar coin series, authorized by the Presidential $1 Coin Act of 2005 and signed into law by President George W. Bush on December 22 of that year. The program began in January 2007 honoring four deceased former United States presidents each year, in the chronological order they served as commander-in-chief.

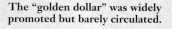

The "golden dollar" was widely promoted but barely circulated.

The first Presidential dollar coin, honoring George Washington.

The Native American dollar is an ongoing series paying homage to contributions by American Indians.

The American Innovation dollars commemorate innovations and inventors.

The discovery of so-called "Godless" dollars—those lacking the edge-inscribed motto IN GOD WE TRUST—stirred national attention during the early days of the series in March 2007 and precipitated a rush of collector interest, with some pieces then selling for more than $500 for a time. However, prices cooled and so did interest in the Presidential dollar series, which sputtered into the next decade.

The Native American $1 Coin Act that was signed by President George W. Bush on September 20, 2007, ushered in the Native American dollar series in 2009. Retaining the obverse design featuring Sacagawea, these dollar coins carry an annually changing reverse depicting "images celebrating the important contributions made by Indian tribes and individual Native Americans to the development of the United States and the history of the United States."

In 2018 yet another multiyear dollar coin program began. Signed into law on July 18, 2018, by President Donald Trump, the American Innovation dollars honor various innovations and innovators from each of the 50 states, the District of Columbia, and United States territories. Still, more than 1 billion "golden" dollar coins dating back to 2000 reside in vaults and may only have a viable chance of seeing the light of day in commerce if the United States stops issuing dollar bills.

AMERICAN SILVER EAGLES BELONG IN THE SILVER DOLLAR CANON

The previous pages of this chapter have just barely scraped the surface in illustrating the story of the United States silver dollar (and related dollar coins). Many whole books have been written about the nation's silver-dollar coins, and certainly compendiums have been penned about individual types and even specific dates within those series.

The American silver dollar is an iconic coin known by many well beyond the boundaries of the numismatic hobby, even if generations have passed since the last true silver dollars were minted for circulation. Mention the term "silver dollar" to anybody, even a child, and chances are pretty good they will have some idea in their mind's eye of what it looks like. Silver dollars thrive in the collective subconscious of Americans.

Not counting the modern commemorative silver dollars that the United States Mint has made since 1983 (and which don't circulate anyway), the nation hasn't struck a real, circulating 90 percent silver dollar since the heart of the Great Depression. Yet, the silver dollar remains an active part of contemporary social culture.

Silver dollars were commonly seen in movies and television shows of the once-predominant Western genre of the 1950s and '60s. It was a time when Americans

The American Silver Eagle, long a favorite coin of bullion investors, is now widely embraced as the "modern silver dollar" or even the "Morgan dollar of today."

could turn on television and encounter collectible coins of every manner, including silver dollars. Consider *Dennis the Menace*, with the titular Dennis (played by Jay North) tormenting middle-aged neighbor Mr. Wilson (Joseph Kearns), a numismatist whose coin collection often made cameo appearances and, on an occasion or two, was the main—and unfortunate—plot device thanks to the young boy and his mischievous ways. The hobby was also a central plot element on certain episodes of other major primetime series of the day, such as *The Dick Van Dyke Show* and *The Lucy Show*, the latter serving as comedienne Lucille Ball's 1960s follow-up to her more famous 1950s series *I Love Lucy*. Silver dollars are even referenced on more contemporary shows, such as the 1980s drama *Matlock* and 1990s hit *Seinfeld*.

Why, even the most repudiated "silver" dollar of all, the Susie B., saw its share of the limelight, even if as the veritable punchline of a joke. A toe-tapping 1979 novelty song by Richard M. Sherman and Milt Larsen, aptly titled "The Susan B. Anthony Dollar," carries lyrics like, "Let's give a great big holler to the Susan B. Anthony dollar/The boys in the mint they got inspired/An 11-sided coin we all desired/Gonna be America's lucky bucka bucka bucka buck buck." Affable *Three's Company* lady's man Jack Tripper, played by late comedy actor John Ritter, in the 1981 episode "Boy Meets Dummy" fights the competing interests of two women by suggesting they flip a coin to decide who gets his attention. "Make it a Susan B. Anthony," he quips. A decade later, the little dollar that couldn't was even parodied on the long-running animated prime-time cartoon series *The Simpsons*. In the show's 1991 episode "Mr. Lisa Goes to Washington," fictional woman's suffrage leader Winifred Beecher Howe, said to have sparked the Floor Mop Rebellion of 1910, "appeared on the highly unpopular 75-cent piece." *The Simpsons* writers took more satiric aim at the Susan B. Anthony dollar in the 2000 episode "Behind the Laughter," in which the obverse likeness of the coin appears on the round shield of fictitious comic book legend Susan B. Anthony Man.

Other dollar coins have largely flown under the levity radar of sharp contemporary comedy writers. However, the American Silver Eagle proudly entered the collective consciousness by way of other, weightier avenues, including advertisements for retirement planning and the realm of home-shopping television programming. In fact, there may be no other silver dollar that has received as much attention as the American Silver Eagle in just this way except the Morgan dollar, another favorite of the promoter.

For many of a certain generation, the Morgan dollar is a highly familiar coin. Many individuals who grew up in the 1950s and 1960s recall loved ones who collected Morgan dollars, which, at the time, could be purchased for face value at banks. This then-easy access to silver dollars is another reason why many children of the mid-twentieth century reminisce over gifts of Morgan dollars for various holidays. By the end of the 1960s, silver prices had already begun rising and instances of picking up silver dollars for a buck a pop were but a fond memory.

Now, many of today's younger people are inheriting Morgan silver dollars from loved ones, and yet another generation is becoming privy to these large silver coins of the past. Just as was the case for a generation of collectors decades ago, the Morgan dollar carries with it the romance and mystique of the Old West, and today's younger collectors embrace a numismatic journey with Morgans, just as their parents and grandparents may have 30, 40, or 50 years earlier.

What many folks may not immediately realize is that of all the silver dollars that have been minted in the United States, no series comes as close to production longevity and overall affordability as the American Silver Eagle. The Silver Eagle has seen more than 35 consecutive years of continuous striking. This places the series ahead of the Morgan dollar, which saw just 28 years of mintage, and even the Liberty Seated series, in existence for 34 years. All other United States silver dollar coins have seen far fewer years of actual production. When it comes to the number of issues struck over the course of the series, the American Silver Eagle comes in with more than 100,

**American Silver Eagles connect the investor and the collector
and have become one of the most popular coins in the world.**

including all mintmarks, Proofs, and major varieties. The Morgan dollar, given its many date-and-mintmark combinations and rambling number of noted die varieties, bests the Silver Eagle in collectible issues and die marriages, but it would take some pretty deep pockets to ever complete that classic series.

If artistic merit has any bearing on the allure of the Morgan dollar, then the American Silver Eagle carries its weight here, too. Adolph A. Weinman's quintessentially American design, as once struck on the half dollar, shines in its full beauty on the large canvas of the Silver Eagle. Weinman's original Liberty Walking design was refined by sculptor-engraver John Mercanti to help areas of the design stand out more boldly upon striking, and Mercanti's vintage-1980s heraldic eagle is as archetypal an elegant design of its time as was Morgan's heraldic eagle of the late 1870s. Both designs can be appreciated as artistic reflections of the aesthetics movements of their eras.

The American Silver Eagle bridges the imaginary gulf between the investor and the collector as a coin of outstanding crossover appeal with a relatively low entry-level cost to both types of buyers. Make no mistake, the American Silver Eagle is a terrific bullion investment vehicle. But the coin has become a true numismatic collectible. In every sense of the word, the American Silver Eagle has everything the collector looks for when deciding what series to collect. Rarity, challenge, beauty, intrigue, and opportunity—all are hallmarks of coins like the Liberty Seated, Morgan, and Peace dollars, and all are to be found with the American Silver Eagle.

3
A Modern Silver Dollar for Modern Times

There is no better way to describe the American Silver Eagle than to say that it is the silver dollar of today's generation. Yes, you can buy them as precious-metal investments, and you can collect them alongside their Morgan and Peace dollar sisters—or all alone, should you choose. But ultimately, the American Silver Eagle is no less a legal-tender silver dollar in reality or in spirit than any of the other large silver coins that have been dubbed "silver dollars" throughout the ages.

In the most basic terms, the Silver Eagle is a legal-tender silver coin denominated as one dollar. However, the glaring distinction is that American Silver Eagles weren't born from a need to fulfill commerce demands; they were originally designed to sell off surplus silver from the U.S. National Defense Stockpile. It just so happens the chosen product took the form of a silver dollar, since the surfeit of bullion could have just as easily been sold as bars, granules, pellets, or numerous other manifestations.

It's fortunate for collectors, investors, silver stackers, and so many others that the United States government bullion reserves were coined into silver dollars. It's reasonable to think that people like Idaho Republican senator James A. McClure, who embraced the concept of

When the American Silver Eagle came on the scene during the mid-1980s, the nation was at a crossroads socioeconomically and technologically.

converting surplus government silver into bullion coins, foresaw these coins selling well. However, it's difficult to believe that anybody truly anticipated the massive and enduring success of the American Silver Eagle. For anybody studying the market viability of a one-ounce silver bullion coin in the mid-1980s, the only numismatic benchmarks they could really look to were the Mexican Libertad, debuting in 1982, and the Chinese Silver Panda, stepping out in 1983.

When the American Silver Eagle finally flew onto investor and numismatic radar screens on November 24, 1986, it received a wide embrace from a marketplace ready and willing for such a coin. Never before had the U.S. Mint produced a legal-tender silver coin of such high purity, not to mention physical size and heft. Offering a full troy ounce of silver, the American Silver Eagle hit the scene at 40.6 millimeters in diameter and tipped the scales at 31.103 grams, with a metallic composition consisting of 99.9 percent silver and 0.1 percent copper.

A total of 5,393,005 coins were struck at the San Francisco Mint bearing the 1986 date. The first-year mintage figure, just short of 5.4 million coins, would eventually prove relatively miniscule compared to later mintages, which neared 50 million. However, few observers in 1986 or 1987 could argue that a distribution tally of over five million was anything less than a stellar success. Bear in mind, these figures don't even account for the 1,446,778 San Francisco Proof coins sold for $21.95, a price point that then represented some four times the coin's intrinsic value of about $5. With collectors and investors alike clamoring for these novel coins, the U.S. Mint clearly had a success on their hands—and they knew this within hours of the coin's official release.

"Sales are phenomenal," noted Mint director Donna Pope to the press in news stories published on November 25, 1986. Pope added that the American Gold Eagle coin, initially released on October 20, 1986, was ranked "product of the year" by *Fortune* magazine. She continued, "To read that we have the number-one selling product in America is a real treat." While the initial inventory of 800,000 American Gold Eagles sold out within two days, the first block of 1.4 million American Silver Eagles was depleted within mere hours, with sales divvied up among bulk orders of 50,000 pieces each to 28 Authorized Purchasers. Pope suspected that many of the initial sales were destined to become gifts for the holidays, just around the corner.

It's clear Americans from inside the hobby, throughout the investor circuit, and well beyond those arenas were waiting for the new coin. Regarded by so many as America's new silver dollar, the American Silver Eagle was clear for takeoff with blue skies ahead. The climate of the United States in the 1980s was just right for the new coin, and with so many who still had memories of growing up receiving or even spending classic silver dollars decades earlier, the American Silver Eagle promised a nostalgic return at a time when the world was rapidly changing, and the future seemed uncertain.

Mint director Donna Pope, circa 1981, alongside Dr. Alan J. Goldman, the U.S. Mint's assistant director for technology.

AMERICA LOOKS AHEAD TO THE 1980S

At the dawn of the 1980s, Americans were still dealing with 1970s problems. Worsening inflation and increasing interest rates were hitting Americans in their pocketbooks. An energy crisis that began in the mid-1970s was pushing prices at the gas pump beyond the $1 per-gallon threshold—an unthinkable figure just a few years earlier. Struggles for oil led to uncomfortable predicaments in the Middle East, a theater for international conflicts.

For many in the 1970s, America became a land of disillusionment, casting a pall upon the early days of the 1980s. Still lingering in the minds of many was the 1974 resignation of President Richard Nixon, disgraced by the Watergate scandal. After the deaths of nearly 60,000 military personnel and injuries to countless thousands more, the Vietnam War came to an end when the South Vietnam capital of Saigon fell to communist North Vietnam forces in 1975; service members returned home to hardly a warm welcome after spending years in a war that was bitterly protested.

President Gerald Ford was commander-in-chief when the United States celebrated its bicentennial in 1976, but many were left to wonder what the future held for the nation. On July 4, 1976, colorful fireworks flew over a nation grayed by the worst economy since the Great Depression. Hanging overhead was a cloud of gloom created by the sobering reality that America was still detested by a nuclear-enabled Soviet Union and frozen in an ongoing Cold War.

President Jimmy Carter was inaugurated in 1977 and soon found himself beset with a host of problems inherited from presidents before, with perhaps none so troubling as the matter of the Middle East. He helmed peace accords between Egyptian president Anwar Sadat and Israeli prime minister Menachem Begin in efforts to soothe tensions between their long-clashing nations. Iran proved to be the biggest challenge when 52 U.S. diplomats and other citizens were taken hostage at the American Embassy in Tehran by college-age followers of the Iranian Revolution on November 4, 1979.

The years leading up to the 1980s were touched by many events that shaped policy for years to come. The Vietnam War raged in the early 1970s, killing thousands. President Richard Nixon resigned in 1974 amid the unfolding Watergate scandal. Lines formed at gas stations in 1979 as an ongoing energy crisis gripped the nation.

The Iranian hostage crisis would continue for 444 days, sharing headlines with economic meltdowns, spiraling inflation, growing unemployment lines, oil shortages, and the ever-looming threat of nuclear war with the Soviets. Throw in the escalating bullion prices sparked by any number of sociopolitical crises and the crazy schemes of the Hunt brothers, and a picture emerges of the consuming angst running through the hearts and minds of many Americans around 1980.

President Jimmy Carter.

The nation of some 226 million residents was 80 percent White and 90 percent Christian, retaining the mostly homogenous demographics that characterized the United States of the mid-twentieth century, particularly beyond the big cities. However, the population profile was on the verge of major changes and a massive population boom fueled by new immigrants from beyond Europe. The United States electorate in 1980 was one of the most diverse in modern history to that point.

In 1980 there were still five million Americans alive who had been born in the 1800s, about 450,000 World War I veterans, and robust numbers of aging but politically active senior citizens who remembered ferrying through Ellis Island as new immigrants from the "Old Country" of Europe. The youngest Baby Boomers were still in high school, while the oldest of that generation were already thirty-somethings who had entered corporate America in the "Me Decade" of the 1970s and were about to define the "yuppie" generation of the 1980s. The plurality of Vietnam veterans were only in their late 20s through early 40s, and so many former flower-child peaceniks were, too. Social movements of the 1950s and 1960s had brought more women and ethnic minorities than ever before to corporate boardrooms and company roundtables, but these numbers were relatively small. America was at a crossroads of every kind, and voters were about to head to the polls to pick a new president—the first to be elected in the 1980s.

Despite a broad range of worldviews in 1980, there was just one consideration that seemed to matter to most voters that year. During a presidential debate on October 28, 1980, with incumbent Democratic president Jimmy Carter, Republican nominee Ronald Reagan asked Americans a question that has since become a keystone campaign inquiry. "Are you better off today than you were four years ago?" Voters resoundingly replied, "No."

Reagan won in a landslide, sweeping into the White House with 489 electoral votes against Carter's 49. Just as Reagan was sworn into office on January 20, 1981, the 52 Iranian hostages were released from their captivity and on a plane bound for the United States. To many, the timing struck the chord of a resolute Reagan forcing the Iranians into submission. However, Carter had been working on negotiations through the last moments of his presidency, and a deal was finally struck with steely Iranian leader Ayatollah Ruholla Khomeini through Algerian mediation.

The nation seemed to transform little under its first months of Reagan's presidency. A world already shaken by the assassination of Beatles musician John Lennon on

December 8, 1980, was stunned when breaking news alerts on March 30, 1981, told of Reagan's shooting in Washington, D.C., in an assassination attempt by John Hinckley Jr., a man obsessed with gaining the attention of young movie actress Jodie Foster. Just weeks later, on May 13, an attempt against the life of Pope John Paul II rocked headlines. Egyptian president Anwar Sadat was assassinated by fundamentalist army officers on October 6, 1981. President Reagan, having just recovered from his bullet wounds months earlier, had fired some 11,000 air traffic controllers striking against the Federal Aviation Authority for better pay and working conditions. Social Security was heading toward insolvency. The U.S. national debt topped $1 trillion for the first time on October 22, 1981.

Were things really going to get any better in the 1980s?

THE AMERICAN SILVER EAGLE TAKES FLIGHT DURING THE REAGAN REVOLUTION

Ronald Reagan was a president who shattered barriers that seemed unbreakable to many Americans of the early 1980s. Born on February 6, 1911, he was 69 years old when he was sworn in as the nation's 40th commander-in-chief on January 20, 1981, then the oldest man to assume the office.

Upon entering the White House, Reagan was only six years removed from a successful two-term run as California's governor. Before that, he spent two decades as a Hollywood star and appeared in more than 50 films. He was married to actress Jane Wyman, with whom he had two children, Maureen and Michael. Divorcing Wyman in 1949, Reagan wed Nancy Davis, herself an actress, in 1952 and together they had children Patricia and Ron.

Ronald Reagan struck many in the early 1980s as unorthodox—a Hollywood star, twice married, and past retirement age. However, he was breaking molds at just the time when Americans were looking for something different in their national leadership. Many Americans felt his patriotism was reminiscent of a more hopeful yesteryear, when the nation was successful at winning major conflicts and the economy was stronger and far more independent. Blue-collar workers and unions broke from their traditional Democratic ranks to vote for staunchly Republican Reagan, on hopes his economic plans would revive a long-languishing job market. Meanwhile, many young voters who would have typically supported the Democratic contender instead pulled the lever for Reagan amid disillusionment with Jimmy Carter, an upstanding man whose presidency—due either to failed policies or simply sheer bad luck—fell short of inspiring much of his voting base.

The American economy didn't automatically whip into shape on January 20, 1981, the day Reagan walked into the White House. The economic malaise and the general mood of the nation had been quite bad for a long time.

One of Reagan's first actions was the Economic Recovery Tax Act of 1981, designed to stimulate the economy and slash federal income tax rates at every echelon. The top individual tax rate plunged from 70 percent to 28 percent, while the corporate tax rate fell from 46 percent to 34 percent. The tax act, signed into law in August 1981, also softened estate taxes and capital gains taxes. The massive tax cuts bolstered the economy for the rest of the decade, but the federal deficit also grew due to revenue shortfalls. This prompted the Tax Equity and Fiscal Responsibility Act of 1982, which revoked some of the rate cuts stipulated in the sweeping tax act of the previous year.

President Reagan's economic policy is often boiled down to the buzzword "Reaganomics." In a nutshell, Reagan believed tax cuts for businesses and fewer regulations would lower costs for employers, who would then have more money to hire more workers, thus eliminating unemployment and helping improve the economy in a "trickle down" pattern.

Amid the myriad changes in tax law, Reagan also took aim at federal spending as the key to achieving a balanced budget by 1984. Federal budget cuts were in full force by the end of his first year as president and saw wide support both inside the Washington, D.C., Beltway and among the majority of Americans. The cuts implemented didn't go as far as Reagan envisioned, but they touched many areas of the government ledger books. Interestingly, one of the casualties was the U.S. Mint Uncirculated coin set program, which returned in 1984 only because of the outcry from the numismatic public.

Despite the budget cuts of the early 1980s, the United States commemorative coin program resumed in 1982 following sweeping support in Congress for a 90 percent silver half dollar honoring the 250th anniversary of George Washington's birth. The George Washington 250th Anniversary half dollar not only signaled the first official United States commemorative coin since 1954 but also would prove highly beneficial to supporting the federal government's bottom line, which would see hundreds of millions of dollars in profit from the commemorative program in the decades ahead.

By the time Reagan ran for reelection in 1984, it was clear the nation's economy was in recovery mode. Unemployment rates, which had reached nearly 11 percent in 1982, fell below 7 percent for the whole of 1984. The economy was looking relatively rosy by the time voters returned to the polls on November 6 to sweep Reagan back into office by even greater margins against Democratic contender Walter Mondale.

President Ronald Reagan signs the Economic Recovery Act of 1981 at his vacation home, Rancho del Cielo, in California on August 13, 1981.

The Reagan Revolution was here, and the United States was an entirely different place than it was at the start of the 1980s. Were Americans really better off in 1984 than they were four years earlier? Many would resoundingly say "yes." Other would argue differently. Yet, the voice of any dissenters barely registered a peep on a political map that showed 525 electoral votes for Reagan and just 13 for Mondale—all coming from the Democrat's home state of Minnesota.

Within months of his second inauguration on January 20, 1985, Reagan would encounter yet another piece of economic legislation on his desk. This time, the bill didn't make mention of tax cuts, federal budget appropriations, or corporate regulation policy. This bill, nondescriptly cataloged in Congressional records as Title II of Public Law 99-61, is known to many by its more patriotic moniker, the "Liberty Coin Act." The American Silver Eagle was ceremoniously signed into law by Reagan's hand on July 9, 1985, and a new era in American numismatics was born.

AMERICAN SILVER EAGLES INCUBATE DURING CHANGING TIMES

The American Silver Eagle arrived during a transitional time for numismatics and the nation as a whole. In the mid-1980s most Americans tuned into only three broadcast networks, listened to their music on the radio, and got their news from the newspaper. Meanwhile, suburban America continued defining what many might consider "mainstream" values and fads, much as they had since the middle of the twentieth century. Families still took vacations in their trusty station wagons or newfangled minivans and usually purchased their clothes and appliances at Sears.

In the 1980s and 1990s many department stores had coin shops, including Sears. The company offered American Eagles through mail-order distribution, and some locations, like this one at University Square Mall in Tampa, Florida, had a coin shop.

Looking at the 1980s as a happier time and place might be a rose-colored nostalgia trip—a trip all generations take when looking at the past. But to say the 1980s was "just a better time" ignores the fact that many of the social challenges and political issues we grapple with today were already fomenting. Beyond the white picket fences and Kenmore kitchens of 1980s middle America, serious issues were bubbling that would eventually shape the nation's social policy in the twenty-first century.

America's inner cities were dealing with a crack cocaine epidemic that left many families physically absent a parent—sometimes both—decimated by premature deaths of loved ones or long-term incarcerations. To combat the crack epidemic, several major anti-drug initiatives sprang up, and Reagan recommitted to the War on Drugs that Richard Nixon had spearheaded in the early 1970s. Reagan signed the Anti-Drug Abuse Act in 1986, by which time First Lady Nancy Reagan's "Just Say No" campaign was already making headway in schoolhouses across the country. In Los Angeles the similar Drug Abuse Resistance Education (D.A.R.E.) program, the brainchild of Los Angeles

Police chief Daryl Gates and the Los Angeles Unified School District, coupled students with police officers to discourage drug use and gang activity.

Acquired Immune Deficiency Syndrome, or AIDS, first clinically reported on June 5, 1981, killed more than 15,000 Americans by the start of 1986. The disease, which knows no demographic bounds, went on to kill more than 700,000 children and adults in the United States by 2021, 40 years after the first handful of cases were identified in New York City, Los Angeles, and San Francisco. More than 30 million people worldwide have died of AIDS during that same timeframe.

Cities were grappling with many other issues, too. The manufacturing economy that had been the backbone of the nation for decades was eroding away. Steel plants in Pennsylvania and Ohio were shutting down, textile mills in New England and the South

First Lady Nancy Reagan led the "Just Say No" anti-drug campaign in the 1980s.

faced stiffer competition from cheaper foreign imports, and tighter fiscal policies at the Federal Reserve dealt heavier debt burdens upon many farmers in the Midwest. Prospects may have been better in the technical and electronic corridor of the Pacific coast, but many Americans were in a state of economic flux. Major players in the nation's once-dominant industrial and agricultural sectors were closing up shop due to bankruptcies and mergers or seeking cheaper labor and material costs by moving abroad.

The globe was becoming ever smaller thanks to the advent of smaller, faster, and more efficient communications technologies. The personal computer began hitting store shelves in the late 1970s, and increasingly powerful models were becoming mainstays in the home and at the office by the mid-1980s. The technology that birthed the commercially successful internet as it is known today was already under development and in early use at many institutions around the world.

Cellular phones were also becoming en vogue in the mid-1980s and, with price points and service fees still out of reach for most Americans, grew in prominence

Personal computers, cellular phones, and compact discs were among the latest technologies of the 1980s.

among an affluent clientele of doctors, lawyers, stockbrokers, realtors, and others who needed to communicate on the go for work.

More and more people were ditching road trips and taking to the friendly skies for long-distance vacations. Air travel, once something only the rich could afford, was deregulated in 1978, opening competition between carriers that made plane tickets much cheaper by the 1980s. People weren't dressing up to fly as much as they had in the 1960s or 1970s, but then again, with legroom and in-flight perks disappearing, why would they?

Music Television, a cable network that debuted on August 1, 1981, and became more widely became known by its acronym "MTV," changed the way Americans consumed music in the 1980s and beyond. So, too, did the compact disc, which was introduced to the mainstream consumer in 1982 and wooed buyers away from records and cassettes. The likes of Phil Collins, Bruce Springsteen, Lionel Richie, and Whitney Houston tore through the radio charts, while individualistic pop icons Michael Jackson, Prince, David Bowie, and Madonna contributed as much to the music scene as they did to the fashion world.

Designers of every stripe eschewed the darker earth tones of the 1970s in favor of neon hues more emblematic of the 1980s. Meanwhile, big hair, legwarmers, spandex, and shoulder pads were all the rage, and it's no exaggeration to say that television crime drama series *Miami Vice* (1984–1989) influenced many of the trendy touchstones of the era. Everybody knew the names of their favorite barflies on Boston-based sitcom *Cheers*, while TV newcomers *The Cosby Show*, *Perfect Strangers*, *The Golden Girls*, and *Murder, She Wrote* joined the primetime ranks with more familiar series such as *The Facts of Life*, *Dallas*, *Dynasty*, and *Hill Street Blues*.

More and more people were beginning to catch the news on cable networks, which began in earnest during the 1970s but had remained little more than a novelty for most Americans. The aptly named Cable News Network (CNN), launched by media mogul Ted Turner and television journalist Reese Schonfeld in 1980, effectively birthed the concept of the 24-hour news cycle. In the mid-1980s CNN offered an immersion of news that few could have dreamt of on broadcast networks, which primarily offered news programs only in the morning and evenings. CNN brought many of the day's breaking stories to the fore, including the disaster at the Chernobyl Nuclear Power Plant in Ukraine, the explosion of the Space Shuttle *Challenger* in 1986, the ongoing scandal of the Iran-Contra Affair, and the evolving relationship between Western democracies and the Soviet Union during the Cold War.

Pop artist Michael Jackson and Great Britain's Princess Diana (seen here with President Reagan in 1985) were two of the biggest celebrities of the 1980s.

The mid-1980s offered budding news junkies a cavalcade of headlining figures, including the Reagans, British prime minister Margaret Thatcher, Princess of Wales Diana (Spencer), Pope John Paul II, Mother Theresa, Russian leader Mikhail Gorbachev, president of Iraq Saddam Hussein, Libyan head Muammar Gaddafi, and Nelson Mandela, then imprisoned in South Africa as an anti-apartheid activist, who later became president of his nation.

NUMISMATICS ENTERS NEW HORIZONS

In the mid-1980s the numismatic scene was undergoing a reinvention. There had been major changes in the hobby in the 1930s and 1940s, when a flurry of new coin products hit retail shelves, including the famous blue Whitman Publishing coin boards (1934) and folders (1940), the *Handbook of United States Coins* (the *Blue Book*, 1942), and *A Guide Book of United States Coins* (the *Red Book*, 1946). The 1950s saw growing popularity of rolls and bags of each year's newly minted coins, bought at face value by collectors and speculators in the hope of future profits. In 1961 Whitman introduced its line of coin *albums* as the hobby and markets continued expanding. The elimination of silver from circulating coinage during the 1960s was a major game changer. But it was the 1980s advent of third-party coin authentication, grading, and encapsulation that would steer the hobby market in the decades ahead.

The concept of third-party coin grading and authentication wasn't completely new in the 1980s. American Numismatic Association Certification Service (ANACS) had introduced its independent grading service in 1972, with ANA experts authenticating coins and photographing them with a grade consensus. In 1986 Professional Coin Grading Service (PCGS) began operations shortly after its founding by dealers David

Professional Coin Grading Service (left) was founded in 1986 and Numismatic Guaranty Company (right) began operations in 1987. Early coin slabs for both companies had simple designs.

Hall, Silvano DiGenova, Bruce Amspacher, Gordon Wrubel, Van Simmons, John Dannreuther, and Steve Cyrkin. Numismatic Guaranty Corporation—now Numismatic Guaranty Company (NGC)—was established in 1987 by John Albanese, another notable dealer who served as an initial partner with PCGS.

PCGS and NGC quickly proved to be popular, providing the coin marketplace with impartial, expert opinions on rare coins that, when encapsulated in their holders, could be reliably traded wholesale between dealers or sold to retail customers on a sight-unseen basis. The emergence of third-party coin grading and encapsulation (so called because the graders neither owned nor were buying the graded coins) helped create an entire new market in the 1980s that came to life just in time to welcome skittish Wall Street investors who lost their shirts during the stock market crash of 1987.

Investors who were used to dealing in paper investments like stocks and bonds were suddenly looking toward alternative assets after the Dow Jones Industrial Average fell 22 percent on October 19, 1987, the notorious "Black Monday" that triggered a decline in stocks around the world. It broke five years of bullish results on Wall Street, where the Dow Jones volume had more than tripled from 777 points in August 1982 to 2,722 points by October 1987. The average dropped 507.99 points on that day—by far the largest single-day drop, by percentage, on record and much worse than any single-day losses seen during the Great Depression, the Great Recession, or the COVID-19 pandemic.

A market correction, rising interest rates, and issues surrounding the strength of the dollar may have contributed to the crash. Some suggest a type of computerized trading formula known as "portfolio insurance," which buys index futures when stocks are increasing and sells futures during stock declines, led to the calamity. Whatever happened, investors panicked. Many threw cash into antique cars, fine art, vintage wines, and old comic books. Others turned to another form of hard asset with built-in value: rare coins.

The advent of PCGS and NGC and their consistent grading, tamper-evident holders, and overall credibility gave investors completely unfamiliar with the numismatic world the confidence to buy high-grade rare coins as assets for their investment portfolios. Investment firms Kidder, Peabody & Company, Shearson Lehman Hutton, and Merrill Lynch all

This 1987 PCGS advertisement appeared in the May 20 issue of the *Wall Street Journal* and introduced a whole new world of sight-unseen trading of rare coins to investors.

created rare-coin funds and invested millions of dollars into numismatic rarities. The Wall Street set favored gem-quality Liberty Walking half dollars, Morgan and Peace silver dollars, pre-1933 common-date U.S. gold coinage, and classic U.S. commemorative coinage. In short order, slabbed examples of these and other high-end U.S. coinage became true blue-chip commodities, with market demand reaching a feverish pitch as 1988 blended into 1989.

"The rare-coin market of 1988–1989 was white hot!" recalls Michael Garofalo, who began working as a coin dealer in the late 1970s. "Prices moved up rapidly week after week, month after month, for certified and uncertified coins. Weekly advances as monitored by *The Greysheet* were commonplace and by the time of the Central States Numismatic Society coin show in mid-April of 1989, in Overland Park, Kansas, we could barely keep up with the price increases." A few coin dealers urged customers to take profits, Garofalo says, but "most dealers simply enjoyed the ride."

During the 1980s, dealers kept pace with the fast-moving markets by using some of the electronic networking technology of the day. "We had the Fox and Crabbe Teletype System (FACTS), and it was a real teletype system," remembers Garofalo. "The 100-plus 'big dealers' who used it had a monster of a machine that ate green-bar paper by the truckload. It began in the 1960s as a teletype network, then went through a number of different owners but was bought by American Teleprocessing Corporation in 1984. Probably around 1985, ATC converted the system to a satellite data retrieval system." He continues, "In the 1990s, it was modified to work on the internet. Collectors Universe owns it today."

Like many others at the cusp of the rapidly moving digital technology curve of the 1980s, Garofalo also had his trusty Commodore 64. "[It] transmitted data (no images) at a baud rate of 300 bytes per second for characters that I used daily to log into my space on Coin-Net. It was an archaic way of transmitting data, but if you had coins to sell, you could list them and people like me could message you to buy them—typical terms were 'COC' (Check on Confirmation). After PCGS started in 1986, the American Numismatic Information Exchange (ANIE) system became the place where PCGS dealers listed their graded coins. ANIE was absorbed by the Certified Coin Exchange (CCE)."

Garofalo notes that the silver price during the time of the April 1989 Central States show was around $6 per troy ounce, while gold tracked close to $380. "At the June [1989] Long Beach Expo, the rare-coin market collapsed," he says. The Wall Street players pulled out of the market. "Prices for nice, rare coins fell precipitously, while gold and silver went lower, but slowly," Garofalo said.

The coin market now entered a prolonged period of slower sales and lower prices spanning roughly from 1990 through 2005, while the bullion market traded in a tight trading range between $300 to $500 per ounce for gold and $4 to $7 for silver. "It wasn't until the 2006 mortgage and housing crisis that bullion prices began to really climb," Garofalo recalls.

The first American Silver Eagles landed in a shifting marketplace scene. In 1986 the vanguard of dealers who had sold their first coins during the Great Depression of the 1930s and post-war boom of the 1940s and 1950s were seeing increasing competition from new market leaders in their late 20s, 30s, and early 40s. These young men and

The mid-1980s was a busy time at coin shows as a slew of new United States commemorative coins hit the streets and the American Eagle program was newly emerging.

women of the Baby Boomer generation had grown up in the 1950s and 1960s, searching their pocket change for Indian Head and Lincoln Wheat cents, Buffalo nickels, and Mercury dimes—coins often destined to fill crisp slots in blue Whitman folders.

These young dealers of the mid-1980s were receiving a torch lit decades earlier during the hobby's mid-century glory years and were carrying it into a brave new world of third-party grading, digital sight-unseen bids, internet trading, modern commemorative coins, million-dollar auction lots, and bullion portfolios for the masses—the latter thanks in large part to the emergence of the American Silver Eagle.

One of many reasons that the American Silver Eagle became so well known among the general public is that in the mid-1980s, numismatic columns were still frequently published in newspapers around the United States. Many of the larger publications had their own columnist or syndicated numismatic stories from larger dailies. All manner of topics were covered. Consider one story from the mid-1970s published by the *San Pedro News-Pilot* in California, when it was reported Whitman Publishing had sent out a survey to dealers and collectors to determine numismatic trends, including preferences for which coins to include in specific folders and albums.

One hot topic of the day was whether to include the recently discovered 1972 doubled die Lincoln cent in the bookshelf album. The poll, overseen by Ken Bressett, revealed 59 percent of respondents felt the variety should be included in the album, and 41 percent did not. "Those speaking against including [the doubled die] were notably strong in their opinions that the 1972 coin is not a normal mint issue, and its relatively high price would discourage many from attempting to complete the set," wrote *Coin Box* columnist Gary Palmer.

A decade later, celebrated numismatic journalist Ed Reiter was covering the coin beat for the *New York Times* and chronicled the emergence of the American Eagle bullion program for millions of readers. "The new coins are expected to generate between $5 million and $8 million in profits for the government during the first year, with higher levels likely in the future," he reported in a September 1986 column touting their impending release.

"Besides attracting customers elsewhere in the world, the American Eagles also figure to divert many American investors away from foreign coins. Market analysts estimate that Americans have been spending up to $1 billion a year on foreign bullion coins," wrote Reiter. He added that in September 1985 President Reagan had banned importation of the gold Krugerrand from South Africa amid sanctions aimed to penalize the country for system of racial segregation known as apartheid. Reiter went on to quote Alan Posnick, vice president of New York coin bullion firm Manfra, Tordella & Brookes, Inc., who said, "I wouldn't be at all surprised if by 1987 the American Eagle is already the number-one-selling bullion coin."

On Becoming America's Modern Silver Dollar

The American Silver Eagle arrived when otherwise few new U.S. coins were coming to the fore. In 1986 the U.S. commemorative coin program was still a young enterprise, having yielded only the 1982 George Washington half dollar, 1983–1984 Los Angeles Olympiad coinage, and the brand new 1986 Statue of Liberty coins. The 1776–1976 Bicentennial coinage of a decade earlier still represented the most popular coin program of modern times, while the beleaguered Susan B. Anthony dollar had quietly faded away in 1981. The Lincoln cent lost nearly all its copper in 1982 in favor of a cheaper zinc composition coated in a thin layer of copper. By the mid-1980s, Americans were used to an otherwise-staid coinage situation.

Then, along comes a new, nearly pure (.999-fine) silver coin sporting a beloved classic design and evoking the grandeur of the silver dollars from an earlier generation. What was old became new again. The coin was immediately embraced as a "silver dollar" in the general media. "Mint Swamped with American Eagle Silver Dollar Orders," screamed a widely syndicated Associated Press story from November 24, 1986, about a month after the release of the first American Gold Eagles. "Dealers figure if the American public loved the gold Eagle so much, then they are going to love the silver Eagle because it is at a price that almost everyone can afford," said Mint director Donna Pope in the story.

The American Silver Eagle has never been widely accessible at its face value of one dollar. Yet, given the legal-tender status of the coin, there is nothing to stop people from theoretically spending these coins in circulation as silver dollars—just as Americans did a century earlier with the Morgan dollar during the peak of its success as a circulating coin. Of course, one was a practical dollar coin that circulated during the heyday of nineteenth-century westward expansion, while the other is a modern coin designed for bullion portfolios and coin collections. Still, they are often compared to each other from the numismatic standpoint.

Just as many collectors will associate the Morgan dollar with the sociocultural milieu of its day, we can also readily make similar connections between the American Silver Eagle and the environmental trappings of its mid-1980s origins. Both coins were conceived during contentious debates about the nation's silver policy and born from controversial silver stockpiles. The Morgan dollar was born in the late 1870s and came of age in circulation during the 1880s, while the American Silver Eagle is a 1980s child whose very existence can trace back to the government's silver selloff efforts that began in the 1970s.

Both coins are also comparable as commodities and collectibles. Morgan dollars are perhaps the most popular and widely collected classic coin series. Meanwhile, the American Silver Eagle is easily the most visible non-circulating coin, familiar not only to investors who embrace these silver dollars as fantastic precious-metals vehicles but also to many Americans who see these modern-day bullion beauties featured on any number of television advertisements and online-based pitches.

American Silver Eagles have long come into their own as numismatic collectibles. More than 100 different issues exist to date, greater than the 96 circulation-strike and Proof-only Morgan dollars struck between 1878 and 1921, which make up a basic date-and-mintmark set. In fact, of all the historic silver dollar series produced by the U.S. Mint, the Morgan dollar comes the closest to rivaling the American Silver Eagle in terms of the number of issues produced.

The Morgan dollar and American Silver Eagle also share the limelight as some of the nation's most widely promoted coins. They appear in advertisements ranging from midnight infomercials to full-color inserts in magazines of all types. Often, the advertisements selling Morgan dollars play up the coin's Old West connections, classic design, and limited availability—even if "limited" means millions versus billions. Meanwhile, the American Silver Eagle is frequently seen in similar advertising spots against a backdrop of patriotism and freedom, hearkening to its gorgeous design symbolic of American liberty and the coin's birth during the administration of Ronald Reagan—widely regarded as one of the nation's most popular presidents.

THE ALLURE OF THE AMERICAN SILVER EAGLE

Some might argue that the excesses of the 1980s opened the door for the success of a coin program that gave Americans the chance to indulge in virtually pure silver. Yes, the American Silver Eagle debuted at a time when the American economy was doing well—

after the era of 1970s stagflation and before the stock market scares that took hold in 1987. However, it's reasonable to assume the American Silver Eagle could have sold itself at any other time in history. When has silver *not* been captivating to the masses?

Yet, there's something more about this coin than its silver content that perpetually lures collectors and investors alike. It's a little difficult to imagine millions of people lining up to buy silver pellets from the United States government. The American Silver Eagle beams a beautiful, inspiring personality that simple granules or non-descript bars could surely never embody.

One of the most important benefits for those who speculate in American Silver Eagles is that these coins are monetized as legal-tender coins and are fully backed by the U.S. government. In the most basic sense, this guarantees that an American Silver Eagle will never be worth less than one dollar. That may be an unnecessary failsafe, but if silver values ever plunged to rock bottom—and stranger things have happened—the coin's monetary value as legal tender is guaranteed. Such a benefit isn't extended to private mint products like rounds or ingots.

A legal-tender coin itself, the American Silver Eagle is partly modeled after one of the most cherished of all. The Liberty Walking motif on the obverse, borrowing from the beloved circulating half dollar of 1916 through 1947, absolutely soars on the larger canvas of the modern bullion coin. The enduring appeal of the Liberty Walking design by Adolph Weinman transcended generations when it appeared for a new audience in 1986, after a nearly 40-year absence from the U.S. Mint production lineup. The Silver Eagle has now carried the famous Weinman design longer than the 32 years it originally appeared on the half dollar.

American Silver Eagles have a perennial appeal.

American Silver Eagles are a proven store of value.

The Liberty Walking design helped the American Silver Eagle become a favorite collectible among numismatists. Numismatic interest in the Proofs was robust from the get-go, but increasing numbers of collectors are pursuing the bullion-finish Silver Eagles that were primarily targeted to precious-metals investors. The groundswell in interest for the bullion strikes suggests shifting tastes in the collector community, which has a growing appetite for modern coinage. However, this also stems from the huge crossover appeal of the American Silver Eagle, which has proven to be a relatively affordable series for collectors who want to both build a bullion portfolio and also assemble a set of attractive coins on a year-by-year basis.

The popularity of the American Silver Eagle spreads around the world. Its beautiful design attracts a following on its own with many international collectors and speculators. However, the coin's backing by the U.S. government as .999-fine legal-tender coinage has earned trust among investors far and wide, many of whom prefer the American Silver Eagle over bullion coins from other countries—in some cases even similar coinage issued by their own nation.

SELLING SILVER EAGLES

It didn't take long for the American Silver Eagle program to soar into the heights of success. All 28 of the bullion distributors authorized at the time to purchase bullion versions of the new coin did so within hours of the coin's release in November 1986. Numismatists and others were also champing at the bit to buy Proofs for their own collections or as gifts for friends and family. Yet, U.S. Mint officials weren't ready to rest on their laurels as the series marched into 1987 and beyond.

A lavish print advertising campaign hit mailboxes, newspapers, and magazines to flood the nation's media landscape with the news that the American Silver Eagle and accompanying American Gold Eagle coins had arrived. "The fall of 1986 marked an historic moment in American history," declares a U.S. Mint advertisement. "The United States Mint struck the American Eagles and America turned to gold." The spot goes on to tout the silver option, "For investors interested in adding silver to their portfolios, there is an American Eagle Silver Bullion One Ounce Coin."

This 1986 U.S. Mint brochure, titled "A Milestone in American Coinage," pitches the brand-new American Eagle coins.

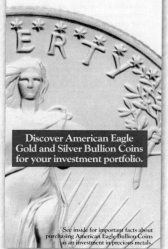

The U.S. Mint touted the American Eagle coins as investment vehicles, even offering a free investors' guide for the asking.

Collectors were pitched a special direct-mail advertisement from the U.S. Mint, introducing Proofs as "the highest form of the master engraver's art." The advertisement continues, "By owning these historic, first-year Proofs you can begin your own family tradition. Struck for the first time in 1986, Proof versions of the bullion coins will be issued in 1987, 1988, and the years to follow."

Another pamphlet targeted the investor: "Recent changes in the federal tax law give you the opportunity to place American Eagle Gold and Silver Bullion Coins in your Individual Retirement Account (IRA)." The "American Eagle Buyer's Guide" was distributed by the Mint for free. Five versions of the guide were tailored to five areas of the United States, including the Eastern Region, Northern Region, South Central Region, Southeastern Region, and Western Region. The guide provided information on different ways the American Eagle coinage, specifically the gold coins, could be incorporated into investment plans and provided resources on where to buy the bullion coins in each geographical region.

"I have exciting news for collectors who wish to combine a lifelong love of coins with one of the world's most preferred forms of gold investment," writes Mint director Donna Pope in a 1988 brochure mailed to Mint customers. "Since their introduction in 1986, American Eagle Gold Bullion Coins have become a convenient way for investors to purchase, hold, and trade gold as part of a balanced investment strategy." Bullion investors, coin collectors, and coin dealers were all in.

Dear U.S. Mint Customer:

All of us here at the Mint are delighted by the growing interest in both traditional U.S. Mint coins and new commemorative issues. One measure of this growth is the influx of new U.S. Mint customers—in the past two years, *over 1 million* new customers have joined the ranks of our valued collectors.

The current year promises to be equally exciting. Already, you have heard from us concerning the pre-issue offer for 1988 Olympic Coins. If you haven't ordered your Olympic Coins yet, look for another mailing from us in a few weeks which will also allow you to order at pre-issue prices.

The 1988 Uncirculated Coin Sets.

As a U.S. Mint preferred customer, you are among the first to have the opportunity to order newly-issued coins. With this mailing we proudly present the 1988 Uncirculated Coin Set, a collection of mint state coins which allows anyone to share in the pleasures of collecting fine U.S. coinage.

Offering you the Lincoln cent, Jefferson nickel, Roosevelt dime, Washington quarter, and Kennedy half dollar, this lovely set adds yet another chapter in an ongoing tradition of uncirculated set issues. Best of all, you still can purchase the 1988 Uncirculated Coin Set for just $7.00—we haven't raised the price in four years!

The 1987 United States Constitution Silver Dollar Coin.

Also available for purchase in this offer are the dazzling proof and uncirculated silver dollars introduced last year to celebrate the 200th anniversary of the U.S. Constitution.

In the months since its original issue, the United States Constitution Silver Dollar Coin has become an important symbol of the promise of American freedom.

Now is the time to add these beautifully crafted heirlooms to your collection...the United States Mint will not produce Constitution Coins after June 30, 1988, and no orders can be accepted after this date. Refer to the enclosed brochure for more details.

Consider "American Eagles"—
An investment you can hold.

I have exciting news for collectors who wish to combine a lifelong love of coins with one of the world's most preferred forms of gold investment.

Since their introduction in 1986, American Eagle Gold Bullion Coins have become a convenient way for investors to purchase, hold, and trade gold as part of a balanced investment strategy. Now, due to recent revisions in Federal Tax law, you can invest any or all of your IRA funds in Eagles. It's an idea you may want to discuss with your investment advisor.

American Eagle Bullion Coins cannot be ordered direct from the Mint—but we've made it easier to locate your nearest source of Eagles with the free "American Eagle Buyer's Guide." To request your copy free of charge, just complete the enclosed order form as indicated. Be sure to refer to the enclosed brochure first.

We're here to serve you.

Occasionally, our customers contact us to check on the progress of an order, or to ask about new issues. If you should have a similar question, please contact our Customer Service Center. Simply call (301) 436-7400, or, if you prefer, address your inquiry to:

(over, please)

This 1988 U.S. Mint pamphlet bills American Eagle gold coins as offering "a convenient way for investors to purchase, hold, and trade gold as part of a balanced investment strategy."

BULLION DEALER MICHAEL GAROFALO
REMINISCES ON THE EARLY DAYS
OF THE AMERICAN SILVER EAGLE

The cat was let out of the bag in 1985 when Congress passed and President Ronald Reagan signed into law first the Liberty Coin Act, approved on July 9, 1985, followed by the Gold Bullion Coin Act of 1985 on December 17. Now the U.S. Mint would be entering the world gold and silver bullion coin business. Coin dealers across the nation scrambled to get information and to figure out how to participate.

Everyone felt that these coins would be successful, but no one knew how to get them, where to get them, who would be selling them, and when they would be available. By November 1986, just as the new Silver Eagle coins were becoming available for purchase, the coin market was awash in rumors. Were all of these coins going to the Mint's Authorized Purchasers? Would any other dealers get any? Do they have them already? There were more rumors than facts.

Since it was already late in November, another important question was, "Would the Mint 'freeze the date' and strike 1986-dated coins into 1987?" Otherwise, how could they strike enough coins to accommodate the demand? We dealers debated these questions, but we had no answers.

Even worse, with silver around $5.40, American Silver Eagles were being offered wholesale from the Authorized Purchasers at $9.50—if you could find a dealer willing to sell! That 75 percent premium over spot meant that unless a dealer sold at $10.50 or more, they weren't making any money on these much-in-demand coins. But what about the end collector/investor? Are they comfortable paying a 90 to 100 percent premium on what is supposed to be a bullion coin? Even worse, if the Mint doesn't strike enough coins in 1986, then they have created a modern rarity instead of the bullion coin they intended.

I was unable to get any 1986-dated American Silver Eagle coins during the calendar year 1986. But in early January 1987 there was the Florida United Numismatists coin show. The FUN show was and still is one of the major coin shows of the year. It especially appealed to dealers in the northern half of the country as a wonderful business

Michael Garofalo was a jet-setting coin dealer in the 1980s as the American Silver Eagle was making waves in the marketplace.

excuse to go to a warmer climate and forget about snow and ice for a week. In 1987 the show was being held at the Buena Vista Hotel in Orlando, so not only would there be great accommodations but it was a great excuse to bring the family along and spend some quality time together—and with Mickey Mouse! More than 12,000 people attended the show, including Mint director Donna Pope.

The flight from Boston, Massachusetts, to Orlando, Florida, on January 6, 1987, was fairly crowded with New England-area coin dealers. There were lots of familiar faces on that flight. Unlike the rules that we all live with today, traveling with coins was a lot easier back in 1987. Many dealers had lots of inventory with them, and trading coins, on some flights, was not at all uncommon. A dealer from Connecticut was seated in my row. I spent a good portion of my flight looking through his new purchases. After buying a couple dozen rare coins, he handed me a box. As I looked in it, I saw rolls of coins that I had never held in my hand before. He didn't realize that he had given me a box of rolls of brand-new 1986 American Silver Eagle bullion coins. I popped one open and just asked him, "How much?"

His reply was, "Sorry! I didn't mean to show you those. I am taking them to the show to sell retail."

"How much?" I asked again.

"I really want to sell them retail!" came back his reply.

I was persistent. "*How much?*" I asked once again.

"Ten bucks a coin!" was his reply.

I wanted to buy all of them. But we agreed on four rolls. Now I had 80 coins, but instead of the $7.95 per coin bid listed in *The Greysheet* as the wholesale price, I paid over retail for these coins. But I held them in my hands, 80 pieces of silver. Either the FUN show had started on a good note, or I had paid too much for those 80 coins and I would have to lug them home.

The rare-coin market was strong, but at this show some dealers restrained their buying. Why? The bullion market was active but there was a great deal of frustration at the show. A large number of dealers had thousands, and in some cases millions, of dollars tied up in physical gold and silver American Eagles, some of which they did not have in hand. While many tried to pre-sell their allotments of Eagles, now they were competing with the 28 original distributors as well as the dealers like me who tried to buy some Silver Eagles and were lucky enough to find a few. With so many people selling what they didn't have in stock, premiums were dropping.

At the show I put the coins out a roll at a time. Every retail customer who walked through the doors when the show opened on Wednesday asked the price. I wanted $12 each. I sold out the first roll within an hour. I put out a second roll. Dealers walking by asked me the prices. $12.50 per coin. The first dealer I quoted that to said, "All sold!"

As retail customers came down the aisle, I spread out a third roll. Many collectors wanted to see and hold the coins. I was quoting $13 a coin. I sold all of them. I waited until Thursday to put out the last roll. Remember, having physical coins in hand that people could see, touch, and buy, really made a difference. These were small purchases. People were willing to "stretch" a little to own them.

Just before the doors opened to the public, I put out the last roll. A dealer walked by, pointed to them, and said, "Is that what I think it is?"

I nodded, "Yes."

He asked, "How much?"

I said, "Sorry, but they are $15 a coin."

All he said was, "Put them on my invoice."

I had sold them all and made a profit on every one. The largest premium I asked for was paid for by a very knowledgeable dealer. However, when I walked the bourse floor, the few coins that were there were being quoted at $16 each.

I was hooked. I knew these coins would be great sellers. But like most U.S. Mint products, the people who made the most profit with them were the people who were lucky enough to have physical coins in stock early—when everyone else wanted to buy them. The January 4, 1987, *Coin Dealer Newsletter* (a.k.a. *The Greysheet*), available at the show, reported that wholesale prices for American Silver Eagles were now down to $7.95.

By May 1987, all 1986-dated American Silver Eagles were trading at $15 to $16 wholesale. The 5.4 million coins that the Mint struck were well absorbed into the marketplace. Now, the 1987-dated Silver Eagles were out in dealers' hands, and they were wholesaling at $10 per coin. Demand was still strong, and collectors had something to collect—a second American Silver Eagle with a *different* date!

AMERICAN SILVER EAGLE PRODUCT OFFERINGS

The U.S. Mint has offered American Silver Eagles in many finishes and product options over the years, catering to the diverse tastes of the numismatic and bullion communities. What started as a simple two-choice program (of bullion strikes and Proofs) blossomed into multiple-coin sets, different mintmarks, new surface finishes, packaged products that included currency notes and various coins, and even a collaboration with the Royal Canadian Mint. These formats and sets are cataloged in detail in chapter 8.

The Novelty Market

Let's be honest about coins that have been colorized or otherwise altered outside the facilities of the U.S. Mint. Yes, they offer little in the way of real numismatic value, but they do have their place of importance in the numismatic market. Colorized American Silver Eagles and other novelty forms of these acclaimed bullion coins appeal to a different kind of buyer than the one typically served by more conventional coin and bullion firms.

Novelty coinage has few exacting definitions and in the more taxonomic sense is probably better classified as "exonumia" (which includes counterstamped and altered coins as well as other numismatic items falling outside of legal-tender coins and paper currency, such as tokens, medals, and scrip). Exonumia is an entire colorful world unto itself—one that some American Silver Eagles populate. These large, round silver coins have been used for making jewelry, holiday ornaments, and just about everything in between. A particularly big seller among the mass-market promoters who advertise in major publications, online, and on television, novelty American Silver Eagles enjoy a robust base of collectors, many of whom also buy collector plates and porcelain figurines.

Some within the hobby's inner circles argue that colorized coins, especially those pitched at often higher-than-retail prices pitched by promoters, are little more than "rip-offs." They suggest that many of the individuals who buy these coins know little about the dynamics of the numismatic marketplace and often buy on the presumption such pieces are rare and will increase in value. Of course, the reality is American Silver Eagles that have been painted, converted into jewelry, or manipulated into other kinds of products are all but certain to never see monetary appreciation as a numismatic collectible.

However, this does not mean that novelty American Silver Eagles are worthless. First and foremost, American Silver Eagles retain their value based on their weight in silver, even if the coin itself is in an altered state, and they could be sold at melt value or as a cull (a coin that has cosmetic problems or other damage); they also still retain their legal-tender value of one dollar. Furthermore, novelty coins—as crossover collectibles—may have monetary value for other reasons not immediately recognized by numismatists who are unaware of market trends or demands in other hobby fields. Finally, any coins sold on the novelty market to collectors who aren't bona fide numismatists serve as ambassadors to the non-numismatic realm and can help create a welcoming bridge into the hobby.

Perhaps this last point is of greatest importance here. The American Silver Eagle is a coin well known beyond the fourth wall of the numismatic hobby, thanks in large part to the marketing efforts of enterprising promoters who pitch these and other iconic coins to non-numismatic audiences. For the hobby to continue expanding its ranks, it must meet the people where they are. For many, that place may be among numismatic novelties, which appeal to a diverse array of individuals whose tastes in art or aesthetics might differ from those of traditional numismatists. Novelty American Silver Eagles and those who collect them deserve a seat at the hobby's table.

One of many American Silver Eagles that have been privately colorized and sold as a special collectible in various television, magazine, and internet advertisements. Such novelties hold little numismatic value, but can inspire an interest in coin collecting among people who otherwise might never have been called to numismatics.

THE AMERICAN SILVER EAGLE'S PLACE IN NUMISMATICS

To say the American Silver Eagle is something of a numismatic cultural phenomenon would hardly be an overstatement. As far as non-circulating coinage goes, it's enjoyed about as much limelight as one could ever dream. Anybody would be hard pressed to identify another coin series that has achieved the same level of name recognition and overall familiarity with the general public despite never seeing the light of day in circulation.

Says Michael Garofalo, "My own experience of a dozen years at APMEX, where American Silver Eagle coins are such a priority, gave me a much greater appreciation for these coins and for both the young and older collectors who drive the American Silver Eagle market. There, I also got to understand how important these coins are in the worldwide silver bullion market. They truly do represent our nation well, both in our country and around the globe."

Gainesville Coins bullion expert Everett Millman suggests the coin's design plays a huge role in why collectors flock to the American Silver Eagle. "Adolph A. Weinman's Liberty Walking theme has long been considered one of the most beautiful coin designs of the twentieth century, and it looks even more impressive on the larger size of the Silver Eagle compared to the half dollar."

Another reason: accessibility. "The American Silver Eagle set is attractive, particularly to new collectors, because it's a fairly short date-and-mintmark set to complete. Nonetheless, in my experience, more than 50 percent of ASE collectors also consider their collection to be a long-term investment in silver. That number may even be as high as 80 percent," Millman said.

When silver prices trek along at recent averages of $20 to $30 an ounce, a collector can continue adding a lovely new addition to their American Silver Eagle set for less than $50 each year—usually under $100 for a pristine, encapsulated example certified by one of the leading grading services as MS-69 or even MS-70. Whether a set of "raw," uncertified coins in an album or a cabinet of top-grade certified coins in an exquisite registry set, the irresistible allure of a Silver Eagle collection is only further enhanced by its tangible value. Owning an attractive collection of large, high-purity silver coins that could readily be liquidated in times of economic need or dire emergency—and later easily repurchased when the opportunity avails itself—instills a tremendous degree of confidence and security perhaps unmatched with other popular sets.

Collectors who sell sets of numismatically rare coins must connect with the right buyer to maximize the opportunity for profit. Even the nicest set of Morgan dollars with "VAM" varieties (those originally cataloged by Leroy C. Van Allen and A. George Mallis in their seminal 1971 book *Comprehensive Catalog and Encyclopedia of Morgan and Peace Dollars*) will probably fail to achieve a decent bid if pitched to anyone but a die-hard collector of Morgan dollars or a dealer who specializes in this area. Meanwhile, consigning such carefully curated sets of rare coins to an auction house may require waiting many weeks or even months before realizing any money from a transaction—assuming the lot sells.

This 1988 United States Mint brochure pitches Proof
American Eagles as wonderful collectibles and gifts.

Should you ever desire to buy back the set you had to sell, good luck trying. Unless we're talking about generic sets of modern-day coinage, you might be years attempting to complete something like a set of Liberty Seated coinage, Morgan dollars, or other scarcer types that are difficult to find in desirable grades. Some of the rarest issues in these series might appear only every few years, regardless of grade or eye appeal.

Of course, the American Silver Eagle series offers no such challenges to the collector. These coins are easy to buy and a cinch to sell. Even the nicest Silver Eagle registry sets—often five-figure assemblages when comprising hefty rarities like the 1995-W Proof in PF-70—can be readily rebuilt by collectors wishing to recapture what they may have once sold.

If the numismatic observer was searching for one word to capture the essence of the American Silver Eagle, perhaps the series can be best described as "versatile." A bullion program in the most basic sense, the Silver Eagle has easily become one of the most complex series, and one worthy of consideration by any numismatist. As long-time dealer and Silver Eagle expert Lee Minshull simply puts it, "For essentially my entire life, the number-one coin for collectors was the Morgan dollar. Today it's the Silver Eagle. I foresee this to continue on."

A New Lease on Life for The Silver Eagle

The American Silver Eagle program has become such a fundamental player on the numismatic and investment scenes that it may be hard to remember the series' original purpose was to dispose of excess bullion in the National Defense Stockpile. In the early 1980s this amounted to more than 100 million ounces of silver primed for dispersal.

Predictably, the size of the stockpile diminished as the successful Silver Eagle program carried on into the 1990s and beyond. By the turn of the new millennium, the American Silver Eagle had proven itself a bullion bestseller. The profits to the U.S. government were monumental. However, the United States was about to close in on its original objective of depleting the National Defense Stockpile's surplus silver.

If the American Silver Eagle was going to continue, something needed to be done on a legislative level to ensure authorization of the program beyond its initial legal parameters approved in the 1980s. Coming to the rescue was Democratic Nevada senator Harry Reid, who introduced bill S.2594, "Support of American Eagle Silver Bullion Program Act," on June 6, 2002. The intent of the bill was "to authorize the Secretary of the Treasury to purchase silver on the open market when the silver stockpile is depleted, to be used to mint coins."

The bill, known as Public Law 107-201, was approved July 23, 2002, and paved the way for the American Silver Eagle program to continue well into the twenty-first century. The years that followed the passage of the Support of American Eagle Silver Bullion Program Act saw record-breaking mintages for the series, with successive mintage records being set almost every year from 2008 through 2015. The all-time record mintage of bullion-finish American Silver Eagles stands at 54,151,500, achieved in 2014. In all, the United States Mint struck more than 600 million American Silver Eagles by the time the last examples bearing John Mercanti's original Heraldic Eagle reverse design rolled off the presses in 2021.

4

Minting a Legendary Coin

★

The American Silver Eagle easily lays a claim to being one of the most beautiful modern coins produced anywhere in the world. If it has any artistic peers in the numismatic sense, they include the various American Gold Eagles that carry Augustus Saint-Gaudens's famous motif of Miss Liberty, alight torch in hand, striding before the U.S. Capitol in Washington, D.C., with the sun rising majestically in the background.

These statements come not at the dismissive exclusion of other gorgeous modern coins produced elsewhere in the world. Surely, cases could be made for the regal splendor of the Great Britain's silver Britannia, the meticulous artistry of the Austrian Philharmonic coinage, the handsomely innovative coinage of the Perth Mint in Australia, or the classic beauty of the Mexican silver Libertad. One might even suggest that criticisms of seemingly uninspired and physically flat designs on coins of more recent vintage have compelled many mints around the world—and their most masterful sculptor-engravers—to cultivate more stunning coinage. This was among the factors that drove thought leaders at the U.S. Mint and the Treasury to call on Adolph A. Weinman's timeless Liberty Walking design for the American Silver Eagle in 1986, nearly 40 years after the motif had been retired.

GAINING WAY FOR LIBERTY WALKING

The Liberty Walking design anchoring the American Silver Eagle since its debut in 1986 first premiered 70 years earlier, in 1916, on the half dollar. The iconic motif of a patriotically dressed Miss Liberty striding across a picturesque landscape, backed by a sunrise peeking over mountains, has resonated with generations of Americans. The design by Adolph A. Weinman has become one of the most enduring in all of American numismatics, rivaling the popularity of the famous Augustus Saint-Gaudens device. The Saint-Gaudens design, following the Weinman classic out of a decades-long retirement, appeared on the obverse of the four American Gold Eagle denominations in 1986.

Like the legendary Saint-Gaudens composition, Weinman's Liberty Walking design was born during the Renaissance of United States coinage, a period many scholars peg to a span of 16 years from 1905 through 1921. During that time, many of the most popular coins in American numismatics came into existence, including the Saint-Gaudens double eagle (1907), his Indian Head eagle (1907), the Indian Head quarter eagle and half eagle by Saint-Gaudens protégé Bela Lyon Pratt (1908), the Lincoln cent by Victor David Brenner (1909), the Buffalo nickel by James Earle Fraser (1913), the Mercury dime and Liberty Walking half dollar by Weinman (1916), the Standing Liberty quarter by Hermon A. MacNeil (1916), and the Peace dollar by Anthony de Francisci (1921).

It was a period of colorful designs by a diverse panel of celebrated American artists and sculptors. But if President Theodore Roosevelt had his way, all the coins would most likely have been designed by Saint-Gaudens. In 1905 President Roosevelt, admiring Saint-Gaudens's soaring sculptures that captured the nation's spirit through symbols and allegorical figures such as stars, stripes, and the bald eagle, commissioned the artist to redesign the nation's coinage.

The Irish-born Beaux-Arts master managed to produce designs for the eagle ($10 gold coin) and double eagle ($20 gold coin), along with a sketch for a new one-cent coin, before succumbing to colon cancer at the age of 59 on August 3, 1907. Roosevelt posthumously honored Saint-Gaudens in a 1908 speech at the Corcoran Gallery, saying that his final works were "more beautiful than any coins since the days of the Greeks, and they achieve their striking beauty because Saint-Gaudens not only possessed a perfect mastery in the physical address of his craft, but also a daring and original imagination."

In the years that followed, the United States government endeavored to replace the aging designs on other denominations with distinctly American themes and classic beauty on par with the work Saint-Gaudens had contributed to the eagle and double eagle. The monumental undertaking shifted predominately to the U.S. Mint and the U.S. Commission of Fine Arts following the end of Roosevelt's second term in 1909; the outgoing president had been far more concerned with numismatic affairs than his successor, William Howard Taft.

Augustus Saint-Gaudens and President Theodore Roosevelt.

The artistry of the Renaissance of
American coinage in the early 1900s.

However, secretary of the Treasury William McAdoo, along with many in the general public and in numismatic circles, was keenly attuned to the aesthetic state of the nation's coinage, and Charles E. Barber's aging Liberty Head motif was increasingly becoming the target of replacement. Debuting in 1892, the "Barber" dime, quarter, and half dollar were appearing artistically subpar in relation to the soaring Saint-Gaudens designs as well as Brenner's Lincoln cent and Fraser's Buffalo nickel.

Among the earliest and most vocal chants against the Barber coinage came from the New York Numismatic Club in 1914. That's when Thomas Elder, a coin dealer and member of the club's executive committee, brought the idea for redesigns before the American Numismatic Society in a presentation in which he asserted, "these [Barber] coins are almost unparalleled in modern issues for ugliness."

Charles Barber's silver coins.

Calls to redesign the Barber silver coinage echoed into the offices of the Treasury, with assistant secretary of the Treasury William P. Malburn broaching the topic to Secretary McAdoo, who responded, "Let the mint submit the designs before we try anybody else." U.S. Mint chief engraver Barber and assistant chief engraver George T. Morgan submitted designs that fell short of the bar raised by the likes of Saint-Gaudens.

As an advisor on the nation's coin designs, the Commission of Fine Arts jettisoned Barber's and Morgan's efforts in December 1915 and instead recommended sculptors Adolph A. Weinman, Hermon A. MacNeil, and Albin Polasek submit their designs. The three, all with ties to New York City, were paid $300 to offer their designs and promised $2,000 for each that was accepted, perhaps with the notion that each would have a design selected for the three silver coins up for grabs. Ultimately, Polasek's offerings didn't make the cut, but MacNeil hit pay dirt with his Standing Liberty design for the quarter. Meanwhile, Weinman scored two wins: his Winged Liberty Head submission was selected for the dime and his Liberty Walking motif was chosen for the half dollar.

ADOLPH A. WEINMAN'S LIBERTY WALKING DESIGN

Weinman's Liberty Walking half dollar and Winged Liberty Head dime designs, along with MacNeil's Standing Liberty quarter, underwent minor tweaks and revisions as they were prepared for production during the spring of 1916. Chief engraver Charles E. Barber was informed of the decision to supplant his designs by way of a March 3, 1916, letter by Mint director Robert W. Woolley, who wrote, "It is understood that satisfactory working models are to be delivered to the Mint not later than May 1st, 1916, and they are to conform in all respects to the requirements of the Mint."

Reportedly, Barber proved stubborn in working with the new designers to bring the new coins to fruition. As Woolley wrote in a March 29, 1916, letter to Philadelphia Mint superintendent Adam M. Joyce, "Confidentially, the sculptors designing the new coins felt that on their last trip [to the mint] Mr. Morgan was much more cordial and cooperative than Mr. Barber was. I realize I am dealing with artistic temperaments at both ends."

Barber, who reported technical issues with Weinman's Liberty Walking design, had his own misgivings about working with the designers. In a letter to assistant secretary of the Treasury Malburn, Barber declared, "Any endeavor to urge the artists to conform to mechanical restrictions was invariably met with objection, that it would interfere with their artistic conceptions of what the design should be." The drama didn't stop there.

Weinman's Liberty Walking caused problematic "fins" of excess metal to develop around the periphery of the die. Revisions were tossed back and forth between Barber and Weinman, the latter electing to revise the size and location of the legend LIBERTY, motto IN GOD WE TRUST, and positioning of Miss Liberty's arms, as well as various elements on the reverse.

Over the course of the late summer and early autumn, more revisions were made to the Liberty Walking design as other changes were happening at the Mint, with Woolley resigning his post as director. He was replaced by Friedrich Johannes Hugo "F. H." von Engelken, who just days into his new assignment wrote to Malburn that the new dime and half dollar sported "a sharp projection of the metal on the edge" and were "decidedly imperfect." In that same September 6, 1916, letter (which numismatic historian Roger W. Burdette suggests was based on Barber's concerns), von Engelken stated, "you will note also, particularly on the half dollar on account of its size, a variation in the thickness of the coin, specifically noticeable at the edge. I went to Philadelphia yesterday to ascertain whether or not this could be overcome, and I find that we are faced with certain

Adolph A. Weinman at work in
his studio on a plaster coin model.

A pattern of the 1916 Liberty
Walking half dollar, Judd-1992.

mechanical restrictions which make it impossible to produce a coin of uniform thickness of edge, and to obviate the fin edge, as long as we maintain the high relief of the coin as it is at present."

The Liberty Walking motif in its original form seemed destined for the slush pile. Barber, seeing an opportunity to craft a suitable design for the half dollar, proposed redesigning the coin himself. But doing so would take six to eight months—much too long for the political sensibilities of Treasurer McAdoo, a Democrat who believed continued delays in redesigning the Barber coinage would give Republicans another bone to pick in the upcoming 1916 presidential election.

McAdoo and von Engelken concluded the best solution for making the design more technically viable for production was for the artist to reduce the size of the main device. Weinman's modifications proved insufficient, so Philadelphia Mint superintendent Joyce gave Barber carte blanche to retool the Liberty Walking design as the chief engraver saw fit. This resulted in the reduction of Weinman's central figure and the addition of a beaded border.

However, Barber's iterations didn't stick. The Mint endeavored to make minor technical modifications that eliminated the finning issues while maintaining Weinman's original Liberty Walking design, which survived some half dozen revisions in the process of perfecting the coin for circulation.

Weinman, who received a shipment of 20 Liberty Walking half dollars from Joyce just before Christmas 1916, was elated to see his new coin had been struck sans beaded border. "Every good wish to you for every day of the New Year," Weinman bade in a letter to Joyce, "and with thanks to the Almighty and yourself that the beads are not on the border of the Half Dollar."

The Liberty Walking half dollar was released in January 1917, just weeks before the passing of Charles E. Barber at the age of 76.

A LIBERTY WALKING TO REMEMBER—
CREATING AN ICONIC DESIGN

It may seem that A.A. Weinman's iconic Liberty Walking design just appeared one day in 1916 as an immaculate stroke of artistic genius. And artistic genius it is!

In the categorical sense, the U.S. Commission of Fine Arts recognizes the Liberty Walking half dollar as an example of the Beaux-Arts style, a French artistic philosophy that became a popular artistic movement in the United States during the 1880s and into the 1920s. The Beaux-Arts style is widely evidenced in the nation's architecture of that period and in many ways was integrated into the Art Deco movement that swept the United States during the 1920s and 1930s.

Many observers consider Weinman's Liberty Walking one of the most beautiful designs ever commissioned for a U.S. coin, in the same league with the Augustus Saint-Gaudens motif of Miss Liberty on the double eagle. Numismatic historian Roger W. Burdette has drawn comparisons of the Liberty motif on the "Walker" half dollar to the *Sower* (*La Semeuse* in French) figure created by Art Nouveau medallist Louis Oscar Roty; dating back to 1887, the *Sower* figure originally envisions a French farm girl sowing seeds upon the land. She is transformed into a likeness of the French symbol Marianne, donning a Phrygian cap for her appearance on France's 50 centimes of yore as well as the one-, two-, and five-franc coinage minted as late as 2001. She lives on today in stylized form as the central figure on France's ten-, twenty-, and fifty-euro cent coins.

Of France's Marianne, numismatic historian Mitch Ernst says, "I find her image to be more of a relatable, national symbol rather than a goddess. She's not a French Ceres in my humble opinion. But rather the symbol of the proletariat."

In his 2005 book *Renaissance of American Coinage, 1916–1921*, Roger W. Burdette wrote, "Weinman has taken the ideal of a 19th-century provincial figure and turned it into an American icon." This echoes what Weinman's son, Robert, told numismatic columnist Ed Reiter in a 2000 interview, calling the design "distinctly American in appearance." At the time, Robert Weinman suggested he hadn't begun hearing connections between his father's Liberty Walking motif and Roty's *Sower* until the latter years of the twentieth century. "As to whether Dad actually used it, I can't answer," Weinman explained. "The only thing I can say is that oftentimes, I think, an artist is guiltless in such situations. He may see something in 1897 that strikes his fancy, and all of a sudden it pops up unannounced two decades later. Is it a steal? Has it been cooking in his subconscious? It's hard to say."

Either way, a French connection in American numismatics is nothing unusual here. Many U.S. coins of the period borrow from France's numismatic influence. Consider the motif that was replaced on the half dollar by the Liberty Walking design; Charles Barber surely found a muse in the French coins of the era when composing his Liberty Head design.

Of the Liberty Walking half dollar, Burdette notes similarities in the head of Miss Liberty and the branches she is carrying to Weinman's *Union Soldiers and Sailors*

France's two-franc coin of the late nineteenth century is among the French silver coinage that may have inspired Charles E. Barber when he created the Liberty Head dime, quarter, and half dollar designs in the early 1890s.

A postcard depicting Oscar Roty's *The Sower*. This design later appeared on French euro coins.

monument, a landmark that was completed in 1909 and stands in Baltimore's Wyman Park. The model for Miss Liberty had long been tied to Weinman's tenant Elsie Kachel Stevens, whose likeness he memorialized in a 1913 bust.

The *Reading Eagle* of Pennsylvania stated on January 7, 1917, that the new half dollars "are reported to bear the profile of Mrs. Wallace Stevens, formerly Miss Elsie Mull, of Reading." This was further substantiated in 1966 by Elsie Stevens's daughter, Holly, who noted that her mom was the model for the Mercury dime and Liberty Walking half dollar. In a 2000 interview, Robert Weinman said, "I think there is some truth to that," adding, "Mrs. Stevens was supposed to have been an unusually good-looking woman, and it wouldn't surprise me at all if this had happened. Whether this got her a percentage back on the rent, I don't know." Despite this, Weinman further stated, "The Walking Liberty of the 50-cent piece was, I believe, based on a professional model. However, she's unknown by name to me."

The reverse of the Liberty Walking half dollar is akin to Weinman's 1907 American Institute of Architects medal. While in the 1907 design the eagle is seen bowing downward with a laurel branch grasped in its beak, the half dollar reverse portrays the eagle on a craggy mountaintop and peering fiercely forward, a pine sapling emerging upward below the legend E PLURIBUS UNUM.

A STANDING OVATION FOR LIBERTY WALKING

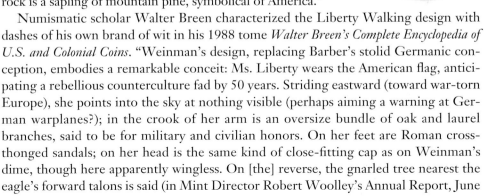

Adolph Weinman's Liberty Walking half dollar received wide praise from the beginning of its run. As Mint director Robert Woolley described in the 1916 *Mint Director's Annual Report*, "the design of the half dollar bears a full-length figure of Liberty, the folds of the Stars and Stripes flying to the breeze as a background, progressing in full stride toward the dawn of a new day, carrying branches of laurel and oak, symbolical of civil and military glory. The hand of the figure is outstretched in bestowal of the spirit of liberty. The reverse of the half dollar shows an eagle perched high upon a mountain crag, his wings unfolded, fearless in spirit and conscious of his power. Springing from a rift in the rock is a sapling of mountain pine, symbolical of America."

Numismatic scholar Walter Breen characterized the Liberty Walking design with dashes of his own brand of wit in his 1988 tome *Walter Breen's Complete Encyclopedia of U.S. and Colonial Coins*. "Weinman's design, replacing Barber's stolid Germanic conception, embodies a remarkable conceit: Ms. Liberty wears the American flag, anticipating a rebellious counterculture fad by 50 years. Striding eastward (toward war-torn Europe), she points into the sky at nothing visible (perhaps aiming a warning at German warplanes?); in the crook of her arm is an oversize bundle of oak and laurel branches, said to be for military and civilian honors. On her feet are Roman cross-thonged sandals; on her head is the same kind of close-fitting cap as on Weinman's dime, though here apparently wingless. On [the] reverse, the gnarled tree nearest the eagle's forward talons is said (in Mint Director Robert Woolley's Annual Report, June

1916) to be 'a sapling of Mountain Pine, symbolic of America.' (A singular choice, as the tree is neither exclusively American nor in any way specially remarkable save perhaps for hardihood near the timberline. This could perhaps allude to the already obsolescent American frontier culture later enshrined in Western movies, though apparently nothing Weinman said on the subject has survived.)"

Though perhaps an unthinkable notion today, the Liberty Walking half dollar did stir some disapproving commentary during its first days in circulation. On January 22, 1917, the *Huntsville Mercury* newspaper in Alabama wrote, "The new coin is radically different from all other monies produced by the government mints. A suffragette is shown sowing small stars in a western field that hasn't been plowed very deeply. The sun is setting and the old girl looks rather tired from her day's labors, in fact, perspiration can be seen trickling from her forehead. The lady wears sandals and her feet are rather dusty. She also appears, to have on overalls under her thin dress. She carries a load of firewood in one arm and wears a large napkin around her neck which leads to the belief that she left a small child at the house. The wind is blowing from the north and the sun has a blizzardly appearance. In great letters LIBERTY is spelled, extending more than half way around the entire surface. On the other side appears an eagle, grown to enormous size and marching madly toward Mexico, a cactus bush being shown in the background. The eagle has raised his wing as if to strike; the old fellow looks like he could put up a good fight if aroused but he has a swell crop of feathers on his legs."

The *Allentown Leader* of Pennsylvania was far more enthusiastic, stating in an editorial of the February 17, 1917, edition that "Any change in the coinage is likely to at first meet with more or less objection because it is a change (most coins are change.) But the appearance of the new half-dollars, following the new dimes, should soon reconcile grumblers who have resented the efforts of the United States Mint authorities to produce something different in the fractional currency. The designs have the merit of being both simple and artistic, and are a distinct improvement in that respect on the pieces so long in use." Adding that the United States, like any government, endeavors to create distinctive coinage that is easily recognizable for its face value and "attractive to the eye," the editorial continued, "this time the United States Mint has succeeded, with the help of the designer, in turning out new silver coins which far surpass in beauty those they replace."

On January 4, 1917, the *Meriden Daily Journal* of Connecticut quipped, "Bet you'll like the new half dollar five times as well as the new dime."

So popular were the new coins that people clamored to get their hands on them in just about any way they could. The January 11, 1917, edition of Connecticut's *Meriden Weekly Republican* reported on a men's clothing store that had depleted one bank's stash of the new half dollars to use in conjunction with a promotion: "The new United States half dollar is in circulation in Meriden and the House of Bernstein is to be credited with causing a big demand for the 1917 coin. All the new fifty cent pieces that the Home National bank had in stock were acquired Friday by the clothing store and the silver displayed in the store window." The story continues, "People were immediately attracted by the display of glistening silver fresh from the United States bakery. [. . .] The store generously exchanged new half dollars for old ones and the pile was cleaned out before night."

Art scholar and noted numismatist Cornelius Clarkson Vermeule III posited the Liberty Walking half dollar "really treat[s] the obverse and reverse as a surface sculptural ensemble. The 'Walking Liberty' design particularly gives the true feeling of breath and sculptural services on the scale of a coin." The Boston Museum of Fine Arts art curator and historian noted the similitude between Weinman's Liberty Walking motif and Roty's *Sower* design but contends the figure on the U.S. half dollar "is an original creation, not a slavish copy." Vermeule bestowed praise upon the reverse of Weinman's half dollar, too, noting the eagle's presence has command but does not overpower the design, while describing the eagle's feathers as "a marvelous tour de force" and hearkening to the touch of Weinman's mentor Augustus Saint-Gaudens. Vermeule concluded the Liberty Walking half dollar is "one of the greatest coins of the United States—if not of the world."

THE LIFE OF ADOLPH WEINMAN

Adolph A. Weinman was born on December 11, 1870, in Durmersheim, a village near Karlsruhe, the capital of the German grand duchy of Baden, and immigrated to the United States at the age of 14 in 1885. By 15, he was taking evening classes at Cooper Union, a private art and sciences college in New York City, and then moved on to the Art Students League of New York, where he studied under notable sculptors of the day.

Weinman honed his craft by assisting renowned sculptors such as Philip Martiny, Charles Niehaus, Daniel Chester French, Olin Warner, and Augustus Saint-Gaudens. In 1904 Weinman opened a studio and charted his career as an architectural sculptor.

Some of Weinman's most important architectural works include sculptures for such New York City landmarks as Manhattan Municipal Building, Prison Ship Martyrs Monument, and Pennsylvania Railroad Station. Sadly, Penn Station was demolished in 1963—barely a half century after its 1910 opening; while much of his work was lost amid the rubble, two of his stately eagles now reside at the modern-day subterranean iteration of the midtown Manhattan transit hub. Other Weinman works include a frieze for the Elks National Veterans Memorial in Chicago, the Jefferson Memorial in Washington, D.C., and interior ornamentals in the U.S. Supreme Court.

Among his most famous sculptures are the *Union Soldiers and Sailors* monument (1909) at Wyman Park in Baltimore, Maryland; *Abraham Lincoln* (1911) at the Kentucky State Capitol in Frankfort, Kentucky; *Rising Sun* and *Descending Night* (1914–1915) for the Panama-Pacific International Exposition in San Francisco, California; and *Fountain of the Centaurs* (circa 1926) at the Missouri State Capital in Jefferson City, Missouri.

His many commissions cemented Weinman's name in the canon of the nation's most respected sculptors. Much of his income came from bronze reproductions of these and other works that he created throughout most of his professional career. Weinman often incorporated in his works expressive figures in draperies and breathed the essence of Neoclassicism. Yet, his work also captures elements of the Art Deco movement that arose around 1910.

For the American Numismatic Society, Weinman designed the Saltus Medal, bestowed since 1913 to deserving artists. In 1920 he became the second recipient of the medal, which over the years has been awarded to other American coin designers including James Earle Fraser, John Flanagan, Victor D. Brenner, Hermon Atkins MacNeil, Laura Gardin Fraser, Chester Beach, Eugene Daub, Anthony de Francisci, and Marcel Jovine.

Weinman was the president of the National Sculpture Society from 1927 to 1930, served on the U.S. Commission of Fine Arts from 1929 to 1933, and was a member of the American Academy of Arts and Letters, the New York City Art Commission, and many other distinguished organizations. His son Robert Weinman became a prominent sculptor. His son Howard Weinman designed the 1936 Long Island Tercentenary commemorative half dollar. Adolph Weinman died at the age of 81 on August 8, 1952, leaving an artistic legacy that remains alive and well in cities and parks around the United States and is preserved on some of the nation's most cherished coins, including the American Silver Eagle and the American Palladium Eagle still in production today.

A 1917 Mercury dime.

A 1916-D Liberty Walking half dollar.

Adolph A. Weinman's 1909 *Union Soldiers and Sailors* monument in Baltimore is one of his most famous works.

A 2016-W gold Liberty Walking half dollar.

A 2017 $25/one-ounce American Palladium Eagle.

The J. Sanford Saltus medal of
the American Numismatic Society.

The design by Weinman for the American
Institute of Architects' 1907 gold medal.

A GOLDEN PATH FOR THE AMERICAN SILVER EAGLE

The American Silver Eagle could have possibly become the only new United States bullion coin of the mid-1980s if not for extenuating circumstances on the world scene. International human rights advocates centered much of their concerns on the crisis of South Africa's apartheid, a structural form of racial segregation implemented by the government. At the time, the nation was ruled by its White minority. Violence along racial lines and growing resistance against apartheid led to clashes in the streets.

Tougher restrictions against Black and other non-White populations in South Africa heightened concerns from many of the world's leaders, who called for immediate and drastic economic sanctions against the country. Among the targets of the sanctions was South Africa's iconic Krugerrand, launched in 1967 as the first gold bullion coin of the modern era. The original Krugerrands contained one troy ounce of gold and were made with a purity of .9167, giving them a higher gold content both in fineness and overall weight than many other large gold coins of the time, including the 90 percent gold United States double eagles—each containing "just" .9675 troy ounces of gold.

The U.S. Congress was taking up legislation to impose economic sanctions against South Africa. However, President Ronald Reagan stepped in during September 1985 with a sanctions package of his own, ensuring the U.S. took a bold stance. One of the toughest economic bites against apartheid came with the ban on importation of the Krugerrand, a coin that singlehandedly accounted for approximately half of South Africa's foreign exchange earnings. At the time, the United States was the largest market for the Krugerrand, with the gold coin posting $600 million in sales in the United States in 1984 alone. So, an American ban on imports of the coin dealt a huge economic blow to South Africa. It went into effect October 11, 1985.

With Americans no longer able to purchase new South African Krugerrands, speculators seeking new U.S. gold were largely limited to the American Arts Commemorative Gold Medallions. Launched in 1980, this series of half-ounce and one-ounce gold medals features a variety of influential American authors, musicians, and other artists.

The gold medals, planned and legislated in the late 1970s and released during the height of gold prices in 1980, were struck at the U.S. Mint's West Point facility, at the time serving as a bullion depository. The coins were sold through the U.S. Postal

A 1981 advertisement for the Krugerrand.

Service with a fairly arduous process that required prospective customers to get the day's prevailing gold price by calling a phone number that provided pricing based on data from the Commodity Exchange of New York, plus fees to cover production and marketing costs. Then the buyer had to go to the post office to pay for the medal by cashier's check, postal money order, or certified check bearing that day's stamp. They would receive their gold purchase from the Mint about six weeks later.

The American Arts Commemorative Series, though successful in fits and starts during its earlier years, saw rapidly falling sales. The American gold medals were canned after 1984, never reaching the lofty goals envisioned by their hopeful advocates years earlier. Congress had sought to make the Treasury Department's gold reserves available to the average American investor. Being non-monetized gold medals didn't help the cause of these pieces. Competing gold bullion coins like the Krugerrand, Maple Leaf, and Libertad had legal-tender status. Investors and other buyers widely preferred monetized precious-metal coins over bullion medals.

With no official domestic gold program in 1985, Congress took up a new cause: creating a gold bullion-coin program that would satisfy the demand of American investors

The American Arts Commemorative Series Gold Medallions program offered half-ounce and one-ounce gold medals commemorating various Americans famous in the arts.

and become the world's number-one gold coin. Within two months of Reagan's October 1985 Krugerrand ban, Congress hammered out the Gold Bullion Coin Act of 1985. The act codified the creation of four bullion coins, including a one-ounce $50 gold coin, a half-ounce $25 coin, a quarter-ounce $10 coin, and a tenth-ounce $5 coin.

As *New York Times* numismatic columnist Ed Reiter noted of the four proposed coins, "these correspond to the sizes in which South Africa strikes the Krugerrand. In addition, they have the same fineness: 22-karat or 91.67 percent. These similarities underscore the fact that Congress intended the new coins as American alternatives to the Krugerrand."

David Harper, then the editor of *Numismatic News*, recalls his impressions of the American Eagle program during its conception: "The gold coin's fineness was taken from the Krugerrand fineness of .9167, ignoring the advice to go right to .999. I also criticized the idiocy of having gold denominations of $50, $25, $10, and $5, but at least the silver American Eagle was $1, and not the $5 or $10 some were advocating at the time." He adds that the legal-tender values were required to monetize them as coins so that they wouldn't be subject to taxes in the way private bullion issues are. "The values needed to be much less than melt value to prevent people showing up at cash registers and trying to use them as money. The Treasury had a great fear of the possibility of the coins in circulation."

NAMING THE BULLION COINS

President Reagan signed the Gold Bullion Coin Act (Public Law 99-185) on December 17, 1985. A new coin program was born, and the United States silver bullion program, legal for barely six months and still uncoined, gained a sibling—or rather four. This posed something of a logistics problem for the United States Mint, which at the time was already juggling an increasingly complex commemorative coin program that in 1986 would see the first-ever trinity of a clad half dollar, silver dollar, and gold half eagle with the Statue of Liberty Centennial commemoratives.

Not only were the new gold coins lacking a design, but they were also without a name. Interestingly, Republican Congressman Ron Paul of Texas footed the American Gold Eagle Act of 1983, a proposal wherein the Treasury would mint two weights of gold coins called American Eagles. However, the bill never made it beyond committee circles and had no direct legislative connection to the American Eagle bullion coins approved in 1985. The Silver Eagles were authorized under the Liberty Coin Act, and the Gold Eagles were brought to life under the Gold Bullion Coin Act. Neither law provided an official name for the coins, whose designs were mandated under the following guidelines:

Silver
"Symbolic of Liberty on the obverse side" and "have a design [. . .] of an eagle on the reverse side"

Gold
"Have a design determined by the Secretary, except that the fifty dollar gold coin shall have – on the obverse side, a design symbolic of Liberty; and on the reverse side, a design representing a family of eagles, with the male carrying an olive branch and flying above a nest containing a female eagle and hatchlings[.]"

The specific wording for the reverse of the $50 gold American Eagle was a reference to a design conceived by Texas sculptor Miley Busiek (now Miley Frost). Though unnamed in the legislation, Frost was an accomplished artist who had conceived the design after watching Ronald Reagan's acceptance speech at the 1980 Republican National Convention.

The Family of Eagles by artist Miley Frost.

Quoted in a 2015 article by Texas coin dealer Mike Fuljenz, Frost recalled, "The theme of his speech that night was 'Together, A New Beginning.' He was encouraging Americans to be thankful for what we have in this country and to act upon that feeling. He was encouraging private-sector initiatives—a willingness to reach out and care about each other and pull together." She went on to say, "Our national symbol, the American bald eagle, had only been depicted as a single eagle, and I liked the idea of thinking of America as a caring family. Therefore, I put together a sketch showing not just one eagle, but a whole family."

Her small sculpture depicting a family of eagles was named *Together, a New Beginning* and it became a favorite of Reagan. He bestowed maquettes of the Frost piece to his inaugural guests as well as the American hostages who returned home from Iran after their 444-day capture at the U.S. embassy in Tehran. Some years later, Frost learned by reading an article in the *Wall Street Journal* that Congress was considering the creation of a new gold bullion coin. "As an artist, it triggered an idea. 'Perhaps there's an opportunity here,' I thought. There couldn't be a more dignified, more positive opportunity for America to subtly state what we stand for in our country than on a gold bullion coin—a coin that would be sold all over the world."

She campaigned leaders on both sides of the aisle in Washington, D.C., as well as a broad range of luminaries in her hometown of Dallas. Among her supporters was Dallas Cowboys football coach Tom Landry, who persuaded Joe Gibbs of the Washington football team, then known as the Redskins, to rally his friends inside the Beltway. Frost then went to Washington herself to lobby members of Congress.

Her crusade was successful. The Gold Bullion Coin Act of 1985 unanimously passed the Senate with the mandate for the $50 gold coin to carry what became known as the "Family of Eagles" on November 14, 1985, just one day after Krugerrand production was suspended in South Africa. The House followed up with unanimous passage of the gold bullion legislation on December 2, with Reagan sealing the deal on December 17. Fuljenz wrote, "Congress stipulated that the Family of Eagles design should appear on the reverse of the one-ounce coin. The Treasury wasn't required to use it on the three fractional coins but chose to do so—and that decision gratified the artist."

Reflecting on the eventual "American Eagle" name for the new bullion coins, Dave Harper remarked, "I remember writing an editorial saying 'American Eagle' would be confused with the old eagle name for the $10 gold." However, he further notes that the Family of Eagles reverse for the Gold Eagles "kind of dictated that 'Eagle' would be referenced in some way." He quips, "Silver kind of was along for the ride on that one."

In a September 21, 1986, column for the *New York Times*, Ed Reiter reported, "American Eagle was chosen as the coins' official name after months of research and discussion. Treasury and Mint officials had some reservations about the term, fearing that it might cause confusion between the bullion coins and traditional U.S. gold coins, whose official denominations include the double eagle, eagle, half eagle, and quarter eagle. They decided that by adding the word 'American,' they were giving the new 'Eagle' a sufficiently distinctive name."

Why the Liberty Walking Design?

In the weeks and months following the passage of the 1985 Liberty Coin Act, the future one-ounce silver coin was a blank canvas.

In the mid-1980s there wasn't nearly the degree of public input on coin design as there is today. Today we have the Citizens Coinage Advisory Committee, chartered by Congress in 2003 (to replace the Citizens Commemorative Coinage Advisory Committee, established in 1993), providing guidance to the secretary of the Treasury on design matters regarding coins and medals. The United States Mint Artistic Infusion Program, a program pooling outside artists to create and submit designs for United States coins, was also nearly two decades distant.

Yet, it wasn't as though the United States Mint and Treasury were acting in an artistic vacuum on the American Eagle. The U.S. Commission of Fine Arts had long been a sounding board for Mint and Treasury officials looking for feedback on coin design proposals. Established in 1910 by an act of Congress, the Commission of Fine Arts provides counsel on design and aesthetic matters to the president, Congress, and other government leads on various projects "as they affect the federal interest and preserve the dignity of the nation's capital," as stated by the organization.

In July 1921 President Warren G. Harding signed Executive Order 3524, which charges the Commission of Fine Arts to advise on the design of coins and medals. While the secretary of the Treasury is not legally required to follow the recommendations of the Commission of Fine Arts, the venerable voice of the organization has been regarded as sound guidance and even a formal blessing on the designs best suited for the nation's coinage.

Choosing the new American Eagle designs was a matter of great importance. "The obverse design of the American Silver Eagle was predetermined," sculptor-engraver John Mercanti wrote in his book *American Silver Eagles: A Guide to the U.S. Bullion Coin Program*; Mercanti devoted 36 years as sculptor-engraver for the United States Mint, from 1974 until his retirement from the post of chief engraver in late 2010.

"It would be Adolph A. Weinman's Walking Liberty originally issued on the half dollar in 1916 and in production until 1947," wrote Mercanti. "I have no idea who made that decision. It could have come from the Mint director, from sales and marketing, or from someone lobbying for it."

"Donna Pope was one of our more engaged Mint directors and was eager to reach out for feedback," remembers Don Kagin, of multigenerational numismatic auction firm Kagin's. "I did recommend the Saint-Gaudens design when asked, but I'm not sure if I suggested the American Eagle name. In 1983 I had hired international artist Peter Max to create the cover of our American Numismatic Association auction catalog using an image of Lady Liberty, since Liberty was the most prominent and popular design on our silver coins. When the idea for a gold and silver bullion coin was contemplated to compete with the South African Krugerrands and other coins, I recommended that we use our most beautiful and popular design for our gold coins. I'm sure I wasn't the only one."

Beth Deisher, who was the editor of *Coin World* in the mid-1980s, suggested Adolph Weinman's Liberty Walking and Augustus Saint-Gaudens's double eagle motifs were perhaps two of the safest bets. "[Mint director] Donna Pope was a person who didn't like a

An American bald eagle named Osceola visits Mint director Donna Pope at the U.S. Mint headquarters.

lot of controversy, and she had a standard line: 'There's no need to change any designs that are on U.S. coins because they are time-honored designs,'" Deisher said. "You have to remember that in 1986, when the United States Mint was creating the American Eagle program, they were under tremendous pressure to get the new designs out. It was the element of time at play." Deisher added, "The Walking Liberty and Saint-Gaudens motifs were widely known American symbols and it was easy for the U.S. Mint to go back and make new hubs and dies from the original models."

Commentary of the period from Ed Reiter also points to the element of time in choosing two existing designs for the obverse: "A high Mint official said time constraints would have made it difficult, if not impossible, for outside designs to have been commissioned. He explained that the obverse design (A.A. Weinman's) and the reverse (John Mercanti's) were chosen almost simultaneously."

MICHAEL BROWN ON STEPPING OUT WITH THE EAGLES

Michael Brown was a close aide for Mint director
Donna Pope at the United States Mint during the 1980s.

The Mint was weary from the experience of the designs for the U.S. Olympic Coin Program [of 1983–1984]. At that time there was no process for coin design development, and our technology was ancient. No one wanted to reopen that debate. We were all disappointed in the 1984 [Olympic commemorative] designs. With the Gold Eagle, we wanted something proven. I also seem to recall that Don Kagin might have suggested this would be a good idea. I remember him visiting with Donna Pope and bringing us a book on American gold coinage with the Saint-Gaudens design embossed on the cover. With James Baker in charge of Treasury, there was assistant secretary John F.W. Rogers, who had an interest in art and architecture. He had led the restoration of the Old Executive Office Building while at the White House and later the Treasury Building. He appreciated the classic coin designs. I don't recall that there were other options put forward. I believe a consensus formed early on this matter. And it was suggested that [Miss Liberty on the Gold Eagle] be slimmed from a size 16 to a size 14.

With the commemoratives, there were photo album books with all proposed designs that were sent to Treasury. They were to permit the secretary to flip through them at his leisure. They went from the Mint to the treasurer to the secretary in the [Donald T.] Regan years. The secretary said he would put them on his coffee table and look at them when he had spare time. In the Baker years they went from the Mint to the treasurer, to John F.W. Rogers, to the secretary. I don't know what happened to those albums.

Grey Advertising developed the branding. The team was led by Bob Ravitz, Dwight Leeper, and Jonathan Baskin. The Mint and Grey had a terrific partnership. I don't know if any other firm ever again understood the Mint and garnered the public interest in coinage. We won many major advertising and public relations awards in that period.

Never underestimate the influence that New York City Mayor Ed Koch had on breaking the logjam on the gold bullion coin. Deep in the Treasury were commodity specialists opposed to gold coinage. Legislation [on implementing gold in the monetary system] offered by Congressman Ron Paul was going nowhere. Then the director was invited to New York City for a press conference on the tenth anniversary of the opening of the gold market. They were displaying a million ounces in gold bullion and had invited Mayor Koch and former Mayor Abraham Beame to the event. Koch was such a showman, he picked up a gold bar and put it in his pocket! But then he turned serious and said the U.S. needed to issue a gold coin to compete against the Krugerrand. On the Amtrak train back to D.C., I used the phone booth in our car to check in with the office. There was a message from Ken Swab [legal counsel for the House Banking Subcommittee on Consumer Affairs

Michael Brown is seen standing on the left alongside his colleagues at the United States Mint in the mid-1980s. Also pictured here, standing from left to right, are Harold Davidson, William Daddio, Kenneth Gubin, and Barry Frere; from left to right sitting are Dennis Fischer, Eugene Essner, Donna Pope, and Andrew Cosgarea.

and Coinage] to call as soon as we got back to D.C. The publicity generated by Koch had already hit Capitol Hill. The next day we were in discussions with the coinage subcommittee about moving the legislation.

Then, out of the blue, we got a call from The Gold Institute and a fellow named John Lutley, who wanted to talk to us about the sourcing of the gold. He came by the office with Ken Canfield of Homestake Mining, who made the case the Treasury should use newly mined gold. They were accompanied by a young and very pregnant woman, Mary Beth Donnelly of Newmont Mining. This was not the Mint's decision, so we sent it up the line to the secretary. We soon heard back from deputy secretary of the Treasury Richard Darman that there was no objection, but with two conditions: (1) Congress had to amend the legislation and (2) the treasury reserved a right to use reserve gold if necessary. Lutley, Donnelly, and Canfield then led the effort to amend the bill. Lutley told me the [Capitol] Hill offices were so concerned that Mary Beth would have the baby in their foyer that they always got right in to see the member. Homestake later furnished the first 5,000 ounces of gold for the Eagles from their mine in South Dakota.

I am a little shaky on this, but I believe that Senator Mayer Jacob "Chic" Hecht of Nevada was supposed to offer the amendment. It was expected he would face a tough reelection against Governor Richard Bryan. The senator was missing, and I believe that Idaho senator Steve Symms had to offer the amendment. Ironically, it was [later] Senator Richard Bryan (he defeated Hecht) who amended the Silver Eagle legislation to permit the Treasury to buy newly mined silver when the national stockpile was depleted at the turn of the century.

The Silver Eagle was promoted by a lobbying group, I think Dutko in its early years with help from the Silver Institute. To stimulate demand, they wanted a classic design. Again, the Mint was weary over the debacle of the [critically panned] designs for the 1984 Olympic coins and did not want to enter into a protracted debate about the coin design. I recall we looked at the Morgan silver dollar, the Peace dollar, and the Liberty Walking. We knew the one-ounce silver coin would be large and the Liberty Walking would be well suited. It also paired well with the Gold Eagle design. There was actually little confidence that the Silver Eagle program would succeed. The decision was made to mint the coins in a little-used room at the San Francisco Mint (then an assay office) because we were not sure the production run justified more investment. We were pleasantly surprised. Demand far exceeded anything the Mint expected.

Anything involving the 140 million ounces of silver in the National Strategic Stockpile was controversial. On one side was Eastman Kodak Corporation attempting to push down the price of silver by dumping the stockpile, and on the other side were the silver producers, led by Senator James A. McClure of Idaho, trying to lessen the impact by diverting the silver into coinage. The Mint was trapped in "no man's land" as these two groups battled it out in Congress. McClure was a loyal Reaganite, but it would have been much simpler to auction the silver reserve. The Kodak office in Washington, and their front-group the Silver Users Association, were very aggressive, to the point of offensive, and that eventually pushed the Mint squarely into the McClure camp.

I organized the first-strike ceremony for the Silver Eagle at the San Francisco Mint with [Mint spokesperson] Hamilton Dix. Secretary Baker and Senator McClure both attended, along with Jack Gerard, the staffer for the legislation. Jack and I became friends and worked on mining issues for another decade. Just before the ceremony in [officer-in-charge] Tom Miller's office, we had this debate if the Silver Eagle was the largest silver coin issued by the Mint. Senator McClure was referencing [the] trade dollar [minted for use in Asia]. I think we got everyone comfortable with the fact [the Silver Eagle] was the largest of the domestic market. Thank goodness there was a *Red Book* handy! I thought it was the best ceremony we ever organized. It was much more of a numismatic family event. The fledgling Financial News Network wanted to feature the coins. We put a Mint policeman on an airplane and flew several coins to Los Angeles to make their deadline. The reporter was Neil Cavuto.

Miley Frost on the American Eagle

Miley Frost created the 1980 Family of Eagles *sculpture that was enshrined on the reverses of the four American Gold Eagles from their inception in 1986 until 2021.* The majestic American bald eagle was truly the guide and inspiration for the gold coin program from the inception. The concept of the design for the reverse of what was to become the American Eagle gold bullion coin began on a mountain top overlooking the Platte River in Wyoming. Observing the attributes of a family of American bald eagles was a profound narrative of all that America represents.

Miley Frost at the first-strike ceremony for the American Gold Eagle on October 10, 1986.

Recalling a small article in the *Wall Street Journal* announcing a possibility that the U.S. Department of the Treasury was considering the creation of a gold bullion coin for the first time in over 50 years, as an artist, I thought, "What could be more appropriate than to have these noble birds carry a message of freedom, peace, and hope for the future to people around the world on the reverse of this proposed American gold bullion coin?"

The original *Family of Eagles* sculpture.

Only in America could such a basic idea become a reality. With the encouragement and support of a wide bipartisan coalition, the Gold Bullion Coin Act of 1985 companion bills passed the U.S. Congress unanimously on December 17, 1985, stating, ". . . On the reverse side, a design representing a family of eagles . . ." The next day I received a call from the U.S. Department of the Treasury, asking, "Do you have a design for the obverse of the coin?" I smiled and said, "No, but I have a suggestion. The best possible way to ensure that it will be a success is to use the Augustus Saint-Gaudens Liberty on the obverse."

With their permission, I contacted the Saint-Gaudens Historic Site Board of Trustees president and asked him if the board would grant permission to the U.S. Department of the Treasury to use the design. They enthusiastically agreed to work with the Mint.

To this day the American Eagle gold bullion and now the American Eagle silver bullion coins would not have achieved their great success without the magnificent, classic obverse designs of Augustus Saint-Gaudens and Adolph A. Weinman. It is with sincere gratitude that I have enjoyed the pleasure and blessing of helping to honor the heritage, values, and hope that America brings to our world. May we always endeavor to seek excellence and dignity for our beloved America's coinage.

CONTROVERSY ENSUES

How much time elapsed between passage of the Silver Eagle legislation in July 1985 and the decision to place the Weinman Walker on the American Silver Eagle may be fuzzy. However, by April 1986, news reports were pointing to the Weinman and Saint-Gaudens designs coming out of retirement for a new role on the bullion coinage. "Reliable sources in Washington, D.C., indicate that the Augustus Saint-Gaudens double eagle design of Liberty—used on double eagles from 1907 through 1933—is likely to grace the obverse of the new gold bullion coins and Adolph A. Weinman's Liberty Walking obverse design and eagle reverse—used on half dollars from 1916 until 1947—are the odds-on favorites for the new silver bullion coin," declared a lead-page story on the April 23, 1986, issue of *Coin World*. The article, citing "reliable Washington sources," reported secretary of the

Treasury James A. Baker III had "approved designs for the new bullion coins in early March [1986] and has ordered that certain 'refinements' be made. It is not clear if the 'refinements' pertain to just one of the coins, some, or all."

Ed Reiter wrote observations on the matter in his June 8, 1986, commentary for the *New York Times*: "Judging from interviews with five of the seven members [of the Commission of Fine Arts], most of the questions and possible objections will center around four gold bullion coins [. . .] Some of the commissioners questioned why the Treasury chose to use older designs, not only on gold coins, but on the obverse of the silver bullion coin. That has the same basic motif as the obverse of the Liberty Walking half dollar, a coin designed by Adolph A. Weinman and issued from 1916 through 1947."

Reiter quoted sculptor and commission member Frederick Hart as saying, "You can't go wrong when you use Saint-Gaudens [. . .] But, on the other hand, it's just such a narrow point of view when you have to reuse a design that's nearly 80 years old in order to achieve some kind of success. These are very special coins, and this is a rich opportunity to do something that is of our age." This same article cited New Yorker Diane Wolf, a public member of the commission, who agreed the time was ripe for new designs. "I love Augustus Saint-Gaudens. [. . .] I think he's a true hero of sculpture in America. However, in every era there are new sculptors and new artists. These coins should have reflected the work of today's most talented people and there should have been a professional competition to obtain all designs." As Reiter also relayed, further dissent concerned the "refinements" to Miss Liberty, something that reportedly rattled "several commissioners" reviewing the designs. Neil Porterfield, a commissioner who also served as chairman of the Department of Landscape Architecture at Pennsylvania State University, raised, "I have a real question about how faithfully the original design has been followed."

Some of the most pointed criticism on the reuse of the Adolph Weinman design came from the artist's son Robert, who, like his father, was a sculptor and medallist of top repute and had served as the president of the National Sculpture Society—as did his dad. Reiter quoted Robert Weinman as saying, "Reusing old designs, however attractive they may be, strikes me as evidence of a paucity of ideas. If we were a nation of 100,000 and there were only two sculptors, and neither of them was up to the task of making a proper design, then I could forgive this reuse. But we've got any of 300 people, I'm sure, who could do a cracking good design, so why are we reusing these old ones?"

"My dad's Walking Liberty and Saint-Gaudens's Liberty gold coin served their purposes admirably in their time. [. . .] But they should be put on the shelf and remembered as outstanding designs, period. To drag them out, dust off the embalming fluid, and try to breathe new life into them is, I think, ridiculous and unnecessary. There are plenty of contemporary artists practicing nowadays who can do as well and possibly even better."

MAKING A MODERN MASTERPIECE

Any disagreement that cropped up when the designs for the new American Eagle coins were selected in the mid-1980s is largely forgotten today. As Mike Fuljenz so matter-of-factly asserts, "The reason the Walking Liberty design was chosen is because it's long been regarded as the most beautiful silver coin ever minted."

The design on the American Silver Eagle is a close facsimile of the one first minted more than a century ago. But some modifications have been made over the years, most notably in 1986 before hubs for the new coin were created. The slightly modified Liberty Walking motif as executed for the Silver Eagle beginning in 1986 was carried out by U.S. Mint sculptor-engraver Edgar Z. Steever IV.

Preparations for the American Silver Eagle were not made with the digital design and modeling programs that are now standard. In the mid-1980s Mint engravers were still creating models for new coins and medals with a Janvier reducing machine, knives, plaster, and clay—all tools of the trade for more than a century by that point. These were the resources with which sculptor-engraver John Mercanti and the team at the U.S. Mint translated the six-inch-diameter master plaster bearing Weinman's motif into working models for the new American Silver Eagle.

Recalls Mercanti in *American Silver Eagles: A Guide to the U.S. Bullion Coin Program*, "Production was begun and dies were cut. Unfortunately, the modifications [to the Silver Eagle design] hadn't been enough to get the level of detail requested. Because we were working with six-inch models for both the obverse and reverse, and because we were still using Janvier reducing machines and hadn't yet moved into the digital arena, the artwork was too small for the tracing stylus to get into small areas of the model to pick up fine detail."

The team had to make the models larger, which was no easy task with the Janvier lathe. "The problem with the Janvier machine is that it's made for reducing, not enlarging. It will create a perfect reduction if the ratios are correct and the artwork is large enough for the stylus to get into the finest element to pick up the detail, but when it comes to enlarging, it's a whole different ball game," observes Mercanti. The process of enlarging the models was painstaking in those days, with larger models recast when necessary and then further engraving executed to fill in details that were muted in the process of enlargement—a procedure that could days, even weeks.

Mercanti's most outward contribution to the American Silver Eagle was the heraldic eagle reverse, which was paired with Weinman's obverse in 1986 and remained in production on the coin well into 2021. "I didn't want a flying eagle for the American Silver Eagle coin," remembers Mercanti in his book. "I didn't go in the direction of soaring eagles with sun rays behind them because it had been [done] so many times before. I wanted something more formal, more heraldic." He adds, "As I think back on the program, I may have submitted an eagle in flight. The drawings are gone and probably lost forever."

Mercanti submitted two versions of his eagle reverse, one showing the eagle straight on and the other with the national symbol turned slightly to the viewer's right. "I don't recall how long we had to work on the American Silver Eagle designs. I would say that, because of the extremely tight deadline, we were allotted no longer than two weeks for finished designs to be submitted," he says. After the designs were sent to the U.S. Mint headquarters for review, Mercanti learned the victor of his two motifs was the formal heraldic eagle facing squarely toward the viewer. "Knowing that the Weinman obverse was six inches required that I make my model the same size, so that we would get the same quality on both sides when we made the Janvier reductions. It was no easy task modeling something so intricate at that scale. It took about two weeks. Dies were then produced and cleaned, and we went into production."

Note the differences between the original Liberty Walking half dollar design
(left) and the version adapted for the American Silver Eagle in 1986 (right).

John Mercanti's
sketches for the
American Silver
Eagle reverse.

John Mercanti working on an enlarged model
of his American Silver Eagle reverse design.

A model of the American Silver Eagle's original reverse.

A Janvier reducing lathe could translate the design on a large
galvano or model for a coin into a smaller version of the art that
would be processed into a hub, from which press-ready dies were made.

1987 Annual Report of the Director of the Mint on American Eagle Coins

The content below is condensed from the 1987 Annual Report of the Director of the Mint for the fiscal year ending September 30, 1987, just as the first complete year of American Eagle sales was drawing near. This was the first such conclusive evaluation of results on the early success of the program.

The United States Mint commenced the sale of American Eagle Gold Bullion Coins on October 20, 1986. The sale of American Eagle Silver Bullion Coins began on November 24, 1986. Initial inventories of the coins were sold out immediately due to the phenomenal demand. So successful was the launch of the American Eagle Bullion Coins that *Fortune Magazine* presented the American Eagle Gold Bullion Coins as one of the "Top Products of the Year" in 1986. In addition, proof versions of the one ounce Gold and Silver American Eagles were offered for sale to the public in FY87 by direct mail order purchase from the Mint.

Secretary of the Treasury James A. Baker III kicked off production of the Uncirculated American Eagle bullion coins at two first strike ceremonies. Production of the American Eagle Gold Bullion Coins began September 8, 1986 following a first-strike ceremony held at West Point. The American Eagle Silver Bullion Coins were first struck during a ceremony held at the San Francisco Assay Office on October 29, 1986.

The Mint commenced sales of American Eagle Gold and Silver Bullion Coins on October 20, 1986, and November 24, 1986, respectively. Initial demand for the gold bullion coins was so strong that the Mint's entire inventory of 845,000 coins was depleted within the first two days of sales. An allocation system for the equitable distribution of sales among the Mint's Authorized Purchasers was immediately implemented. An allocation system for the sale of the American Eagle Silver Bullion Coins was instituted from the commencement of silver coin sales due to the incredible demand for the new U.S. bullion coins.

The U.S. Mint entered the bullion coin market utilizing the already well-established distribution network used by other successful foreign mints. For the sale of the new bullion coins the U.S. Mint initially approved a total of 25 Authorized Purchasers for the gold bullion coins and 28 Authorized Purchasers for the silver bullion coins. Each Authorized Purchaser met strict qualifying criteria in order to guarantee a buy-back market for the coins during both stable and unstable economic periods. By the end of 1987, 3 additional gold purchasers and 6 additional silver purchasers had been approved by the Mint for a total of 28 Authorized Purchasers for the gold bullion coins and 34 Authorized Purchasers for the silver bullion coins. These distributors market the American Eagles in over 20 countries. Markets represented by the Authorized Purchasers include the United States, Canada, England, Switzerland, Luxembourg, Japan, Hong Kong, and Germany. Through this distribution system, the coins are widely available throughout world markets.

Initial projection for the first year of sales for the American Eagle Bullion Coins were 2.2 million ounces of gold bullion coins and 4 million ounces of silver bullion coins. By March 30, 1987, sales of American Eagle Gold and Silver Uncirculated

Bullion Coins had surpassed all projections. Final sales figures for FY87 totaled 2,659,250 ounces of gold bullion coins and 11,806,000 ounces of silver bullion coins.

Gross receipts for the year totaled more than $1.1 billion in the sales of American Eagle Gold Bullion Coins and over $85.7 million in the sales of American Eagle Silver Bullion Coins.

Comprehensive marketing plans have been developed to support the sale of the American Eagle Bullion Coins in both the domestic and international markets. A major component of the plans is print advertising. The Mint selected Grey Advertising of New York to implement the introductory phase of print advertising announcing the availability of American Eagle Coins in the world marketplace. Advertisements for the American Eagle Coins first appeared domestically in November 1986. However, due to the strong demand for the coins domestically, worldwide advertising was delayed a few months until sufficient coin inventories were available to meet the market demand. The introductory phase of advertising ran from January through June 1987. An expansion phase advertising

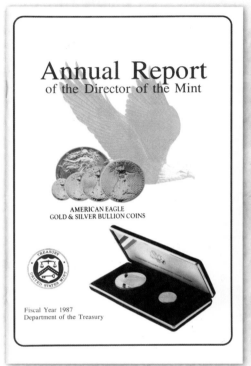

Annual Report
of the Director of the Mint

AMERICAN EAGLE
GOLD & SILVER BULLION COINS

Fiscal Year 1987
Department of the Treasury

**Donna Pope, James Baker, and Katherine Ortega at
the first-strike ceremony for the American Gold Eagle.**

campaign was launched in June 1987 with advertisement [sic] appearing in national newspapers and magazines as well as in 12 of the top metro market newspapers. Internationally, advertisements ran in newspapers throughout Germany, Japan, Hong Kong, Belgium, Holland, Switzerland and Luxembourg. The advertisement campaign was scheduled to continue into the new FY88.

The United States Mint has also created and produced point-of-sale materials to support the new American Eagle Bullion Coins. Point-of-sale kits consist of several elements including posters, brochures, stuffers, advertisement slicks, logo and line art, window decals and counter cards. Point-of-sale materials have been produced in six languages: English, French, Dutch, German, Japanese and Mandarin Chinese. These materials are provided without charge to retailers and Authorized Purchasers to enhance the sales of American Eagle Bullion Coins.

Proof versions of the one ounce Gold and Silver American Eagle Coins were offered for sale to the public in FY87 by direct mail order from the U.S. Mint. Unlike the Uncirculated investment coins, the proof bullion coins carry the Mint mark of the producing facility ("W" designating the West Point Bullion Depository for the gold bullion coins and "S" denoting the San Francisco Assay Office for the silver bullion coins). The ordering period commenced November 1, 1986, and ended December 1, 1986. During the direct mail ordering period customers purchased 446,290 gold proof one ounce coins and 1,446,778 silver proof one ounce coins.

BECOMING AN AUTHORIZED PURCHASER

Thinking about becoming an Authorized Purchaser so you can buy newly struck American Eagle bullion coins directly from the U.S. Mint? The Mint has a pretty stringent set of requirements for those who want to join of the network of official distributors who create a two-way market trading among wholesalers and other secondary market players, including financial institutions and retail outlets.

Criteria for becoming an Authorized Purchaser depends on if the applicant wishes to purchase American Silver Eagles or other American Eagle products, which include gold, platinum, and palladium coinage.

The Mint's wholesale pricing for all American Eagles is contingent on the bullion price of silver, gold, platinum, and palladium and also includes premiums to cover the cost of minting, distributing, and marketing. Prices changes

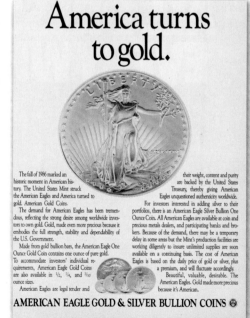

One of several advertisements introducing American Eagles to the world soon after the bullion coins were released.

daily. Silver Eagle prices are based on the prevailing price of silver according to the London Bullion Market Association (LBMA) plus a premium charge of $2.35 per coin (as of late 2022). So, if an Authorized Purchaser wishes to buy American Silver Eagles on a given day that the precious metal is trading for $22.50 per ounce, they would expect to pay $24.85 per coin to buy the coin directly from the Mint. The U.S. Mint further imposes a minimum order requirement of 25,000 ounces of American Silver Eagles in order to become an Authorized Purchaser of Silver Eagles.

Those who wish to become Authorized Purchasers must furnish documentation showing they have a tangible net worth of at least $10 million for the last three years, or have at least $5 million in tangible net worth and offer a letter of credit favoring the U.S. Mint that covers the difference between their net worth and the $10 million threshold. This is to help protect the Mint in the event of the Authorized Purchaser failing to meet its financial obligations as dictated in its purchasing arrangement. After approval of these prerequisites, the Authorized Purchaser candidate must undergo review and approval, as well as vetting of the business as a two-way market maker. There may be additional requirements depending on the results of the review.

SOURCING SILVER

Silver doesn't grow on trees—it is mined, straight from the earth. It is a dirty, laborious, dangerous job, but someone has to do it. Pickaxes and hammers were tools of the trade for silver miners in days of yore. Today silver ore is mined with heavy machinery in underground mine shafts and open pits.

About 24,000 metric tons of silver is mined annually, and India consumes about 12 percent of it, making that nation the largest consumer of the metal. Even as the various uses for silver have changed during the evolution of human society from the analog world of the Industrial Age to the rapidly advancing digital environs of the Information Age, the principal science behind silver mining has changed relatively little. On occasion, silver is found in pure form, but it is also encountered in stephanite, acanthite (silver sulfide), chlorargyrite (silver chloride), and polybasite. About half of the silver

This open-pit mine yields silver, gold, copper, and other minerals.

mined today is found alongside other ores, including gold, copper, lead, zinc, argentite, pyrargyrite, and cerargyrite. Tons of material might need to be pulverized to obtain even just a few ounces of silver.

The silver ore is broken away from large deposits using any of several techniques, depending on the kind of rock surrounding the silver, and it may be extracted from the ground in the form of solid nuggets or in flakes interspersed in other minerals. Once silver has been mined, it then undergoes refinement, which purifies the silver by separating it from other elements.

Silver may be removed from lead ores through a process known as cupellation, which involves heating the ore in a furnace. Another refinement system utilizes froth flotation; in this case, crushed ore is placed in a bath and air bubbles push silver upward toward the frothy surface, where the precious metal can be skimmed and then smelted to further separate it from other metals present. Once refined, the silver is usually shaped into .999-fine or .9999-fine ingots (or bars) ready for shipment to vendors, some of whom manufacture blanks and planchets for mints around the world, including the U.S. Mint.

Pouring molten silver into a mold at Sunshine Minting.

Finished planchets ready to ship to the Mint.

Turning Silver into Planchets:
An Interview with Sunshine Minting
President and CEO Tom Power

Tom Power is the president and chief executive officer of Sunshine Minting, Inc., which is the largest supplier of silver planchets for the U.S. Mint. Planchets from the Coeur d'Alene, Idaho, company are used for striking American Silver Eagles and many other silver coins. Founded in 1979, Sunshine Minting started providing the Mint with silver planchets for the American Silver Eagle program in 1997 after Canadian firm Johnson Matthey shifted its business focus and the Mint needed a new supplier. Power, who had been with Johnson Matthey since 1988, assisted the Mint during its transition to a new vendor, which eventually became Sunshine Minting.

Q. *What was the process like in becoming the primary vendor for the United States Mint?*

A. It was challenging, but very rewarding. In 1996 Johnson Matthey (JM) corporate [headquarters] in the United Kingdom decided to exit the production of silver products due to the low margins involved. This included jewelry products and industrial products, which included silver brazing products, and Mint products. This created a challenge for JM Canada as they had a supply contract with the U.S. Mint for silver planchets. In early 1997 I was part of the team responsible for working with the U.S. Mint to help relocate this production to another vendor. I was asked to fly to Idaho to meet with Sunshine Minting to look at the transition of this production. Sunshine Minting at that time was a very, very small company located in Coeur d'Alene and was working to become an approved supplier to the Mint. However, without technical and operational expertise, they were struggling. They could not get "production" volumes of planchets approved by the U.S. Mint in West Point, as they were not meeting the very stringent quality standards. During my initial visit to Sunshine Minting, Inc. (SMI), I was able to identify the areas that they needed to improve, suggest some much-needed capital investment, and work with training the employees on the quality standards as required by the U.S. Mint. Shortly after my initial visit, SMI was able to get approved by the Mint as a supplier and now needed to focus on building their capacity to meet its needs. Upon my return to JM, I decided to take advantage of a corporate restructuring that was happening, as a result of the decision to exit the production of silver products, and tendered my resignation. With the assistance of the owner of SMI at the time, Marvin Otten, I was able to quickly secure my work visa and relocated to SMI in May of 1997 as the new director of operations. Within a short period of time, I was able to get SMI to meet the production numbers required by the U.S. Mint, and the rest is history!

Q. *Where does the silver comes from for production of these planchets?*

A. The silver used to produce silver planchets for the American Silver Eagle blanks comes from the open market and is delivered to us in 1,000-ounce Good

Delivery Bars from recognized refineries. In the early days of the program, silver bars were supplied from the U.S. Mint to help reduce the strategic stockpile of bars. However, for over 15 years, the bars have been purchased on the open market based on the U.S. Mint's specifications.

Q. *What are some of the challenges of running an operation that supplies planchets to the U.S. Mint?*

A. The planchets are a fully engineered product, meaning that in addition to meeting size and minimum weight requirements, there are a number of metallurgical properties that the planchets must meet in order to pass their quality standards. The biggest challenge with running a planchet operation is the fact that the precious-metals industry globally is very small, as compared to other industries, so the equipment and resources needed are not readily available. In addition to machinery, finding people with direct experience in our industry is very challenging. That goes all the way from direct labor to engineers, quality technicians, and management.

Q. *Has much changed over the years in terms of the process or procedure of manufacturing the American Silver Eagle planchets?*

A. The biggest change we have seen in our industry has been focused on automation and robotics. Most of our equipment vendors are now focusing in on automation for their specific equipment to improve efficiency and minimize any potential long-term health and safety issues, such as automated weighing cells, automated material handling systems, vision inspection systems, robotics and collaborative robot systems in manual processes such as packaging, and digitization of process such as tool and design to utilize new computer numerical control and laser technologies.

Q. *How did Sunshine Minting maneuver through the darkest days of the COVID-19 pandemic?*

A. Obviously, the very early days of the pandemic were a challenge for everyone as we all tried to figure out our next steps. SMI was very fortunate in that it was immediately deemed an "essential service" within days of the start of the pandemic because we are a critical part of the supply chain for the U.S. government and the Department of the Treasury. The challenge then became, "How do we keep employees safe and engaged at work to minimize disruptions in service?" This was a key issue for us. As a precious-metals producer, many of our employees were already accustomed to wearing high levels of personal protective equipment, including masks and gloves, so we had to ensure that we had an abundant supply as these items became mandated by state and federal entities. We had to modify our inventory levels of critical items, including silver from "just-in-time" to "just-in-case," as the interruptions in the global supply chain were difficult to predict and manage. The biggest change came with our workforce. We focused on cross-training and workforce flexibility to help overcome the challenges of dealing with COVID in the workplace. We socially distanced where possible, created safe workspaces where applicable, engaged in a huge program to clean and disinfect our operations on a regular basis, and educated our employees on how to deal with COVID, using sound medical facts and reliable information, not social media! As a result of this, we were able to minimize interruptions. To this day, we still employ the cross-training and workplace flexibility and are able to maintain our operations and output with about 20 percent less labor than pre-COVID levels. We are continuing to invest in automation and integration of our processes with robots and co-bots. We are constantly re-evaluating our supply chain based on the lessons learned during COVID to ensure we have a robust supply of critical supplies.

THE UNITED STATES MINT: PRODUCER OF THE AMERICAN SILVER EAGLE

The United States was founded on July 4, 1776, with the signing of the Declaration of Independence. Other establishing documents were drafted in the coming years, including the Articles of Confederation, adopted on March 1, 1781, that permitted Congress the sole right to regulate the value and alloy of coins struck under its authority and by the states. Throughout the 1780s, various forms of coinage were concocted by different states, though the most widely used currency were copper and silver foreign coins and tokens, such as British pieces and the Spanish milled dollar and its fractions.

Some of the nation's leading minds, including Thomas Jefferson, Benjamin Franklin, and Alexander Hamilton, addressed the need for a national monetary system. Several kinds of pattern coins and related proposals were made. On March 3, 1791, Congress passed a resolution to establish a national mint and give President George Washington the latitude to seek coin designers and procure the equipment necessary for striking coins. President Washington would directly address the matter of founding a national mint in his third national address, and action soon followed.

The United States Mint was authorized with the Coinage Act of April 2, 1792, otherwise known as the Mint Act. This law formally established the U.S. Mint and called for its construction in the nation's then-capital city of Philadelphia. The Coinage Act also stipulated the core elements of the nation's new monetary system, including the basis of a decimal system built around the dollar as a unit and cents making up

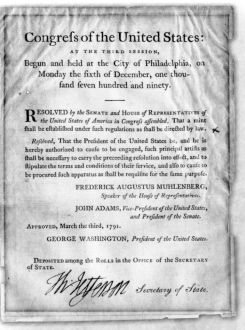

The United States Senate and House of Representatives approved the U.S. Mint in a joint resolution on March 3, 1791.

fractions thereof. The Coinage Act predicated the production of a variety of new coins in denominations ranging from the half cent to the eagle (the name of the circulating $10 gold coin).

The United States Mint eventually grew into eight domestic minting facilities in the following locations:

Charlotte, North Carolina: C mintmark (gold coins only; 1838–1861)

Carson City, Nevada: CC mintmark (gold and silver coins only; 1870–1885; 1889–1893)

Dahlonega, Georgia: D mintmark (gold coins only; 1838–1861)

Denver, Colorado: D mintmark (1906 to date)

New Orleans, Louisiana: O mintmark (gold and silver coins only; 1838–1861; 1879–1909)

Philadelphia, Pennsylvania: P mintmark (mintmark used only since 1942 for some coins; 1793 to date)

San Francisco, California: S mintmark (1854 to date)

West Point, New York: W mintmark (1984 to date)

Today four of these facilities operate, with the Philadelphia, Denver, San Francisco, and West Point Mints handling all coin production for the United States.

A LOOK AT AMERICAN SILVER EAGLE PRODUCTION

While planchets are made by private vendors, West Point Mint chemist and chief assayer Jeanette Grogan says she and her team subject every shipment to a battery of tests to ensure they are up to the Mint's standards. "We sample everything, and the two most important things we look for is the weight of each planchet and that they are of the correct purity—99.99% silver," explains Grogan, who says silver shipments usually come in weekly. "We visually inspect them to ensure they are free from surface defects, and we make sure the hardness of the planchet meets the minimum criteria."

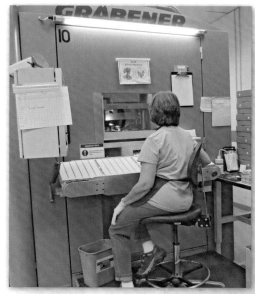

A mint worker oversees production of 2014 American Silver Eagles at the West Point Mint.

She says they also sample one blank per lot for its chemical composition. "We roll the coin blank flat and then dissolve it in nitric acid. The results are summarized." If there any issues, her team generates a nonconformance report for corrective and preventative actions. "Quality is very important to us, whether it is a bullion, Proof, Uncirculated, or another type of coin," Grogan says.

Dies are manufactured at the Philadelphia Mint and finished at the West Point Mint. Die finishing is usually performed only for dies intended for production of numismatic coinage, not bullion strikes, according to Grogan.

The West Point Mint operates on a three-shift schedule, meaning coin production is nearly nonstop. Bullion coins receive two blows by the die, while most numismatic versions receive three strikes. A typical American Silver Eagle die on the bullion production line will produce 10,000 to 12,000 coins, while a numismatic strike might produce a few thousand. Output varies depending on consumer demand for bullion and a variety of other factors, says West Point Mint deputy superintendent Tom DiNardi. In 2015 the West Point Mint made 47 million Silver Eagles. That breaks down to about 903,850 per week and 129,120 per day on a seven-day operating schedule—or nearly 181,000 daily during a five-day workweek.

Grogan notes that one of the most important parts of striking Silver Eagles is to make sure the struck coins match the design specifications. This was particularly vital in 2021, when the Mint introduced the reverse design and subtle obverse refinements to the American Silver Eagle. "We wanted to make sure the employees were well versed in the new design. We posted templates on every press to help the operators know what to look for." She adds, "The production people are quite astute."

WHY NO MINTMARKS ON BULLION-STRIKE AMERICAN SILVER EAGLES?

Bullion-strike American Silver Eagles do not carry mintmarks, in keeping with their more utilitarian purpose as coins primarily intended to be bought and sold on the basis of their precious-metal content. However, series experts have discovered that some American Silver Eagles can be traced back to their mint of origin based on specific markings noted on their mint shipping crates. More information about this can be found in chapter five.

THE UNITED STATES MINT POLICE

The United States Mint Police was established in 1792 and is one of the nation's oldest federal law enforcement agencies. The police force protects the more than 1,650 employees who work for the Mint, the tens of thousands who tour the facilities each year, and more than $100 billion in coins and bullion. Their mission is to ensure each mint is "As Secure as Fort Knox," a reference to the iconic gold bullion facility in Kentucky that is among their jurisdictions; they also serve the Philadelphia Mint, Denver Mint, San Francisco Mint, and West Point Mint as well as the United States Mint headquarters in Washington, D.C.

U.S. Mint police guard a U.S. Mail truck laden with gold destined for Fort Knox, 1937.

A more modern (circa 2009) U.S. Mint Police vehicle.

The Mint Police protect lives and property, prevent and detect crimes, investigate criminal acts, make arrests, collect and preserve evidence, and enforce local and federal laws, among other duties.

The Mint Police force includes officers, detectives, and supervisory personnel. Before reporting for duty, prospects must undergo three months of training at the Federal Law Enforcement Training Center in Glynco, Georgia, near Brunswick, or Artesia, New Mexico. Then they must complete specialized onsite training at the Mint facility where they will work, plus successfully complete further training sessions throughout their tenure as a Mint Police officer.

Dennis Tucker, publisher at Whitman Publishing and a member of the Treasury Department's Citizens Coinage Advisory Committee, has seen the Mint Police in action at all four operating Mint facilities and at headquarters in Washington. "The Mint Police are the most professional and dedicated law-enforcement organization you'll encounter," Tucker says. "Hundreds of officers and their chiefs are all devoted to a hugely important mission spread out across the country. Imagine the law-enforcement logistics and training involved in protecting a typical large bank. Now think of the West Point Mint, the largest producer of American Silver Eagles, which also holds about a quarter of the nation's gold reserves. Talk about high security!"

The Mint's 2021 *Annual Report* laid out the Mint Police's work in contact-tracing for COVID exposure among Mint employees, in addition to normal activities—conducting more than 73,000 vehicle searches, almost 100 asset transfers, and 150 personnel background checks, and "maintaining security of the high-value assets in our custody, and physical security of all our facilities."

MINTING CHANGES OVER THE YEARS

The U.S. Mint has seen plenty of changes since the original Philadelphia Mint was established in 1792. It has gone from flywheel presses and hand-cut dies to computer-driven design and fully automated coin production. Some of the most notable changes in the

Mint's day-to-day operations have been implemented just since the American Silver Eagle was first struck in 1986.

As detailed within the accounts by John Mercanti earlier in this chapter, the Mint was still using decades-old sculpting, engraving, and design tools in the mid-1980s. In those days the two main types of coin finishes from the United States Mint were circulation strikes and Proofs. Regarding the Cameo Proof, with frosted designs (devices) and lettering (inscriptions) against a deeply mirrored background (field): This had really only been perfected five to ten years before the first American Silver Eagle. Before the late 1970s and early 1980s, Cameo Proofs were generally seen only on the first coins struck by a new die. Average Proofs dating before the mid-1970s and carrying a strong cameo effect on both the obverse and reverse are relatively rare.

American Silver Eagle dies.

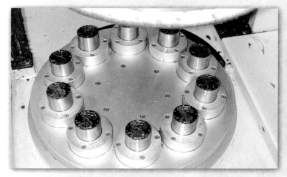

Dies prepared for polishing.

Advances in designing and engraving coins digitally began early in the twenty-first century, as Mercanti remembers in *American Silver Eagles: A Guide to the U.S. Bullion Coin Program.* "On or around the year 2003, under the directorship of Henrietta Holsman Fore, there suddenly appeared in the Mint a young engineer by the name of Steve Antonucci. I would go into the chief engraver's office and see Steve working on his laptop, not really knowing what his official capacity was. He was on board for weeks before I even had a proper introduction. Little did I know how he would ultimately change the face of numismatics."

Mercanti recalls that Antonucci was brought in to help the Mint team transition from the ages-old drawing, modeling, and reduction procedures to new and more efficient digital technologies. "There was a great amount of resistance—from older members of the staff and a few individuals who couldn't see the benefits of digital technology—but the decision had been made, and in spite of the pushback we were resolved to move forward. My immediate supervisor gave me a mandate, in jest: 'Those machines will go to the Smithsonian or you will.' That pretty much sealed the fate of the Janviers as far as I was concerned."

The digital designing and engraving technology was rolled out in phases, with a medal dedicated to Mint director Fore among the earlier trials of the futuristic tools, followed by cutting a mintmark into a die. "This mintmark was an incredible leap forward for us," says Mercanti. Joining the U.S. Mint around that time was classically trained but digitally skilled sculptor Joseph Menna, someone who Mercanti says, "was just what the doctor ordered."

Joseph Menna.

Existing physical models of various coins, including the American Silver Eagle, were scanned in, and from these files new dies could be cut and refined using lasers and other precision tools. Mercanti relates that the changeover to digital technology did result in some minor variations to the American Silver Eagle. "At the time I modeled the original artwork I didn't use a standard alphabet; a font close to the original was used. Ultimately this caused a problem that resulted in the manufacture of an error coin (or, more accurately in numismatic language, a die variety). The letter U in the selected font had a bar on one side and didn't curve around like my original."

The changeover occurred beginning with 2008 American Silver Eagles and can also be seen in the curving of the tilde (or squiggle) between the words SILVER and ONE on the reverse, which is curvier beginning in 2008. Mercanti notes the changes for the 2008 reverse were made in 2007 to be placed into use the following year. "Both Philadelphia and West Point were instructed to purge their inventory of Janvier-cut dies," says Mercanti. But West Point apparently did not take all of the 2007 reverse dies out of the production pool. "They were inadvertently put into the mix at the striking of the 2008 American Silver Eagles and resulted in a number of 2008 coins that had 2007 reverses—a variety that was a boon to the collecting fraternity."

Laser die polishing is another breakthrough that has aided in the creation of fascinating new types of American Silver Eagles, including the Reverse Proofs and Enhanced Reverse Proofs. Years ago, Proof dies were prepared using a sandblasting technique.

The American Silver Eagle's reverse font of 1986–2007 shows no stem on the bottom right of the letter "U" in UNITED.

A little stem appeared on the bottom right of the "U" in UNITED on the reverse of American Silver Eagles struck from 2008 through 2021.

With computer technology, dies can be textured to emulate the appearance of sand-blasted features. Mercanti says creating just the right look was "no easy task," adding that "the laser produced a discernable pattern." Over the years, the texturing has been refined to better replicate the patterns created by natural sandblasting of yore.

"Repeatability is one of the major benefits of digital technology," Mercanti concludes.

FINISHES GALORE

In 1986 there were just two kinds of American Silver Eagles being made: bullion strikes and Proofs. Today there are all kinds of exciting options with the Silver Eagle program:

Bullion

When the bullion strikes rolled off the presses in 1986, they were largely marketed as "Uncirculated" coins. This remained the case for many years to come, in part due to the fact that there was little need to distinguish these coins from anything other than Proofs. Bullion strikes generally

A bullion-strike American Silver Eagle.

have a matte appearance, though some are more brilliant than others, depending on die preparation and the planchet itself. While American Silver Eagles are generally struck well, the bullion strikes represent the basic production quality of an American Silver Eagle in any given year and are not made with any special preparations beyond what is standard at that time.

Proof

The U.S. Mint has been striking Proof coins since the early nineteenth century. These gorgeous coins represent the epitome of a mint's production abilities and are revered by numismatists as the finest of the fine. However, it should be remembered that Proof is not a

A Proof American Silver Eagle.

"condition" or "grade" but rather a method of manufacture. Modern Proofs are typically made with polished planchets that are intentionally struck twice (or more) by specially prepared dies on high-tonnage presses to ensure even the most minute of details is clearly rendered on the finished coin. In recent decades the cameo effect that contrasts frosted devices and inscriptions against deeply mirrored fields has become commonplace due to advances in the preparation of Proof dies.

Burnished

Marketed by the United States Mint as "Uncirculated" coins, Burnished American Silver Eagles appeared on the scene in 2006 in time for the 20th anniversary of the series. Burnished Silver Eagles undergo a special treatment process wherein the planchets are tumbled inside drums containing seemingly countless miniscule balls that polish the surfaces of the blanks and eliminate imperfections. The planchets are then hand-fed into a press and struck just once before being carefully packaged and sent to customers.

A Burnished American Silver Eagle.

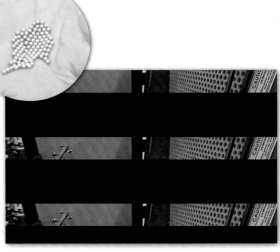

Burnished Silver Eagles have a matte finish and appear very similar to bullion strikes. However, the presence of a mintmark is what helps distinguish these special coins from their more ordinary counterparts.

Planchets intended to become burnished American Silver Eagles are tumbled and polished inside a Spaleck machine. Inside these machines, hundreds of little balls are used to polish burnished Silver Eagle planchets.

Reverse Proof

Debuting in 2006 alongside the Burnished Silver Eagles was the Reverse Proof. This finish displays mirrored devices and cameo fields, which is a reversal of the mirror-like fields and cameo-contrasted design elements and lettering typically seen on a Proof. Reverse

A Reverse Proof American Silver Eagle.

Proof coins have now been issued for many years and remain highly popular with collectors, widely enjoyed for their distinctive appearance. Once an unusual offering, Reverse Proofs are a mainstay in the U.S. Mint catalog.

Enhanced Uncirculated

The first Enhanced Uncirculated American Silver Eagle was released in 2013 and became an instant hit. The Enhanced Uncirculated coin features three distinct types of finishes, including a brilliant mirrored

An Enhanced Uncirculated American Silver Eagle.

finish on the obverse in the date, the "red" stripes and "blue" field of the American flag, the lines of Miss Liberty's dress, and the mountains, while on the reverse the mirrored finish appears in the arrows and branch, banner, and parts of the shield held by the eagle. A light frosted finish is employed on the fields of the obverse and reverse. Other parts of the design and inscriptions are given a heavy frosted finish. The dies used for striking the Enhanced Uncirculated Silver Eagles are burnished with stainless steel shot, cleaned with soap and water, and polished with horsehair brushes. Mint officials contend that none of this—including handfeeding of the dies onto the presses and the triple-striking process—constitutes these coins as Proofs, which are manufactured using a different process that produces coins of their own quality.

Enhanced Reverse Proof

The Enhanced Reverse Proof American Silver Eagle has frosted fields and polished devices akin to Reverse Proof coins, but "what sets it apart are the multiple polished and frosted finishes applied to different isolated elements," as the U.S. Mint explained. Meanwhile, dies used in the production of the Enhanced Reverse Proofs are fully "Proof polished," with various designated elements receiving various magnitudes of laser-applied frosting as dictated by computer programming.

An Enhanced Reverse Proof American Silver Eagle.

American Silver Eagle dies with different numismatic finishes.

The Nation's Other Bullion Coin Programs

The American Silver Eagle and American Gold Eagle were the first bullion-coin programs offered by the U.S. Mint. Their successful entry into the marketplace in 1986 inspired the creation of many other such programs, and special gold coins.

American Platinum Eagle Bullion Coins

A one-ounce American Platinum Eagle.

This series debuted in 1997 as the third member of the American Eagle family of bullion coins. They have been produced in four denominations, with the $100 coin containing one troy ounce of platinum. Fractional denominations include the half-ounce ($50), quarter-ounce ($25), and tenth-ounce ($10) issues, though these fractional coins have not been minted since 2008. Proof Platinum Eagles carried the same reverse design as the regular strikes, though Proofs struck from 1998 through 2016 offer a different reverse motif each year. Beginning in 2018, Proofs have been struck with a new common reverse and various obverse designs.

American Buffalo .9999-Fine Gold Bullion Coins

An American Buffalo one-ounce gold coin.

The American Buffalo gold coins were first released in 2006 and carry a faithful reproduction of the Buffalo nickel design by James E. Fraser that appeared on the nation's five-cent coin from 1913 through 1938. The American Buffalo coins were originally produced in only a one-ounce format with a denomination of $50 in 2006 and 2007. This changed in 2008, when fractional variants were struck in half-ounce ($25), quarter-ounce ($10), and tenth-ounce ($5) sizes.

First Spouse $10 Gold Bullion Coins

A First Spouse gold coin.

The First Spouse $10 gold bullion coin series ran in conjunction with the Presidential $1 coin series, produced contiguously from 2007 through 2016 and 2020. These coins contain one-half troy ounce of .9999-fine (24-karat) gold and honor the nation's first spouses on the same schedule as each respective first spouse's presidential partner. In cases where a president was not married during the time of their tenure in the Oval Office, the first spouse coin carries "an obverse emblematic of Liberty as depicted on a circulating coin of that era and a reverse image emblematic of themes of that president's life." Bronze medals of similar designs were issued in concert with the First Spouse series and offered collectors and others an affordable alternative to buying the gold coins.

MMIX Ultra High Relief Gold Coin

A modern version of the 1907 Ultra High Relief double eagle was produced in 2009 using techniques that were unavailable back when this coin, designed by Augustus Saint-Gaudens, was first created. The original

The MMIX (2009) Ultra High Relief coin.

1907 double eagles featured a relief so proud that it made mass production infeasible. The issues that plagued the coin in 1907 had been overcome with the new technologies available at the U.S. Mint, including digital design and engraving procedures that allowed Mint technicians to recreate the Saint-Gaudens design and strike it on a coin containing one troy ounce of 24-karat gold. Aficionados of the original 1907 Ultra High Relief coin will note some differences on the new coin, including the addition of four stars to represent the 50 states now in the Union, the motto IN GOD WE TRUST, and the date—MMIX—declaring in Roman numerals the year 2009.

America the Beautiful Silver Bullion Coins

America The Beautiful quarter dollars were struck from 2010 through 2021 honoring various national parks and landmarks in each of the 50 states, the District of Columbia, Puerto Rico, Guam, the Virgin Islands, American Samoa, and the Northern Mariana Islands. The bullion coins carry designs that are virtually identical to their circulating quarter-dollar counterparts, with the exception that the large .999-fine silver coins are three inches in diameter and are inscribed on the edge with the phrase .999 FINE SILVER 5.0 OUNCE, instead of carrying reeding as with the regular quarters. All of the five-ounce silver bullion quarters were struck at the Philadelphia Mint.

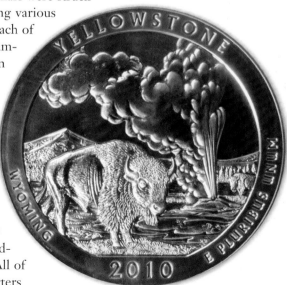

An America the Beautiful five-ounce silver coin.

American Liberty High Relief Gold Coins

American Liberty High Relief gold coins were launched in 2015 and are .9999 fine, contain one troy ounce of precious metal, and carry a denomination of $100. Struck at the West Point Mint, the American Liberty High Relief gold coins are known for featuring modernized renditions of "Liberty" and are struck biannually, with tenth-ounce versions bearing the same design issued between the release of the one-ounce coins.

Two coins from the American Liberty high-relief gold series.

American Palladium Eagle Bullion Coins

A fourth constituent of the American Eagle bullion program came aboard in 2017 with the one-ounce palladium coins. Adolph A. Weinman's Winged Liberty motif, as produced on the obverse of United States

An American Palladium Eagle.

dimes from 1916 through 1945, graces the front of this newest American Eagle coin. The reverse depicts an eagle carrying a branch, a reappropriation of Weinman's 1907 American Institute of Architects gold medal.

400th Anniversary of the *Mayflower* Gold Coin

The U.S. Mint struck a quarter-ounce $10 gold coin in 2020 marking the 400th anniversary of the Pilgrims' landing at Plymouth Rock aboard the *Mayflower* in 1620. The coin was issued by the sec-

The *Mayflower* gold coin.

retary of the Treasury under authority granted by Congress and was struck in a .9999-fine gold composition.

75th Anniversary of the End of World War II Gold Coin

This $25 gold coin honors the 75th anniversary of the end of World War II, which drew to a close in 1945. The coin contains a

The 75th Anniversary of the End of World War II gold coin.

half ounce of .9999-fine gold and honors the millions of American citizens who fought in the bloody international conflict. A corresponding silver medal with a virtually identical design was also issued.

THE DESIGN SO NICE, THEY MINTED IT THRICE

No in-depth survey of the American Silver Eagle would be complete without a brief shout-out to another coin that contains the magnificent Adolph A. Weinman Liberty Walking motif. Alongside the Liberty Walking half dollar and the American Silver Eagle, the third appearance of the Liberty Walking design was on a special 2016 gold coin commemorating the 100th anniversary of the classic Weinman masterpiece.

The 2016 Liberty Walking Centennial gold coin.

The 2016-W Liberty Walking Centennial gold coin was struck at the West Point Mint in a half-ounce format and bears a design virtually identical to its silver anteced-ent, and is denominated at 50 cents. Interestingly, this was not the first time the U.S. Mint struck a gold coin with a nominal face value of 50 cents. A gold Kennedy half dollar was produced in 2014 to honor the 50th anniversary of that coin.

The 2016-W Liberty Walking Centennial gold coin was minted alongside similar gold coins struck in the style of the 1916 Mercury dime and 1916 Standing Liberty quarter. This reimagined Liberty Walking half dollar saw a mintage of 65,509 and trades today for a small premium over its spot value.

A Guide Book of United States Coins catalogs these gold offerings alongside their respective silver series. While many collectors of the original series from the twentieth century may wish to add these gold coins as modern-day appendices to the main sets, many others view the 2016-W Liberty Walking half dollar and the other gold pieces as distinct and separate collectibles.

DEALING WITH COVID-19

The COVID-19 pandemic that swept the world in early 2020 halted all areas of com-merce and industry, and that includes the U.S. Mint. The virus-related shutdowns affected not only coin production but also the flow of planchets and distribution of coins from the Mint to the Federal Reserve, and from there to banks, stores, and other outlets. Hiccups in the flow of new coins out to the public—and the fact that many people were not spending coins back into circulation due to safer-at-home orders, quarantines, or fear of handling money during the spread of a highly contagious and deadly illness—led to a lasting coin shortage.

Supply issues also affected some programs, notably the cancellation of the second year of striking the 2022 centennial Morgan and Peace silver dollars. A March 14, 2022, press release from the Mint promised the coins' return in 2023.

Difficulties mounted at the Mint, which grappled with staffing reductions, limited contact between employees, and many people staying home from work due to illness and to help improve social distancing. "It was challenging from the production standpoint, as we were not able to produce [coinage] at the usual rate," said West Point Mint superintendent Ellen McCollum. "The director [David Ryder] wanted to make decisions as to whether the West Point Mint would operate full out, and we had a COOP [continuity of operations plan] with regard to what we'd be doing with the three shifts that operate here."

The West Point Mint reduced their staff on the floor by about half and the facility was shut down for a week. "It was a scary situation, especially here in New York where COVID really hit hard early on. Many employees were scared, some saying, 'We don't understand this.'" Despite reducing the number of shifts, the West Point Mint still turned out about 20 million American Silver Eagles during the first year under COVID-related protocols. "It was done under new ways of operating—plastic partitions, wearing masks, social distancing, and other things that were new to us at the time. My hats off and credit to the employees for maintaining normal quality. They were dedicated and loyal to the cause. We were very proud of them." She said one of the keys to successfully navigating the pandemic during the height of the crisis was communication. "Communication is key to everything—and it's communicating to everyone, including everybody on the [production] floor."

COINING DURING COVID: DAVID RYDER LOOKS BACK

David Ryder served as the director of the United States Mint from 1992 to 1993 and again from 2018 through 2021, helming operations during the scary heyday of the worst pandemic since the Spanish Flu of 1918–1920.

When COVID came along, it really upset the apple cart in terms of production, but also the supply of silver planchets used in making many of the Mints products—being able to get the number of blanks that were required to meet demand became difficult. In early 2021, during the height of COVID, we had been working on the legislation for the new Morgan and Peace silver dollars, the new designs for the American Eagle, and putting together a new quarters program. President Donald Trump signed both the quarters program and the Morgan/Peace legislation prior to leaving office in 2021. It all hit at the same time, creating a difficult problem in supplying certain products. With a silver shortage problem, we really couldn't deliver all the silver products we originally wanted to.

As for the COVID problems, I took them all very seriously. Since there was no operational plan developed for a pandemic like COVID for a manufacturing facility like the U.S. Mint, the Mint team rewrote our continuity of operation plan (COOP) and presented it to the Treasury. It was accepted and eventually used by several other bureaus within the Treasury as a roadmap of what could be done. The Mint followed that plan every day. We had meetings every morning and spent $4 to $5 million to improve safety procedures throughout the entire U.S. Mint. We kept our employees safe and kept the Mint open for business. I received many comments from employees—some liked the procedures, some didn't. I felt we did an outstanding job protecting all the employees of the U.S. Mint.

We were the only mint at the height of COVID in the world to stay open. And not just to stay open, but we were producing record amounts of circulating coins—going from the typical 12.5 billion a year to 20 billion. When you look at that from a supply point of view during that crisis, our suppliers did a remarkable job keeping our near-record circulating coinage supplies coming. Additionally, our bullion suppliers providing planchets did an outstanding job given the circumstances under which we were forced to operate.

We had a relatively small number of cases and two deaths due to the COVID-19 pandemic. In almost every instance, the cases that we did have emanated from outside the Mint. We monitored the situation very carefully. When an employee got infected with the COVID virus, we reviewed security camera video tape to ensure that social distancing was in place and being practiced. Anyone who came in close contact with an infected employee was asked to go home for the required period of time prior to returning to the Mint. Our security team did a great job keeping track of where everybody was at any given time—as you might expect, the Mint has an excellent security surveillance system in place that was a huge asset from a monitoring point of view. I think overall the Mint fared pretty well with COVID.

David Ryder.

5

The American Silver Eagle: Collecting and Investing

The crossover appeal of the American Silver Eagle lends exciting collecting and speculating opportunities, whether you consider yourself a numismatist or investor. As the popularity of the series has grown over the decades, more and more numismatists have embraced the American Silver Eagle as a true collectible rather than "just" a bullion coin.

A look back at advertising and press reports shows the bullion coins were originally targeted to investors, while the Proofs were aimed at collectors. However, collectors quickly migrated toward collecting both types, as well as Burnished, Reverse Proof, Enhanced Uncirculated, and Enhanced Reverse Proof issues that later followed. Meanwhile, many investors were lured the other direction, willingly paying much more than spot values to acquire Proofs to aesthetically diversify their holdings and wager their bids in the formally numismatic arm of the Silver Eagle program.

A set of Silver Eagles pleases the eye of the discriminating collector, brings fortune to the lucky silver stacker, and even provides peace of mind to strategic investors who roll these coins into Individual Retirement Accounts (IRAs). Whether pursuing them for future profit or building a complete set of the series —or chasing both goals—there are many investment principles and much numismatic wisdom the buyer should know before going all in on the American Silver Eagle.

COLLECTING AMERICAN SILVER EAGLES

As is the perennial wisdom throughout the rest of the numismatic sphere, collectors have no limitations on how they can pursue a collection of American Silver Eagles. Among the decisions a collector must make when embarking upon Silver Eagles: Do you want your coins certified by a third-party grader, or "raw" (uncertified)? And what type of set do you wish to build?

A Guide Book of United States Coins Senior Editor Jeff Garrett says, "American Silver Eagles are an interesting series in that there are many ways to collect them. As this book illustrates, there have been many special-issue American Silver Eagles produced over the years."

PCGS Director of Numismatic Education and Grading Team Leader Steve Feltner says American Silver Eagles have played a role as a sort of numismatic ambassador. "While most individuals purchasing American Silver Eagles are doing so for the bullion value, they are a wonderful gateway coin to pursuing other collecting or investing interests. Over the decades that I have been actively involved in the numismatic arena, I have heard countless stories of people gaining interest in American numismatics due to their initial involvement with Silver Eagles." He adds, "In more recent years, and especially with the formation of Registry Sets, American Silver Eagles have found their moment for the spotlight."

Certified Versus Raw

Collectors of any series will eventually encounter this dilemma, and it's pertinent to the Silver Eagle collector, who must ultimately make a determination based on their overall budget, desired grade, and storage considerations. When it comes to going certified or uncertified, there is no ideal or "better" method to collecting American Silver Eagles. Both approaches have their pros and cons.

BENEFITS OF BUYING RAW

Prices are generally lower than for graded examples

Much wider availability

Unholdered coins can go right into a coin album

Raw coins save space in vaults

BENEFITS OF BUYING CERTIFIED

The labeled grade and condition of the coin is ascribed by an independent party and authenticity is guaranteed

Slabbed coins are better protected from the elements

Certified coins tend to bring higher prices when sold

Collectors can build registry sets and compete with other collectors for accolades and prizes

DRAWBACKS OF BUYING RAW

There is no guarantee the coin is authentic

Uncertified coins are exposed to elements with little protection

Many unslabbed coins tend to be overgraded

Raw coins can be perceived as less desirable to other collectors

DRAWBACKS OF BUYING CERTIFIED

Certified Silver Eagles tend to sell for much higher prices over spot than their raw counterparts

If submitting the raw coin for slabbing, the price of shipping and encapsulation fees

Slabbed coins take up more vault space

Encapsulated coins require special albums for displaying

Bear in mind, a collector is never "stuck" with the set they build. If you start out building a raw set only to later decide you would rather own certified coins, either to upgrade your collection or to compete in a set registry, you could always sell your set to a dealer and apply the funds toward building an assemblage of certified Silver Eagles. Vice versa for the collector who has a complete collection of certified Silver Eagles but wants to pare down on storage space or buy a greater quantity of raw Silver Eagles, using the equity of any numismatic premiums built into the value of the slabbed coins.

Set-Building Strategies

There are as many ways to collect Silver Eagles as there are collectors, though there are some common approaches to building sets of American Silver Eagles:

Some people prefer their American Silver Eagles certified by a third-party grading company, while others rather own "raw," unencapsulated coins. There are benefits and drawbacks to both approaches.

- Year sets and date sets
- Inclusive series sets (every date-and-mintmark combination, finish, etc.)
- Type sets
- Collecting dates of personal importance (birth year, graduation, etc.)
- Toned coins

YEAR SETS AND DATE SETS

This is a widely preferred path for collecting the American Silver Eagle series and is also the most likely to convert the diehard investor into becoming a collector—or vice versa. "American Silver Eagles are 'gateway' coins for discovering the hobby of numismatics," remarks Jeff Garrett. "Many buy an American Silver Eagle as their choice of bullion and quickly discover the fun of collecting them by date."

There are many albums accommodating one dated slot for each year of the American Silver Eagle series, including a Whitman Classic album for assembling a single bullion strike from each year of the series going back to 1986. Building a date set is an affordable way to build a "complete" assemblage of American Silver Eagles. Moreover, a basic date set avoids the pricier Proofs and more expensive special releases that have come in more recent years. The biggest challenge for the date-set collector is buying the 1996 issue, which is the undisputed key date for the bullion arm of the series.

If you pursue a date set of bullion strikes, you should have little difficulty obtaining the coins you need to finish your collection. The price of building a complete date set from 1986 to the present is largely determined by the prevailing bullion value. Most bullion-quality American Silver Eagles are obtainable for prices a few degrees north of the bullion price. However, it should be noted that in recent years American Silver Eagles before the year 2000, and especially those from 1986 through the mid-1990s, have begun seeing numismatic premiums significantly above their bullion value. This is particularly so with the 1986 and 1994 issues, notwithstanding the aforementioned 1996 bullion strike, which has long been priced at multiples of its spot price in the open marketplace.

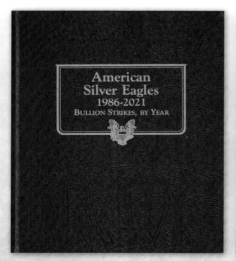 

For a date set of bullion Silver Eagles, you have two basic options: go raw or aim for certified. The potential low-end price of building a date set of raw coins is temptingly close to the current spot price, and the cost of an album for storage and organization is nominal. Conversely, a "premium" version of a bullion date set would include Silver Eagles graded MS-70, certified by a reputable third-party grader. However, certified coins in "perfect 70" grades are far beyond the going price for raw coins in "average" Mint State grades. Decisions, decisions . . .

A raw date set may be most appealing to the precious-metals investor who wants to take an entry-level step into building a numismatically minded assemblage of Silver Eagles without the costs of high numismatic premiums. This approach could whet the appetite of neophyte "collectors" into building more elaborate sets of Proof Silver Eagles or even pursuing other series altogether. It would be remiss to omit mention of another important crowd who might be turned on to building a raw date set of Silver Eagles: collectors on a shoestring budget.

On the other hand, certified date sets could be what lures a diehard numismatist into pursuing the American Silver Eagle series. "A basic MS-69 set of the yearly issues is easily accessible. Even collectors with a modest budget can enjoy the sense of accomplishment that comes from completing a 1986-to-present set," comments Jeff Garrett.

Then again, what collector's collector could resist the tempting beauty of lustrous, white MS-70 American Silver Eagles, neatly ordered by date from their inception in 1986 to the present day? Even the most ardent of numismatic collectors, studiously focused on acquiring every obscure die variety from the scarcest nineteenth-century series, have been known to own a handsome date set of certified Silver Eagles to be enjoyed for their modern beauty and investment potential.

Ultimately, a date set can stand alone as a "complete" collection of American Silver Eagles or serve as a springboard for building an expanded collection of die varieties, Proofs, Reverse Proofs, Enhanced Reverse Proofs, and Burnished examples. One might even use a year set of Silver Eagles as a cornerstone for a numismatic cabinet or investment portfolio incorporating American Gold Eagles, American Platinum Eagles, and/or American Palladium Eagles. The versatility and functionality of an American Silver Eagle date set is essentially endless.

INCLUSIVE SERIES SETS

Up for a challenge? Building an inclusive series set of American Silver Eagles will test your numismatic agility and certainly your pocketbook. Whether expanding upon a year set or starting from scratch, endeavoring to build a complete set of American Silver Eagles—one that is *truly* complete—will rank as one of the nobler feats for a collector. It's not to say that completing a set of American Silver Eagles is necessarily a difficult task. Unlike the sheer challenges that come with chasing low-population key dates for a classic series, the Silver Eagle series will pose no such obstacles of availability to the financially well-heeled collector. All the coins necessary for completing a set of American Silver Eagles should be readily available today, for a cost.

So, what makes such a collection so difficult? For one, expense. Another consideration is the absolute size of such a set. The U.S. Mint has issued a labyrinthine array of Silver Eagles since 1986—particularly so since the dawn of the twenty-first century, when new numismatic finishes were added to the mix as well as a larger spectrum of issues distinguishable by mintmark.

Back in 1986, the American Silver Eagles took flight with two annual issues: a bullion issue distributed to the public via a small network of Authorized Purchasers and a Proof version marketed by the Mint directly to collectors. This was the modus operandi until the mid-1990s, when the first special issues were released. This came in the form of the longstanding series key date, the 1995-W Proof, which was sold only in a special five-piece American Eagle Proof set honoring the 10th anniversary of the nation's bullion-coin program. Other scarce issues include the 2008-W, Burnished, Reverse of 2007, and the 2019-S Enhanced Reverse Proof.

In recent years numismatists have begun to identify pseudo-mintmark issues for earlier bullion releases, determining that all 1986 and 1987 bullion strikes came from San Francisco but that those from 1988 through 1998 were split between production runs at the San Francisco and West Point Mints. Additionally, bullion-strike Silver Eagles have been minted at the San Francisco, West Point, and on some occasions the Philadelphia Mints since 2011, with none of these bullion coins bearing identifying mintmarks. It can be determined which of these unmintmarked Silver Eagles came from Philadelphia, San Francisco, or West Point if the coins are still in their original mint shipment boxes, which are banded with identification markers revealing their origin.

As a collector, do you pursue each of these pieces with latent "mintmarks"? Do you also include the die varieties, such as the comparatively rare 2008-W, Burnished, Reverse of 2007? What about other entries, like the small handful of errors and other oddities that weren't necessarily regular issues but nonetheless round out a comprehensive representation of the series?

These are questions you must answer as you meander through a series that grows increasingly complex by the year. Another consideration is whether to pursue such a set with raw coins or certified. This revisits the same dilemma posed in the rundown on year-set collecting and can be resolved by deciding whether you want to house the collection in an album, submit it for display and competition in a registry set, or if—regardless of how the set is physically presented—you aim for MS-70, PF-70, and SP-70 examples.

Cost will become the main factor if your goal is to obtain coins with a numerical grade of "70." Even though American Silver Eagles are categorically modern coins, MS-70 bullion strikes from the earlier days of the series are remarkably scarce, many commanding significant premiums over those graded MS-69 or lower. You shouldn't

assume PF-70 Deep Cameo was the norm for Proof strikes, either. Many Silver Eagle Proofs are relatively rare with a "70" certification label, as seen in the example of the esoteric 1995-W Proof American Silver Eagle—a coin that as of this writing trades for five-figure prices when graded PF-70 Deep Cameo.

Therein lays the type of difficulties you will have in completing this set. Yes, you shouldn't have any real trouble finding any of the regular issues, even with a grade of "70," if you're really looking for them. A couple dates might prove tougher than others but they're still obtainable at the right price. But that's where the real obstacles come in for collectors on a budget.

Perfect coins exist, but at that level they are cost-prohibitive for all but those with the deepest of pockets. A collector could theoretically set out and, with the aid of a well-connected coin dealer, cobble together all the coins necessary for completing the American Silver Eagle series to date, with varieties and other goodies included, in short order. But to do so at a certified grade level of "70" could easily mean spending six figures. Then again, owning a set of such extraordinary quality and true completeness is a meaningful numismatic achievement that few collectors of this series can claim.

A collector who wants to go all the way on a comprehensive American Silver Eagle set should absolutely insist on acquiring coins with the crispest surfaces. No matter what grade of American Silver Eagle you pursue, avoid any coins with "milk spots," a pervasive detraction with this series theorized to originate with a washing process at the U.S. Mint. Milk spots will be examined in detail later in this chapter and are of primary concern to the buyer seeking bullion strikes.

Another factor to consider, especially if you're building a registry set, is whether to buy coins certified by PCGS or NGC. Both companies are highly reputable and offer registry-set platforms, though rules generally dictate that the majority if not all of the coins in your registry set be certified by that company. Beyond that, you may find some personal satisfaction in having all the coins in your set certified by one company or the other. This might come down to your personal affinities, or to apples-to-apples comparisons.

TYPE SETS

Not many collectors will build a type set specifically around American Silver Eagles. That is not to say the number of people who include Silver Eagles in type sets is small. Many will buy at least one to include in a type set of U.S. coins from the twentieth or twenty-first centuries. And American Silver Eagles have also been popular in silver dollar type sets, which typically include one example of each design produced.

In favor during the early 2000s were silver dollar sets pairing a 2000-dated Silver Eagle with a 1900 Morgan dollar; another variation on that set was a twentieth-century type offering a 1900 Morgan dollar and a 1999 American Silver Eagle, representing the "first" and "last" silver dollars of the twentieth century.

However, a type set involving *only* American Silver Eagles has not yet been widely done, perhaps because of the perception that there really aren't many "types" of Silver Eagles to collage. At least, that may have been the case in the 1990s or early 2000s, but the situation has since changed for the American Silver Eagle series. The most obvious difference now is the reverse design by sculptor-engraver Emily S. Damstra that debuted in 2021. This means there are at least two distinct types: the original John Mercanti heraldic eagle design and Damstra's flying eagle motif. But if we dive a little deeper, we find a few more entries worth including in an American Silver Eagle type set.

The 2008-W, Burnished, Reverse of 2007, transitional variety arose when a die impressed from an outdated hub was put into production. In 2008 the U.S. Mint was creating new hubs during a time of transition to digital engraving methods, which manifested in new fonts for the lettering on the reverse of the American Silver Eagle. These changes are most evident in the "U" of UNITED, which on the proper 2008 reverse shows a little base stem on the lower right side of the vowel. This new font remained on the reverse for the duration of the American Silver Eagle run through early 2021. The dash between SILVER and ONE also differs from earlier issues.

Thus, this constitutes a modified reverse that some type collectors might deem worthy of collecting as a separate type.

Another important piece worth mentioning here is the 2016-W, Lettered Edge, American Silver Eagle, struck to commemorate the 30th anniversary of the series. Many heralded the release of this special piece as the first Silver Eagle bearing a significant design change, with the edge incused with 30TH ANNIVERSARY rather than the typical edge reeding. This marked a major diversion from the norm for the series, becoming the first and so far only Silver Eagle with edge lettering.

Finally, one might consider each of the various finishes employed in the series as important additions. While numismatic finishes are not usually seen as separate "types" in and of themselves, it's difficult to imagine a "complete" type set of American Silver Eagles—a series very much defined by the various finishes among its offerings—without at least one representation for each of these special formats. The classic bullion and Proof offerings may come immediately to the top of the mind, but thorough collectors will also want at least one example each of Burnished, Reverse Proof, Enhanced Uncirculated, and Enhanced Reverse Proof.

COLLECTING SPECIFIC DATES

There is a certain appeal to collecting coins from certain memorable dates. Consider the whimsy behind wondering if that 1989 American Silver Eagle was struck the very same day as your wedding, graduation, or even birth! For related reasons, Silver Eagles

are also treasured gifts. They're the modern silver dollar, every bit as much a keepsake memento for the child of the twenty-first century as a Morgan or Peace dollar may have been for children during the twentieth century. Silver eagles are just as treasured by adults, many of whom will remember exactly what they were doing during the date emblazoned upon a particular Silver Eagle.

An assemblage of American Silver Eagles from incontiguous dates may appear random, even disorderly, to someone uninformed about the collecting methodology behind the set. But if the dates are significant to the collector, then it does it matter what anyone else thinks?

While a set of coins from disconnected dates may only be sellable to a coin dealer as a "random-date" holding, there are advantages to building such collections. Such a collection permits for an entirely customizable set. There are absolutely no external rules except for the self-imposed "requirement" of acquiring Silver Eagles from the dates meaningful to the collector. This may or may not circumvent expensive key dates, but nevertheless the collector need not worry about filling any holes for years that are not significant to their overarching set objectives.

There are also many choices available if you want to attractively display a set of coins of various inconsecutive dates. Frameable display boards exist for coins from a specific year alongside a photograph of, say, loved ones connected with the year on those coins. Whitman Publishing offers folders and albums with blank, unlabeled slots for arranging coins of any combination of dates, including American Silver Eagles.

TONED AMERICAN SILVER EAGLES

Toning is a highly subjective, even controversial, area of the hobby. Years ago, there were many products on the market targeted to collectors who wanted to rid their coins of any color other than that of the metal in its cleanest and brightest state. However, in recent years more and more collectors have begun valuing natural patina on their coins. Some collectors like a little color, while others like a lot. Some numismatists want every hue of the rainbow in their American Silver Eagle collection.

Toning is something for which there is little set market. When an attractively toned American Silver Eagle crosses the auction block or is offered for sale, it can take huge sums over the value of a similar but untoned coin. Collectors generally prefer coins certified by one of the major third-party graders since so many colorful coins in the marketplace are *artificially* toned—something the certification companies look for and avoid encapsulating without notation on the label.

Toned American Silver Eagles are highly popular and can make a wonderful collecting objective for collectors who love naturally colorful coins.

It can take years to assemble a complete set of Silver Eagles with the desired toning, costing many tens of thousands of dollars. But the fruits of this labor can dazzle the eyes!

SPECIAL LABELS GALORE

Collectors who seek certified coins have no shortage of attractive options. Certainly, there are the gorgeous "70" coins out there—and these can add a degree of brilliance to any collection, whether or not it is listed in a set registry. Beyond super-grade Silver Eagles, certified coins offer another degree of collectability that is worthy of consideration.

PCGS, NGC, and other third-party graders offer a wide variety of special labels that identify a noteworthy aspect of the encapsulated coin. It might be that the coin was one of the first to roll off the presses, belonged to an exceptional hoard, was recovered from a shipwreck or other historic site, or was struck during a unique occasion.

Some special labels are significant not because of the coin but rather because of the nature of the label itself. Many special labels are hand-signed by individuals somehow connected with the coin. In some cases, it is the coin's designer, a Mint official who was in office when the coin was struck, or a celebrity who may have an association with the coin or something depicted on it.

FIRST STRIKE AND EARLY RELEASE LABELS

Both PCGS and NGC offer label programs specially tailored to recognizing coins distributed within a short time after their initial release. These have been popular with many American Silver Eagle collectors since their launch in 2005.

PCGS offers the First Strike label, which designates coins that were distributed within 30 days of that issue's initial release. The submission must either be made by the customer within 30 days of the coin's release, or the coin must be retained within its original, unopened mailer and postmarked no later than 30 days from the coin's release. PCGS also awards First Day of Issue labels to certain qualifying coins, accompanied with proof they were obtained on the first day of their striking.

PCGS and NGC have labels recognizing coins submitted for encapsulation within 30 days of that issue's initial release.

NGC has several special label designations relating to coin release dates. These include Early Release, First Release, and First Year of Issue. Early Release and First Release designations are synonymous with NGC and must be received by the company within 30 days of the coin's release. First Year of Issue applies to coins bearing the date of their first year of release (such as 1986 American Silver Eagles).

Two other major grading companies, Independent Coin Graders (ICG) and ANACS (formerly known as American Numismatic Association Certification Service), also furnish special labels for holders. ICG offers Initial Release designations for certain U.S. Mint coins (including American Silver Eagles) submitted within 30 days of the new coin being issued. ANACS also offers First Release attribution and designates qualifying examples with First Day of Issue or A First Strike Coin.

It's important to note that these special adjectival terms relating to when specific coins were struck are designations used by third-party graders and do not relate to terminology used by the United States Mint in describing these coins. Mint officials stated in a press release that "The United States Mint has not designated any coins or products as 'first strikes' or 'first releases,' nor do we track the order in which we mint coins during their production. The United States Mint strives to produce coins of consistently high quality throughout the course of production." The Mint goes on to say, "United States Mint products are not individually numbered, and we do not keep track of the order or date of minting of individual coins."

While the Mint does not generally keep tabs on which coins are the earliest ones off the presses, collectors still place value on coins bearing First Strike, Early Release, and similar slab labels. Such coins have long enjoyed premiums in the numismatic marketplace and are widely enjoyed by collectors, many of whom build elaborate sets of American Silver Eagles encapsulated with these noteworthy inserts.

EMERGENCY-ISSUE LABELS

The COVID-19 pandemic that overwhelmed the globe beginning in early 2020 threw the world into socioeconomic chaos. The virus caused workplace shutdowns around America. The U.S. Mint saw temporary closures of some facilities and production restrictions across its network during the height of the pandemic's first wave of illnesses in spring 2020. Meanwhile, many individuals were turning to American Silver Eagles, as these silver coins enjoyed twofold heightened demand from both collectors and investors.

Many speculators opted for silver bullion over traditional paper investments as the stock market tumbled at the start of the pandemic. Concurrently, the collectibles industry saw unprecedented growth with millions of Americans stuck at home during quarantines, lockdowns, and safer-at-home orders. Many people in hunker-down mode at home were flush with newly distributed federal economic stimulus money sent to millions of households. It was the perfect storm for Silver Eagles, sought after but in short supply.

Even as businesses, including the U.S. Mint, began resuming some modicum of normal operating hours as 2020 turned into 2021, the demand for new American Silver Eagles didn't let up. Much of the increased pressure on 2021 American Silver Eagles was related to the widely publicized design change that came to the coin that year; however, many Wall Street–wary investors also clamored for Silver Eagles as ongoing economic tumult drove millions toward the relatively safe haven of precious metals.

COVID-safety protocols and market pressures forced the Mint to expand production of bullion-strike Silver Eagles beyond their usual origin at the West Point Mint. As a result of these extenuating circumstances, relatively small numbers of bullion American Silver Eagles were struck at the Philadelphia and San Francisco Mints to help supplement the West Point bullion output.

Bullion-strike 2020 and 2021 American Silver Eagles from the Philadelphia and San Francisco Mints bear no mintmarks and look exactly like the typical strikes from West Point. Even though these Philadelphia and San Francisco strikes have no outward distinguishing

The U.S. Mint struck a limited number of American Silver Eagles to meet urgent demands during the height of the COVID outbreak in spring 2020.

factors, they have enjoyed strong demand in the numismatic market. PCGS labels these emissions from Philadelphia and San Francisco as "Emergency Issue," while NGC declared them "Emergency Release."

There are two ways to determine if you have one of these emergency coins. One way is to simply buy so-labeled certified pieces. The other is to purchase unopened, sealed monster boxes, which are packaged by the Mint, contain 25 nylon tubes with 20 coins each, and are wrapped with labels bearing serial numbers that can be used to identify the mint of origin. Dealers who ship these unopened, sealed boxes with proper identifying marks and accompanying paperwork to a third-party grading company that offers the "Emergency" label may be able to have those coins encapsulated, with either an implied Philadelphia or San Francisco "mintmark" listed on the insert as appropriate.

However, there is absolutely no method or known diagnostic for determining if any given raw Silver Eagle is in fact an emergency issue.

Why would a collector pursue emergency-issue Silver Eagles? One reason might be their limited mintages. For example, the 2020 (P) Silver Eagle saw a mintage of 240,000, as deduced by the packing numbers on monster box labels ranging from 400,000 to 400,479. The 2021 (P) emergency-issue American Silver Eagle had a mintage of just 495,000. Some of the 2021 (P) coins sold for nearly $800 when they first came to light, while others traded for lower but still lofty sums. There is the additional historical novelty of owning emergency issues due to their connection to the COVID-19 pandemic, a watershed crisis that will be remembered for generations to come.

PARENTHETICAL MINTMARK LABELS

In a similar vein to the emergency-issue labels, other third-party grading labels identify American Silver Eagles that have been struck at places other than the usual West Point Mint. As with the emergency-issue American Silver Eagles, the parenthetical mintmark designations rely on the subject coins being shipped directly to a third-party grader in sealed, unopened monster boxes with identifying labels still on the crate.

Professional coin dealer Troy Thoreson remembers the awareness of and market for the implied mintmark taking off during the early 2010s, by which point bulk submissions of American Silver Eagles to third-party graders had become popular. "Bulk submissions were no doubt fueled because of the 2011 San Francisco–issued Uncirculated coin issued in the monster green boxes. This was the first time the Mint obviously identified the contents of a monster green box of Silver Eagles other than West Point. They used two bright yellow San Francisco straps that had to be cut to open the box. The problem, once the strap is cut, is there is no mintmark on the coins, therefore, the entire sealed box had to be bulk-submitted in order to prove which mint made the coins. The labels for these certified coins used parentheses to signify the mint, for example *2011 (S)*, versus a coin with an actual mintmark, such as *2011-S*. To add to the confusion, this is also the first year for a bullion-strike San Francisco–mintmarked coin, which appeared in the five-piece anniversary set. This S-mintmarked coin only had an authorized mintage of 100,000 coins."

Nylon strapping stating the mint of origin was used until 2014. In the years since, labels with serial numbers and other stampings are the key to determining where the coins originate. As with the emergency issues, there are no mintmarks or other outward diagnostics or distinctive die characteristics permitting collectors to distinguish at which mint a single raw example was struck.

Curiosity around these parenthetical mintmarks began growing in the early 2000s as the Mint began farming out production of American Silver Eagles to multiple facilities when demand for the silver bullion coins exploded. NGC began the practice of

Various U.S. Mint facilities have struck bullion-finish American Silver Eagles. Examples still in their original shipment boxes from the Mint may be traceable as to where they were minted and may be encapsulated by a third-party grader with a label recognizing that Mint facility.

issuing labels with parenthetical mintmarks in 2011 when it was discovered that some bullion American Silver Eagles dated for that year were being shipped in monster boxes originating from the San Francisco Mint.

PCGS soon began recognizing these parenthetical mintmarks as well. As these coins do not carry a mintmark, third-party labels will generally declare something to the effect of "Struck at the San Francisco Mint" (NGC) or "Struck at San Francisco" (PCGS) alongside the parenthetical mintmark next to the date.

These pieces may be of greatest importance to collectors who want a thorough set of American Silver Eagles from all mints where they were struck. For such a collection you must opt for certified examples, as there is absolutely no difference in appearance between, say, a 2011 (W) Silver Eagle—a typical example of that year's output—and a 2011 (S), which sells for significant premiums due to its lower mintage.

HAND-SIGNED LABELS

Another exciting objective for some collectors is to purchase certified examples of American Silver Eagles that are paired with labels carrying the autograph of somebody associated with the encapsulated coin. This represents the intersection of two very popular hobbies: numismatics and autograph collecting. The latter has long been associated with hand-signed memorabilia, such as photographs, boxing gloves, and even automobiles. Imagine the thrill of owning a baseball signed by early-twentieth-century home-run hero Babe Ruth (also known by beloved nicknames "The Bambino" or "Sultan of Swat") or a tennis racket signed by 1980s court champion John McEnroe (famously known for spewing "you can't be *serious!*" to line judges upon unfavorable calls during matches).

When it comes to autographed labels, John and Jan Hancocks may be signed by any number of luminaries from within the

Many famous individuals tied to certain coins have signed encapsulation labels for third-party graders, like this one signed by engraver John Mercanti. These hand-signed inserts can add a new degree of collectability to slabbed coins.

world of numismatics and beyond. There are labels by the likes of U.S. Mint directors such as David Ryder, former Delaware governor and numismatic advocate Mike Castle, American Silver Eagle Type I reverse designer John Mercanti, Type II reverse designer Emily S. Damstra, U.S. Mint engraver Michael Gaudioso, and *Red Book* editor emeritus Ken Bressett, among many others.

The reason hand-signed labels are important in the numismatic hobby is multifaceted. Part of their appeal is in owning authentic, hand-signed memorabilia bearing the signatures of favorite numismatic personalities and hobby figures. "I like the inserts signed by designers of the coins or by people responsible for permitting the minting of those coins during their tenure as Mint director or something similar," says professional numismatist Michael Garofalo. Bullion dealer and market expert Lee Minshull agrees: "There are many great signed labels including figures who are becoming historic in the scope of U.S. Mint history, including sculptor-engraver John Mercanti and Mint directors Ed Moy and David Ryder, the latter being the only person to serve as Mint director on two separate occasions."

But the significance of these hand-signed programs extends beyond the hobby itself. In many cases, labels paired with coins are autographed by widely recognized figures such as athletes, astronauts, actors, ex-politicians, and others who are adored by millions of people.

These hand-signed label programs can help make coin collecting more appealing for those who do not consider themselves numismatists. And when the numismatic door cracks ajar, it often swings wide open as these newcomers become familiar with other areas of the hobby. Thus, lifetime coin collectors are born.

WORLD TRADE CENTER SALVAGE LABELS

On September 11, 2001, the course of human history changed in a matter of three hours as commercial airliners hijacked by terrorists were flown into the Twin Towers of the World Trade Center in New York City and the Pentagon in Washington, D.C.; another jet, reportedly heading for the U.S. Capitol Building in Washington, was commandeered by passengers on the plane and crashed into the rolling hills of Pennsylvania minutes before it would have reached its intended target. In all, 19 terrorists aboard four planes killed 2,977 people and further injured tens of thousands on that bloody day now ubiquitously known simply as "9/11."

While only a portion of the Pentagon was damaged when a plane flew into the building (which was later fully rebuilt), the World Trade Center was completely destroyed. Many unfamiliar with New York City's original World Trade Center, officially dedicated on April 4, 1973, often believe the financial hub consisted of just the iconic 110-story twin skyscrapers. However, the first World Trade Center in Lower Manhattan was a complex consisting of seven large buildings that on any given day accommodated 50,000 workers and hundreds of thousands of tourists. Most of the World Trade Center buildings were situated on a multi-story subterranean structure housing a massive parking garage, dozens of stores and restaurants, a subway transit station, and huge vaults where millions of dollars in precious metals were stored.

Approximately $250 million in bullion (in 2001 dollars and metals prices) were stored in a massive vault located below 4 World Trade Center, which stood at the southeast side of the complex and was the home of the Commodities Exchange Center (COMEX). The vault was owned by Scotia Mocatta Depository Corporation, a bullion and metals division of the Bank of Nova Scotia in Canada, and at the time of the attacks contained 379,036 ounces of gold and 29,942,619 ounces of silver. Around half was the bank's holdings and the balance belonged to businesses and individuals, and it was held there on behalf of the COMEX bullion trading division of the New York Mercantile Exchange, serving as a security against COMEX futures contracts. On the afternoon of September 10, 2001, when the vault was locked overnight for the last time, the price of gold closed at $272.30 per ounce, while silver was $4.19 an ounce.

Retrieval of the bullion was no easy task. Fires burned for several weeks in the pit known as "Ground Zero." For months, acrid air hung heavy over the site littered with some 1.8 million tons of rubble and debris, much of it laden with asbestos from the 1970s-era buildings and made even more dangerous by smoldering toxic chemicals. As recovery crews sifted the rubble for human remains, many of which sadly have yet to be identified to this day, risks of cave-ins at the site grew. The "bathtub," as many called the cavernous World Trade Center foundation, was seven stories deep and partly damaged—a major risk considering the Hudson River lay a mere block to the west.

Hundreds of police officers and agents from the Federal Bureau of Investigation

An encapsulated 2000 American Silver Eagle that was recovered from the World Trade Center after the September 11, 2001, terrorist attack.

guarded the recovery zone, with many staking out the region of Ground Zero where the vault was located. The bullion, while insured, remained virtually unscathed despite being buried under hundreds of tons of debris and was securely removed from the site. The coins situated in a secure vault under custody of Scotia were soon purchased by a major coin dealer, who submitted more than 100,000 of them to PCGS for encapsulation with a special label declaring their recovery from the World Trade Center site.

Coins from various nations were stored at the World Trade Center, including those from Australia, Austria, Canada, Jamaica, Great Britain, Hungary, Mexico, South Africa, and Uruguay, ranging across many dates. There were also one-ounce Swiss gold bars and a few ten-ounce Swiss gold bars. The holdings representing the United States included a tremendous array of American Gold Eagles and American Platinum Eagles, and several dates from the bullion American Silver Eagles series that include 1987, 1989, 1991, 1993, 2000, and 2001.

Buyers should beware that any coins dated after 2001 and appearing in holders labeled as World Trade Center recovery coins (and similar verbiage) or advertised as such are illegitimate and either in faked holders or are themselves of questionable authenticity.

Early PCGS holders sealed from December 2001 until June 2002 grade the coins only as "Gem Uncirculated," while those encapsulated later declare a numerical grade. Due to changing protocol involving the presence of a barcode on the labels, rendering population reports for these coins is effectively impossible. Some 100,000 coins were verifiably recovered from the World Trade Center and submitted for encapsulation. So, while these coins may possess sentimental value for many and are rightfully respected as somber artifacts from the fallen World Trade Center, they are not rarities—even if advertisers suggest they are. All told, total charitable proceeds related to the sale of these coins, not counting profit Scotia Bank made from the purchase (which was all donated), well surpassed $1 million.

Additional products tying back to the World Trade Center that collectors must approach with discernment are Silver Eagles advertised as having been minted with silver recovered from the World Trade Center. These are not Silver Eagles that were actually made with planchets sourced from silver that once resided at the World Trade Center. Rather, they are regular coins that were struck at the U.S. Mint from regularly procured ore and then plated, post-mint, by a private company that purchased bullion recovered from the site, melted it, and then applied a thin layer upon the outside of the advertised coin.

Numismatists can essentially categorize such pieces as altered or novelty coins, though their collectible appeal is understandable. Those who wish to purchase them should not do so on the basis of rarity, as these are neither scarce nor special-issue coins. Buy them with no expectation of any marked increase in future financial appreciation beyond what the prevailing price of silver may dictate.

American Silver Eagle Hoards

The thousands upon thousands of American Silver Eagles recovered from the World Trade Center may be among the most well-publicized hoards containing these bullion coins, but many others have appeared on the marketplace over the years. Lee Minshull of Minshull Trading became a coin dealer in the mid-1970s, a decade before the debut of the American Silver Eagle that would later become the core of his business.

In the mid-2000s he entered the Silver Eagle market following a massive hoard purchase involving 100 sealed boxes of the coin dated 1994, 1995, 1996, and 1998. Today Minshull is one of the nation's top dealers in American Silver Eagles, with annual sales well into the millions of dollars. He deals in hundreds of thousands of coins in any given year.

Minshull has also handled many smaller hoards, including one containing 20 boxes of 1987 Silver Eagles and some 20,000 certified pieces that encompassed just about everything, including many complete basic date runs ranging from 1986 to the present. "We have bought over the last five years four date-run sets (1986–2015) as sealed box sets," he notes. Minshull can turn around and sell these coins just about as quickly as he procures them. "We sell more than 5,000 complete sets of American Silver Eagles each year. That's nearly 40 coins per set (in 2022) or 200,000 coins a year right there."

Jeff Garrett has handled countless high-end American Silver Eagles. "Sealed boxes of 'vintage' Silver Eagles (1986–2000) show up with some regularity on the wholesale market," Garrett says. "These sealed boxes trade for prices that make them essentially expensive lottery tickets. I have seen boxes of some of the rare issues, such as 1999, submitted to NGC or PCGS and yield zero MS-70 coins, and the buyer loses over $10,000 for the bet. Occasionally, the quality of one of these boxes is extraordinary and the payoff is spectacular."

Overall, when you consider the purchase of coins advertised as hailing from a "hoard," make sure you're not overpaying. Silver Eagles are often recovered in quantities consisting of rolls or boxes, but they don't usually have a collectible premium because of this alone. The American Silver Eagles recovered from the World Trade

Center and labeled with this pedigree have a highly notable connection to a well-documented vault discovery. So, even if they aren't rare, they could lay fair claim to being at the very least sought after by collectors and others who want to own something of value that once called the World Trade Center home.

However, buyers should carefully discern before paying massive premiums for coins that are patently marketed as hoard finds. Third-party coin grading companies often label submitted coins that were discovered in a hoard with pedigrees linking the encapsulated coin back to its origin. At a minimum, these pedigreed hoard labels are informative and oftentimes denote a coin with historic or illustrious ties. Such coins may carry some real collectible premium due to their pedigree.

Monster boxes are the plastic cartons in which groups of 500 American Silver Eagles— 25 rolls of 20 coins—are sent from the U.S. Mint to its authorized distributors.

Yet, while such coins may be perfectly authentic expats from a legitimate hoard, this doesn't mean they are necessarily worth paying extra for, and it certainly doesn't guarantee they are rare. By the very definition that the coins turned up in a hoard, the implication is that many identical (or at least similar) coins share a similar provenance. When talking about hundreds, thousands, or even tens of thousands of modern Silver Eagle coins emerging from the same place, how could they be rare? Novel? Sure. Historic? Maybe. But "rare"? Most likely not.

69 Or 70? That is the Question . . .

Whether collecting only a few American Silver Eagles or chasing after the entire series in every possible finish and variety, the deliberation many collectors have is in what grade to collect these beautiful modern coins. The decision usually comes down to two close but distinct grade points: 69 and 70. What's the difference in a point? With Silver Eagles, just about everything. To the naked eye, a Silver Eagle in MS-69 or PF-69 will look virtually the same as a similar example in the numismatically "perfect" grade of MS-70 or PF-70. However, whip out that little 5x or 10x loupe and the presence of a hairline or two will change the entire game.

If you're buying American Silver Eagles for their bullion content, you probably aren't as concerned about whether they grade 69, 70, or even if they're graded at all. A great many precious-metals speculators buy these coins "raw" and in rolls, and the matter of grade hardly enters the picture for them, and that's totally fine. But numismatists, and especially those collecting coins on the basis of grade and eye appeal, will not find the differences between 69 and 70 a trifling matter. In many cases, an MS-70 Silver Eagle is at least marginally scarcer than its MS-69 brethren, and in some situations the "perfect" coin is genuinely rare—some of the pre-2002 dates in the series confirm that fact.

"A set of MS-69 American Silver Eagles is easy to complete with modest effort," Jeff Garrett remarks. "Some collectors prefer to buy the sets already completed. The MS-69 coins are much more closely related to a bullion play than the MS-70 counterparts. Many bullion buyers gravitate to one of each date Silver Eagle as they discover coin collecting. The MS-70 American Silver Eagles are much more difficult to collect."

Garrett says he rarely sees complete sets of MS-70 American Silver Eagles offered on the market. "The coins will most likely need to be found individually and many are quite rare." Yet, he adds that many MS-70 American Silver Eagles are coming out of the woodwork and being graded all the time. "That is the biggest risk for collectors buying MS-70 Silver Eagles. More will be produced for years to come. The population numbers will continue to grow, and this should be factored in when buying the more expensive issues," Garrett says. Regardless, a major part of the marketplace for MS-70 Silver Eagles comes from the ever-growing number of registry collectors. "Set-registry collecting has had a tremendous impact on the hobby in recent years. Collectors truly enjoy competing with each other, and some will pay nearly insane prices for a leg up on the competition," Garrett says.

Numismatic author and market analyst Scott Travers says set-registry collectors constitute a major segment of the demand for high-end American Silver Eagles. "There are certain percentages of buyers from every part of the collecting and investing spectrum that buy certified high-grade American Silver Eagles and pay large premiums to

Deciding whether to buy American Silver Eagles numerically graded 69 or 70 may come down to cost and your collecting strategy.

secure them. I've advised people against buying these for monster sums in the past, and many persons specifically went against my advice, bought the coins on their own, and later sold them for impressive profits." He points to populations as being a major driver of where the market goes for top-grading examples. "Sometimes a low-population MS-69 or MS-70 coin can have a high value because few received a high grade. If more coins receive lofty grades, that high value can easily dissipate," Travers says.

CDN Publishing Vice President of Data and Content and *Greysheet* Editor Patrick Ian Perez points to populations as the most important factor on pricing differences between 69- and 70-graded American Silver Eagles: "The greatest influence on the spread, or lack thereof, between a given date in MS-69 and MS-70 is certified population. The Silver Eagle set is very attractive to a huge amount of collectors and rare coin marketers, and there will always be those who only want the finest-known coins. Thus, MS-70 coins, especially those dates in which the population is stable (i.e., new MS-70 coins are not being 'made' at the grading services), will remain in demand and have potential to grow in value."

STORING AMERICAN SILVER EAGLES

There are a multitude of methods for storing American Silver Eagles, whether you are collecting them as a set or accumulating them as part of an investment strategy. Let's break down the most common storage solutions below:

ALBUMS

One of the most popular ways to store a collection of American Silver Eagles is displaying them in an album. Coin albums offer long-term protection for coins while also keeping them well organized and easily viewable. Whitman Classic albums are available for American Silver Eagles, including those suited for widely collected year-by-year sets as well as collections encompassing the bullion strikes and numismatic issues.

CERTIFIED HOLDERS

Third-party grading companies will, for a fee, evaluate, authenticate, and grade coins, then encapsulate them in tamper-evident holders. ANACS began the first grading service in 1972 under the tutelage of the American Numismatic Association but did not encapsulate coins authenticated and graded under this service in sealed holders. The first company to do so at scale was Professional Coin Grading Service (PCGS) in 1986, followed shortly thereafter by Numismatic Guaranty Corporation (NGC, now Numismatic Guaranty Company) in 1987. Certifying American Silver Eagles in third-party holders provides for easier sight-unseen trading, provides superior protection to other types of holders, and, in the case of PCGS and NGC, permits collectors to include their coins in online registry sets that provide a venue for displaying one's collection and competing against other collectors for awards. Quantities of certified coin slabs can be held in boxes designed to hold 20 (or more) encapsulated coins. The major grading companies sell plastic row boxes specifically sized to the specifications of their own holder and that will attractively store and organized these coins.

Display Cases

There are a number of displays on the market that accommodate various types of sets involving the American Silver Eagle. Some of these sets might provide a portal for just one Silver Eagle as part of a type set. Others have slots for a much larger run of American Silver Eagles, perhaps representing an entire date run from a certain period of time

or some other arrangement. The quality and format of display cases for coins runs the gamut in quality, materials, and price. Some less-expensive displays involve a board with holes in it that can be secured in a picture-style frame and hung on a wall or displayed on a shelf. Some of the priciest displays are made from museum-quality Lucite and provide for the secure display of coins in an opaque center panel, sandwiched between two outer transparent panels that are screwed together in triplicate. An affordable and safe display case is the Whitman Snaplock holder, which is made from two inert plastic panels that snap together around a coin. The Snaplock product line offers holders for individual American Silver Eagle that can be stored in Whitman's classic blue plastic row box.

U.S. Mint Presentation Cases

The U.S. Mint sells its numismatic American Silver Eagles directly to the public in various kinds of presentation cases that are referred to as "original government packaging" (OGP). While many Proof, Uncirculated, and other types of American Silver Eagles are sold in the secondary market, oftentimes these coins are broken out of their original government packages and sold in other types of housing—flips, 2x2s, and the like. Collectors who wish to return their numismatic Silver Eagles to their original government packages can find these empty cases in aftermarket settings. These cases are sometimes sold by dealers who kept the holders they had tossed aside after removing the coin(s) from within for individual sale; some coin supply dealers also sell U.S. Mint presentation cases.

Capsules

Coin capsules consist of two clear plastic lenses that completely envelope an individual coin within an inert, airtight case. Some capsules provide for clear viewing of all three sides of a coin—obverse, reverse, and edge—while others come with a soft ring or collar that cradles the coin within the lenses but provides for viewing of only the obverse and reverse. These disc-shaped capsules can be inserted into larger square cards or panels that allow them to be more easily stored inside a row box.

ROLLS AND TUBES

Those who are tight on space might consider storing their American Silver Eagles in rolls or tubes. These products are also among the least expensive of the coin storage options on the market, but their major disadvantage is they do not provide for the display of any coins—they are designed as vessels to hold larger quantities of coins in as small a space as possible. Ideal candidates for buying rolls or tubes are silver stackers, dealers, or those who are holding large numbers of Silver Eagles bearing random dates. Large-scale investors will also find rolls and tubes a space-efficient solution for storing huge quantities of American Silver Eagles in safety-deposit boxes or vaults.

2X2S, FLIPS, AND ENVELOPES

The most economical method for storing American Silver Eagles is in 2x2s, plastic flips, and paper envelopes. These solutions cost just pennies per coin and offer decent short-term protection. Cost is the biggest advantage of these holders, which are commonly used by dealers for presenting coins in display cases at a shop or coin show. These are not designed as long-term solutions for storing coins because they don't seal out air from getting inside the holder, leaving the coin susceptible to mishandling, and may contain chemicals that will eventually harm the coins contained within.

THE INTERSECTION OF COLLECTING AND INVESTING IN AMERICAN SILVER EAGLES

There are many collectors who have purely numismatic ambitions—they collect to collect and pay little regard to whether they make a profit if they ever sell their coins. Then there are investors, who are driven by the overarching objective of making more for their coins than they pay and won't be happy unless they beat inflation with their portfolios. And then exist the folks who are a bit of both collector and investor. There are no polls out there that reliably track how many people consider themselves collectors, investors, or somewhere in between. Ultimately, many if not most people who are involved in the arena of buying and selling coins are something of a hybrid—they both appreciate coins as collectibles and have ambitions to make money from their collections.

This is where the intersectionality of collecting and investing occurs, and it happens far more frequently than many may guess—certainly more than some diehard numismatists or steely investors are willing to admit. There is probably no greater niche of the numismatic realm where this occurs than with the American Silver Eagle series, which arguably draws the largest share of investors due to its popularity, accessibility, and affordability, as well as its alluring connections to the historic numismatic legacies it draws from.

Expert market analyst Jeff Garrett has been asked countless times if rare coins are a good investment. "My answer has always been that you should never buy coins as an investment, but that if you collect rare coins, they are usually a good investment," he says. He believes education is vital in any numismatic pursuit. "Collecting coins means choosing a series, learning about that series, and buying coins over time. Becoming an educated collector is your best chance when collecting American Silver Eagles or Lincoln cents." Garrett encourages those who want to build a collection or portfolio do so with a long-term perspective: "The advantage of cost averaging over time helps you avoid the stress of buying a market peak and feeling the pressure when prices fall. The most successful collectors I have observed over the years are very patient and look for opportunities. I like to say, 'Investors are sold coins and collectors buy coins.'"

Gainesville Coins precious-metals editor and market analyst Everett Millman says, "I've seen a fair amount of crossover from both directions, perhaps more so with bullion investors becoming interested in year-date collecting and other numismatic concepts, like special finishes on coins, through pursuing American Silver Eagles."

Lee Minshull challenges the idea that one is either a collector or investor. "Everybody is an investor," he asserts. "Once you spend $2,000, $3,000, or $5,000 on coins, in the back of your mind you're hoping to see the value of your coins grow."

Stack's Bowers Galleries Sales Manager Andrew Bowers has encountered many

American Silver Eagles over the years. "I find that these are far and away the most requested form of silver bullion that customers want when they come into our New York City gallery, even despite the higher premiums they command compared to other forms of silver bullion. I think aesthetically they are superior to many other options out there, and I believe that people may have more confidence in buying something from the United States Mint."

Bowers says, "Beyond the bullion aspects of the Silver Eagles, they have certainly become numismatically collectible as well over the years. With pieces such as the Proof 1995-W, various Reverse Proof and Enhanced finishes, the 2020-W with V75 privy mark, and grading considerations, the Silver Eagle series can present many fun challenges and opportunities for new and old collectors." He says with prices for Silver Eagles starting right around $35 (as of summer 2022), the series is approachable for virtually anyone. "Stack's Bowers certainly has handled our share of Silver Eagles through our various auctions as well, with more and more appearances each year—a trend that I am sure will continue!"

THE DIFFERENCES BETWEEN COLLECTORS AND INVESTORS, ACCORDING TO SCOTT TRAVERS

Coin collecting and investing exist on a spectrum or continuum. Collectors on one side of the spectrum buy coins for their cultural, artistic, and historic significance. Collectors are often not completely focused on value and grade, but on the suitability of the coins for their collections. Coin collecting is a project mentality, and collectors focus on completeness (e.g., one of each date and mintmark) and how the coins appear together (e.g., matching grades and toning). Collectors often don't sell their collections during their lifetimes, as they are not focused on market trends or financial implications.

In the 1980s, word of the highly publicized, exceptional profits of coin collector Harold Bareford, whose collection was sold at auction in October 1981, made its way through the press. What many neglected to disclose was that Bareford was dead when his collection was sold.

Collectors of American Silver Eagle coins maintain the same project mentality that their counterparts in high-value vintage coins hold. But the exception is that American Silver Eagle collectors don't have to have large sums of money available to complete a set, especially a raw or uncertified one.

Bullion-strike American Silver Eagles, uncertified, are popular with budget-minded collectors. But those collectors often transition to acquiring one of each year of the Proof coins (except for 2009, when none were struck). These are all affordable raw or uncertified, except for the 1995-W, which carries a low- to mid-four-figure price.

Investors exist on the other side of the spectrum and acquire coins to make a profit or so they can go to the cash window and celebrate. Self-educated investors are focused on the suitability of a coin for appreciating in value and often don't appreciate the aesthetic beauty. Investors often buy multiple coins of the same date and type (what collectors would consider "duplicates") and focus on value opportunities.

American Silver Eagles are very popular with investors because they contain exactly one ounce of silver and are very liquid: published two-way markets are widely made, with bid and ask spreads facilitating transactional transparency. Helping to make these coins attractive is that they are accepted in

Scott Travers, at the lectern, holds a seminar with fellow market analyst Maurice Rosen before a full house at the 2020 Florida United Numismatists Show in Orlando, Florida.

Individual Retirement Accounts (IRAs), so long as the coins are held by an Internal Revenue Service–approved custodian.

But collecting and investing are not mutually exclusive. Collectors-investors, a hybrid of collector and investor, buy coins for the magnificence of the coins and for the investment potential. If a coin owned by a collector-investor increases in value, the collector-investor might well go to the cash window and celebrate, but retain a photo of the coin as a memento to appreciate that small work of art.

American Silver Eagles are especially attractive to collector-investors because their magnificent designs, precious metal content, affordability, and variance of dates all combine to form the possibly ultimate collector-investor series.

American Silver Eagles appeal to the greatest number of collector-investors. Over the last eight years, when I've surveyed my audiences at seminars I've given at the American Numismatic Association and Florida United Numismatists conventions, a large percentage of audience members respond to this request: "Please raise your hand if you are a collector-investor active in American Silver Eagle bullion coins."

INVESTING IN AMERICAN SILVER EAGLES

Investors have flocked to American Silver Eagles since they took flight in 1986. Should anyone be surprised? Bullion investors have had a love affair with United States coinage for decades, tracing back to at least the mid-1970s, when sanctions were lifted on the ownership of gold coins, and farther back to the early 1960s, when rising silver prices led to a run on circulating 90 percent silver coinage.

Humanity's love affair with silver goes back to at least 3000 B.C., and as we've seen in earlier pages of this book, the American Silver Eagle represents but a short though popular chapter in the ongoing saga of silver bullion coinage. As we progress through the rest of this chapter, we will examine some of the most common and lucrative ways that people use American Silver Eagles as an investment vehicle and how you can turn these attractive silver coins into a high-performance liquid asset.

Silver Stacking

"Silver stacking" is the accumulation of silver coins, silver bars, and any other mechanically created, hand-made, or hand-poured silver items, regardless of their origin. While many silver stackers may also be silver investors or precious-metals speculators by definition, stackers are not necessarily stockpiling silver for the sake of investing, at least in the traditional sense of "buying low and selling high."

Not all silver stackers are minted the same, though their general ambition is to gather as much silver as they can, usually regardless of the physical form or other qualities that may be of prime concern to a numismatist, such as date, condition, or origin. Some silver stackers are motivated to gather silver in an effort to cash it in at some point when silver markets are favorable or when a financial emergency arises and they need ready cash.

Silver stackers could be endearingly described as a motley bunch, ranging from white-collar professionals earning six- and seven-figure incomes in bustling downtown skyrises to hunters and farmers living in relative social isolation amid some of the most remote stretches of the country. Their motivations for stacking silver are just as diverse. Most silver stackers are tight-lipped about their hoards. While some may be characteristically taciturn anyway, others are social butterflies—but few want people to know about their silver stacking proclivities because they don't want to risk getting robbed. After all, silver stackers tend to keep their hoards in a home vault to ensure ready access, to save money on storage fees in a bank safe deposit box or bullion depository, or simply because they don't trust keeping their physical assets out of sight.

Not all silver stackers are created from the same mold. Cruise YouTube, Facebook, Instagram, or other social media and you will readily find videos, photos, and posts with silver stackers proudly displaying their stash. These digital alcoves are brimming with posts by people showing off their latest silver acquisition or clips giving virtual "tours" of their stack. It's safe to assume many individuals publicly posting about their silver stacks are broadcasting under pseudonyms and are likely heavily armed. If you have ambitions of showing (and telling) the world about your silver stack, it's wise to adopt a pseudonymous online identity to help protect yourself and your loved ones.

For some, silver stacking has a game-like element, with the goal being to stack, say, a certain amount of silver by a certain date, or to cobble together a specific quantity of silver each week or each month. Such objectives can be as challenging as they are fun for the silver stacker, who might be just as content to add an American Silver Eagle to their pile as they would a broken sterling-silver necklace chain—so long as the item helps them reach their goal.

In some cases, the silver stacker may create stockpiling parameters. For example, while self-declared "stackers," they might prefer acquiring only coins, or only bars, or perhaps restricting their hoard only to silver coins from a particular nation. At this point, the stacker may have some hybrid collecting tendencies, whereby they aren't indiscriminately purchasing silver, but rather targeting certain pieces with some degree of bias, artistic, patriotic, or otherwise.

Others may identify less as "silver stackers" and are rather silver *hoarders*, with survivalist philosophies of preparing for some type of future socioeconomic tragedy. It's safe to say that a significant, though indeterminate, percentage of silver stackers don't put much faith in fiat currencies. In many

Silver stackers generally aim to acquire as much silver as they can get.

cases, these individuals are anticipating the collapse of well-established monetary systems or global political disasters that they believe will cause monetary systems unbacked by precious metals, and digital forms of money, such as cryptocurrency, to lose all value.

Frequently, these silver stackers are also accumulating other provisions for the theater of overthrown governments and broken commercial supply chains. Such silver stackers aren't typically planning to receive a monetary return on their silver "investment," but rather expect to use their silver as barter for housing, food, or other necessary supplies in a worst-case scenario. Survivalist silver stackers usually prefer American Silver Eagles as well as vintage (pre-1965) 90 percent silver dimes, quarters, half dollars, and dollars due to their familiarity with the public, their patriotic themes, and their convenient size (smaller than, say, 10-ounce or 100-ounce bars).

In all cases, silver stackers need to beware of getting wrapped up in misleading claims or hysteria about the silver market, silver prices, or hypothetical events that could cause panic buying. Hasty purchases can lead to buying counterfeit goods, including fake American Silver Eagles or other bullion products purported to be authentic. Beware buying bogus items only because they were offered at prices substantially lower than fair market rates. Later in this chapter, we will cover a number of keys to safe silver shopping, including how to avoid getting scammed with fake items, avoiding grossly overpriced coins, and other tips to help you be a smart buyer.

Bullion Investing

Silver stacking is an activity that can be pursued by both collectors and investors, just as many individuals are hybrid collector-investors. So, is there a delineation between silver stacking and investing? There's no formal distinction, per se. However, it could be said that while the silver stacker might be squirreling away bullion for profit, for a rainy day, or for the pure pleasure of building a cache of shiny silver, the investor may have a more clearly defined intention of, at some point, turning their silver in for a profit, or at the very least the best money they can get from their bullion holdings. In other words, there's usually an endgame objective in mind for the investor, whether the point at which they seek a return on their investment be tomorrow, next year, or decades from now.

You don't need to be financially well heeled to become a silver investor. You can begin investing in silver with the simple purchase of just one

Many people take a strategic approach to investing in American Silver Eagles.

silver coin. Indeed, the democratization of bullion investment is one reason the United States government launched the American Eagle program, which offers something for just about every level of investor, from beginners on shoestring budgets to seasoned speculators rolling seven figures into precious metals on an annual basis.

"Many high-net-worth families acquire large quantities of American Silver Eagles and American Gold Eagles to fill out the physical metal asset class of their holdings," notes Scott Travers. "Working-class investors would often be best suited to buy quantities of the raw coins but, instead, sometimes buy a small quantity of certified coins with the budgeted funds. Ironically, many of these investors would do better financially with the raw coins. Lower-budget collectors sometimes compete for high-grade certified American Silver Eagle through auction online facilitators such as eBay and pay top dollar. Or they buy these certified coins from TV infomercials." Travers goes on to say, "Investors like that there are many of these coins, which allows for a fluid market and transparent pricing, and that the price over the melt value of the metal is not prohibitive."

The American Silver Eagle is often touted as a gateway coin for investors. With wide aesthetic appeal to those inside and outside the numismatic and investment arenas, a relatively low cost over spot, easy availability, and broad familiarity around the globe, the American Silver Eagle is a go-to coin for those who have made the decision to build an investment portfolio. Once you decide you want to build a silver investment portfolio, the next logical step might be deciding your financial goals, how much silver you need to meet your goals, your budget, and where and when you intend to purchase and liquidate your assets.

While it doesn't cost much money to get started in building a silver portfolio, the investor should do some soul searching before plunking serious money on bullion. Why are you choosing silver? Why now? What's the goal? What percentage of your income will you dedicate to bullion? What piece of your investment pie will be consumed by silver? What are the risks and rewards? Can you eat losses without losing your shirt? How much time do you have to monitor the performance of your portfolio? Will you store your physical bullion at home or in an offsite location? Do you have the space and security necessary for at-home storage? Do you have the funds to afford storage at a bank or depository? Who will be the beneficiary/beneficiaries of this portfolio in the case of an unforeseen or unfortunate situation?

These questions are posed not to dissuade the prospective investor from going full throttle on Silver Eagles, but rather to spark a brainstorm and help the future speculator create a plan for success from the start of the investment journey. Entire books can be written to answer each of the questions above, but let's briefly address them.

Why choose silver? Silver is affordable, readily obtainable, and a store of value with demand in industrial and recreational circles. If you've decided to invest in silver exclusively or as part of a larger precious-metals portfolio, continue studying this area of the bullion market to become an educated investor and help develop a greater passion for it. This book is one of many resources you should include in your investment library, and you should continue to ask experts questions, seek out reliable information from reputable sources, and only spend significant sums of money on silver products you know about and are comfortable buying.

Should you invest now? This is one question only you can answer. There are no crystal balls in the bullion industry, and you can never really know if this moment represents the last time silver will be this expensive—or this cheap. Besides, the first qualification in determining when to invest is ascertaining whether you have the funds to invest in silver. Even if you need to delay your formal entry into silver investing, now is the perfect time to study and learn, to make wiser decisions when the time comes to buy.

What's your goal? As an investor, you'll be served well in making some clear goals for yourself and your investment portfolio. What is your strategy and what is your timetable? Are you looking to buy now, hold for a few years, then sell? Investing in silver for retirement? Looking to sell the minute silver prices reach a certain threshold? Develop a laser focus on your investment plan and know when and how to react as various events occur in the marketplace and in your personal life.

What percentage of your income should you dedicate to bullion? Only you can determine how much money you can spend on silver, but be careful when arriving at a figure. Think rationally, and resist the temptation to spend all of your disposable income on a single asset, like silver. Don't put all your eggs in one basket. Diversify your assets.

What share of your investment portfolio should be silver? A good rule of thumb is spending $5 to $10 on silver for every $100 you devote to your overall investment portfolio. This will provide you with enough silver to enjoy marked gains in positive markets but soften the blow during periods of negative movement. Remember, silver—and precious metals in general—tend to provide better results for investors as a hedge against inflation and especially currency devaluation than as an investment in the traditional sense of making huge profits. Except for a few moments in history where silver posted unsustainable short-term blowout spurts of growth (almost always followed by a sharp correction), bullion is rarely friendly to those looking to make a fast buck. Forget *sprints* and think *marathons*.

What are the risks and rewards? Silver could tank tomorrow. Silver might reach for the stars next week. Silver might hold steady for a few years and make a pronounced move neither up nor down. Silver can behave with volatility during periods of market unrest. Balancing the risks and rewards can be frustrating, and you may find more peace of mind in an assertive but not overly aggressive stance. Ultimately, investing in silver or any precious metal is akin to gambling. Although you likely will not lose all the marbles in bullion, you might drop a handful of them. Or, you could luck out and win big in a bull market. Let the chips fall where they may . . .

Can you afford to take a loss? If you plunked $100, $1,000, or $10,000 in silver today and lost half that amount next year, would it financially disable you? Avoid spending more than a small percentage of your income on silver, and never more than your disposable income or dedicated investment budget permits.

Do you have time to manage your portfolio? If you're just buying a few American Silver Eagles here and there, you likely have no problem keeping track of what you're spending and how much your silver holdings are worth, and planning what to buy next. But some individuals have millions of dollars tied up in precious metals and are simply too busy to keep their bullion house in order. It might make sense to build your silver portfolio with the assistance of a bullion broker or other trusted intermediary who can help administer your assets.

Where will you keep your bullion? A small bullion holding can easily be stored in your home vault if you prefer, but in some cases it might be more practical to keep your silver in an offsite location with larger accommodations and better security. Make this decision based on the size of your holdings, your desire to procure appropriate vault space, your comfort with the protection your home can offer, and your willingness to entrust custody of your physical assets with an agent.

Do you have the space and security necessary for at-home storage? Depending on the size of your digs, you might barely have room for a half-cubic-foot lockbox capable of holding a small number of American Silver Eagles, or you might be easily able to tuck away a large vault perfect for housing literal tons of bullion. Take into account how secure your home is, protecting your valuables against flood and fire (burglary isn't your only risk), and factor in the costs of the necessary components for safe and secure storage.

Can you afford storage at a bank or depository? If you decide on offsite storage, the next factor to consider is the fees you'll incur. Banks charge for use of safety deposit boxes, and bullion depositories also levy dues. Prices will vary based on where you choose to house your silver, how much space you need, whether you need insurance, and other costs.

Who will be the beneficiary/beneficiaries of your portfolio should unforeseen or unfortunate events occur? When investing significant sums of money, it's wise to think about where your assets will go in the event you are unable to use them down the road as expected. Speak with an attorney about drafting a will if you don't have one, amending it to include your bullion holdings if these aren't addressed in your directives, and take care of any other matters related to your unique circumstances.

As you map out your investment strategy, consider other factors that are unique to your circumstances and influential in the whys, whens, and hows of your silver speculation journey. Create a well-composed plan with defined targets and goals, doing your best to stick with it. But also remember that some of the most successful bullion investors are nimble, ready to roll with the unexpected punch, and are adaptable to unforeseen marketplace realities. Create a Plan A, Plan B, and Plan C, and keep doing your best to educate yourself on how to become a better bullion investor.

Can You Retire on American Silver Eagles?

One of the wonderful things about American Silver Eagles is that they can make a terrific investment vehicle when market conditions are favorable for bullion. They can also be a lucrative addition to your retirement portfolio.

How do you begin incorporating American Silver Eagles into a retirement plan? What are the costs and considerations? How does this all even work?

It's possible to purchase a bunch of American Silver Eagles, save them for a period of years—even decades—and then when you're ready to bow out of your career, cash these coins in for at least enough to have beaten inflation. But there are many things that can go against your long-term plans with this approach.

Consider the issue of taxes. What you earn from the sale of those American Silver Eagles may be subject to taxation, both federal and state. You might encounter other tax quandaries upon selling or soon after, including capital gains taxes or other forms of levy based on where you live, your personal financial situation, or other legal circumstances. Not paying these taxes could land you in court opposite Uncle Sam on federal charges of tax evasion.

So, is there a way to safely incorporate Silver Eagles into a retirement plan while mitigating the tax blow? The short is yes—yes, you can. The long answer is what follows.

Building a Silver IRA

Individual retirement accounts, or IRAs, have been around for decades and have long been touted as a safe and effective method for building wealth that can be used for retirement. Authorized under the Employee Retirement Income Security Act (ERISA) of 1974, IRAs were designed to give workers who did not have pension coverage a tax-sheltered means for building a nest egg for retirement. IRA eligibility expanded to include all workers and their spouses with the passage of the Economic Recovery Tax Act on August 13, 1981, signed by President Ronald Reagan as part of his overarching tax overhaul.

Over the years, the maximum yearly contributions permitted under the IRA tax code has grown from $1,500 per year in 1974 to more than $6,000 in 2019, with accommodations for additional "catch up" contributions for those 50 years of age or older. Rules and eligibility on withdrawals differ depending on whether you elect a traditional IRA or Roth IRA. For traditional IRAs, penalty-free withdrawals can begin as early as 59-1/2 provided the IRA is at least five years old, with mandatory distributions kicking in at age 72 and taxes assessed against all withdrawals. With the Roth IRA, you can withdraw against the after-tax contributions at any time with no additional tax levies or penalties

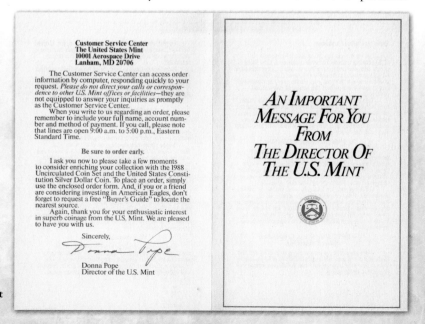

A U.S. Mint brochure encouraging investment in Silver Eagles and other Mint products.

provided the account is at least five years old. The rules are always changing with IRAs; seek the counsel of a savvy financial advisor whenever making decisions about these widely embraced tax-sheltered accounts.

The most common types of investments under current IRA laws include bonds, mutual funds, certificates of deposit (CDs), money market accounts, common stocks, savings accounts, exchange-traded funds (ETFs), Treasury inflation-protected securities (TIPs), and real estate investment trusts (REITs). Less-common permitted investments range from residential and commercial real estate to oil and gas royalties and dozens of other novel assets. Additionally, you can invest in U.S. bullion coins as well as a variety of other related bullion products hailing from the U.S. Mint and beyond. Included among these are American Silver Eagles.

Can all types of coins similarly be included in IRAs? Unfortunately, no. There was a window of time between 1979 and 1981 when the U.S. Labor Department relaxed ERISA regulations and a variety of non–income-producing assets were permitted in IRAs, including collectible coins, stamps, diamonds, rugs, artwork, and other items. However, sweeping changes under the umbrella of the Economic Recovery Act of 1981 dramatically shifted the scope of the IRA.

Scott Travers offers his perspective on the matter of IRAs: "I don't like the concept of any coin in an IRA because you don't have the physical coins in your possession. Now, I like the very fact that any U.S. coin, bullion or otherwise, is allowed by law in an IRA. It helps the value of the coins that aren't in IRAs. But if you're putting a coin in an IRA, you better educate yourself as to what you're doing and get the appropriate legal and financial advice in advance to be sure that you know what you're getting into. Personally, I buy and sell gold and silver exchange-traded funds (ETFs) for my own IRAs. Hard-money asset fans call this 'paper' gold and silver."

Is it ever too early to start investing in a retirement plan? No! Some of the most successful investors began planning for their retirement in their 20s and early 30s. Never underestimate the power of compound interest. Even if you're in your 50s, 60s, or older, there are accelerated investment strategies that can help you maximize your investment in a shorter period of time, not to mention the aforementioned catch-up contributions permitted for older investors who own IRAs.

PROS AND CONS OF SILVER IRAS

Precious-metals specialist Everett Millman offers three questions investors needs to ask themselves before they pursue a silver IRA, as well as some pros and cons of these precious-metals accounts.

The key questions an investor needs to ask before opening a silver IRA are:

- Do I plan on selling my metals within the next few years, or do I at least want the flexibility to do so?

- Am I interested in any potentially collectible coins with a numismatic premium (outside of the Proof Silver Eagles and Proof Gold Eagles)?

- Do I care if I get to admire, display, or otherwise hold my silver?

If the answer to any of these is "yes," then a silver IRA may not be the best choice.

Advantages:
Your silver investment is either tax deferred (Traditional IRA) or tax free upon redemption (Roth IRA).

The requirement to store your IRA silver in a vault ensures its safety.

Holding your silver in an IRA encourages long-term saving.

Disadvantages:
Your silver is not easily liquidated while it's part of your IRA.

Not all types of silver bullion are eligible for IRA inclusion.

There is an annual contribution limit ($6,000 to $7,000, depending on your age).

IRA-APPROVED BULLION COINS

Whether you choose a traditional IRA, permitting tax-deductible contributions, or a Roth IRA, which provides for tax-free growth on contributions as well as untaxed retirement distributions, the same rules apply when it comes to the types of bullion coins you are allowed to enroll. The coins must meet certain minimums of precious-metal fineness and should generally not be considered collectible coins—i.e., 1909-S V.D.B. Lincoln cents, 1804 Draped Bust dollars, and other coins whose marketplace values are virtually centered around their numismatic qualities are not permitted.

Below is a general list of minimum precious-metal fineness for bullion coins in an IRA:

- Silver coins: .999 fine or finer
- Gold coins: .995 fine or finer
- Palladium coins: .9995 fine or finer
- Platinum coins: .9995 fine or finer

Bear in mind there are exceptions, and one may be glaringly obvious to those who collect or invest in American Gold Eagles. While the typical minimum fineness for IRA gold is .995 fine, American Gold Eagles are "only" .9167 fine. Yet, American Gold Eagles *are* approved for IRAs (note that South African Krugerrands, also boasting a .9167-fine gold composition, are presently *not* IRA approved). American Silver Eagles, which are .999 fine, are among the many types of silver bullion coins approved for IRAs. Unfortunately for silver stackers, pre-1965 90 percent silver coinage and other popular "junk" silver are not acceptable for inclusion in IRAs.

Does this mean that *all* American Silver Eagles are allowed in IRAs? The late Diane Piret, who spent the last 25 years of her life serving as the industry membership and affairs director for what was then known as the Industry Council for Tangible Assets (ICTA), authored an article for *Coin Dealer Newsletter* in 2010 addressing such questions. She pointed out that the legislation for the American Silver Eagle and American Gold Eagle programs in 1985 expressly addressed the definition of the term "collectibles" (which have not been allowed in IRAs since revisions to the law in 1981), which deemed that such terminology did not apply to the new bullion coins. "There is no differentiation between Proof and Uncirculated, and both versions are allowed," wrote Piret.

She noted that the matter of submitting certified American Eagles in such plans was much iffier. "This depends on the IRA company, because there are no government regulations concerning it." What about sets of coins issued by the U.S. Mint that includes a mix of American Eagles and other coins that are not permitted under IRA regulations? She remarked the law on such matters very specifically permits "Eagles or any gold, silver, platinum, or palladium bullion of a fineness equal to or exceeding the minimum fineness that a contract market (as described in section 7 of the Commodity Exchange Act, 7 U.S.C. 7) requires for metals which may be delivered in satisfaction of a regulated futures contract." On that legal note, she advised, "check with the IRA company you choose. You may find that a depository will reject coins that [don't] meet its criteria. We are aware of errors that have occurred in the past where the transaction proceeded all the way to the metals arriving at the depository only to be rejected."

As lawyer and numismatic expert David L. Ganz advises, "the best thing an IRA investor can do is read the disclosure material they are furnished for their account and ask their agent for specific details as to what is and is not allowed in their holdings." And when it comes to selling? Ganz's key piece of advice for those who are ready to liquidate their bullion IRA portfolio is "to pray." He goes on to say that even though IRAs are generally tax-sheltered in one form or another, this doesn't mean there aren't opportunities for Uncle Sam to make a cut from the sale of your bullion profits. "Make sure you're aware of the possibility of paying capital gains taxes," Ganz says. This does not apply in all cases, and this is why he again urges those who are looking to contribute Silver Eagles into an IRA plan or cash one out to read the fine print on the disclosure materials and consult their financial advisor. Ganz, declaring the American Silver Eagle series "a dynamic program," remarks that laws are apt to change, and thus investors need to keep up to date with the latest requirements whenever considering the next move with their bullion IRAs.

WHAT ABOUT KEEPING YOUR IRA BULLION AT HOME?

It's natural for many who start a silver IRA to want to physically keep the bullion they purchase as part of the plan in their own home vault or maybe a bank safety deposit box. However, IRA regulations require all tax-deferred precious metals enrolled in these retirement plans to be physically stored with an approved and offsite custodian, such as a bullion depository. Remember there are fees involved with storing bullion at a depository, and this could factor in as one of the disadvantages of owning a silver IRA. Of course, years of steady gains in the precious-metals market or potential peace of mind in owning a well-diversified account may offset the sting of bullion-storage fees.

Some may try avoiding these fees or skirting the offsite-storage requirements altogether by seeking so-called "home storage" bullion IRAs. Such schemes aren't usually self-concocted. Rather they are inspired by numerous misleading or simply downright false advertisements on television, the internet, and elsewhere claiming that investors can purchase American Silver Eagles and other bullion coins under the guise of depositing them into an IRA and store them in their home vault or a safety-deposit box.

These advertisers will invariably suggest launching a limited liability corporation (LLC) as part of a two-step transaction that involves the investor physically purchasing the bullion and then transferring it to another "party" that then holds the assets in its own vault—which just so happens to be located in, say, the investor's home. Such plans are in direct opposition to tax laws, which are designed to prevent investors from directly possessing their own IRA assets. The Internal Revenue Service has unequivocally spoken out on the matter saying that home-storage IRAs are absolutely prohibited. When, not if, Uncle Sam discovers someone is trying to circumvent the law concerning bullion IRAs, the unfortunate investor could face major tax assessments, heavy penalties, and/or other counterproductive legal ramifications.

Case in point? Check out the final verdict of *Andrew McNulty et al. v. Commissioner of Internal Revenue*, wherein the defendants tried storing $411,000 in gold and silver American Eagle coins in their home safe under a separate bank account opened under an LLC. Donna McNulty claimed that the purchases of the coins were documented and labeled as the property of her IRA-owned LLC. The judge ruled that the McNultys storing the American Eagles at home resulted in "unfettered control" of the investment and hence rendered a taxable payout from the IRA amounting to the full $411,000 value for the coins. The couple was levied tax assessments and penalties of more than $300,000.

As summarized by the National Coin & Bullion Association (www.nationalcoinbullionassoc.org): "Purchasing and holding assets in an IRA on a pre-tax basis is a great benefit. To continuously receive that benefit, the IRA assets must be held by a financial institution or an IRS-approved nonbank custodian."

SELF-DIRECTED IRAs: WHAT THEY ARE AND WHAT THEY ARE NOT

A self-directed IRA (or SDIRA) is the type of account you will need to start if you wish to include silver or other alternative investments in your retirement plan. It can take the form of either a traditional or Roth IRA and offer the commensurate tax benefits, but these differ in the sense that the owner will be the one responsible for making investment decisions, rather than the custodian, who can't offer any financial advice. The other key difference is that the owner of a self-directed IRA can reach beyond the traditional realm of stocks, bonds, mutual funds, exchange-traded funds, and certificates of deposits.

The major advantages are that you can diversify your portfolio with bullion, real estate, and a number of other alternative assets that you ordinarily couldn't utilize. However, you will need to be savvy and prepared for risks, including major losses, that you might otherwise be sheltered from when dealing with regular IRAs, which are built around traditional investments and continuously managed by the custodian to maximize gains and optimize long-term results. When embarking on a self-directed IRA you also need to be wary of fees, fraud, and other pitfalls that you might not normally encounter with a regular custodian-driven IRAs. Consider, for example, what happens if you own real property as part of your SDIRA. While it's easy to sell stocks, bonds, and mutual funds, it might be hard to unload that 10-acre rural parcel or Midtown Manhattan apartment if the real-estate market is sour. Do your homework, invest wisely, and create various liquidation strategies should Plan A flop.

Additionally, you will need to find a specialized provider to open an SDIRA, with your sights set on someone who specifically assists in opening a bullion IRA, if that's your preference. Bear in mind that the same contribution limits and withdrawal stipulations apply whether you own a regular IRA or self-directed plan. This also means that collectibles, including numismatic coins, are *not* permitted with self-directed IRAs.

Don't get excited at the perceived prospect that, due to the seeming autonomy of a retirement account with the word *self* in the name, you get to take physical custody of any silver or other bullion you own as part of the plan. Unfortunately, this is not legally permitted. Silver IRAs, regardless of how they are formally managed, absolutely require all silver or other IRA-eligible bullion be physically held by a custodian at an approved depository. Among the most popular is Delaware Depository, though one of the benefits of holding a self-directed IRA is that you get to choose which approved and independent depository holds your bullion. Before choosing a depository or custodian for your bullion IRA, check with the Better Business Bureau and make sure they have an A+ rating and no outstanding consumer issues or unresolved complaints.

No matter what route you take when investing in a silver IRA or any type of retirement plan, do your due diligence. Tax rules and IRA protocol are subject to change at any time. Therefore, it's best for anyone considering a silver IRA to consult with a financial adviser for more information on the latest requirements and to further discuss your options for building a lucrative bullion-backed retirement plan.

Being a Smart Buyer

Collectors, investors, and everyone in between should always do their best to be market savvy when it comes to buying American Silver Eagles. The best advice you can ever receive is to buy the book before the coin. That's a phrase attributed to numismatic book dealer Aaron Feldman, whose now-famous numismatic mantra appeared in an advertisement in a March 1966 issue of *The Numismatist*.

Knowledge is power, and owning this knowledge can mean the difference between being a successful coin collector or bullion investor and getting scammed out of your money through deceptive marketing practices or out-and-out fraud. Unfortunately, fraud, fakes, and shams are rampant in the back alleys of numismatics, and this is why it pays to understand what you're buying, know who you're buying from, and do your dealings under the light.

Avoid buying bullion in deals listed on swap-meet websites or on websites where you need to meet people in fast-food restaurant parking lots to make the trade of cash for coins. The risk of buying counterfeit or stolen goods through these backdoor transactions is just too high, and your chances of recourse are virtually zilch.

When buying coins from e-commerce and auction websites, stick to coin dealers who are vetted, offer return policies, and have plenty of positive feedback and good reviews from actual customers. The major U.S. online marketplaces and the noteworthy numismatic auction houses provide buyers with many safeguards for buying coins.

Choose a good coin dealer who is experienced in buying and selling bullion and has affiliations with some of the industry's most important organizations. Some of these include:

> **American Numismatic Association (ANA)**—Founded in 1891 and chartered by Congress in 1912, the nonprofit American Numismatic Association

is the largest coin club in the United States, boasting around 25,000 members. The ANA is committed to advancing education, advocating for history, and spreading the joy of the hobby. The ANA hosts two large shows every year, has an award-winning monthly magazine known as *The Numismatist*, offers a variety of educational courses to the public, and operates the Edward C. Rochette Money Museum at the organization's headquarters in Colorado Springs, Colorado. www.money.org.

American Numismatic Society (ANS)—Headquartered in New York City, the American Numismatic Society was founded in 1858 and is dedicated to the preservation and study of coins, currency, medals, and tokens. The nonprofit museum and educational organization holds more than 1 million pieces of money, literature, and other items related to numismatics. The ANS offers courses and other resources for those interested in pursuing academic careers in numismatics and has defined itself as an institute of numismatic education. www.numismatics.org.

ANACS—Founded in 1972 as the American Numismatic Association Certification Service, ANACS became the first third-party authenticator and grader of coins and remained for more than a decade the only such major service to offer these services, providing a certificate and photograph of the coin declaring its authenticity and grade. In 1989 ANACS began encapsulating their coins in plastic slabs, inserted with a label declaring the grade. The grading service has been managed by various firms over the years and continues to operate today with the ANACS name. www.anacs.com.

Better Business Bureau (BBB)—While not specifically related to numismatics, the Better Business Bureau remains one of the most important consumer-protection agencies, serving as a place to file complaints against businesses that fail to uphold their promises or otherwise conduct unethical or questionable practices. The BBB awards businesses that go above and beyond to both ensure customer satisfaction and quickly rectify any issues that do arise with an A+ rating. www.bbb.org.

Combined Organization of Numismatic Error Collectors of America (CONECA)—Formed in 1983, this organization focuses on educating the collecting community on errors and varieties. The club publishes its popular bimonthly educational journal *Errorscope* and offers a lending library, listing and attribution services, and its well-attended Errorama conventions. www.conecaonline.org.

Independent Coin Graders (ICG)—Independent Coin Graders was founded in 1998 and has built a name on providing fast, affordable, and reliable authentication, grading, and encapsulation of United States and many world coins. ICG handles individual and bulk submissions and offers same-day and walk-up grading services at several coin shows each year. www.icgcoin.com.

National Coin & Bullion Association (NCBA)—The National Coin & Bullion Association (formerly known as the Industry Council for Tangible Assets) is a tax-exempt trade association aimed at advocating for fair tax laws and favorable regulations to support the numismatic and precious-metals bullion industry. NCBA worked with the Professional Numismatists Guild (PNG) and the ANA to create the Anti-Counterfeiting Task Force and Education Foundation (ACTF/ACEF), now run by PNG. www.nationalcoinbullionassoc.org.

National Silver Dollar Roundtable (NSDR)—This nonprofit organization was founded in 1982 and is dedicated to advancing knowledge on silver dollars, including American Silver Eagles. All members must comply with the NSDR's code of ethics. The NSDR publishes a journal three times a year and helps coordinate many educational exhibits and seminars focusing on various aspects of United States silver dollars. www.nsdr.net.

Numismatic Guaranty Company (NGC)—Founded in 1987 as Numismatic Guaranty Corporation, NGC is one of the leading third-party coin grading and encapsulation services. It certifies coins submitted by NGC-member dealers and collectors and has encapsulated many prestigious seven-figure coins. www.ngccoin.com.

Professional Coin Grading Service (PCGS)—Professional Coin Grading Service became the first company to authenticate, grade, and encapsulate coins at scale when it was founded in 1986. PCGS accepts submissions from members of its Collectors Club and PCGS Authorized Dealer network and graded the most valuable coin sold to date, a 1933 Saint-Gaudens double eagle that sold for $18,872,250 in June 2021. www.pcgs.com.

Professional Numismatists Guild (PNG)—A nonprofit founded in 1955 on the principles of "knowledge, integrity, and responsibility," the Professional Numismatists Guild serves as a clearinghouse of the hobby's most ethical and professional coin dealers. All members must pass a criminal background check, meet requirements of net wealth and knowledge, and rigorously comply with a strict code of ethics. www.pngdealers.org.

Bear in mind that new dealers who haven't yet joined the likes of the ANA, NCBA, or other leading organizations aren't necessarily dishonest or shady. Many of the hobby's most ethical and trustworthy businesspersons started out as so-called "vest pocket" dealers roaming the floors of coins shows and selling coins toted around in their pockets, with nary a professional address or phone number attached to their names.

Still, you as a consumer drastically reduce your chances of getting rooked if you work with vetted dealers who operate with physical addresses and phone numbers, belong to professional organizations that enforce penalties against fraudulent activity, and are highly recommended by both buyers and other dealers. Don't forget to do some of your own research before committing to a coin dealer by checking their reputation through the Better Business Bureau. Customer feedback on Google Reviews, Yelp, Facebook, and other online mediums can also be very helpful.

Why You Can't Buy Silver Eagles at Spot

Some beginners pursue silver bullion with the idea that it should be available at its spot price—the actual value of the silver itself. With rare exceptions, this is simply not possible due to a number of factors, including market dynamics, scarcity of product, and the cost of doing business. Even the wholesalers—the U.S. Mint's network of Authorized Purchasers who buy the coins directly from their source—have to pay a fee over spot to buy these silver coins.

As Patrick Ian Perez notes, "The U.S. Mint only sells bullion Silver Eagles to Authorized Purchasers at a fixed amount above spot that is based on demand and availability. These Authorized Purchasers then sell the coins on to wholesale accounts. Some of these wholesale buyers sell direct to the public (retail sales) and others supply coin shops, online dealers, etc., who then sell to the public."

Perez says there can be as many as four tiers in the market between the U.S. Mint and the end user (the collector or investor). "Since even the top of the food chain—Authorized Purchasers—cannot buy Silver Eagles at spot, the public will never be able to. In a market environment that we have had recently, which combined huge demand for rare coins and increasing monetary inflation, the premiums surge. Recently, among the lowest wholesale prices for a bullion Silver Eagle was $9.50 over spot. On the other hand, which is often overlooked by collectors, is that dealers are willing to pay $5 or $6 over spot to buy Silver Eagles back." He adds, "For bullion issues, the dealer profit margin is very small—usually 1 percent to 5 percent."

To take this point to another realm, there is a reason that the regular issues—though classified as "bullion" strikes by the plurality of the marketplace—don't all sell for the same price. There are numerous Silver Eagle issues that are well recognized as scarce dates, and these pieces are duly in demand by collectors who are willing to pay premiums—sometimes substantial.

Insight on Pricing Dynamics for American Silver Eagles

Pricing within the space of the American Silver Eagle market is nuanced and complex—and is certain to throw for a loop those who believe pricing of these "bullion" coins is strictly based on silver value. While it is true that prevailing bullion values are a major influence on the more recent and common bullion strikes, this is not always the case with the scarcer issues and numismatic releases.

Those who follow the market will notice this when they turn to the pricing data in *A Guide Book of United States Coins*, which generally reflects retail values. Pricing for Silver Eagles of particular numismatic significance, such as key dates and Proofs, is usually based less on bullion trends alone and more on multiple market factors. CDN Publishing President and CEO John Feigenbaum describes some of the considerations that go into tracking market pricing for his company's wholesale and retail price guides. "The pricing mechanics as *Greysheet* reports them are based on live bids from market makers on CDN Exchange and auction data at major firms like Heritage Auctions, Stack's Bowers Galleries, David Lawrence Rare Coins, Legend Rare Coin Auctions, etc. *Greysheet* pricing follows and reflects the market levels as best as possible."

Patrick Ian Perez, who serves as vice president of data and content for CDN Publishing, elaborates on the pricing structure for the most collectible Silver Eagles. "I would say that the silver spot price is only incidentally influential in the pricing of numismatic Silver Eagles. Of course, the Mint factors in the prevailing spot price at time of issue, but other factors are much more important when it comes to aftermarket pricing. These factors include mintage, collector demand, and the state of the overall rare-coin market."

Perez says set building is the most important influence on the pricing of the key dates in the Silver Eagle series. "Each year that passes means that the earlier dates [1986 to 1996] become less available on the market in quantity because any significant amount is quickly absorbed by the wholesale market. Compared with a decade ago, in which there were only three or four dates people considered 'better,' I believe that we will get to a point eventually in which all the early [issues] trade for different prices based on scarcity."

Bullion dealer Troy Thoreson, a special consultant for the *Red Book*'s American Eagle pricing, recalls seeing numismatic premiums really escalate for older dates during the Great Recession, when many collectors and investors flocked to Silver Eagles amid rising bullion prices. "From late 2008 through 2011 silver demand started to increase, and this played a major role in the disappearance of older-year Uncirculated Silver Eagle dealer stock," he says. "Up until this time it was possible to travel the country and find pockets of Silver Eagle dealer stock where the dealer really didn't care if one was buying earlier-date Silver Eagles. The exception to this rule was the first-year issue and the 1996. In general, deals could be found in solid rolls of scarcer coins. Then when the big silver rush of 2011 happened, demand for anything silver skyrocketed. This silver rush took out many of the pockets of older Silver Eagles, therefore helping to start a healthy secondary market for older years. Future rushes for silver will continue to put pressure on supplies of these classic issues."

Getting The Best Deal for Your Money

How do you avoid getting ripped off and ensure you're paying a fair price for American Silver Eagles? Buy from a reputable dealer, be cognizant of current market pricing, and know what you're buying. In the previous section we discussed choosing a reputable coin dealer or precious-metals broker. Next is the issue of pricing: a subject that can get particularly complicated in the volatile metals markets.

The diverse American Silver Eagle market can be easily divided into five basic categories:

> **Commoditized Bullion Strikes**—All non-mintmarked bullion strikes in the American Silver Eagle series (with some exceptions; see the next bullet point). The most recent and most common issues see the lowest prices. Given the bullion-related facet of this series, pricing for common bullion strikes prevails with the winds of the precious-metals market and is expressed not by a fixed dollar amount, which is subject to change by the day or even the minute, but rather as "spot + $X.XX." The spot price is the full price of silver per ounce at the moment of sale, while the second half of the equation reflects a built-in premium, which may vary from dealer to dealer and often by date of the coin purchased.

Scarcer Bullion Strikes—Certain issues produced as normal bullion strikes sell for premiums well north of the "standard" price of a Silver Eagle, particularly the pre-2000 dates and especially the 1996 bullion strike, a relatively low-mintage issue that is widely regarded as the key bullion date. There tends to be some marketplace uniformity in pricing, especially for coins in the most actively traded grades. Also, none of the bullion strikes in grades lower than MS-69 are yet considered so scarce that they are outside the influence of the current silver price, which at the very least is a secondary factor in determining prices for more run-of-the-mill examples of these tougher dates.

Standard Numismatic Finishes—The standard Proofs, Reverse Proofs, Enhanced Reverse Proofs, Burnished examples, and other regular offerings are considered common and have a strong and active presence in the marketplace. Unless dealing with condition rarities (i.e., uncommonly high grades), which are more prevalent among the earlier dates, there are few surprises to be had when it comes to pricing. Premiums for numismatic coins are much higher over spot than for bullion, so this segment of the market is occupied mainly by collectors. That's not to say there aren't bullion investors looking for some "prettier" pieces to spice up their portfolio or, perhaps, buying such pieces as gifts for others or as mementos for themselves.

Ultra-Rarities, Errors, and Varieties—Large amounts of money are dropped very quickly in this sector of the Silver Eagle marketplace. Unlike the bullion issues and the more commonplace Silver Eagle collector formats, the special pieces draw big attention from collectors with deep pockets. Pricing rules may go out the window when fervent bidding between two or more hungry collectors is underway for a PF-70 Deep Cameo 1995-W American Silver Eagle. Ditto for the 2019-S Enhanced Reverse Proof and 2008-W, Burnished, Reverse of 2007, or any of the rare errors, the latter offering the least amount of marketplace pricing guidance given their relatively scant trading data.

Culls, Colorized, and Damaged Silver Eagles—Some of the best opportunities for retail buyers (collectors or investors) to score really good deals on American Silver Eagles will be found among the marketplace rejects, so to speak. Dealers are usually eager to unload their less-than-desirable material. When most of the marketplace wants blast-white American Silver Eagles, those that don't fit the bill move out of the sales case a little more slowly. Culls (pieces that are cleaned scratched, or otherwise damaged), colorized coins, spotted coins, and other misfits are frequently offered at prices very close to spot. Such deals may be most attractive to silver stackers or others who really don't care what their Silver Eagles look like. Collectors building low-ball sets—collections wherein the coins are at the lowest wear-based grade obtainable—may land some terrific finds with dealers who sell off-quality Silver Eagles.

Regardless of what you're buying, stay up to date with pricing and get a concept in mind as to what is fair. It can be difficult to make a judgement call in the case of bullion coinage, especially as precious-metals pricing fluctuates throughout the day and a spontaneous spike or drop in silver values could occur literally at the moment of your transaction. Keep an eye on the metals market on days you're purchasing American Silver Eagles and work with dealers whose pricing structures are fair and forthright.

Milk Spots, Fakes, and Phonies—Oh, My!

Some of the most common American Silver Eagle pitfalls, and how to overcome them, are addressed here.

MILK SPOTS

One of the biggest problems with American Silver Eagles is milk spots, so dubbed because they take the form of cloudy white splotches that commonly crop up on the surface of these silver coins. They may appear as a single small spot or as broad blotches across the entire surface. They are extremely problematic because they can begin to appear many years after a coin was minted and are very difficult to remove safely, if at all.

While reported on Silver Eagles of all finishes, milk spots are generally most prevalent on bullion issues. This may be of little concern to investors, stackers, and others who buy Silver Eagles primarily as bullion. However, it becomes a problem to the many numismatists who collect bullion strikes, and especially those who buy encapsulated versions grading MS-68, MS-69, or MS-70—where the presence of milk spots could nullify the labeled grades. This means evaporating value for collectors. As Scott Travers cautions buyers, "even if a holder has the MS-70 grade, look at the coin yourself. If it has white, milky-like stains or scratches visible with a five-power magnifying glass, I'd pass on the coin."

The problem has dogged collectors for years. In 2012 U.S. Mint Quality Division Chief Stacy Kelley-Scherer declared a thorough investigation into the cause of the milk spots, including the cleaning and brightening agents used to prepare the planchets, rinses used on the planchets during production, drying procedures, and other factors, including the planchets themselves.

Buyers are advised to avoid milk-spotted Silver Eagles.

West Point Mint chemist and chief assayer Jeanette Grogan says milk spots are "a latent defect," and she and her team test the coins to observe changes in the surface over days or weeks and will report the issue to vendors when samples begin showing spotting. She adds that spotting often doesn't show up until after the coins leave the

Examples of milk-spotted Silver Eagle obverses.

Mint, and sometimes the variable elements of how and where collectors store their coins may exacerbate the issue. Temperature, humidity, and chemicals in a coin holder can all play a role in when or if the spots show up and at what magnitude.

Examples of milk-spotted Silver Eagle reverses.

In addition to American Silver Eagles, milk spots have been found on U.S. commemorative coins and many other modern silver coins, and they're turning up on silver bullion coins from Australia, China, and Canada. Officials at the Royal Canadian Mint have said milk spotting can be traced back to the first silver Maple Leafs struck in 1988 but the source hasn't been identified, nor do they say anything can be done to prevent the issue.

Steve Feltner of PCGS said the problem has long plagued American Silver Eagles: "The best working theory has to do with the rinsing and annealing of the planchets prior to being struck, much like Peace dollars in the early 1920s. These planchets were bathed in a solution to remove any debris or imperfections before striking. Unfortunately, the planchets weren't properly rinsed afterwards to remove any of the solvents that remained on the surface, and the planchets were subsequently struck." He said that in some extreme cases coins must be called "environmentally damaged" due to the severity of the blotching; no numeric grade can be formulated.

"For the most part, milk spots cannot be removed by traditional conservation methods," Feltner commented. "It is the policy of Professional Coin Grading Service to formulate a grade for American Silver Eagles while taking spots into consideration. Obviously, any coin exhibiting a spot will not be in contention for a grade of 70—they must be inherently flawless to achieve this level. Most would be in the 69 or lower category based upon the location, amount, and severity of the spot(s)." He said if a coin begins to exhibit spots subsequent to grading, the guarantee does not cover this: "We guarantee the coin as it was seen while at PCGS, not what happens after it leaves our facility."

In a 2012 policy statement PCGS stated, "We have received Silver Eagles in sealed Mint boxes [the 500-ounce green "monster boxes"] and opened them to find coins that have already spotted. We have also graded spot-free coins, sent them to customers, and then had them returned to us months later after they had developed spots. There seems to be no rhyme or reason as to why some coins spot and some don't." Numismatic Guaranty Company offers similar sentiments on the matter, saying, "There is no known method to determine whether a modern silver coin will develop white spots, or how large these spots will be. Some modern silver coins never develop white spots. Others develop white spots immediately after they are struck. The development of white spots appears to be entirely unpredictable."

Both the major services will account for milk spotting on Silver Eagles already showing evidence of the blemishes. However, development of milk spots is not covered by either company's guarantees, as the situation is random and not the fault of either company's authenticating, grading, or encapsulation services. Both PCGS and NGC offer conservation and restoration services that aim to minimize the appearance of milk spots, but their complete removal isn't guaranteed, nor do they offer any way to completely prevent future spotting.

There are many collectors looking for a do-it-yourself option, a fact illustrated by the 16,500,000 results on Google for the phrase "remove white spots Silver Eagles." Pure acetone, a solution used for removing polyvinylchloride (PVC) damage from coins, has provided favorable results for some collectors but offers no guarantees. The somewhat more controversial technique of using silver dips to remove white spots can yield some success, though purists might consider these coins "cleaned" afterward.

Collectors should always avoid the temptation to use more abrasive agents, such as baking soda and toothpaste, for removing milk spots. While these harsher methods may work in removing the spots, they will impart minute hairlines, permanently damaging the coin's surfaces and decimating any numismatic premium.

Avoiding Counterfeits

There has never been a time when more counterfeit Silver Eagles were floating around than right now. "I know people who buy American Silver Eagles because they think they are safe—that there's no risk in buying these coins as opposed to rare ones, which they may think are more commonly counterfeited," remarks longtime ICG Senior Authenticator Randy Campbell. "But they're dead wrong." He has seen more counterfeit American Silver Eagles than he can count, with many turning up in the most surprising of places, including government packaging.

"I can't stress strongly enough that the counterfeit problems with Silver Eagles and other coins is worse than 98 percent or 99 percent of the people in the hobby think it is." Campbell noted that many buyers often have more confidence in their counterfeit-detecting skills than they should and that buying raw coins online, particularly from overseas markets, is "dangerous." He says there are ways to combat the dangers of buying counterfeit American Silver Eagles. "One way to stay safe is to buy slabbed coins. The other way is to educate yourself," remarked Campbell, who additionally serves as the education director for the Florida United Numismatists. "The info people need is available in states where coin collecting is popular," he said, referencing educational seminars held at coin shows. "Among these states are New York, Pennsylvania, California, Texas, and Florida," the latter being where Florida United Numismatists has held its major coin shows since the club's founding in 1955.

This counterfeit coin purports to be a 1986-S Proof American Silver Eagle, graded PF-70. The NGC holder is also counterfeited.

While many counterfeit American Silver Eagles might fool some new collectors, Steve Feltner said the bulk of these fakes have some giveaway features. "Most have a 'cartoonish' look and lack many of the fine details that are put into the genuine article by the U.S. Mint. Many exhibit more bubble-font numerical devices and lettering. Most are made out of a base metal, like copper, and then plated with silver to try and confuse individuals." He advises collectors and investors to check the weight and diameter of any Silver Eagles they're considering for purchase. "Comparing the design elements to known genuine examples is always a great first step. Using a non-invasive precious-metal detector like a Sigma or XRF gun can also be very useful, although expensive."

Says Doug Davis, director of anti-counterfeiting at the Anti-Counterfeiting Educational Foundation (ACEF), "One-ounce American Silver Eagles are one of the main U.S. coins being counterfeited and are flooding the U.S. marketplace."

He explains advanced designing, engraving, and minting technology is getting into the wrong hands. "Sophistication in counterfeit technology by counterfeiters increases daily and the quality can fool any level of numismatic experience if not carefully examined. Counterfeit coins and precious metals pose a significant threat to the numismatic industry," Davis says. They're popping up in the most seemingly benign of places, including coin shows, coin shops, and antique malls. Counterfeiters are also hawking their bogus "Silver Eagles" on fraudulent websites, various popular e-commerce and auction websites, and social media platforms.

Davis cautions buyers from being tempted by advertisements selling coins and precious metals at below-market prices. "Counterfeiters, organized groups or individuals who buy counterfeits in quantities from sites such as Alibaba, are looking for the easy target, such as the elderly or uneducated person in the area of coins and precious metals who is looking for an alternative investment venue."

The former law-enforcement officer of 30 years has helped bust many counterfeit operations, though he recalls some of the worst have involved thousands of fakes. "ACEF and the Anti-Counterfeiting Task Force (ACTF) assisted Customs and Border Protection in the seizure of over 5,000 counterfeit 'Silver Eagles' being shipped from China to a distributor in the Dallas–Fort Worth area. ACTF also assisted in the investigation of a case involving the purchase of 1,500 counterfeit 'Silver Eagles' from a fraudulent website located in the United Kingdom," Davis says.

He adds, "Based upon the current proliferation of counterfeits within the U.S. marketplace, investors and the general public should educate themselves about the coin and precious-metals business and buy only from established and professional dealers." Davis advises collectors and investors to buy their coins from a dealer affiliated with the Professional Numismatists Guild (PNG), a PNG-accredited precious-metals dealer, or a well-referenced local dealer.

This bogus material posing as numerous American Silver Eagles and an American Gold Eagle was purchased by a coin buyer and reported to the Anti-Counterfeiting Task Force, which intervened.

Counterfeit Expert Jack Young Reveals What to Look for with Fake Silver Eagles

Unfortunately, we can find counterfeits in practically every area of numismatics. As a member of a group of experts who spend a large part of their spare time looking for counterfeits, I see them every day! I actually enjoy researching, documenting, and reporting these threats to our hobby in an effort to make others aware of some of the things to look for when reviewing a coin to add to their collection; this includes one of the very popular series, the American Silver Eagle.

The following images showcase examples available to purchase in many of the current online selling venues, most listed as genuine "coins"!

This 2004-dated example is technically a "reproduction" with the word COPY stamped on the reverse. The concern is a buyer would receive one with the word omitted, making it a counterfeit. Even properly labeled, this one would violate eBay's stated coin-listing policy and would be removed when reported.

With COPY removed, there is still a pretty simple test for this one as a counterfeit. One of the fatal and common mistakes is the use of the wrong reverse as the model for examples dated 2007 and earlier, since the reverse style changed in 2008 as illustrated below:

The problematic 2004 shown here has the features of 2008!

Reverse of 2007

Reverse of 2008

The example on the following page, dated 2017, is an abomination when you really look at it.

This one clearly has a face only a mother could love! Once you get past the face, there are so many things wrong with this that comparing it to a genuine example is like looking through a *Where's Waldo?* book to find anything correct, although it did use the correct version of the reverse for its model.

While the following "2020" has a more convincing appearance, it used the 2007 reverse instead of the correct one for the date.

And a second "2020" example images the original box and holder to showcase the counterfeit.

The coin needs only to be compared to a genuine example to confirm any suspicion that it is a counterfeit.

As a researcher and author on the subject of counterfeit coins in our hobby, I cannot stress enough the importance of attributing any coin considered for purchase—compare the subject example with images of known genuine ones from any number of great internet sources. If it doesn't match, then more than likely, "Houston, we have a problem!"

6

Key Dates, Varieties, and Errors

American Silver Eagles may not be widely known for their rarities, but a deep dive into the series reveals numerous gems hiding in plain sight. The series offers keys, semi-keys, varieties, and errors. Some of these coins are expensive but readily obtainable, while others could take months or even years to track down. All are worthy, scarce, and valuable collectibles that prove a coin series long perceived as "bullion" or perhaps "semi-numismatic" to be a true numismatic principality.

In this chapter the most challenging and enigmatic issues will be examined in much greater detail, including their collectability, collecting strategies, and how they came to be some of the toughest coins in the American Silver Eagle series. Some pieces are familiar even to silver stackers and investors who may not be as keenly aware of the numismatic rarities in the series, while others have largely remained obscure except to the most seasoned of Silver Eagle specialists. Yet, all rightfully summon the attention of collectors and can help bolster the quality and scope of an American Silver Eagle collection.

KEY DATES

Virtually every series has its keys, and the American Silver Eagle series offers three indisputable contenders for that lofty title, each presenting its own challenges to collectors. These three key dates are the 1995-W Proof, the 1996 bullion issue, and the 2019-S Enhanced Reverse Proof. The most expensive of these is the 1995-W Proof, the lowest mintage among regular-issue bullion strikes is the 1996, and the overall lowest-mintage regular-issue entry is the 2019-S Enhanced Reverse Proof.

1995-W Proof

The 1995-W Proof American Silver Eagle is by far the most expensive, and one might dare say the most iconic, issue in the series. Ranking fourth in the *100 Greatest U.S. Modern Coins* (fourth edition) by Scott Schechter and Jeff Garrett, the 1995-W Proof Silver Eagle is in a class all by itself. As Schechter and Garrett remark, "The mystique and desirability of this coin have only grown over time. To say that the 1995-W is the 'key' to the series is an understatement." They go on to say that "Its value is nearly equal to that of all the other coins in the series combined. By any measure, the Proof American Silver Eagle program is more popular today than at any point in its past, which only continues to bolster demand for its king rarity, the 1995-W."

The 1995-W Proof American Silver Eagle became the first special-issue coin in the series, which up until 1995 had largely followed a formulaic production schedule of bullion strikes and Proofs either from the San Francisco Mint (1986 through 1992) or the Philadelphia Mint (beginning in 1993). Even the 1993 Philadelphia Mint Bicentennial Set does not include any novel Silver Eagles. It encompasses the regular-issue 1993-P Proof American Silver Eagle, regular-issue 1993-P Proof versions of the tenth-ounce through half-ounce American Gold Eagles, and a special .76-ounce, .900-fine silver commemorative medal illustrating a famous painting by John Ward Dunsmore of First Lady Martha Washington examining the first U.S. coinage. However, this special set does not contain any exclusive-production American Silver Eagle coinage (nor Gold Eagles, for that matter).

The 1995-W American Silver Eagle emerged as the key date of the series with a mintage of just 30,125 pieces.

The tenth anniversary of the American Eagle bullion coin series in 1995 inspired the creation of a special coin set honoring the occasion. The 1995 American Eagle 10th Anniversary Proof Set contains all four of the American Gold Eagles struck in Proof at the West Point Mint as well as a W-mint 1995 Proof American Silver Eagle—a special bonus included only with this set. As a *Washington Post* story noted of the tenth anniversary Proof set, it was priced at $999, which was the usual price of the four Proof American Gold Eagles, making the 1995-W Proof Silver Eagle a true bonus. That set and other special Mint offerings were released earlier in the year than usual, with hopes of spurring sales ahead of gift-giving holidays such as Mother's Day and Father's Day as well as graduations, weddings, and other events that occur during the summer months. "It makes real good business sense to make them available nine months of the year instead of two months," stated U.S. Mint director Philip Diehl in the story. "It's a shot in the dark for us," he continued.

While many 1995 U.S. Mint products saw high sales numbers, the nearly four-figure price tag for the anniversary set proved a big pill for most collectors to swallow, given that the year's average price for an ounce of gold was $385. Few collectors could ante up nearly $1,000 for this special set, leading the set to fall well below its production cap of 45,000 units. Most collectors wanting a 1995 American Silver Eagle opted for the more affordable P-mint version, which had an issue price of $23 and saw total sales of 438,511 pieces.

Hindsight being 20/20, collectors and investors who received sales fliers for the much-heralded tenth-anniversary set may now regret not scraping their proverbial pennies together at the time to buy one, given today's incredible desirability and astronomical cost of the 1995-W Proof American Silver Eagle. Mint director Philip Diehl had predicted the 1995-W Proof Silver Eagle might one day become a high-ticket collectible.

"I acknowledge that the $999 purchase price for the 10th anniversary set with the 1995-W Proof Silver Eagle seems high and that not every collector of Proof Silver Eagles can afford it," wrote Diehl in the June 26, 1995, issue of *Coin World*. "However, that price is more affordable than you might think. I've just finished scanning the 'buy prices' for 1994 American Eagle Proof gold coins in the coin market section of several numismatic publications. I see that collectors can, on average, sell unpackaged, individual Proof gold American Eagles in each of the four denominations to a dealer for $949. And that's an average resale price; by shopping around, you could do better than this." He reasoned that, "Using the $949 price as a guide, a single Proof Silver Eagle from the 1995 10th anniversary set has an effective price of $50 for collectors of eagles who buy the five-coin set and immediately sell the four gold coins to a dealer." Diehl concludes, "Other things being equal, a $50 effective price seems like a reasonable, reachable, and even tempting price for one of the lowest-mintage U.S. coins in this century."

As goes a famous internet meme starring actor Morgan Freeman, "He's right, you know." Anyone following Diehl's line of thinking as he couched it in that guest commentary spot would've made huge profits within mere months of buying a tenth-anniversary Proof set from the Mint. Diehl also makes a salient point regarding the low mintage of the 1995-W Silver Eagle. Relatively few regular-issue coins minted during the twentieth century saw lower mintages than the 1995-W Proof. Few other U.S. coins from the previous century, not including Proofs or varieties, even come close to the tiny mintage of the 1995-W. Some of the nearest competitors include the 1913-S Barber quarter, with a mintage of 40,000, and the 1916 Standing Liberty quarter, which yielded a production run of 52,000. Famous rarities of the period, including the 1916-D Mercury dime and 1901-S Barber quarter, witnessed much higher mintages of 264,000 and 72,664, respectively. The 1909-S V.D.B. Lincoln cent, another famous key date, was struck to the tune of 484,000 coins.

The 1909-S V.D.B. Lincoln cent was struck at the San Francisco Mint with the initials for designer Victor David Brenner. The coin is a popularly sought-after key date. Its low mintage of 484,000 is still much higher than that of the 1995-W Proof American Silver Eagle.

A raw 1995-W Proof American Silver Eagle is now worth multiples of the entire set's original issue price of $999. Coins grading PF-70 regularly take five-figure prices, with the all-time record registering at an astounding $86,654.70 in a March 31, 2013, Great-Collections online auction. That price, notched for a coin encapsulated by PCGS and grading PF-70 Deep Cameo, was one of the few certified at that level by any of the services. Prices have since softened for PF-70 coins as more have surfaced. However, as the flow of fresh PF-70 examples slows in the years ahead, and should the scarce coin see greater demand as the number of collectors grows, values could rise once again.

1996 Bullion Strike

The undisputed key date among bullion Silver Eagles, the 1996 issue is a challenging coin. An honoree in the *100 Greatest U.S. Modern Coins* book, it claims the lowest mintage figure among all regular-issue bullion Silver Eagles, and its output of just

3,603,386 pieces marks the nadir of the bullion strikes. As with virtually all Silver Eagle bullion strikes, mintage is a direct reflection of demand, and in the mid-1990s many regular customers were backing off from buying U.S. Mint products—most notably due to an overwhelming number of offerings at the time.

In 1995 and 1996 the Mint released to the public a cumulative 46 different commemorative coins (including Uncirculated and Proof variants). Most of these belonged to the two-year commemorative program honoring the 1996 Summer Olympics held in Atlanta, Georgia. The Olympiad inspired the creation of 16 distinct commemoratives, including different designs among four clad half dollars, eight silver dollars, and four gold half eagles. These, along with other commemoratives themed around Civil War battlefields, Special Olympics, national community service, and the Smithsonian Institution, simply over-whelmed collectors and dealers. Proof-set and Mint-set sales also lagged somewhat around this same time.

The Olympic coins were offered individually, but collectors wanting the entire series found it far more cost effective to buy the entire kit and caboodle as a 32-piece set that, packaged in a locking wooden presentation case, was offered at a price of $2,261.

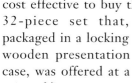

The 1996 is a key date among the bullion strikes.

The massive 1995–1996 Olympic commemorative set from the U.S. Mint involves 32 coins and had an original issue price of more than $2,200.

A thicker U.S. Mint catalog during the mid-1990s may put in better perspective why the 1996 Silver Eagle and, perhaps to a lesser extent, the 1995-W Proof saw relatively light sales. However, this reasoning alone dismisses another key factor in the scant sales, and that has to do with the relatively stable silver bullion prices of the mid-1990s.

While younger or newer collectors may be accustomed to great volatility in the bullion markets as we have witnessed in recent years, there was a time in the 1990s when silver and gold didn't see those kinds of drastic swings. Consider the price of silver during the period from December 1993 to November 1997, when silver had a low monthly average of $4.49 (July 1997) and a high monthly average of $5.79 (March 1994). Bluntly, silver was not an exciting commodity in the mid-1990s.

There were always silver investors, but the white metal wasn't inspiring many people to "buy the dips" in the mid-1990s, especially when silver had just come off a decades-long low of $3.59 in February 1993 and there were still plenty of folks who recalled the sting of the bullion crash of the early 1980s. Who knew that in the next decade of the 2000s silver would rocket to the stars again, this time with sustainable and persistent growth? Suffice it to say, those who bought silver in the mid-1990s and held it until 2008, 2009, or later did well for themselves, but there was little compelling buyers to stock up on new Silver Eagles in 1996.

Today the low-mintage 1996 Silver Eagle is a highly desirable coin—one that dealers typically sell for huge premiums. But mintage and price aren't necessarily what make this Silver Eagle so tough. It's quality issues that can thwart the buyer. Many 1996 bullion strikes exhibit varying degrees of irreversible and unsightly milk spotting, which might make buyers apprehensive—especially if buying an example that does not (presently) reveal this hazy imperfection. As with any coin, buy the best examples you can afford. There are thousands in MS-69 but only a fraction thereof grading MS-70, and those pieces easily snatch four-figure prices.

2019-S Enhanced Reverse Proof

If any American Silver Eagle had the wherewithal to unseat its kingly 1995-W Proof brethren from the throne, it would be the 2019-S Enhanced Reverse Proof. Released at noon on November 14, 2019, it was issued at $65.95 with a production limit of just 30,000 pieces. Virtually all 30,000 pieces sold out within 15 minutes under a strict guideline of one coin per household. The U.S. Mint website was buzzing, as were the Mint's customer-service phone lines. Meanwhile, at the Whitman Baltimore Expo lines had begun forming around 2:30 the morning of the coin's release; many of these folks were paid by dealers to stand in line and buy the coin for a tidy reward if they in turn sold the coin back to the dealer.

Such scenes had become familiar to hobbyists, with the U.S. Mint coordinating the release of some major items during the landmark coin shows. Mint representatives have been setting up shop at these shows with the anticipation of selling thousands of coins to eager customers awaiting the release of a much-publicized new coin. In many cases, these special releases fizzle out in the secondary market as demand for the new coin wanes.

Yet, the 2019-S Enhanced Reverse Proof Silver Eagle was a different story. To be sure, some of the incredible demand for this coin was coming from speculators looking to flip the coin for a quick buck; within hours, examples of the 2019-S Enhanced Reverse

Proof were selling on eBay for $1,000, with mass promoters offering First Strike and Early Release examples grading PF-70 for more than $2,000. However, a major segment of the marketplace for this coin stemmed from collector demand. Here was a Silver Eagle that would genuinely become the lowest-mintage issue in the entire series.

Incredibly, the 2019-S Enhanced Reverse Proof managed to retain the vast majority of its peak secondary market value. Today this coin trades in PF-69 for around $1,050, with PF-70 examples fetching closer to $2,500. Although these are remarkable prices for an American Silver Eagle, these still fall significantly short of the 1995-W Proof, which has a floor price of around $3,000, even in PF-65.

As the 1995-W Proof and 2019-S Enhanced Reverse Proof show, some U.S. Mint products not only hold their value after they are released but in fact climb to astronomical heights. However, many limited-edition items, even those that sell out in mere minutes or hours—as seems to be common these days—tend to soften in value after their prices peak in the secondary market. Jeff Garrett says that when it comes to buying certain challenging American Silver Eagles, patience is key: "Many of the

Only 29,909 2019-S Enhanced Reverse Proof American Silver Eagles were minted, even lower than the 1995-W Proof.

limited-edition coins are fiercely fought over when they are sold by the U.S. Mint with household limits. Often, the coins soar in value in the days and weeks after release. If you were not able to buy the coin from the Mint in the initial release, it is often more prudent to wait for prices to settle down in the after-market before jumping in."

Should the 2019-S Enhanced Reverse Proof be crowned as "the" series key? The verdict is still out. With a mintage differential between the 1995-W Proof and 2019-S Enhanced Reverse Proof of just 216 pieces, the 2019 rarity has a small but technically sound edge. But it's difficult to see hearts changing on the status of the 1995-W as the "King of American Silver Eagles."

SEMI-KEY AND SCARCE DATES

While the series boasts a trinity of keys, semi-key dates also keep collectors occupied as they build their sets. These include:

1986 Bullion—This first-year-of-issue Silver Eagle has been atop collectors' wish lists since the beginning of the series. With its mintage of 5,393,005 now among the 10 lowest for the bullion strikes, this date usually commands notable premiums regardless of grade.

1994 Bullion—The 1994 bullion strike has a mintage of 4,227,319 and has emerged in recent years as a desirable date. It is also a condition rarity that offers few certified coins in a "perfect" numismatic grade. Small surface blemishes usually keep this coin from reaching a 70, though there are tens of thousands in MS-69.

1994-P Proof—With its mintage of 372,168, the 1994-P Proof is one of the scarcest regular-issue Proofs in the American Silver Eagle series. It is listed in *100 Greatest U.S. Modern Coins*, which says this issue "has emerged as a key date, often more difficult to locate than the 2006-W Reverse Proof issue, and therefore it can also be more expensive."

2006-P Reverse Proof—Issued in the U.S. Mint's three-coin 20th Anniversary Silver Eagle set, the 2006-P Reverse Proof has a small mintage of 248,875 and holds a special allure as the first Reverse Proof of the series. Ranking 31st in *100 Greatest U.S. Modern Coins*, it is noted to have a "look so distinctive within the series that the Reverse Proof will always be a curious standout among Silver Eagles."

2006-W Burnished—The first of the so-called Burnished Silver Eagles, this 2006-W piece has few obvious surface distinctions from the regular bullion-strike 2006 Silver Eagle except for the presence of the "W" mintmark. Only 468,020 examples were struck, making this a scarcer entry in the series. Ranked 64th in *100 Greatest U.S. Modern Coins*, the 2006-W Burnished Silver Eagle has enjoyed continued popularity with collectors.

2011-S Burnished—Just 99,882 examples of this special S-mint Silver Eagle rolled off the presses at the San Francisco Mint. It was issued exclusively in the five-coin 25th Anniversary Silver Eagle Set. The coin, placing 47th in *100 Greatest U.S. Modern Coins*, is coveted by collectors as the only Uncirculated S-mintmarked Silver Eagle in the series to date.

2011-P Reverse Proof—Another issue unique to the 25th Anniversary Silver Eagle Set is the 2011-P Reverse Proof American Silver Eagle, which saw a mintage of 100,000. As with the 2011-S Burnished Silver Eagle, the 2011-P Reverse Proof is ranked 18th in *100 Greatest U.S. Modern Coins* and sees buoyant demand in the collector community.

2012-S Reverse Proof—Only issued in a special two-coin 2012 San Francisco Proof Set, this Reverse Proof saw a mintage of 224,935 pieces and became a collector favorite due to its low mintage and distinctive appearance. It is ranked 87th in *100 Greatest U.S. Modern Coins*.

2013-W Enhanced Uncirculated—This first-of-its-kind Uncirculated coin broke the mold with its tri-level finish, including brilliant, lightly frosted, and heavily frosted details. Sold in a two-piece set with the 2013-W Reverse Proof American Silver Eagle, the 2013-W Enhanced Uncirculated issue saw a mintage of 281,310 and is sought by collectors for its novel finish and overall scarcity.

2020-W Privy Mark—This special West Point release includes a seldom-seen privy mark, a small marking that incorporates a special design and lettering, on the obverse. This privy mark includes the alphanumeric characters "V75" to honor the 75th anniversary of the Allied victory in World War II in 1945. The outline of the privy mark mimics the shape of the Rainbow Pool at the World War II Memorial in Washington, D.C. The coin saw a production limit of 75,000 and quickly sold out upon its release on November 5, 2020.

AMERICAN SILVER EAGLE DIE VARIETIES

Varieties are extremely uncommon in the realm of American Silver Eagles, whose dies are meticulously cut and carefully prepared for use in production. Yet, a few notable varieties have been reported over the years and include the following:

1992-S, Doubled Die Reverse

Hub doubling is evident in the mintmark, stars, and the word SILVER. The spread is considered medium, and this piece is notable for being the first reported Silver Eagle with hub doubling evident in the mintmark.

The 1992-S, Doubled Die Reverse, shows notable spread on the word SILVER, the stars, and "S" mintmark.

2008-W, Burnished, Reverse of 2007

Listed in *100 Greatest U.S. Modern Coins*, this is the most significant and widely collected of Silver Eagle varieties. It arose when old dies that had been hubbed during usage of the traditional Janvier reducing machinery were inadvertently paired with the 2008 obverse, which was supposed to be paired with a new die reflecting changes related to the Mint's new digital engraving procedures. The key diagnostic is found on the reverse in the font for the "U" of UNITED, which shows the curved "U" seen on the 1986–2007 reverse instead of a "U" with a little stem on the bottom right, as seen from 2008 to 2021. This exciting transitional variety spawned an estimated 47,000 examples, and many collectors don't consider their sets of American Silver Eagles complete without one.

The 2008-W, Reverse of 2007, is the most significant die variety in the American Silver Eagle series.

2011 Bullion, Doubled Die Obverse

This doubled-die variety shows strong thickness across many obverse features, including the date, the stars in the flag, the motto IN GOD WE TRUST, and the skirt, flag, and feet of Miss Liberty. The discovery was made by collector Wayne Perry, who found this doubled die in a 25th Anniversary Silver Eagle Set and reported it to variety expert Dr. James Wiles.

Thickness is seen in the date and motto IN GOD WE TRUST
as well as in the stars in Miss Liberty's flag and her feet and skirt.

ERROR HIGHLIGHTS

NGC grading finalizer David Camire says most of the mint errors that collectors will come across on the American Eagle coins are struck-through errors: "The majority of these involve grease, lint, or plastic. Most are small fragments of a couple millimeters in length or less." He notes, "Larger struck-through errors that are very noticeable, covering an area of the coin, are far scarcer and demand a good premium over a normal coin. Of these coins, they can be found with or without the debris struck into the coin. On rarer occasions, there can be a progression set where a bunch of coins will show an area of struck-through, ending with the actual debris being struck into the last coin."

Camire says errors that are far less frequently encountered on the American Silver Eagle include die cracks, misaligned dies, clashed dies, and die-adjustment strikes. "We have seen only a handful of all these coins, and all have been relatively minor. The two exceptions are a run of 2016 Silver Eagles that have very strong clashed dies and a run of die-adjustment strikes around the same time frame," he says. The rarest Silver Eagle errors, Camire says, are curved clips and multi-struck coins: "All the curved, clipped planchets that we have seen are very minor in nature and do not exceed more than 5 percent. The multi-struck coins, for the most part, have been in-collar double strikes that show a double height to the edge reeding and occasional doubling of the design elements. Since the production of Silver Eagles has become almost fully automated, over time, these types of errors rarely get out."

In 2013 *Coin World* ran a story on an impressive 1998 American Silver Eagle that was struck on a planchet intended for a commemorative silver dollar. The coin, discovered by a West Coast collector, was evaluated by error expert Fred Weinberg, who found the coin weighed 26 to 27 grams—right in line with the 26.73-gram standard planchet weight of a traditional silver dollar. PCGS, which encapsulated the coin, confirmed the coin weighs 26.7 grams—significantly less than the standard weight of an American Silver Eagle, which tips the scales at 31.103 grams.

Error dealer Jon Sullivan eventually tracked this coin down and sold it to a client for $50,000. "While this is a high price for any error, the coin is the only known wrong-planchet error for the entire silver American Eagle series, making it a highly desirable coin and something that any serious collector would love to own," he wrote in a 2015 *Coin World* guest commentary. "Whoever found the coin originally made an incredible cherrypick, and certainly a large profit!"

Sullivan, a foremost expert on the subject of American Silver Eagles, delineated the types of errors that a collector is most likely to find in the series, as he explains in the following section.

Struck-Through Errors

This runs the gamut of struck-through grease and small pieces of clear plastic (the plastic, I believe, is used to cover the dies during storage to prevent contamination, rust, etc., and is removed for striking the coins). If some sticks to the die, you get a strike-through.

A surprising number of Silver Eagles have the plastic retained in them, so this plastic has a problem with "sticking" to the dies. Other strike-through types include colored pieces of plastic and bits of wire (possibly from wire brushes or from the descaling brushes used for cleaning planchet strips). Strike-throughs with small, unknown struck-through areas are very common on Silver Eagles. The larger the strike-through, the more valuable the error, and if the strike-through object is retained, the coin will be worth typically three to ten times more than if the item fell away. Building a collection of strike-through errors by year is very doable, although some dates and mints would be scarce.

Partial-Collar Strikes

These coins were struck only partially within the collar die, and the strike causes the planchet to expand beyond its normal diameter where it fails to meet the collar die. The result is an edge with reeding around only part (usually about half) of the edge.

These are scarce but are known for probably all dates of Silver Eagle bullion strikes. Special surface issues, special mintmark issues, and Proof issues are very rare with partial collars. These are usually worth around $1,000, give or take. For most years, there are probably five to eight known for the date, though these errors are more common in some dates than others.

Misaligned Dies

These are coins with one die slightly misaligned. This error type looks like a minor off-center strike at a glance, but the difference is that the coin will usually have a fully struck, reeded edge (sometimes this error type is in conjunction with partial collars) and will almost always have a properly aligned reverse. Misaligned dies almost always occur on the obverse side for Silver Eagles. These are typically worth somewhere in the hundreds of dollars.

Laminations

Sometimes impurities get into the planchet metal, causing the metal to flake or small pieces to fall off. This is a lamination, an error that occurs when impurities get into the metal as it is refined or rolled out. Planchets of precious metals such as silver are carefully made so that the metal is free of impurities. As a result, laminations are typically minor on Silver Eagles. A major example would be worth a large premium, but minor laminations are worth a few hundred dollars.

Struck-Through Sanding Discs

These are really neat items and have not received the publicity they deserve, in my opinion. I have bought and sold probably 50 or so of the Silver Eagles struck on sanding discs. These discs are emery paper and were apparently used, according to a press worker as told to me secondhand, for keeping the Silver Eagle planchets in 1986 and 1987 from sticking to the dies during striking. This, he said, was because of new technology being used in creating the Silver Eagle dies, which caused the surfaces of the dies to frequently "stick" to the planchets.

The press worker said the Mint tried numerous things, before finally figuring out that occasionally running a particular grit of emery paper through the press would keep the dies from sticking. This problem was corrected in 1987 and the Mint no longer used the emery paper, which is why you only find these struck pieces of emery paper on 1986 and 1987 Silver Eagles. I'd estimate there are around 100 to 150 discs in existence, including 1986, 1987, and "reverse" Silver Eagles. All dates and the reverses are probably equally rare.

There are probably three to five sets of Silver Eagles known with the emery discs struck in and retained. Examples struck on emery discs (you will see them alternately described as "sanding discs" or "emery discs," but both refer to the same thing) typically sell for $800 to $2,000. Coins with the disc retained typically sell in the $10,000 to $20,000 range.

Clips

Very rare, with existing examples typically being so minor that they only effect the rim. These are rare because the Mint puts great care into making sure the coins are of "full weight," since they are valued for their precious-metal content. Depending on the size of the clip (the larger, the more valuable), these sell for $500 to $1,500.

Clashed Dies

There are not many clashed dies known for Silver Eagles. For the year 2016, there were a number found, and there are at least many dozens of them existing. Clashed dies occur when there is no planchet between the dies, causing the dies to collide directly with each other, and so imparting some of the design detail from one die to the other. Coins struck from these dies will have portions of design details from the opposing die on them. Such clashed dies typically sell for around $750 to $1,500, depending on the grade and how strong the clash marks are.

Other American Silver Eagle Errors

The above isn't an exhaustive list of the kinds of errors you may encounter on American Silver Eagles. Other types range from minor to major, less expensive to quite lofty in price. They may include indents, blank planchets, and other anomalies. The bottom line? Don't assume all Silver Eagles are perfect, and be on the lookout for prime cherry-picking opportunities!

Indent errors are some of the rare, infrequently seen errors on American Silver Eagles that can be worth many hundreds of dollars.

7

A New Generation of American Silver Eagles

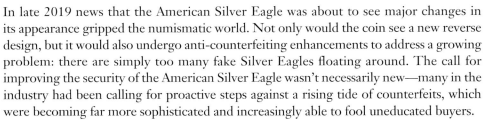

In late 2019 news that the American Silver Eagle was about to see major changes in its appearance gripped the numismatic world. Not only would the coin see a new reverse design, but it would also undergo anti-counterfeiting enhancements to address a growing problem: there are simply too many fake Silver Eagles floating around. The call for improving the security of the American Silver Eagle wasn't necessarily new—many in the industry had been calling for proactive steps against a rising tide of counterfeits, which were becoming far more sophisticated and increasingly able to fool uneducated buyers.

There was ample discourse on changing the American Silver Eagle reverse as the design was reaching its 25th year in production in 2011. As John Mercanti, designer of the original reverse, remarked about the possible replacement of his heraldic eagle, "I figured it was a matter of time before they did something with that."

The Citizens Coinage Advisory Committee (CCAC) acknowledged the pivotal 25-year anniversary, which signals when a U.S. coin design can be changed without congressional approval, in its 2009 annual report, stating:

In 2011, the current design of the American Eagle Silver Bullion Coin will have been in use for 25 years. Recognizing an opportunity to advance efforts to pursue a renaissance in the design of U.S. coinage, the CCAC recommends the American Eagle Silver Bullion Coin be redesigned within the requirements of the coin's original enacting legislation, Public Law 99-61. This statute requires an obverse design symbolic of Liberty and a reverse design of an eagle. In an effort to create continuity between the obverse and reverse designs selected for this coin, the CCAC further recommends that the design selection process focus on selecting obverse and reverse designs created by the same artist.

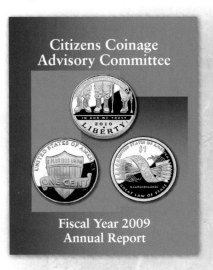

The U.S. Mint redesigned the American Silver Eagle in 2021, giving it a new reverse and slightly modified obverse as well as enhancing it with anti-counterfeiting elements.

The topic was formally brought to the fore by the CCAC in its April 2014 meeting, where members had a chance to review various eagle-themed designs that had been proposed in recent years, including several that had been proposed, but not accepted, for the 2015 U.S. Marshals Service 225th anniversary commemorative coin program.

TALKING UP THE NEW AMERICAN SILVER EAGLE REVERSE

What follows are snippets of key CCAC meeting minutes concerning the proposal for and approval of the American Silver Eagle redesign. Complete CCAC transcripts can be read at www.ccac.gov/calendar/notices.html.

April 8, 2014, CCAC Meeting Transcript Highlights

Before the April 8, 2014, CCAC meeting, 44 design candidates had been winnowed down to 16, which were considered by the panel. Text is condensed and in some places lightly edited for clarity.

CCAC Member Erik Jansen: [J]ust as the reverse of the penny was changed in the anniversary of Lincoln, just as the ongoing features of the quarter have always been considered substantial, the portrait of George Washington, here we have something a little different and more special, in a way, than a circulating coin. We have a bullion coin, a bullion coin which carries the sovereign assay, the assurance, I don't know if it's a legal term, the guarantee, represented by the reputation of the U.S. government that this coin is in fact the purity and the metallic content that it is advertised to be. [. . .] This coin circulates worldwide. And over a long period of time stays in possession of a store of wealth. This is a bullion coin, and so I believe it must demonstrate and show the very, very core of what this country stands for. And if a picture's worth a thousand words, and we have a few words that have to be on there by statute, the picture is what people will remember. What it makes them feel, what it makes them emote, what it makes them sense, what it makes them believe about this country. [. . .] This is an iconic, iconic production of the U.S. Mint and I'm just pleased that we're going to take the time to review some really quality art and see if the committee believes it's of the caliber to be considered.

Design 1.

Design 10.

Design 16.

Design 18.

Design 19.

Design 22.

Design 23.

Design 24.

Design 25.

Design 30.

CCAC Member Michael Bugeja: I just wanted to point out something numismatic that I hope will inform the process of our selection. By the very nature of choosing the eagles from various coin proposals, we're going to get a number of different types of eagles. [. . .] There are four types of eagles that we find at this posed selection. [. . .] One is a stylized eagle. [. . .] The other would be a personified eagle, you would see that on Number 1. It's an eagle holding lightning. It's personified and those typically are not very well thought out for a coin. The third is just a bird, a bird flying [. . .] They would not be appropriate for the reverse of a coin. And then the rest are symbols. Those are what we often find on the reverse of coins and have found since the beginning of coinage by the U.S. Mint. And that is not a bird, it's not a drawing, it's not an animation, it's a symbol of power, a symbol of peace, something that would go on the reverse of one of America's most popular bullion pieces. We have one right now on the reverse that is a symbol. [. . .] And it was heartening to see that the committee was drawn to symbols.

CCAC Member Michael Olson: This is certainly the coin of the realm, for folks that are selecting and building up their stellar reserve. [. . .] My belief is this is a flagship coin for the United States and therefore it needs to demonstrate the strength and majesty and greatness of the United States. [. . .] I would prefer to see more emphasis on the eagle, less emphasis on shields and other devices. My belief is that the eagle should occupy as much real estate on the reverse of this coin as possible. It needs to be a bold eagle, a strong eagle, as it is the representation of our country and all that's good about our country.

Design 36.

Design 38.

Design 39.

Design 40.

Design 41.

Design 44.

CCAC Member Jeanne Stevens-Sollman: I first of all want to comment on Erik's introduction, which I think was very inclusive and very thoughtful. Thank you, Erik, for stating those thoughts for us all. I had been thinking we need to make this coin be fully fantastic in the eyes of the world, as well as in the eyes of our own people and collectors. And for that reason, my top pick was 41.

CCAC Chairperson Gary Marks: Thank you, Jeanne. I think I'm going to go ahead and offer my comments here. I, too, am very favorable to number 41. And I guess I'll talk about a couple things that we haven't really touched on yet. One is the pairing. That is, how does the design picked pair up with Adolph Weinman's Walking Liberty image, which of course is on the obverse. I believe this eagle that's represented on 41 is a beautiful pairing.

Heidi Wastweet, an artist and sculptor from California, was a member of the CCAC from 2010 to 2018.

CCAC Member Heidi Wastweet: I think that we are headed in the right direction, and we clearly have a favorite. I would like to see a couple variations of Number 41. The thing that strikes me about this is, the beak is a little crowded towards the edge of the coin. I'd like to see a little more breathing room around the eagle. And in looking at the existing design that we have, it has an olive branch, it could be laurel, I think it's olive and arrows. I would be open to adding some arrows next to the branch [in design 41], as it symbolically stays in line with what we already have, sending the message of strength and peace, as part of our national goal.

CCAC Member Donald Scarinci: I think I'd be pretty happy, I'd be pretty excited if we didn't have to have the olive branch with Number 41, and I'm certainly very interested in a lot of the comments that have been made so far in this discussion. We always tend to look at things differently after we hear each other speak, than we do prior to getting together, whether it's in a meeting or a phone call. [. . .] I'm hearing people liking the olive branch, I just don't. I wish it was just an eagle.

Marks: Thank you, Donald. Donald, I would suggest that if we do indeed go ahead with a recommendation for 41, given your feelings about the olive branch, we make a motion and that would give the committee a chance to discuss your specific concern there.

Jansen: I see a train leaving for 41 and I'm really sad about that, quite frankly. I think that is cutting short this process. I think this process needs to highlight our first, second, third, fourth, or a basket of four ideas, maybe in order of preference. But I would encourage you, when you vote try not to vote to make a single selection, but vote so as to show a series of preferences, because today is not the end of this process, today is the beginning of a sacred review here. If I dare use the word sacred, I'll replace that with sovereign. [. . .] Now, this is a large coin. This is not a dime, this is not a penny, this is not a nickel, this is not a quarter, this is a large design. Today and in the future, I'm going to up the charge to the sculptor that inherits the charge to sculpt whatever design we end up with in the weeks or months ahead. Because I would feel really, really, really let down if we got the bird-feather equivalent of "Spaghetti Hair" here [referring to Mint engraver William Cousins's retooling of George Washington's hairstyle on the quarter dollar in 1999]. I look at Design 40 and 41—those aren't feathers, those are scales. [A lot of these designs, if] these are sculpted in a way to maximize die life and throw away artistic intent, I am going to be very, very, very disappointed. And I will encourage the public audience to weigh in on that issue.

Mint sculptor-engraver Don Everhart (left) and Citizens Coinage Advisory Committee senior member Donald Scarinci discussing coin designs.

We all hated Spaghetti Hair, and it was listened to and changed on the America the Beautiful Washington quarter, and that Washington image is gorgeous, again, as it was in '32, when it was originally designed, sculpted, and implemented. And so I'm going to put the charge out there, to the sculptors to use relief and sculpt detail and not Photoshop this stuff. If we've got to strike 50 million of these a year, quite frankly I think it would be tragic to say, "No more than 500 dies, guys" and require that they get 100,000 strikes per die. I just think that is a misplacement of this country's sacred integrity and trust in the world. I feel pretty strongly about that. I don't like Item 41. It was part of my list, because I was one of these that submitted preferences. Forty-one, the beak is crowded, that could be fixed. The leading edge of the olive branch, there is no way an eagle is going to carry an olive branch, in the wind, and have the leading edge of that olive branch look like that. Ain't gonna happen. He's not going to grab the olive branch that way. The leading edge would be blown back in the wind, so that needs to be corrected, if it's included. Adding arrows, it's certainly more consistent with the historical presence of eagles and talons. I think this thing looks European, 1910 to me, and that's not America, 2014. So, 41 would barely make my list. And I'm going to ask you guys to please reconsider jumping on 41 as you think the train is leaving the station.

CCAC Member Thomas Uram: I look at it and say, "What's the upside of changing an already successful design, number one?" And we've heard some of that in [Gary Marks's] opening remarks, as well as Erik's in regards to the stability of the bullion piece. It's recognized and importantly has international acceptance. So, from my opinion, and the comments that I'm going to make in regards to the designs here, would be related to the Proof version, if we go down the row. I'm totally against any kind of change in the bullion coin as it stands. I think it represents exactly what we want it to represent. And it reminds me of Coca-Cola wanting to change their taste. I think we've got the best coin and I think if we change it, I haven't found our upside yet. Now, having said that, on the Proof, we have an anniversary of this coin coming in 2016. In 2016, when we have the 30th year, a couple things. I thought a high relief of the coin would be an outstanding compliment to the other metal techniques that the Mint has used in the past anniversaries. And that would be the ideal time to change, from a collector's point of view, unlike the bullion point of view. Collectors might like to see something different in 2017.

After more than an hour of discussion, the CCAC motioned to recommend Design 41 to the U.S. Mint for review by its artists, with consideration to the concerns about the design as raised by some committee members. Any design revisions offered by the Mint would be reviewed by the CCAC and undergo an approval process, with input and feedback from the U.S. Commission of Fine Arts. As history now shows, this proposal never gained traction and John Mercanti's heraldic eagle reverse remained intact on the American Silver Eagle for several more years.

CCAC Chair Gary Marks Remembers the 2014 Discussion

Q. *How long had the idea of changing the American Silver Eagle reverse been in the works before a formal announcement, and who was involved in proposing this idea for debate?*

A. When I became the CCAC chairperson in 2010, my overarching goal for the committee was to spur the Mint toward design excellence for the nation's coins and medals. I figured a great place to start would be with the American Silver Eagle, the flagship coin of the U.S. Mint. I made the first public remarks on this subject at the March 1, 2011, CCAC meeting as part of a discussion on the committee's 2009 annual report. I informed the committee that the Act of September 26, 1890 (Federal Code Section 3510), allows designs on U.S. coins to be changed every 25 years without a specific act of Congress. I pointed out that the American Silver Eagle was first introduced in 1986, making 2011 the 25th year of the design.

The committee unanimously supported adding a recommendation in our 2009 annual report to redesign the obverse and reverse of the American Silver Eagle. The recommendation was included in each subsequent annual report through 2014. Unfortunately, the recommendation went nowhere at the Mint. We were told the Treasury Department did not want to tinker with the designs of this very popular and recognizable bullion and numismatic coin. There was no mention of counterfeiting concerns at that time. The evening of March 10, 2014, I was enjoying dinner with a few other CCAC members. We discussed the candidate designs that we had been provided from the Mint for the U.S. Marshals Service 225th Anniversary Commemorative Coin Program. We were slated to discuss these designs at the CCAC meeting the next day. We all agreed that design USM-G-R-11 of a flying American bald eagle was exceptional. (We would later learn the design was the work of the Mint's Artistic Infusion artist Paul Balan.) It was beautiful and uncluttered, with an elegant and dignified presence reminiscent of classic U.S. coin designs from the early 1900s. I suggested to the others that Balan's design would be perfect to pair with Adolph Weinman's classic Liberty Walking obverse design on the American Silver

Paul C. Balan's design for the reverse of the U.S. Marshals Service $5 gold piece—a design highly praised by the CCAC and recommended in 2014 for the American Silver Eagle.

Eagle. The others agreed. Based on that discussion, we agreed to *not* select it for the Marshals program. The members at dinner agreed to talk with other committee members ahead of the next day's meeting to ask them to join us in avoiding any recommendation to use the Balan flying American eagle design for the Marshals program. Instead, I would use my statutory authority as the committee chair to call a special meeting to potentially recommend the Balan design as a new reverse for the American Silver Eagle; this despite Treasury's ongoing resistance to our previous recommendations to redesign the American Silver Eagle.

Balan's flying eagle found a perch not of silver, but of gold—on the reverse of the 2015 American Liberty High Relief $100 gold coin, as sculpted by Don Everhart.

The next morning I gaveled the meeting to order and immediately announced the committee would hold a special meeting on April 8 to consider a recommendation to change the reverse of the $1 Silver Eagle coin. Subsequently and leading up to the special meeting, I asked Mint staff to assemble a portfolio of eagle designs that had been proposed but not used for various coin programs dating back to 2008. The resulting 44-design portfolio would serve to give the committee the opportunity to review other eagle designs in addition to the Balan design. I wanted any recommendation to withstand the comparative scrutiny of the committee. But I was fairly sure a clear majority would agree that Balan's design should be the recommended design. I was correct. The committee concluded the April 8 meeting with a unanimous vote to recommend the Balan design. The committee took the idea of changing the ASE design very seri-

CCAC Chair Gary Marks.

ously. One does not change the design of such an iconic coin without first finding designs that attain a very high standard of excellence. The committee felt Balan's design gave us an opening that could appropriately complement the Weinman obverse, so we made our move. But, as history records, the Treasury was not impressed, and no change happened.

Q. *Was the obverse design ever in play for a redesign, or was it deemed untouchable?*

A. Yes, it was in play initially. The committee's annual reports for 2009 through 2014 all recommended a redesign for both the obverse and reverse. But the Treasury Department's resistance to those recommendations made it clear that a wholesale change of both sides of the coin was simply not going to happen. When the Balan design was presented to us, we saw a chance to present a less-threatening option for the Mint and Treasury to consider. The beloved Weinman design would be preserved and would be paired with a stunning eagle reverse. It seemed like a potential way to make a positive change.

Q. *What are your thoughts on the passage of several years between the time the reverse redesign came up in 2014 for debate and the eventual redesign in 2021?*

A. In the aftermath of the committee's ASE recommendation of the Balan design being rejected, the Mint convinced Treasury to support the creation of a Liberty-themed gold coin and silver medal program for 2015. A coin bearing the Balan Flying Eagle design was used for the 2015 American Liberty program. I'm not sure why a design change couldn't happen in 2014 but could in 2021. I assume change in leadership at Treasury and/or the Mint was the difference. They say the 2021 change was necessary as an anti-counterfeiting measure. While this may have had something to do with it, I also think it's likely new leadership simply decided it was a good idea.

If at First You Don't Succeed, Try, Try Again . . .

By 2019, much had changed in Washington, D.C., and the United States Mint had a new director in David Ryder—who had previously served in the same role from 1992 through 1993. The nation also had secretary of the Treasury Steven T. Mnuchin, who along with Ryder was an appointee of President Donald Trump. American Silver Eagle redesign proposals were coming to a head by the end of the decade. There was a new rationale behind making a change. It was more than aesthetics; the very integrity of the coin was at stake.

Paul Gilkes of *Coin World* wrote in an October 26, 2018, article recapping that year's United States Mint Numismatic Forum (an event attended by journalists, dealers, and other key figures in the hobby) that "U.S. Mint officials were surprised that most of the more than 100 individuals invited had seen an example of a counterfeit United States bullion coin." Gilkes continued, "[U.S. Mint Manager of Design and Engraving Ron] Harrigal said Mint officials have not been directly exposed to counterfeit U.S. bullion coin products, made aware only through what they have read in the numismatic press. When he asked how many of those in attendance had seen a counterfeit U.S. bullion coin, nearly all hands were raised."

Over the next months, the ball got rolling to create a new type of American Silver Eagle that would be harder to counterfeit. There was a prime opportunity to redesign the coin in conjunction with its upcoming 35th anniversary.

In a *Coin World* story on October 11, 2019, then-acting chief for the Mint's Office of Corporate Communications Todd Martin announced the plans to redesign the silver and gold American Eagles. Martin added that Ryder had "assembled an anti-counterfeiting interdisciplinary team within the Mint that is researching and reviewing both overt and covert options to enhance the protection of our bullion products."

While the degree of anti-counterfeiting technology to be employed on the new American Silver Eagles was unknown then and has likely not been completely publicized by the U.S. Mint today, other mints around the world had already begun implementing advanced technology to safeguard their coins. Among the nations leading the charge was Canada. The Royal Canadian Mint started using Bullion DNA technology. "Every die used to produce the Gold and Silver Maple Leaf coins is laser micro-engraved with an anti-counterfeiting security mark: a textured maple leaf," states the

Royal Canadian Mint website. "Our registration process—digital non-destructive activation (DNA) technology—captures images encrypted with a string of codes, and stores these in our secure database." The coins can then be scanned with a special device (linked to the Mint's database of registered coins) by "approved Bullion DNA dealers [to] easily verify the authenticity of registered Gold and Silver Maple Leaf bullion coins." In Great Britain the Royal Mint launched its Integrated Secure Identification Systems technology, which has been used in the production of that nation's circulating £1 coin.

After U.S. Mint officials announced in fall 2019 that they were ready to redesign the silver and gold American Eagle coins, the designers in the U.S. Mint Artistic Infusion Program were called to submit their proposals. After considering 39 reverse designs, the CCAC came to a recommendation over the summer of 2020. What follows is a brief recap of the discussion CCAC members had when reviewing finalists to make the Committee's recommendation to Treasury Secretary Steven T. Mnuchin.

June 23, 2020, CCAC Meeting Transcript Highlights

At this CCAC meeting 39 designs were up for consideration for the silver and gold American Eagle coins. Text is condensed and lightly edited for clarity, and, while quotes are in order of their occurrence at the meeting, comments not published here may have occurred between those selected below.

CCAC Chair Thomas Uram: This is a really significant change over 35 years. We're going to be selecting a design that will be here for another probably 25 to 35 years. So I look forward to our discussion. [. . .]

CCAC Member Donald Scarinci: I discounted designs that were just too busy. I don't think it should be too busy. I think it's [a Silver Eagle], and it should be an eagle, a majestic eagle. [. . .] So I discount the ones with two eagles or anything too busy for the reverse. You don't really want anything detracting from the obverse. I felt the same way with the use of the flag. I don't think we need to put the American flag on the reverse. I think the obverse of both coins after all these years makes a statement: These are American coins. This is America. The obverse says that loud and clear. [. . .] The things I like the most would be Reverse 2, Reverse 12A. This is

Thomas Uram was chair of the CCAC when the new reverse design of the American Silver Eagle was deliberated in 2020.

actually one of the most exciting things I think we've been called upon to do. [. . .] To have the opportunity to pick the reverse of the most iconic, the two most iconic coin designs that identify the United States around the world is just a very humbling experience, and this is a very exciting opportunity for us on this committee.

CCAC Member Michael Moran: As I approached all of these, I had three rules: One, is it consistent with the obverse it will be paired with and not jarringly different, as I think the current designs are? Two, [. . .] it needs to be significantly different from the original reverses that the coins embodied in the first designs by Saint-Gaudens and Weinman. We are in the twenty-first century, we can come up with different reverses. And finally, three, I look at whether the design was scalable down to the quarter-ounce [gold] coin. Because to me that dictated whether we used it on the gold coin or not. I liked Reverse 2. It is clean, it's simple, and it's scalable. And it's consistent enough with the obverses that it goes with them. It basically transcends time. I also [like] 11. I particularly liked 11A. I think that the eagle says something there. I also agree with Donald on 12 and 12A. Those are both excellent designs. [But] you need to get the landscape out of there and that gets messy.

CCAC Member Robin Salmon: I found myself counting primaries. I was really amazed at how detailed some of these drawings were in terms of accuracy, anatomical accuracy. I too looked for designs that would complement the obverse. [The eagle head on number 38,] I thought it was really powerful and particularly representative of what we're hoping to convey in some of the new designs. Number 10, the overhead view of the eagle flying, was very interesting and I think could make a very beautiful design. I opted, though, in my favorites to choose the full eagle or mostly the full eagle in flight.

CCAC Member Sam Gill: Well, I'm sure everyone would agree that this is probably the most important and challenging coin that we've had the pleasure of working on. I consider it a real privilege and a pleasure to be a part of the [group] that has the responsibility to weigh in on such an important design. And I want to pay homage to the reverses that these new designs will replace. I always thought they were classic and beautiful. And that's certainly what I'm striving for here. This is what I was looking for, the lens I was looking through: The designs have to be emblematic of our country and they should show strength and pride, which is what the eagle does. The gold and silver are such an important part of the financial world, and this coin must represent our country as the leader in the world financial community.

CCAC Member Dennis Tucker: This is one of the best groupings that we've seen in a while, and a very important subject. Miley Busiek was the artist of the "Family of Eagles" on the gold coin back in 1986. When that design debuted, it was something unusual in an American coin design. Did its style and theme match the strength of Augustus Saint-Gaudens's obverse?

Dr. Lawrence Brown, a noted collector of modern U.S. Mint coins and a CCAC member representing the general public, praised the potential new American Silver Eagle designs in the Committee's June 2020 meeting: "This is impressive. I would like to commend all the artists, because these designs were fantastic."

That's a matter of debate in the hobby community. But at the time it did offer a different view of the bald eagle than what American coinage had seen from the 1790s to the early 1980s. Keeping in that spirit with this portfolio, I tried to look closest at designs that offer a fresh perspective. Many of the designs I discounted because they don't do anything new with the subject matter. We've seen many eagles in flight in the platinum bullion series and elsewhere, in the American Liberty High Relief gold coins. So I discounted quite a few of the designs that simply show an eagle flying. We've also seen eagles crouching, we've seen them getting ready to fly, we've seen them standing and in similar poses. I discounted a good number of those designs. I liked the fresh perspective of Reverse 3, but I don't like its symbolism. The oak tree is traditionally a symbol of strength, and here we see the oak tree being broken, so I didn't think that that worked. Reverse 16—I actually liked this. To me it was something of an extension of the family concept in the gold design, the Family of Eagles design. This theme of family, of community. I think this would be a good successor to the original Family of Eagles. Design 25 struck me as having that same continuity with the concept of family and of group, of a community. Eighteen and 18A, I must admit, I found my eye drawn to these. I found these to be really powerful eagle designs even though they are one of many eagles in flight that we see. I think these would make a nice, bold silver dollar taking over for John Mercanti's heraldic eagle. And also with 18 and 18A, this eagle is actually kind of simple. He's not trying to do too much. He's not wrestling with olive branches or banners or ribbons or what have you. It's bold and active. And I also liked 38. I was drawn to that one, and I think that would make a nice design.

CCAC Member Dean Kotlowski: I picked one that was a full eagle, one that might be called a partial eagle, and the other was a portrait. I'm not sure that these are going to surprise anyone. I picked for the full eagle number 2. And I thought that was a good design. Very familiar, very classic. Very safe, but very, very good. The one that I really fell in love with, well, the two, were number 10—that's my partial eagle. I liked the perspective. I liked the fact that we're looking down. I think this would stand the test of time. I liked the circularity of it. I think it probably could work on either the gold or the silver, but I'm going to defer to some of the experts there. And I really loved 38. I thought the portrait was fine. I thought it was striking. I thought it was different, but again, something that could become a new classic.

CCAC Member Jeanne Stevens-Sollman: I think that this is a fabulous portfolio. We were definitely gifted to have so many wonderful designs to choose from. I compliment the artists on really going far out to articulate all the feathers. Robin mentioned she counted the feathers, and of course I did, too. Some of them are more credible than others. But as I went through the portfolio, I tried to look also at designs that were more innovative. I wanted to say that we are going to do Page 70 some contemporary work here. And I disregarded some of these designs because I think we've seen them so many times even though they are good. But I wanted this particular design because of the gravity of—the longevity that it will have, we need to look at something fabulous. The first thing that I was drawn to was 38. Thirty-eight is powerful, a powerful portrait. The detailing is spectacular. [. . .] Also it would be a great piece because on any scale of the gold coins, it would be simple. [. . .] Number 2: I think it's just too traditional and I didn't feel like it was giving me enough power for a contemporary piece. I liked Donald's concept of number 12 and 12A, but I would like not to see the rays of the sun. That eagle is beautiful. Kudos to the artist who did that. So those are my choices, 38 being number one.

Scarinci: I understand that 38 seems to have gotten a lot of votes. I just—for those people who voted for 38, it's a portrait on the reverse of a coin. I just don't see it. I just don't see how that looks right.

Uram: When I looked at these designs, I really saw three concepts. We have eagles in flight, we have eagles landing, and we have eagles on watch. When I think of the gold, I think of maybe an eagle that's more stoic, an eagle that's more on watch. And I chose three designs that I thought would fill that category. And number 38 as my first choice. [. . .] I also looked at number 34 and number 16. [. . .] I thought silver would be in flight. I know that there's a lot for number 2, and I think it's a great design. But I don't know, maybe I'm reading too much into it . . . I just don't want to see an eagle landing necessarily. America should be in flight and looking up. If we have an eagle that's landing, I'm just not comfortable with the symbolism, although I like the design. So, for my eagle in flight, I looked at 12A. [. . .] The wings are spread. It's upward-moving—the negative space would be great. [. . .] And then number 10 I agree, too, that's interesting.

U.S. Mint Chief Engraver Joseph Menna: Artistically speaking, I always like when an obverse/reverse complement each other in terms of their compositional elements. The gold is a very strong vertical composition, which I think would benefit from a composition that was perhaps maybe a little more dynamic or had some diagonals. The silver, while it has a strong vertical in the center, has a lot going on. There's an arc across the top, there's a diagonal going towards the sun. Her other leg creates a diagonal. So maybe something a little more static on the reverse would complement that artistically.

Tucker: On Reverse 10, can anyone comment on the anatomical correctness of the layout of the eagle's feathers?

Stevens-Sollman: Yes.

Tucker: Is it good?

Stevens-Sollman: No, no.

Tucker: Is it bad?

Stevens-Sollman: I would hope that if this were chosen, that the sculpting would be more accurate. These feathers are definitely not in alignment. I mean, it sort of looked like it damaged itself by flying into a tree. It's just not correct. If you look at a bird, the feathers are going to go in one direction. These feathers don't do that. They're kind of willy-nilly, sorry to say. The head feathers are fine. And these—how can I say? These wing feathers—there's a set of feathers, the primary feathers, the secondary feathers that go over. And they're very much in alignment so that through the air they're going to not get into any distress. They're going to fly through the air, they're going to be smooth like an airplane. So these feathers are not correct.

Salmon: This is Robin, and I agree.

Tucker: So, what would we do about that? This design was mentioned several times in our conversation as being innovative and attractive. But how do we vote on that then? How do we rank this if there's work that still needs to be done?

Scarinci: The popularity of 10 surprised me only a little, I guess, because it is a very attractive design. [. . .] But it's just not as compelling as number 2 and number 12A. It just seemed to me that number 2 and number 12A were the two most compelling reverses, one being for the gold, one being for the silver. It's a question of which one to pick.

Uram: Which one would you like to see between those two, gold and silver?

Scarinci: For the gold, I would probably see number 2. And for the silver, I would probably see 12A.

Moran: I have a hard time arguing with Donald on any of what he said. I guess my problem, or what I have to get over, and I think everybody else on the committee does, is 38 is an exceptional design. I certainly want to see it somewhere, sometime, someplace. It's the best head of an eagle I've seen in my time on the committee. But at the same time, it's not as compatible with the obverses, obviously. Whatever we choose, it is going to be with us for a long time. Two and 12A are good designs. They are compatible with the obverses. And 12A will look good on the larger planchet of the American Silver Eagle bullion coin. So unless somebody can tell me that I need to choose the head of an eagle for the reverse on [the Silver Eagle], I really think it's more experimental. We've not done that in American coinage ever that I'm aware of. We're far better off experimenting with it on a commemorative coin, a one-off, and seeing what it looks like.

Uram: Okay, so what are you picking for your top two? Gold, give me the gold first.

Moran: Gold is 2.

Uram: Silver?

Moran: Yeah, silver is 12A.

Tucker: My understanding is that the silver will be the more popular and more popularly sold coin. I would make a motion that we vote on 38 for the silver and 12A for the gold.

This meeting went on for more than two hours. In an initial vote among the 11-member panel, designs 2, 10, 12A, and 38 were favored. After a series of votes and motions recommending several combinations of designs, the CCAC voted 6-5 to recommend design 38 for the Silver Eagle and 12A for the Gold Eagle. Ultimately, with guidance from the CCAC and the Commission of Fine Arts, as well as advice of top officials at the Mint, Treasury Secretary Steven Mnuchin chose design 2 for the silver eagle and 38 for the gold eagle.

AES-R-01.

AES-R-02.

AES-R-03.

AES-R-05.

AES-R-06.

AES-R-07.

AES-R-08.

AES-R-10.

AES-R-11.

AES-R-11A.

AES-R-12.　　　　AES-R-12A.　　　　AES-R-13.

AES-R-15.　　　　AES-R-16.

AES-R-18.　　　　AES-R-18A.　　　　AES-R-19.

AES-R-19A.　　　　AES-R-20.

AES-R-21.

AES-R-22.

AES-R-23.

AES-R-24.

AES-R-25.

AES-R-27.

AES-R-27A.

AES-R-28.

AES-R-28A.

AES-R-29.

AES-R-30.

AES-R-31.

AES-R-32.

AES-R-33.

AES-R-34.

AES-R-35.

AES-R-36.

AES-R-37.

AES-R-38.

DAVID RYDER TALKS ABOUT THE REDESIGN OF THE AMERICAN EAGLES

When the Silver Eagle started, there had never been a silver or gold bullion program before. Congress passed the legislation in 1985 and the Mint was mandated to start production of the program in 1986, and it has been one heck of a great program ever since—a program that has sold hundreds of millions of dollars of Eagles for quite a long time. The way the law was written allowed the secretary of the Treasury to make a design change to the American Eagle program after the coin had been in existence for 25 years.

When I learned that, I started asking questions about that program. We spent a great deal of time considering how best to go about this change. One of my biggest concerns was what the numismatic collectors would think about changing John Mercanti's iconic heraldic eagle design to something brand new. I received a lot of pros and cons from a lot of different people. It was a matter of changing a hugely popular product—even large corporations refrain from changing a product that is so popular. But I came to the belief, after talking to many different people and my staff at the Mint, that it was not a bad idea at all.

The Citizens Coinage Advisory Committee (CCAC) and Commission of Fine Arts (CFA) take the responsibility of recommending the designs for coins and medals very seriously. When it came time to pick the design for the silver and gold American Eagle, they were sincerely interested in making historically correct decisions. After all, these two designs will be around for the next 25 years, unless someone decides to make a change, or if mandated by legislation, which could happen, but I don't think it will. Everyone involved, including Secretary Mnuchin, wanted to develop designs that would be timeless from the design point of view.

Before I moved forward with the designs, I called each of the artists who had created the original motifs for the coins. John Mercanti is a good friend of mine, and I asked him if he minded that we change the design. He said certainly not—adding that the design had already been around for 35 years. He was also very supportive of Emily Damstra's new reverse design for the Silver Eagle. It was the same case with Miley Busiek, who designed the original Family of Eagles design for the gold coins—she was also very supportive of the changes.

Originally, the CCAC had decided to use the Type II Gold Eagle design on the Silver Eagle and the Silver Eagle design on the Gold Eagle. It was a very close decision, and ultimately, I took the designs to Treasury Secretary Mnuchin and it was decided to change it around to what you see today. So the team moved the eagle head intended for the Silver Eagle to the Gold Eagle, which I thought was a bold change for the American Gold Eagle. And the traditional eagle in flight for the Silver Eagle—it's just an iconic-looking design.

I also made a number of marketing decisions regarding the Mint's release of the new Eagles—we decided to release the Type II designs mid-year, meaning that in 2021 collectors could collect both the original Type I design during the first half of the year and the new Type II design in mid-year 2021. I think collectors enjoyed it, and it was a good move from the standpoint of revenue for the government. It was also the first time that something like that was done for the American Eagle program.

The author and Mint director David Ryder at the U.S. Mint Headquarters in Washington, D.C., in 2019.

A CONVERSATION WITH AMERICAN SILVER EAGLE REVERSE DESIGNER EMILY S. DAMSTRA

Emily S. Damstra is an artist who has parlayed her successful career in scientific illustration into an exciting journey as a numismatic designer. After growing up in Grand Rapids, Michigan, Damstra now lives near Guelph, Ontario. Her work has appeared on nearly 20 United States coins and medals as well as some 50 Canadian coins and numismatic pieces. Her artwork is in numerous science and nature publications and can be seen in many museum and educational institutions.

Q. *Let's start with your early life and first bit of your career. How did you discover the arts and what were your college years like? How did you transition into the career you have now as a professional artist?*

A. My mother set the stage for my career in art and for my interest in nature. She nurtured my interest in drawing and her curiosity about nature inspired mine. Both of my parents supported my choice to major in studio art in college, despite their misgivings about a career in art offering any kind of financial security. Truthfully, I wasn't quite sure what I'd do with my art degree from Alma College. Then I heard about a master of fine arts degree program in science illustration at the University of Michigan, and this felt like a great way to combine my artistic side with my appreciation for the natural world. Through the guidance of an excellent instructor and advisor—Joe Trumpey—that program gave me just the foundation I needed. I embarked on a career as a self-employed natural science illustrator immediately after graduation.

Q. *What is your career in scientific illustration and design like, and what type of work have you done? How did you venture into numismatics? Did you ever expect to work in the numismatic realm?*

A. As a graduate student, I held a work-study job drawing fossil fish bones for the [University of Michigan] curator of fishes, Gerald R. Smith. He was a superb mentor who gave me a lot of confidence in my work, and he commissioned some fish illustrations for a book he was revising, *Fishes of the Great Lakes Region*. That was my first real job as a freelance illustrator, and that work led to other work, and so on. I've probably illustrated more fishes than any other group of animals, but my portfolio is pretty diverse. It includes a multitude of plants, animals, and fossils, as well as some archaeology-related illustrations and a variety of infographics. Some of the work is published in books, magazines, journals, or websites, and some illustrations are for interpretive signs at museums, zoos, and nature centers.

In 2005 I moved to Canada, and in 2010—a decade into my career as a natural science illustrator—I received a phone call out of the blue from the Royal Canadian Mint, asking if I'd be interested in submitting a design for a coin. I found out later that an acquaintance who'd done some coin designs for the Royal Canadian Mint had given

Emily S. Damstra created this colored-pencil illustration for *Guide to Great Lakes Fishes* by Gerald R. Smith (University of Michigan Press, 2010).

them my name; I'll always be grateful to that person: Celia Godkin. Of course, I said yes to the Royal Canadian Mint's invitation, and while my first submission wasn't selected, they liked it well enough to continue offering me invitations, mostly for nature-related coins.

I had never imagined that I would be designing coins, but I have found that the practices that made me a successful science illustrator also translate well to coin design.

Q. *What's it like working in the U.S. Mint Artistic Infusion Program? How did you join the program? In general, is working with the AIP a daily involvement or more episodic as the need for a new coin design comes up from time to time?*

A. I responded to a call for applicants to the United States Mint's Artistic Infusion Program (AIP) in 2014 after hearing about it from my sister Carolyn, who is also an artist. The first stage of the application process was to submit ten samples of my work along with my resumé and a statement. Artists who reached the second stage were invited to create a coin design. From that pool of artists, the Mint selected about 20 of us to be part of (or continue being part of) the AIP.

As an AIP member, I typically work on a few to several coin or medal programs per year. I love the variety of subjects that I'm assigned, and it is truly a joy to work with the people in the Mint's Office of Design Management—a highly capable, enthusiastic, and dedicated group. It's incredibly rewarding when one of my visions for a coin or medal ends up resonating with the stakeholders and committee members involved in a given program. Being part of the AIP is also challenging. More often than not, the designs I submit are not selected; after all, I'm competing against some extraordinary artists.

Q. *What comparisons do you draw between working with the U.S. Mint and the Royal Canadian Mint? How are they similar and how are they different from your viewpoint as a coin and medal artist?*

A. There are quite a few similarities in the design development process for each mint. The biggest difference is that the U.S. Mint's design selection process is guided by legislation, resulting in a longer process with more revisions but also more transparency than the RCM's selection process.

As a dual citizen, it's been a privilege to work with both the Royal Canadian Mint and the United States Mint. I feel honored to see my work become a small part of the numismatic history of both countries.

Q. *What were some of your early experiences like in working with numismatic art? Did you find it challenging to work within such small canvases?*

A. I think the biggest challenge I had—and continue to have—is coming up with ideas that are unique and that also honor the subject as completely as possible. The small canvases really amp up the pressure to come up with design ideas that have some impact at a glance.

Q. *Do you have a particular artistic philosophy or school of thought you work with? How does this influence your approach to any project, numismatic or not?*

A. As a graduate student, I absorbed the idea of the importance of accuracy in my work. Since science illustration's primary goal is to communicate a message about science or nature, it makes sense that the illustrator must be thorough in their research. Most of the time, my inclination to strive for accuracy works well for coin design, though there are instances when "artistic license" might be the best solution and I can have a hard time allowing myself this license. There are also situations where I may spend more time in the research phase than is necessary, but since that is my favorite part of the work, I tend to allow myself the indulgence.

Q. *Please do share on the journey with the American Silver Eagle. How did this come about and how did you approach this project? Did I read somewhere you had originally worked on your Type II reverse under the impression it would potentially be used for the American Gold Eagle?*

A. As a member of the AIP, the United States Mint invited me to submit designs for the American Eagle gold coin. I took to heart Miley Tucker-Frost's inspiration for her original gold reverse design, which the U.S. Mint shared with the AIP artists who were working on designs for this coin:

> Her design was inspired by the hopelessness she saw in the face of a lonely youth she witnessed, and a wish to utilize this tiny billboard, this coin's design, to send a message to every American—a reminder of how much we care for our people. She chose to depict a family of eagles as a symbol of what we stand for as Americans, noting eagles will steadfastly withstand all kinds of weather to protect and nurture their eaglets. She had observed an American eagle pair as they took turns refreshing their nest over the Platte River. She posited that eagles return year after year to the same nest and mate for life. In her observations, she noted that eagles were not only strong and courageous, but also compassionate, caring, and dedicated (much like America itself).

Tucker-Frost's approach appealed to me, so I considered what aspect of a bald eagle's life cycle might be symbolic of American values. Because both male and female of a mated pair build and repair their nest, I liked the idea of showing nesting eagles because this could symbolize diligence, care, protection, and cooperation.

I used photos and videos of eagles building nests, carrying branches, and landing as inspiration and reference for my initial sketches. The only reason an eagle would be carrying a branch is if it were involved in building or repairing a nest, so in my design the nest isn't shown but it is implied.

I spent hours selecting the typefaces and tweaking the placement and spacing of every word. I chose typefaces that are readable and coinable at a small size and offer a sense of gravitas and grace, sifting through many to find ones designed by Americans. I wanted every aspect of this coin to be American.

If I left it at that, one might be led to believe that my process involves a lot of action, but in reality most of my time is spent staring at my sketchbook or my computer screen and just thinking. I took great care and pride in designing the reverse side of this coin, and I feel very fortunate to have had this design opportunity.

Q. *How long did it take you to work on early sketches, and what was your inspiration and goal with the design?*

A. I had about five and a half weeks to work on the project once I received the assignment in the fall of 2019. I didn't keep track of the number of hours I spent on each stage of the process, but certainly more than half of the time would have been spent on research and idea development (early sketches).

Q. *There's a lot of action in your eagle design. Can you provide some detail about what exactly is happening in your flying eagle design? I imagine there is a very realistic bent to this depiction of the eagle carrying an oak branch.*

A. For a couple reasons, I decided from the outset that I would create a design that wasn't heraldic. One reason is that a number of heraldic eagle designs are already part of the United States' numismatic history. A bigger reason is that I revere the bald eagle, and I feel that showing it in a lifelike pose, informed by its natural history, is the best possible way to showcase our magnificent national bird. In my design, the eagle is about to land on its nest. With its feet, the eagle grips an oak branch that it collected for its nest. One can discern that the branch is from a bur oak by the few leaves that are still attached to it. At some point during my design development, I was alarmed when I recalled that bald eagles typically build their nests before the oaks leaf out. Fortunately, a bit of research reassured me that eagles also occasionally add to or repair their nests throughout the year, so leaves on the branch are realistic.

Q. *About that oak branch. This, of course, is another type of departure—that is, away from the olive branch and arrows so commonly associated with this type of imagery on U.S. coins. Why did you choose an oak branch here? What patriotic symbolism do you connote with this?*

A. This is a great question, and the answer is a bit of a long story. It starts with my passion for native plant gardening. I became interested in gardening with native plants over a decade ago after reading the book *Bringing Nature Home* by Douglas Tallamy. I learned that native plants—as compared to non-native plants—are more valuable to wildlife because many insects need native plants, and insects are a critical part of the food web for many other animals. Most North American songbirds, for example, raise their young almost exclusively on insects.

I became more aware of how the native plant species in any given location make that place unique and special and can define a landscape.

For those reasons, when I considered the symbolism of the tree species involved in my design for an American coin, I felt that it must be a species native to the United States. Although species of olives occur in many places around the world, including North America, the olive traditionally used as a symbol for peace is Mediterranean. In my view, a much more logical (and more American) choice would be an oak, which is historically associated with strength. There are numerous oak species native to the U.S., and the oak is America's official national tree. Moreover, Tallamy reports that oaks support more forms of life than any other tree genus in North America. I ended up realizing that oaks are one of America's best symbols, and that planting an oak tree native to one's region might be one of the most patriotic things an American could do.

Emily S. Damstra painted this watercolor and gouache illustration of a bald eagle for the Smithsonian Institution.

Q. How many iterations did this design endure between concept and unveiling, and please talk a bit about the competition process. What was it like? Was this the sole design you submitted for this redesign, or did you have others in the running, too? How many other artists were you competing against, and what was it like being in contention among them?

A. I submitted a total of five designs for this program, three of which made it into the pool of submissions presented to the CFA and CCAC. Before the committees reviewed all of the candidates, I was asked for two revisions to the design that was ultimately selected: a small tweak to the oak branch, and then a version with inscriptions for the silver coin.

With every coin or medal program, I know from the start that it's going to be a tough competition. The other AIP artists are a hard-working, creative group; I have to submit my best possible work in order to have a chance at success, so there's a good deal of pressure.

Q. How much time passed between the opening of competition, revealing finalists, and choosing the eventual winner (your design)? Did you have to answer a lot of questions from panelists / the public on this or make many tweaks to the design during the CCAC design-selection process?

A. I received the assignment in October of 2019, submitted my designs in early December, and the CCAC and CFA reviewed designs for the American Eagle gold and silver coins in June of 2020. The Mint notified me on August 3, 2020, that my design had been selected.

As mentioned earlier, I was asked to make two tweaks to my design, and these happened before the committees reviewed the design candidates. When an artist submits a design, the Mint requests that the artist compose a paragraph or so of text about it, and the committees typically receive some version of this text. That's the extent to which the artists might communicate with committee members. The committees review the designs without knowing which artist submitted which design, so in order to maintain anonymity there is no artist participation in the committee review process.

Q. *How did you feel when you learned your design was selected as the winner? What about when you found out it was destined for the American Silver Eagle?*

A. I was elated to hear that one of my designs was selected. I don't think I could concentrate on anything else for the rest of the day. With every coin or medal program, the design process can be an emotional rollercoaster; I alternate between feeling confident in my design idea and feeling despair that it's not nearly good enough. Thus, when the people who recommend and choose the designs land on one of mine, it's very gratifying.

Although I was aware that the American Eagle silver coin was an important program because it's such a widely sold coin, I don't think I fully understood the regard that many numismatists have for this program, nor did I anticipate the amount of publicity that would accompany the unveiling of the design and the release of the coin. I was happy that my design would be paired with Adolph A. Weinman's iconic obverse design on the silver coin.

Q. *What was it like to finally see your new American Silver Eagle reverse on a coin, in hand? How did this compare to seeing your other coin designs come to fruition?*

A. It's always a delight to hold a coin that I designed, and to see how the engraver interpreted my drawing.

Q. *Did you feel a certain responsibility in working on this particular design? How does it feel to know that your flying eagle design may very well be in active production for many decades to come?*

A. With every coin program I work on, I feel a sense of responsibility to honor the subject in the best possible way. The American Eagle silver coin was a little different from most U.S. programs because an external stakeholder was not part of the equation. Stakeholders are involved in most of the programs I work on, including commemorative coins, American Innovation coins, the America the Beautiful Quarters, the American Women Quarters, and every Congressional Gold Medal. For example, the Breast Cancer Research Foundation was involved with the Breast Cancer Awareness commemorative coins; they helped lay the groundwork for the design brief and commented on the design candidates. With no external stakeholder (that I know of) giving input on the American Eagle silver coin designs, I had less direction than usual at the outset. This can be both freeing and challenging, and in this case, I think it took me longer than usual to convince myself that I was heading in the right direction with the ideas I'd developed.

I'm not sure anyone can predict how long my design will be in production, so I don't think much about its longevity; it's out of my control.

Q. *Beyond the American Silver Eagle Type II reverse, could you share some other career highlights?*

A. In my Canadian numismatic work, I'd consider my reverse design for the 2012 Lucky Loonie to be a career highlight, since it's the only circulating coin I've designed for Canada. As for American coins and medals, my reverse design for the 2022 Maya Angelou quarter and for the 2020 Tallgrass Prairie quarter are ones I'm especially proud of.

In my work as a science illustrator, the projects that stand out in my mind are the ones where I was able to work with an enthusiastic scientist. There were a few different books on fishes where I collaborated with Gerald Smith; the most involved was *Guide to Great Lakes Fishes*. More recently, I had the pleasure of working with author Stephen B. Heard on illustrations of plants and animals that are named after people, for his book *Charles Darwin's Barnacle and David Bowie's Spider*.

Q. *How do you see your art serving a role in the greater world? What type of message do you hope it delivers? What do you want someone to glean from your works, whether it be the new American Silver Eagle reverse or a sketch in a museum pamphlet or nature book?*

A. It's my hope that my art gives the viewer a greater appreciation for or understanding of the subject. When I illustrate some aspect of nature, I'm aware that connecting people to nature is the best way to inspire people to care about it.

Q. How do you spend your down time?

A. I spend my free time gardening, baking, sewing, swimming, walking, or traveling with my husband, George.

Emily S. Damstra has created highly detailed renderings of a diverse range of creatures great and small for the education and enjoyment of many kinds of audiences. Seen here: an early Jurassic creature known as a Sunrisites brimblecombei; the golden soldier beetle; and a wading bird named the ruddy turnstone.

Emily S. Damstra U.S. Coin/Medal Designs

2017 Boys Town Centennial
silver dollar, obverse.

2017 Boys Town Centennial
silver dollar, reverse.

2018 Breast Cancer Awareness
coins, obverse.

2018 Breast Cancer
Awareness coins, reverse.

2018 World War One
Centennial medal,
U.S. Army, obverse.

2018 Office of Strategic
Services (OSS) Congressional
Gold Medal, obverse.

2018 Office of Strategic
Services (OSS) Congressional
Gold Medal, reverse.

2019 Frank Church River
of No Return Wilderness
quarter dollar, reverse.

2019 Native American
dollar, reverse.

2019 American Innovation
dollar, Georgia, reverse.

2019 Steve Gleason Congressional
Gold Medal, reverse.

2020 Tallgrass Prairie National
Preserve quarter dollar, reverse.

2020 American Innovation dollar, Massachusetts, reverse.

2021 Christa McAuliffe silver dollar, reverse.

2021 American Silver Eagle, reverse.

2022 American Women quarter, Maya Angelou, reverse.

2022 American Women quarter, Anna May Wong, reverse.

CHATTING WITH AMERICAN SILVER EAGLE REVERSE ENGRAVER MICHAEL GAUDIOSO

Michael Gaudioso was a sculptor-engraver at the U.S. Mint from 2009 until 2020. During that time, he designed or sculpted dozens of coins and medals. One of his final projects as a Mint artist was sculpting Emily S. Damstra's design for the American Silver Eagle. Gaudioso lives in Saint Augustine, Florida, and is involved in a wide range of sculpting and artistic mediums.

Q. What were your early years like? How did you become a sculptor and engraver, and what was your formal education in the arts?

A. As a young child, I was interested in art. I enjoyed drawing and painting. My father was a painter and artist. My mother sent me to Fleisher Art Memorial in South Philadelphia, where the neighborhood kids could learn painting, drawing, and sculpting for a

Michael Gaudioso with his sculpting of Ronald D. Sanders's design for the 2013 5-Star Generals gold coin.

few dollars a week. As a kid, I would ride my bike around the city discovering the public statues in Fairmount Park and on the parkway. I remember in grade school my notebooks were filled with sketches. In art class I would get an A throughout my primary education. When I found out I could go to high school for art, I seized the opportunity and was accepted to the Philadelphia High School for the Creative and Performing Arts. In high school I studied visual arts. After completing high school, I applied to the University of the Arts in Philadelphia on Broad Street and was accepted. After college, I continued my education at the New York Academy of the Fine Arts and obtained a master's degree in sculpture.

Upon graduation from the New York Academy of Fine Arts, I sought out a classical training that led me to apply to the Repin Institute in Saint Petersburg, Russia, also known as the Saint Petersburg Academy of Fine Arts. The Repin

Stained glass by Michael Gaudioso.

Institute was able to provide me with a classical sculptural training that was equivalent to American sculpture of the 1910-1920 era. The sculpture program was a rigorous and strict program where the students learned intensive anatomy, physiology, and studied the Old Masters from Greek and Roman all the way to the Russian masters of the twentieth century.

While studying in Russia, I realized exactly what I did not know and what I needed to know to become a master sculptor. After five years of intensive study, I arrived home to South Philadelphia and did what most sculptors did and landed a job in a plaster shop, working for other sculptors until I established my own career.

Q. *What did you do prior to working at the United States Mint?*

A. I was a painter at one of America's oldest stained-glass companies, where I painted church windows. I enjoyed this work because I find great beauty and peace in religious iconography. Throughout my career as a sculptor, I continued to work on private commissions and compile personal work to fill my studio.

Q. *How did you land your role at the U.S. Mint?*

A. Living in a big-small city like Philadelphia, word gets around quickly when a U.S. Mint sculpting and engraving job opens up. I compiled my CV and portfolio, submitted those with the U.S. Mint application, and patiently awaited the good news that I was hired as a U.S. Mint sculptor and engraver.

Q. *What was it like working at the Mint? Was the workflow pretty steady, or more episodic as the need for certain projects came up?*

A. In general, the workflow at the U.S. Mint was always steady. In the few slow periods between sculpts, I worked on reference material, design work, sharpened my skillset, made sculpting tools, and occasionally took group field trips. One of my favorite times as a U.S. Mint sculptor was the Code Talkers series. This was an intensive program lasting three to four months, consisting of 59 sculpts in total. I personally sculpted and designed seven Code Talker Congressional Gold Medals.

Q. Did you ever use any of the traditional engraving tools, such as Janvier reducing lathes and plaster models, at the Mint, or did you do most of your work there using computers and lasers? Any philosophical thoughts you want to share on one technique versus another and their role at the Mint in the modern era?

A. My personal work at the Mint was strictly traditional. What I mean by this is that I enjoyed working in clay and plaster. Eventually, I utilized much of the technology to resolve details of sculpts and quicken production. In all of our designs, the sculptors and engravers use Photoshop. After scanning my plasters, I used ZBrush to fine detail and final rendering for submission to headquarters. I do not believe there are many people who could differentiate a sculpt in ZBrush from a traditional plaster. Both ZBrush and plaster, in my opinion, are a means to an end producing the desired sculptural image.

Q. Diving into the American Silver Eagle adventure, what was it like working with Emily S. Damstra? Was there a lot of direct back and forth between you and her to refine various elements of her art for use on the coin?

A. There is very little collaboration required between the designer and the sculptor. Normally, the aesthetic decisions are made by the chief engraver, the director, and sales and marketing. These decisions include finishing, details, the height recommendations, what parts of the sculpt need enhancement, and what parts need to be pushed back. On occasion the designer and sculptor will have some contact and discuss design intention. Our training and sculptural/design knowledge are enough to produce the final product without the need for discussion. This option is always available if needed.

Q. How long did it take you to render Damstra's design for the first dies?

A. Emily Damstra's design was completed within 12 days. This is the average expected timeframe. I have sculpted so many eagles over the years that it becomes a skill set or methodical system of sculpting. The sculpt came back two times. The first time I refined the feathers. The second time I sharpened the beak. This was a normal part of the process at the U.S. Mint, as headquarters in D.C. scrutinized each design to perfection.

Q. Are you able to share any details relating to new security details on the coin?

A. I do not take part in the security details. For instance, the edging around the coin, the fonts, and the basin/field measurements are handled by the security personnel at the U.S. Mint and D.C. headquarters. The chief engraver and the director play an active role working with security personnel on those details. For the sculptor and engraver, it's business as usual as we sculpt and design the coins.

Q. *How long did it take to go from initial engraving duties on this coin to trial strikes? What was this process like?*

A. From start to finish, the American Silver Eagle was sculpted and minted in the normal timeframe. The dies are always a challenge. It is rare to have an initial coin strike that is perfect. During my career at the Mint, I have had one or two coins that were a perfect initial strike. The American Silver Eagle was not very high in depth, [and] the coin came back one or two times for minor revisions. I worked within the wing that went into the side of the basin; it wasn't filling properly. The American Eagle went back to the die cutters and they pushed it up, down, much of the rendering was done digitally, and a new die was struck. In the old days they polished out any imperfections and fixed the coin manually.

One of Michael Gaudioso's plaster models for the American Silver Eagle Type II reverse.

Q. *Were there any technical challenges that arose in translating the design from concept to die? Or was this a fairly straightforward leap from sketch to production?*

A. From sketch to production, the American Eagle was a straightforward leap. The design committee knew what type of

Tools in Michael Gaudioso's work area at the Philadelphia Mint's artist studio, March 2013.

design they wanted. The first American Eagle done by John Mercanti was very regal and symmetrical. The design committee knew they wanted something completely different. When the design was finished, there were no refinements or alterations to do. It went right to production.

Q. *How did it feel to hold an American Silver Eagle bearing a design you helped bring to life?*

A. As a sculptor, seeing the end product of any of your medals or coins is always exciting. But, to see the reverse of the American Eagle that I had a part in creating, and knowing that Adolph Weinman was the sculptor of the obverse and that I shared a coin with him, is a dream come true.

Q. *And what about the legacy of having a hand in this next chapter of the American Silver Eagle? What's that like?*

A. It is an absolute honor to see my initials on the reverse of the American Silver Eagle. When I see ads in magazines, on TV, or the internet, I think to myself, "Wow, I did that." I have the American Silver Eagle all around the house and in my studio. I look forward to sharing the adventure with my granddaughter when she gets older.

Q. *What are some other career highlights you wish to share?*

A. One of the highlights in my career at the Mint was sculpting the reverse of the Washington Crossing the Delaware quarter. The quarter was only in production for one year. This was one of my favorite sculpts. Being from Philadelphia and having spent much time at Washington Crossing State Park, I felt a connection to this coin.

The Code Talker designs that [were] selected—I enjoyed this program because it gave us an opportunity to design a historical culture within our culture. I used design elements of Native American iconography and symbolism combined with the history of World War II.

The Montford Point Marines medal was another highlight. I went to Congress and presented the medal to some of the World War II veterans—this was a huge honor.

Q. *What would you tell anybody wishing to get into sculpting as a career?*

A. To become a successful sculptor now, one would want to study traditional sculpture, go on to relief work, and study numismatics, study abroad, work at a foundry or casting studio and seek out classically trained teachers. My wife and daughter are starting a YouTube channel that will allow me to share some tips for those interested in pursuing a career or just sculpting for pleasure. I highly encourage those interested in sculpture to pursue their dream.

Q. *Are there any mentors you want to tip your hat to?*

A. I would like to thank John Mercanti, Joe Menna, and Ron Harrigal for their support and mentoring. They were wonderful bosses that encouraged teamwork and artistic expression. They showed me how to become solution based. I appreciated their professional input and friendship.

Q. *Can you shed a little bit of light on what your personal life is like?*

A. Currently, I live with my wife, Linda, our daughter, Jessica, and granddaughter in Saint Augustine, Florida. Just as I enjoy fishing, for me sculpting is relaxing, enjoyable, and my vision becomes material. Recently we purchased a train station in Satsuma, Florida, that we are converting into a sculpture studio. We are excited to begin a new chapter in our life.

American Silver Eagles: 2021 Type I vs. Type II

As part of its redesign of the American Silver Eagle, the U.S. Mint made enhancements to the Liberty Walking obverse in an effort to restore elements in Adolph Weinman's motif. The new 2021 obverse (second row of images below), which more closely reflects Weinman's original design, was created by referencing historical models made by Weinman in 1916. This included the addition of Weinman's original artist mark below IN GOD WE TRUST on the obverse.

A security feature: the notched edge.

Then-Mint director David Ryder ceremoniously struck the last 500 of the Type I American Silver Eagles and first 500 of the Type II American Silver Eagles at a special event marking the transition between the old and new designs in April 2021.

WHAT THE AMERICAN SILVER EAGLE DESIGN CHANGE MEANS FOR COLLECTORS

It's natural to wax poetic about the symbolism behind a transition like the 2021 change in American Silver Eagle designs. Numismatic philosophers could, if so inclined, write entire volumes on what the various designs mean for the hobby and, in the greater sense, what they speak to on historical, political, and societal fronts.

There are some very tangible implications behind the changing of designs on the American Silver Eagle. What collectors now have with the creation of a new type in the Damstra/Gaudioso reverse is a numismatic bookend for a series that was growing longer and more complex by the year. While countless collectors will continue building a run of Silver Eagles extending well beyond 2021, those who wish to focus their attention on a particular segment of the series now have 2021 as both a coda and an intro.

Some of the most popular U.S. coin series boast these organic chapters—compartmentalized segments that allow collectors to focus on one area or another. Take, for example, the Lincoln cent, which has several of these chapters: the Wheat Ears (1909–1958), Lincoln Memorial (1959–2008), and Shield (2010 to present) reverses. Any one of these segments makes for an exciting numismatic pursuit and can keep a dedicated collector busy for years, even decades, chasing just the right coins to complete their set. The Jefferson nickel, Roosevelt dime and Washington quarter also have natural "chapters" in their series created by changes in design or metallic composition.

As for the American Silver Eagle, the end of the Mercanti reverse type and beginning of the Damstra/Gaudioso design in 2021 gives collectors who are just entering the American Silver Eagle arena an opportunity. If you focus only on the Type II design, at least for the time being, you have a chance to jump into the series starting with the 2021 coin and "catch up" with the purchase of the other coins made since then, with the aim of completing a set that can grow year by year. Imagine having started a set of Silver Eagles in, say, 2010 or 2015 and jumping into a series that had been in existence for many years and had by then already spawned numerous pricey issues. With the changes in 2021, the series saw something of a reset.

The American Silver Eagle series deals collectors its fair share of delights and challenges, no matter how you define your collection. The question is, how do you want to chart this journey? Starting with Type I or Type II could lend a natural springboard into collecting the other. So, too, could beginning with only the bullion strikes before chasing after the Proofs, Burnished coins, and other more expensive issues. Or you might decide to simply enjoy the American Silver Eagle buying one coin at a time and letting the shifting numismatic winds of the day navigate your way—no set plan, no hard objectives necessary.

It's a new day for the American Silver Eagle. Carpe diem!

8

Analysis and Market Guide to American Silver Eagles

INTRODUCTION

As this chapter clearly illustrates, the American Silver Eagle series is massive. With one exception, each year at least two and often three, four, or more different Eagles have been released. The lone exception came in 2009, for reasons explained later.

Mintages range from small to quite large—some downright enormous. Something that becomes evident as we trace through the following listings year by year is just how much this series has grown since its inception decades ago. It started off with a predictable dualism of bullion strikes and Proofs and culminated in some of the impressive sets of more recent vintage containing Silver Eagles of various finishes and design enhancements. The growth of the series correlates with emerging trends in the hobby of numismatics as well as the evolving popularity of the Silver Eagle. It's fascinating to see how this dynamic series has come of age as the world's leading silver-bullion coin.

Grading American Silver Eagles

The American Silver Eagle is legal tender but not intended to serve as a circulating coin. Therefore, relatively few will ever be encountered in circulated grades. That is not to say there aren't Silver Eagles with some degree of wear. Friction and rub are common on coins that have been mishandled, leaving the appearance of wear on high points of the design like Miss Liberty's outstretched hand, her gown, or various points on the shield and feathers of the eagle on the Type I reverse. There are also rare cases where an American Silver Eagle has been exchanged as money.

Precious-metals specialist Everett Millman recounts, "I have heard some humorous stories of people spending their Silver Eagles as legal tender—for one dollar—at a Publix supermarket [in Florida]. . . . It goes to show that even though there are hundreds of thousands of American Silver Eagle collectors and investors, the vast majority of the public is still totally unfamiliar with these coins (and what they're worth!)." There is also a small but growing number of well-circulated American Silver Eagles encapsulated by PCGS and NGC and being included in low-ball registry sets.

Essential elements of the American Numismatic Association Grading Standards are presented here for Proof and bullion-strike coins. While it's possible to find an American Silver Eagle in any grade, the vast majority are in the higher Proof and Mint State conditions.

PROOF

A specially made coin distinguished by sharpness of detail and usually with a brilliant, mirrorlike surface. Proof refers to the method of manufacture and is not a grade. These ANA grading standards are modified slightly to reflect that "average" quality for an American Silver Eagle Proof is about PF-69.

PF-70: The perfect coin. Has a very attractive sharp strike and surface (mirror or other style) of the highest quality for the variety. No contact marks are visible under magnification. There are absolutely no hairlines, scuff marks, or defects. Eye appeal is attractive and outstanding.

PF-69: Has a very attractive sharp strike and surface (mirror or other style) of the highest quality for the variety, with no more than two small, non-detracting contact marks or flaws. No hairlines or scuff marks can be seen. Eye appeal is exceptional. Note that Proof-69 is a common level for American Silver Eagles.

PF-68: Has an attractive sharp strike and full mirror (or other style Proof) surface for the variety, with no more than four light, scattered contact marks or flaws. No hairlines or scuff marks show.

PF-67: Has full mirror (or other style Proof) surface and sharp strike. May have three or four very small contact marks and one more noticeable, but not detracting, mark. A few hairlines may show under magnification, or one or two partially hidden scuff marks or flaws may be present.

PF-66: Has high quality of strike and full mirror (or other style Proof) surface, with no more than two or three minor but noticeable contact marks. A few light hairlines may show under magnification, or there may be one or two light scuff marks showing on frosted surfaces or in the field.

PF-65: Shows an attractive high quality of mirror (or other style Proof) surface and strike. A few small, scattered contact marks, or two larger marks, may be present, and hairlines may show under magnification. Noticeable light scuff marks may show on the high points of the design. Overall quality is below average for an American Silver Eagle, though overall eye appeal is still very pleasing.

PF-64: Has at least a typical mirror (or other style Proof) and strike for the issue. Several small contact marks in groups as well as one or two moderately heavy marks, may be present. Hairlines are visible under low magnification but are light. Noticeable light scuff marks or defects might be seen within the design or in the field. Overall quality is attractive, with a pleasing eye appeal.

PF-63: Mirrored (or other Proof style) fields may be slightly impaired. Numerous small contact marks and a few scattered heavy marks may be seen. Hairlines are light but extensive and are visible without magnification. Several detracting scuff marks or defects may be present throughout the design or in the fields.

PF-62: An impaired or dull character may be evident in the Proof fields as well as on the higher areas. Clusters of small marks may be present throughout, with a few large marks or nicks in prime focal areas. Hairlines are heavy and very noticeable. Large, unattractive scuff marks might be seen on major features. Overall eye appeal is barely acceptable.

Milk spots or "milkiness," such as seen on this 1995-W Proof, can keep an American Silver Eagle from a higher grade than its strike and other characteristics would otherwise warrant.

PF-61: The mirror (or other style Proof) fields may be diminished or noticeably impaired, and the surface has clusters of large and small contact marks throughout. Hairlines dominate the fields, taking away from most of the original mirror (or related) characteristics. Scuff marks may show as unattractive patches on large areas or major features. The quality may be noticeably poor. Eye appeal is somewhat unattractive. Proofs at this level are usually marketable only to bargain hunters, and for a sharp discount.

PF-60: Unattractive, dull, or washed-out fields exhibit little if any mirror characteristics. There may be many large, detracting contact marks or damage spots. There is a heavy concentration of hairlines, possibly in combination with unattractive large areas of scuff marks. Rim nicks may be present, and eye appeal is very poor. Proofs at this level are usually marketable only to bargain hunters, and for a sharp discount.

MINT STATE

The terms Mint State (MS) and Uncirculated (Unc.) are interchangeable and refer to coins showing no trace of wear from circulation. Such coins may vary slightly due to minor surface imperfections, as described in the following subdivisions:

MS-70: The perfect coin. Has very attractive sharp strike and original luster of the highest quality. No contact marks are visible under magnification. There are no noticeable hairlines, scuff marks, or defects. Eye appeal is attractive and outstanding.

MS-69: Has very attractive sharp strike and full original luster, with no more than two small, non-detracting contact marks or flaws. No hairlines or scuff marks can be seen. Has exceptional eye appeal.

MS-68: Has attractive, sharp strike and full original luster, with no more than four light, scattered contact marks or flaws. No hairlines or scuff marks show. Has exceptional eye appeal.

MS-67: Has original luster and normal strike for date and mint. May have three or four very small contact marks and one more noticeable, but not detracting, mark. On comparable coins, one or two small single hairlines may show, or one or two minor scuff marks or flaws may be present. Eye appeal is above average.

MS-66: Has above-average quality of surface and mint luster, with no more than three or four minor or noticeable contact marks. A few light hairlines may show under magnification, or there may be one or two light scuff marks showing. Eye appeal is above average and very pleasing.

MS-65: Shows an attractive high quality of luster and strike. May have a few small, scattered contact marks, or two larger marks may be present. One or two small patches of hairlines may show. Noticeable light scuff marks may be seen on the high points of the design. Overall quality and eye appeal are very pleasing.

MS-64: Has at least average luster and strike. Several small contact marks in groups as well as one or two moderately heavy marks may be present. One or two small patches of hairlines may show. Noticeable light scuff marks or defects might be seen within the design or in the field. Overall quality is attractive, with a pleasing eye appeal.

MS-63: Mint luster may be slightly impaired. Numerous small contact marks and a few scattered heavy marks may be seen. Small hairlines maybe visible without magnification. Several detracting scuff marks or defects may be present throughout the design or in the fields. Overall, the coin is rather attractive.

MS-62: An impaired or dull luster may be evident. Clusters of small marks may be present throughout, with a few large marks or nicks in prime focal areas. Hairlines may be very noticeable. Large, unattractive scuff marks might be seen on major feature. Overall eye appeal is below average.

MS-61: Mint luster may be diminished or noticeably impaired, and the surface may have clusters of large and small contact marks throughout. Hairlines could be very noticeable. Scuff marks may show as unattractive patches on large areas or major features. Small rim nicks and striking may show, and the quality may be noticeably poor. Eye appeal is somewhat unattractive.

MS-60: Unattractive, dull, or washed-out mint luster may mark this coin. There may be many large, detracting contact marks or damage spots, but no trace of circulation wear. There could be a heavy concentration of hairlines or unattractive large areas of scuff marks. Rim nicks may be present, and eye appeal is very poor.

THE YEAR 1986

"I don't need a pick and shovel to start the San Francisco Silver Rush of 1986," declared Secretary of the Treasury James Baker as he reached for a button on Mint press No. 105 on October 29, 1986. With that, the long and enduring chapter of the American Silver Eagle began at the U.S. Mint Assay Office in San Francisco, the facility now known as the San Francisco Mint.

What began as a relatively non-descript silver-bullion distribution proposal in the 1970s, a contentious legislative football in the early 1980s, and an initiative authorized by U.S. law with the Liberty Coin Act of 1985, had finally come to fruition as the nation's American Eagle bullion-coin program.

Nobody then knew if the fledgling silver coin would be a hit. It surely had all the right ingredients: one ounce of nearly pure silver content, a patriotic design, and price points that were reasonable for the average American consumer. But what if nobody gave the coin a chance?

This wasn't a problem. From the get-go, millions demanded American Silver Eagles of their own. The 1986 Silver Eagle was a hit, with nearly 5.4 million bullion strikes filtering into the public through Authorized Purchasers and more than 1.4 million Proofs being sold in quick succession by the Mint directly to collectors, dealers, and investors. There was no turning back. The 1986 American Silver Eagle quickly became one of the most sought-after coins in U.S. history.

Current Events in 1986

NASA Space Shuttle *Challenger* exploded 73 seconds into its mission on January 28. All seven crew members aboard were lost, including New Hampshire high school teacher Christa McAuliffe, who would have become America's "teacher in space" and conducted experiments to help inspire the nation's youth to pursue a path in the sciences.

More tragedy came on April 26 when a power surge at the Chernobyl Nuclear Power Plant in Soviet Ukraine led to one of the worst nuclear disasters in history. While fewer than 100 deaths are directly attributed to the nuclear meltdown, countless medical maladies, including cancer and birth defects, have been linked to the release of nuclear material over much of Europe in its wake.

Halley's Comet lit up the night sky in early 1986 as the interstellar voyager passed near Earth on an orbit that takes around 75 years to complete. The Soviets pushed into the heavens with the February 20 launch of their Mir international space station, which operated in low orbit about 223 miles above Earth until 2001.

Crossing the contiguous United States were the outstretched arms of more than five million people in "Hands Across America," an effort that raised some $15 million to fight hunger and homelessness.

The evening news covered details about the emerging Iran-Contra Affair.

The newly refurbished Statue of Liberty celebrated her 100th anniversary on Liberty Island and was reopened during July 4 weekend in a gala ceremony attended by President Ronald Reagan, French President François Mitterrand, and hundreds of thousands of revelers.

The average price of a new house in 1986 was $92,000, while a base-model Chevrolet Chevette sold for $5,645 and a Ford Escort went for $6,052. Gas averaged 86 cents a gallon, while milk sold for $2.05 per gallon. Bread was 56 cents a loaf and eggs were 87 cents a dozen. The national minimum wage was $3.35 per hour. On the radio were hits like "Manic Monday" by The Bangles, "Say You, Say Me" by Lionel Richie, and "On My Own" by Patti LaBelle and Michael McDonald. Millions were watching hit TV shows like *Cheers*, *The Cosby Show*, and *The Golden Girls*, while *Top Gun*, *Crocodile Dundee*, and *Ferris Bueller's Day Off* drew throngs to the silver screen.

On the Numismatic Scene in 1986

"1986 was a colorful year in the hobby," remembers Beth Deisher. "We had the new American Eagle bullion program and all the news coming out of the Mint with that, and the Statue of Liberty Centennial commemorative coins, which were a huge hit. There were controversies on the grading scene, and then there was the advent of PCGS and the certified coins. As editor of *Coin World*, I was especially busy having to choose which stories would lead. Ordinarily it was pretty easy to decide what the biggest story of the week was going to be, but in 1986 I could've chosen three or four lead stories at any given time!"

Professional Coin Grading Service (PCGS) launched operations on February 3, 1986, to become the first company to offer third-party authentication, grading, and encapsulation at scale.

Coin collecting was enjoying steady popularity in 1986, with hundreds of thousands of active hobbyists. While the roll-collecting craze of the early 1960s was a distant memory, plenty of collectors were busy building sets. Many of the hobby's most familiar periodicals were flying off newsstands, with *Coin World* carrying a circulation of 80,394, *COINage* fielding 60,367, *Numismatic News* standing at 35,923, and the American Numismatic Association's monthly *The Numismatist* at 33,072. Meanwhile, hobby columns were well read in many of the nation's daily newspapers, with witty coin observer Ed Reiter leading his popular numismatic column in the *New York Times* throughout the 1980s.

Silver averaged $5.47 per ounce in 1986.

The 1986 United States Mint catalog offered collectors one of the last opportunities to purchase 1776–1976 Bicentennial coin sets directly from the United States Mint.

1986, Bullion Strike

Mintage: 5,393,005

Minted at San Francisco with no mintmark

The first American Silver Eagles were struck in October 1986, with sales of the coin beginning on November 24. Each of the U.S. Mint's then-28 Authorized Purchasers maxed their orders of 50,000 coins, and sales topped 1 million units within hours of the coin's release. Nearly 5.4 million of the new bullion coins were produced to satisfy the number of orders that stacked up. With silver around $5.25 an ounce on November 24, 1986, a typical buyer at the time could expect to pay $6 to $7.50 for a bullion strike.

Minting of the Silver Eagles occurred at the San Francisco Assay Office, though no mintmarks distinguish the origin of the bullion coins. The 1986 bullion Silver Eagle was ranked 83rd in the *100 Greatest U.S. Modern Coins*, in which authors Scott Schechter and

Jeff Garrett note this historic issue as "the coin that started it all." They further comment, "the American Silver Eagle was an instant success and has become the most popular silver bullion coin in history."

Scott Travers recalls, "the American Silver Eagle bullion coin was just that in 1986: a bullion coin for investors. But with each passing year, it appealed more and more to collectors because they have different dates to collect. As the years pass and more coins of different dates are issued, collectors who maintain a project mentality accept the challenge and attempt to assemble a full set."

The all-time-record price for the most valuable 1986 American Silver Eagle was notched on February 8, 2013, when an MS-70 example hammered for $21,150 including fees. That lofty price was no doubt inspired by fervent bidding from collectors looking to achieve a top score in a registry set.

1986, Bullion Strike

MARKET VALUES

	Raw	MS-69	MS-70
Value	$65	$110	$1,000

Note: "Raw" values are for average coins that are not professionally graded/slabbed.

CERTIFICATION DATA

	Total	<MS-69	MS-69	MS-70
# Certified	217,022	6,710	204,931	5,381
Percentage		3.09%	94.43%	2.48%

Note: Data compiled from NGC and PCGS reports, September 2022.

1986-S, Proof

Mintage: 1,446,778

Minted at San Francisco with S mintmark

The first-year Proof maintains the highest mintage of any single Proof in the series, with a total of 1,446,778 pieces being struck at the San Francisco Mint. For perspective, the next-highest Proof mintage belongs to the 2006-W Proof, which saw 1,092,477 coins struck. Interest in the American Silver Eagle series was understandably high during the inaugural year of the coin's reign. This naturally led to outstanding sales of the Proof, which was issued for $21 and could be purchased directly

from the U.S. Mint by the public, as opposed to the bullion coins distributed only through Authorized Purchasers. Virtually all 1986 Proof Silver Eagles grade PF-68 or better, with large numbers certified as a perfect PF-70. While populations of PF-70s are well into the thousands, heavy demand for these top-shelf coins against a comparatively small available supply keeps premiums quite lofty at that grade.

1986-S, Proof

MARKET VALUES

	Raw	PF-69	PF-70
Value	$85	$105	$450

Note: "Raw" values are for average coins in original Mint packaging, not slabbed.

CERTIFICATION DATA

	Total	<PF-69	PF-69	PF-70
# Certified	93,988	2,709	75,347	15,932
Percentage		2.88%	80.17%	16.95%

Note: Data compiled from NGC and PCGS reports, September 2022.

THE YEAR 1987

The American Silver Eagle had already proven its mettle by the second year of the program. The Silver Eagle and its four American Gold Eagle counterparts had quickly become the most popular bullion coins with U.S. investors and collectors and had even begun building a following with international speculators.

The American Gold Eagle was vying for a piece of the pie also held by South African Krugerrands, Canadian Maple Leaf gold coins, Mexican Libertads, and Chinese Pandas. However, the American Silver Eagle was up against only the Mexico Libertad and China Panda silver coinage—silver bullion coinage like Canada's Maple Leaf, Austria's Philharmonic, Australia's Kookaburra, and Great Britain's Britannia had not been released yet. The Silver Eagles were, nearly single-handedly, filling a large precious-metals niche and establishing dominance in the silver marketplace.

Current Events in 1987

The savings-and-loan crisis of the mid-1980s, stirred by poor lending decisions, risky speculation, and lack of oversight by many of the nation's banks, worsened in 1987. The shakeup made many Wall Street investors skittish and was one of many factors that could have led to the stock market crash that year.

The situation with the Dow Jones Industrial Average started off rosily enough in 1987, with the stock index surpassing 2,000 points on the closing bell for the first time on January 8. However, markets were in a tailspin by autumn. On October 19, 1987, a day known among investors as "Black Monday," the Dow Jones Industrial Average fell from an opening stance of 2,247 points and shed 508 points to close at 1,739, resulting in a nearly 23 percent drop to mark the largest one-day loss in volume ever recorded for the Dow.

Prevailing economic issues could have culminated in the loss, but many analysts suggest computerized trading hastened a selloff that was already in motion, and this triggered investors to get rid of even more shares, compounding the situation. Whatever the cause of the 1987 stock market crash, it ended a five-year bull market on Wall Street.

President Reagan, embroiled in continued fallout from the Iran-Contra Affair, claimed no involvement with the situation. However, after congressional investigations proved the arms deals were facilitated by individuals very close to the commander-in-chief, Reagan took full responsibility for the matter in a nationally televised speech in March 1987. Later that year, in June, the president gave another speech that received much less attention at the time but ultimately became one of his most important. Orating before a crowd of hundreds of thousands to commemorate the 750th anniversary of the founding of Berlin, a city ripped in two by the Berlin Wall, Reagan beseeched Soviet leader Mikhail Gorbachev to "tear down this wall." Many historians today widely declare Reagan's 1987 speech at Brandenburg Gate to be a definitive moment that

...ed thaw the four-decade-old Cold War and precipitated the eventual fall of the ...lin Wall and collapse of the Soviet Union over the next few years.

Debuting on ABC in 1987 was beloved family sitcom *Full House*, joining television favorites like the *Cosby Show*, *Cheers*, *Murder, She Wrote*, and *Married... with Children*.

Three Men and a Baby, *Fatal Attraction*, and *Dirty Dancing* were some of the top films in 1987, while top tunes on the radio included Michael Jackson's "Bad," Whitney Houston's "I Wanna Dance With Somebody (Who Loves Me)," Rick Astley's "Never Gonna Give You Up," and George Michael's "Faith."

New homes averaged $104,500, a 1987 Ford Tempo was priced at $9,238, and videocassette recorders—still a hot-ticket item—were selling for $250. A gallon of milk was $2.28 and a dozen eggs cracked in at 78 cents. A gallon of gas went for 95 cents and first-class postage stamps were 22 cents each. The world added its five billionth living person in July 1987.

On the Numismatic Scene in 1987

Numismatic Guaranty Corporation (NGC) began operations in 1987 as a third-party grading service to rival PCGS. NGC, now formally known as Numismatic Guaranty Company, joined PCGS as a major player in what was then a rapidly expanding third-party-graded rare-coin market.

As the year progressed, slabbed rare coins were also enjoying attention from a new set of buyers: Wall Street investors spurned by sputtering stocks and looking for alternative investments. Coins proved a viable vehicle for many investors who eschewed paper commodities in favor of hard assets with known value, inherent rarity, and aesthetic merits. It would seem that third-party graders, with their standardized grading and tamper-evident encapsulation methods, arrived on the scene at a serendipitous time, just as waves of investors wanted something new to speculate in that could be safely traded sight unseen, much like stocks, and this opened the floodgates for affluent Wall Street capitalists and multimillion hedge funds managers to dump tons of new cash into slabbed coins.

The 1987
United States Constitution
Silver Dollar Coin.

Legal tender coinage designed and struck to commemorate the Bicentennial of the United States Constitution.

Designed to convey the strength and integrity of America's most precious document, and struck with exacting care by the U.S. Mint, each United States Constitution Silver Dollar Coin has earned a place among America's finest commemorative coins and serves as an important reminder to hold on to the promise of freedom.

A remarkable tribute in Proof or Uncirculated Quality.
Available in your choice of Proof or Uncirculated Quality and designed by Patricia L. Verani, each finely crafted commemorative coin is struck in .900 fine silver and enclosed in a crystal clear capsule for lasting protection. The obverse features a sheaf of parchment and a quill pen with the inscription "We the People." The reverse displays a cross-section of Americans from past and present.

Presented in strictly Limited Edition.
As required by law, the United States Mint will not produce these coins after June 30, 1988. After this date, the dies will be destroyed—assuring the coins' status as treasured heirlooms for generations to come.

Order your precious heirlooms today!
To secure your selection of United States Constitution Silver Dollar Coins, simply use the Order Form enclosed in this mailing and return it in the reply envelope.

Use the enclosed Order Form.

Constitution Coin Sales
End June 30, 1988

The United States Constitution Silver Dollar Coin is 1.5 inches in diameter and contains 0.76 troy ounces of pure silver.

The 1987 United States Constitution silver dollar was among the commemorative offerings from the U.S. Mint that year, which also included the related United States Constitution $5 gold coin.

No 1987 Kennedy half dollars were minted for general circulation, with all business strikes being issued only in that year's mint sets. The coin had been waning from circulation for about a decade. The Mint was also busy striking the 1987 U.S. Constitution Bicentennial silver dollar and gold half eagle in both Uncirculated and Proof formats. In 1987 the price of silver hovered around $7.02.

1987, Bullion Strike

Mintage: 11,442,335

Minted at San Francisco with no mintmark

Coming off tremendous momentum from its late-1986 release, the American Silver Eagle was soaring into the stratosphere by the time 1987 rolled around. A total of 11,442,335 were struck, more than double the production during the coin's inaugural year. This was the high-water mark for the series' mintage in the twentieth century. The 1987 bullion mintage would not be surpassed until 2008. Rising silver prices in 1987 prompted bullion speculators to stock up on the new coin, with silver prices flirting with $11 an ounce during the spring. All told, silver threw its lariat around the $7 price point, which was higher than 1986 averages but still well off early-1980s highs.

Some 1987 American Silver Eagles are encapsulated by PCGS with a "WTC Ground Zero Recovery" label, indicating the coin was found in the bullion vault once housed under the World Trade Center in New York City.

Collectors should keep an eye out for bullion examples that are free of marks, spots, and scratches. As is par for the course, most 1987 bullion Silver Eagles are found in grades ranging from MS-66 to MS-68, with MS-69 coins scarce and MS-70 still scarcer and more in demand. The record price for the 1987 American Silver Eagle was achieved in March 2013, when GreatCollections offered an MS-70 example that commanded $9,075.

1987, Bullion Strike

MARKET VALUES

	Raw	MS-69	MS-70
Value	$38	$47	$1,200

Note: "Raw" values are for average coins that are not professionally graded/slabbed.

CERTIFICATION DATA

	Total	<MS-69	MS-69	MS-70
# Certified	194,532	6,819	185,390	2,323
Percentage		3.51%	95.30%	1.19%

Note: Data compiled from NGC and PCGS reports, September 2022.

1987-S, Proof

Mintage: 904,732

Minted at San Francisco with S mintmark

While the 1986-S Proof Silver Eagle was struck to the tune of nearly 1.5 million pieces, the 1987-S offering came in at just a little over 900,000.

In retrospect, that is still a lofty number for a series wherein typical mintages infrequently surpassed 800,000 or 900,000 for any single issue bearing a premium-quality numismatic finish. The slippage might be explained in part by a $2 increase in price for the Proof, which was now issued at $23.

By all accounts, the 1987-S Proof Silver Eagle is a standard release, offering few curveballs or pleasant surprises for the collector. As is typical for 1980s Proof Silver Eagles, PF-70 coins are scarce and expensive, a factor tracing back to extraordinary demand by set registry collectors looking to complete a "perfect" assemblage of Silver Eagles. Most collectors building sets in albums or acquiring one of every Proof will be amply satisfied with a blazing PF-69. Regardless of grade, American Silver Eagles are known for spotting and thus collectors should avoid blemished coins. There are plenty of pristine Proof examples on the market.

1987-S, Proof

MARKET VALUES

	Raw	PF-69	PF-70
Value	$85	$105	$625

Note: "Raw" values are for average coins in original Mint packaging, not slabbed.

CERTIFICATION DATA

	Total	<PF-69	PF-69	PF-70
# Certified	52,976	1,889	45,134	5,953
Percentage		3.57%	85.20%	11.24%

Note: Data compiled from NGC and PCGS reports, September 2022.

THE YEAR 1988

The American Silver Eagle program sailed into its third year with weaker mintages but continued dominance as *the* silver coin for collectors and investors, even as Mexican Libertad production remained strong and Canada unveiled its similar Maple Leaf offering. Suppressing sales of the Silver Eagle was the slipping price of silver, which had slid from multi-year peaks in 1987.

Current Events in 1988

On September 29, 1988, the Space Shuttle *Discovery* took to the heavens, marking NASA's "Return to Flight" after grounding its shuttle fleet for more than 30 months due to the *Challenger* tragedy of January 1986.

A wave of the future was laid below the Atlantic waters with the first-ever transatlantic fiber-optic cable. The fiber-optic line could carry as many as 40,000 simultaneous calls. A more nefarious peek into the world of tomorrow occurred in 1988 when the "Morris worm" became one of the first known computer viruses to affect computers linked to the internet.

In June 1988 NASA Goddard Institute for Space Studies director Dr. James Hansen spoke at a historic Senate hearing on climate change. In the report, he stated that Earth had reached its warmest point in modern history and there was 99 percent certainty that man-made greenhouse gases like carbon dioxide emissions from burning fossil fuels were influencing the warming trend.

The 1988 U.S. presidential election pitted Republican Vice President George H.W. Bush against Democratic Massachusetts governor Michael Dukakis. Bush, who had been serving as vice president under President Ronald Reagan since 1981, was a national household name and was running with the relatively young and unknown Indiana Republican senator Dan Quayle. Meanwhile, Governor Dukakis—who had been active in state-level politics in Massachusetts since the early 1960s—was paired with Democratic Texas senator Lloyd Bentsen, an elder statesman capable of garnering votes south of the Mason-Dixon Line. Dukakis went into the fall of 1988 atop Bush, but the vice president performed well in two debates and ultimately carried 40 states and 446 electoral votes to win the election with nearly 48.9 million votes.

While Americans claimed only two gold medals and medaled six times during the Winter Olympics in Calgary, Canada, the United States saw a much stronger performance a few months later at the Summer Olympiad in Seoul, South Korea, where the nation took home 36 golds and 94 total medals.

Cheers and *The Cosby Show* continued in popularity in 1988 alongside *Growing Pains, The Golden Girls, Roseanne*, and *Alf. Rain Man, Who Framed Roger Rabbit?, Coming to America, Twins*, and *Big* were all the rage in theaters while top radio hits included "Get Outta My Dreams Get Into My Car" by Billy Ocean, "Don't Worry Be Happy" by Bobby McFerrin, "Heaven is a Place on Earth" by Belinda Carlisle, "Sweet Child O' Mine" by Guns n' Roses, and "Kokomo" by The Beach Boys.

A typical new home cost about $113,000 in 1988 and a new Ford Taurus took $9,996. The IBM personal computer, boasting 30 megabytes of hard drive and a monitor, clocked in at $1,249, while a Logitech computer mouse ran for $89.99. Gas was 91 cents a gallon, while a gallon of milk and loaf of bread were $2.19 and 60 cents, respectively. The average price of silver for the year was $6.53.

On the Numismatic Scene in 1988

The West Point Bullion Depository, which had opened in 1937, officially became a United States Mint facility on March 31, 1988. West Point had been intermittently striking legal-tender coinage since 1973, beginning with unmintmarked supplies of Lincoln cents and Washington quarters in the 1970s and culminating in 1983 with the production of the 1984 Olympic $10 eagle, the first legal-tender gold coin struck by the U.S. Mint since 1933 and the first U.S. coin to ever bear the "W" mintmark of West Point. Beginning in 1986, West Point was striking bullion coinage without a mintmark. It still holds bullion and conducts other business not directly pertaining to the striking of coinage. The United States Mint facility in San Francisco also regained its "Mint" status, having become an assay office in 1962 after coining had come to a pause in 1955—101 years after the first San Francisco Mint opened in 1854.

The slabbed rare-coin market was really heating up in 1988. Wall Street investors seeking alternative assets were lured by sight-unseen trading made possible by standardized grading and tamper-evident encapsulation.

This helped fuel tremendous growth in the coin marketplace, though many feared the quick and pronounced upswing in pricing was little more than a bubble bound to burst. Even with the safety net of third-party grading, the complex world of rare coins met newbie investors with a steep learning curve, and some were taken for a ride by unscrupulous sorts. The American Numismatic Association and the Federal Trade Commission embarked on a partnership to release an educational brochure entitled "Consumer Alert: Investing in Rare Coins."

1988, Bullion Strike

Mintage: 5,004,646

Minted at West Point and San Francisco with no mintmark

The year 1988 saw the lowest mintage figures yet for the young American Silver Eagle series, with the bullion finish logging fewer than half of the sales it saw in 1987. Some in Congress suggested the limited sales network of a couple dozen or so Authorized Purchasers was to blame. Distributors suggested the coin had lost its novel appeal. But a drop-off in sales back in 1988 can just as well be attributed to lower silver prices, which had fallen a notable 7 percent from 1987 averages, and the American Silver Eagle perhaps saw some of its market share siphoned off by the new one-ounce silver Canadian Maple Leaf.

All in all, a production run of 5 million later proved to be about on par with or even better than most of the annual outputs for the bullion Silver Eagle during the remainder of the twentieth century. The relatively anemic mintage figures for the 1988 American Silver Eagle contribute to robust prices for better-grade coins, especially the MS-70 examples. The record price for the bullion 1988 American Silver Eagle goes to an MS-70 example sold by GreatCollections in April 2013 for $27,500.

1988, Bullion Strike

MARKET VALUES

	Raw	MS-69	MS-70
Value	$38	$48	$1,925

Note: "Raw" values are for average coins that are not professionally graded/slabbed.

CERTIFICATION DATA

	Total	<MS-69	MS-69	MS-70
# Certified	139,318	4,263	133,707	1,348
Percentage		3.06%	95.97%	0.97%

Note: Data compiled from NGC and PCGS reports, September 2022.

1988-S, Proof

Mintage: 557,370

Minted at San Francisco with S mintmark

The 1988-S Proof Silver Eagle endured its lowest mintage yet, though that was not necessarily saying much for a series that had been around for only three years. Even with its overall output of 557,370 pieces, lower than mintages from either of the previous two years, the 1988-S Proof posted significantly higher numbers than would be seen by many of the Proof issues yet to come. Issue pricing can't be fingered as the culprit for lower sales in 1988, as the Proofs were offered for $23, the same price as in 1987.

Collectors will find the vast majority of 1988-S Proofs grade around PF-69, with a small but significant minority earning a PF-70 grade. Expect to pay a strong premium for the 1988-S in PF-70. The record price for the 1988-S Proof is $2,185, paid in January 2008 for a PF-70 coin that crossed the block of Heritage Auctions.

1988-S, Proof

MARKET VALUES

	Raw	PF-69	PF-70
Value	$85	$105	$550

Note: "Raw" values are for average coins in original Mint packaging, not slabbed.

CERTIFICATION DATA

	Total	<PF-69	PF-69	PF-70
# Certified	40,459	1,034	33,903	5,522
Percentage		2.56%	83.80%	13.65%

Note: Data compiled from NGC and PCGS reports, September 2022.

THE YEAR 1989

American Silver Eagle sales were a touch stronger in 1989, but it wasn't necessarily because of the intense investor speculation in rare coins, which peaked that year. Many of the hobby's most popular series were cresting in value at prices never before seen, but the feverish activity eventually broke later in the year.

Current Events in 1989

President George H.W. Bush was inaugurated on January 20, 1989. The savings-and-loan crisis was coming to a head in 1989, with nearly a quarter of financial institutions and associations needing help via government bailouts totaling $150 billion. In the spring, calls for freedom and democracy in China led to massive demonstrations in Beijing's Tiananmen Square.

The Berlin Wall fell on November 9, 1989, following a decree by the leader of the East German Communist Party that citizens of the German Democratic Republic were free to cross the border at will. The Berlin Wall, constructed in 1961, was demolished by throngs of sledgehammer-wielding revelers in what became a memorable live television news feed. The Cold War was beginning to wane as free elections took place in Poland and talks occurred at the Malta Summit between President Bush and Soviet General Secretary Mikhail Gorbachev.

More horrific was the news coming out of Prince William Sound, Alaska, where the Exxon *Valdez* oil supertanker spilled 10.8 million gallons of oil into the region's pristine waters on the morning of March 24, 1989. Hurricane Hugo raked through the Caribbean islands before slamming into South Carolina's shores on September 22, 1989. The storm killed 67 people and caused $11 billion in damage. A major explosion at the Phillips 66 polyethylene plant in Pasadena, Texas, leveled the facility, killing 23 and injuring 314.

On October 17, 1989, the Loma Prieta earthquake rocked the San Francisco Bay area with 6.9-magnitude forces. The devastating earthquake killed 67 people and injured thousands, with many of the casualties resulting from the collapse of the double-decker Nimitz Freeway.

Nintendo's handheld videogame system known as Game Boy was released in the United States on July 31, 1989, selling one million units within the first week and becoming one of the most successful and iconic gaming consoles of all time. A day after Game Boy hit the streets, Microsoft released Microsoft Office, which originally included Microsoft Word, Microsoft Excel, and Microsoft PowerPoint.

"My Prerogative" by Bobby Brown, "Wind Beneath My Wings" by Bette Midler, and "Every Rose Has its Thorn" by Poison were working their way up the Top 40 charts. Meanwhile, *Cheers, The Cosby Show*, and *Roseanne* maintained a lock on television ratings, with other popular programs such as *A Different World, The Wonder Years*, and newcomer *America's Funniest Home Videos* rounding out the primetime schedule. Some of the big screen favorites were *Batman, Driving Miss Daisy, Indiana Jones and the Last Crusade, When Harry Met Sally, The Little Mermaid*, and *Honey, I Shrunk the Kids*.

Prices for new homes climbed to an average of $120,000. A new Ford Probe cost $10,459, while the slightly tonier BMW 325 was $21,400. Gas prices registered at $1 per gallon and a gallon of milk was $2.30. A first-class postage stamp was 25 cents, and a Casio handheld liquid-crystal display color television set back on-the-go couch potatoes $249.99.

On the Numismatic Scene in 1989

If there was a high-water mark for the numismatic industry in the last decades of the twentieth century, then 1989 may have been it. The coin-market boom that began in late 1987 rose to its zenith by the spring of 1989, when market prices—driven by unprecedented (and since unmatched) investor interest in slabbed rare coins—were climbing for some pieces by 10 or 20 percent or more each week.

A story in the January 21, 1990, edition of the *Chicago Tribune* summarized the rare-coin market of 1989: "Investors in extremely rare coins enjoyed a profitable 1989, according to comprehensive price surveys compiled by the hobby's two larger newspapers." The story went on to report that the Trends Index by *Coin World* reflected a 50.6 percent increase in value for "Choice Uncirculated" coins over a period of 12 months ending November 30, 1989, while a coin index by *Numismatic News* highlighted a 45.5 percent increase in prices during 1989.

What wasn't necessarily reported in the general media was the bloodbath on the ground over the summer of 1989, when the bubble burst. Price increases across much of the marketplace appeared to halt over early June, during the Long Beach Expo in California. Investor groups began to pull out of the market, pulling the plug on the runaway prices.

By the end of 1989, it was clear the coin boom went bust. Many dealers had to close up shop, while unlucky investors who didn't sell at the peak of the market in spring 1989 were left to lick their wounds. Those holding a position in bullion were also recovering from losses, as average silver prices dropped to about $5.51 an ounce—off a little more than a dollar from 1988.

1989, Bullion Strike

Mintage: 5,203,327

Minted at West Point and San Francisco with no mintmark

Mintages were up slightly for the 1989 bullion Silver Eagle over the production figures for 1988. A drop in silver prices may have helped inspire some investors to "buy on the dip," thus edging up demand a hair. Collectors need to be choosy about their 1989 Silver Eagles, many of which have seen undesirable toning, milk spots, and other issues over years of mishandling and poor storage—nothing unique to 1989, per se, but certainly much more prevalent among older issues in the series. Conversely, nicely toned examples can and deservedly do take beaucoup bucks at auction.

Many 1989 bullion Silver Eagles were recovered from the vaults of the World Trade Center after the 9/11 terrorist attacks. PCGS authenticated and encapsulated these in holders bearing patriotic labels emblazoned with the phrase "WTC Ground Zero Recovery."

The record price for a 1989 American Silver Eagle was claimed by a coin graded MS-70 that crossed the block at a September 2016 Heritage Auctions event for $5,170.

1989, Bullion Strike

MARKET VALUES

	Raw	MS-69	MS-70
Value	$38	$48	$1,225

Note: "Raw" values are for average coins that are not professionally graded/slabbed.

CERTIFICATION DATA

	Total	<MS-69	MS-69	MS-70
# Certified	158,274	5,518	150,925	1,831
Percentage		3.49%	95.36%	1.16%

Note: Data compiled from NGC and PCGS reports, September 2022.

1989-S, Proof

Mintage: 617,694

Minted at San Francisco with S mintmark

Mintages for the 1989-S Proof were up significantly—better than 10 percent—over the 1988-S offering. Perhaps some of the investor interest in rare coins spilled over to the Proof American Silver Eagle, an attractive lure for novice and advanced collectors alike. The U.S. Mint issued the 1989-S Proof for $23, the same price pegged for S-mint issue since 1987.

Most 1989-S Proofs offer remarkable surface and strike quality. PF-70 examples really aren't rare for this issue, though premiums remain much higher than for PF-68 and PF-69 examples. Collectors should focus on the best they can find, as some Proof examples offer sharper cameo contrast and nicer surfaces than others.

1989-S, Proof

MARKET VALUES

	Raw	PF-69	PF-70
Value	$85	$105	$320

Note: "Raw" values are for average coins in original Mint packaging, not slabbed.

CERTIFICATION DATA

	Total	<PF-69	PF-69	PF-70
# Certified	43,474	969	35,115	7,390
Percentage		2.23%	80.77%	17.00%

Note: Data compiled from NGC and PCGS reports, September 2022.

THE YEAR 1990

If 1989 marked the peak of the rare-coin market, then 1990 represented a valley. It was during the start of the 1990s that the real fallout from the collapse of the rare-coin market was felt, with prices for many series in free fall. In retrospect, classic commemorative coins probably fared the worst of all, with some issues falling in price by more than 90 percent from their mid-1989 highs. Morgan dollars, Liberty Walking halves, and other popular coins also endured staggering slides in value throughout 1990 and beyond. The American Silver Eagle, on the other hand, was on an upswing, with mintages climbing for a second straight year.

Current Events in 1990

In August 1990, under the leadership of Saddam Hussein, Iraqi military forces invaded neighboring Kuwait. The setting was more peaceful for the Germans, who celebrated the official recoupling of East and West Germany. A different kind of connection was made under the waters of the English Channel, where British and French crews linked both sides of a tunnel eventually serving as a rail line between Great Britain and France.

NASA endeavored upon its own expensive pie-in-the-sky dream: the April 24 launch of a massive telescope that could see to the edges of the universe. The multi-billion-dollar Hubble Space Telescope was based on an idea first proposed in the 1940s and was funded in the 1970s.

New satellite technology allowed Mazda to introduce the first car with global positioning system technology for navigational use. Software consultant Tim Berners-Lee published the first website on the World Wide Web.

A catastrophic 7.7-magnitude earthquake in Iran left 50,000 dead, and in the United Kingdom, Prime Minister Margaret Thatcher resigned after helming the nation since 1979. The television world was never the same after *The Simpsons* debuted on FOX in December 1989, taking pop culture by storm in 1990. *Cheers* remained atop the primetime ratings, with *60 Minutes, Roseanne, A Different World*, and *The Cosby Show* also in tight contention for viewers. On the radio were "U Can't Touch This" by MC Hammer, "Groove is in the Heart" by Deee-Lite, and "Vogue" by Madonna. The top box-office draws included *Home Alone, Dances with Wolves, Pretty Woman*, and *The Hunt for Red October*.

Prices for a new home rose to $130,000, while the price for a Toyota Camry LE was $14,658. A gallon of gas lifted to $1.10. A loaf of bread was $1.29 and a gallon of milk cost $2.15, but a first-class postage stamp remained at 25 cents. The United States economy was heading toward a recession as consumer confidence sunk and oil prices rose amid the specter of war in the Middle East. International tensions were on the rise and so was inflation.

On the Numismatic Scene in 1990

If prices were about to rise for the typical American consumer, they might have found a little relief if they were shopping for collectible coins. The numismatic marketplace crashed in 1990. Popular Gem Uncirculated rare coins that had been widely promoted as surefire investments in 1988 or 1989 could be had for a fraction of their prices just months earlier. The Wall Street investor had all but disappeared from the coin community. Left to pick up the pieces were bargain-seeking coin collectors, many of whom had willingly stood by the sidelines as they watched the action unfold.

Many dealers lost their shirts in the fallout, and so, too, did those who bought rare coins thinking they had a foolproof investment on their hands. The marketplace activity of the late 1980s was a boom-bust cycle that had happened before and happened again, though perhaps never before or since with the same magnitude of growth.

The bearish marketplace lumbered through most of the 1990s, a period that was very friendly to collectors who bought coins for the love of the hobby and their particular numismatic niches. Many series offered deals not seen in years, and collectors—particularly those building type sets or assembling date-and-mintmark runs of classic coins—did very well for themselves. Collectors of gold coins were aided not only by the softening of pricing for high-end material but also by low bullion prices, with gold averaging a closing price of $386 per ounce in 1990. Silver, meanwhile, clipped along at $4.83 an ounce that year.

The 1990 United States Mint Proof set was one of the many U.S. Mint offerings that year.

1990, Bullion Strike

Mintage: 5,840,110

Minted at West Point and San Francisco with no mintmark

The bullion arm of the American Silver Eagle series saw its third consecutive year of production increases, a direct reflection of building demand for the coin. Softening bullion prices made the coin more affordable for investors, perhaps many of whom were also growing increasingly nervous about the deepening geopolitical conflict in the Middle East and the possibility that energy prices would subsequently skyrocket.

The 1990 Silver Eagles offer a mixed bag of coins, some discolored or spotted, others sporting flashy white surfaces, and a small number awash in gorgeous toning. While bullion investors may pay little attention to the lesser-quality examples—perhaps even preferring them due to lower numismatic premiums over spot—the diehard collector will take great pains to seek the nicest coins with the best eye appeal. An example graded MS-70 realized $13,200 in a June 2018 Heritage Auctions sale.

1990, Bullion Strike

MARKET VALUES

	Raw	MS-69	MS-70
Value	$38	$48	$2,900

Note: "Raw" values are for average coins that are not professionally graded/slabbed.

CERTIFICATION DATA

	Total	<MS-69	MS-69	MS-70
# Certified	118,435	5,491	112,361	583
Percentage		4.64%	94.87%	0.49%

Note: Data compiled from NGC and PCGS reports, September 2022.

1990-S, Proof

Mintage: 695,510

Minted at San Francisco with S mintmark

Proof 1990-S Silver Eagles touched nearly 700,000, a figure to that point last surpassed in 1987 and not to be reached again until 2001. The U.S. Mint offered the 1990-S Proof for $23, pricing that had remained in effect since 1987. The 1990-S Proof is usually encountered in the grade of PF-69, with PF-70s much scarcer but still attainable. Collectors should always be choosy with their Proof Silver Eagles, selecting the nicest examples they can find with deeply mirrored fields and heavily frosted devices.

1990-S, Proof

MARKET VALUES

	Raw	PF-69	PF-70
Value	$85	$105	$300

Note: "Raw" values are for average coins in original Mint packaging, not slabbed.

CERTIFICATION DATA

	Total	<PF-69	PF-69	PF-70
# Certified	46,168	911	36,660	8,597
Percentage		1.97%	79.41%	18.62%

Note: Data compiled from NGC and PCGS reports, September 2022.

THE YEAR 1991

The U.S. coin market continued to shed its late-1980s gains, with prices still falling on many of high-end coins from popular series. Meanwhile, silver and gold also continued sinking in value, even as the recession that began in 1990 languished into the first quarter of 1991. Inflation rates, which reached 5.40 percent in 1990, settled back to 4.21 percent in 1991 and would continue sliding downward as the 1990s progressed.

Current Events in 1991

Following Saddam Hussein's march into Kuwait in August 1990, the United States and North Atlantic Treaty Organization (NATO) situated troops in Saudi Arabia under Operation Desert Shield, with the United Nations promising military action if Iraq didn't vacate Kuwait by January 15. Iraq stood its ground, leading the United States to start attacks shortly after the UN's expiration date passed, beginning the multinational coalition effort known as Operation Desert Storm. Weeks later, ground forces entered Kuwait and southern Iraq in Operation Desert Sabre, with President George H.W. Bush calling for a ceasefire in February. Iraq agreed to keep the peace and calm returned to Kuwait.

The June 12 election of Boris Yeltsin as president of the Russian Soviet Federative Socialist Republic served as real hope that the region's communist regime was eroding away. The Soviet Union dissolved on December 25, 1991, officially ending the Cold War and bringing independence to more than a dozen Eastern European nations.

A terrible cyclone killed more than 135,000 in Bangladesh and massive fires in the hillside of Oakland, California, destroyed thousands of homes, with 25 people perishing in the flames. A widespread tornado outbreak on April 26, 1991, spawned more than 50 twisters, including an F-5 in Andover, Kansas, with winds topping out at 268 miles per hour. The storms killed 21, injured hundreds, and caused more than a half billion dollars in damage.

The most popular primetime shows were *60 Minutes, Roseanne, Murphy Brown, Cheers,* and *Designing Woman.* Debuting in September 1991 was *Home Improvement.*

Topping the charts in 1991 were "Black or White" by Michael Jackson, "Rush, Rush" by Paula Abdul, "Motownphilly" by Boyz II Men, "Losing My Religion" by R.E.M., and "It Ain't Over 'til It's Over" by Lenny Kravitz. *The Silence of the Lambs, Terminator 2: Judgment Day, Father of the Bride,* and *Beauty and the Beast* scored big crowds at movie theaters.

The typical cost of a new home topped $140,500, while the price for a 1991 Dodge Caravan started at $12,427. First-class postage stamp prices rose to 29 cents in February 1991, while the price for a gallon of gas hovered around $1.14. Milk was $2.80 and a dozen eggs were $1.01, with a loaf of bread costing $1.25 and a pound of bacon about $1.49. The Dow Jones Industrial Average closed above 3,000 points for the first time on April 17, 1991. Silver prices ticked downward from the previous year to an average of $4.06 per ounce.

On the Numismatic Scene in 1991

The American Numismatic Association, widely known as the ANA, celebrated its centennial in 1991 with a monumental World's Fair of Money event in Chicago. The club was founded in 1891 and has since grown to become the largest numismatic organization in the United States, with some 25,000 members.

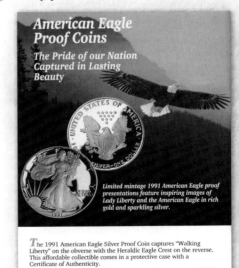

American Eagle Proof Coins
The Pride of our Nation Captured in Lasting Beauty

Limited mintage 1991 American Eagle proof presentations feature inspiring images of Lady Liberty and the American Eagle in rich gold and sparkling silver.

The 1991 American Eagle Silver Proof Coin captures "Walking Liberty" on the obverse with the Heraldic Eagle Crest on the reverse. This affordable collectible comes in a protective case with a Certificate of Authenticity.
$11 American Eagle Proof Silver One Ounce Coin.............................$ 23.00

The 1991 American Eagle Gold Proof Coin features a modified version of Augustus St.-Gaudens "Liberty" on the obverse. A modern impression of a family of Eagles is featured on the reverse. The coins are struck at least twice with special dies to ensure that the detailed images are captured in shimmering beauty.

By 1991, the Proof American Silver Eagle had become a seasoned part of the U.S. Mint product lineup.

1991, Bullion Strike

Mintage: 7,191,066

Minted at West Point and San Francisco with no mintmark

Falling silver prices helped contribute to an uptick of buyers snatching silver bullion at a perceived "low," and the American Silver Eagle hence performed quite well in 1991. Selling nearly 7.2 million units that year, the 1991 American Silver Eagle saw its highest mintage since 1987 and wound up posting the second-highest sales total for the 1990s, bested only slightly by the 1999 bullion Silver Eagle, which notched a mintage just north of 7.4 million.

A small number of 1991 Silver Eagles have been holdered by PCGS as "WTC Ground Zero Recovery" coins, meaning they were legally removed from the large bullion vault that was located under New York City's World Trade Center.

Many 1991 Silver Eagles are toned or show other signs of surface aging, none necessarily bad but some boasting better eye appeal than others. Collectors wanting blast-white coins can find them, though MS-70 is a particularly elusive grade. The record price for a 1991 American Silver Eagle was hammered by Heritage Auctions in September 2009, when a coin graded MS-70 sold for a stunning $34,500.

1991, Bullion Strike

MARKET VALUES

	Raw	MS-69	MS-70
Value	$38	$47	$2,500

Note: "Raw" values are for average coins that are not professionally graded/slabbed.

CERTIFICATION DATA

	Total	<MS-69	MS-69	MS-70
# Certified	141,682	6,091	134,675	916
Percentage		4.30%	95.05%	0.65%

Note: Data compiled from NGC and PCGS reports, September 2022.

1991-S, Proof

Mintage: 511,925

Minted at San Francisco with S mintmark

Demand for Proof Silver Eagles tapered off throughout the 1990s. Bearing this out is the anemic mintage of barely over a half million for the 1991-S Proof, which continued to be sold by the U.S. Mint for $23. Most 1991-S Silver Eagles grade around PF-68 or PF-69, but PF-70 pieces are plentiful enough for the collectors who want them.

1991-S, Proof

MARKET VALUES

	Raw	PF-69	PF-70
Value	$85	$105	$500

Note: "Raw" values are for average coins in original Mint packaging, not slabbed.

CERTIFICATION DATA

	Total	<PF-69	PF-69	PF-70
# Certified	36,307	1,017	30,712	4,578
Percentage		2.80%	84.59%	12.61%

Note: Data compiled from NGC and PCGS reports, September 2022.

THE YEAR 1992

The United States Mint celebrated its bicentennial, having been established in Philadelphia in 1792. The occasion was marked by the minting of special commemorative medals and a new 90 percent silver Proof coin program. Meanwhile, American Silver Eagle mintages fell as silver prices sank below $4 per ounce, discouraging many investors from dumping funds into bullion coins. Also continuing their slide were the prices of collector coins, with the marketplace still reeling from the mass exodus of Wall Street investors in late 1989 and 1990.

Current Events in 1992

The North American Free Trade Agreement (NAFTA) was signed by President George H.W. Bush, who entered into the agreement with the Canadian prime minister and Mexican president. NAFTA aimed to ease trade restrictions between the three nations, allowing for more open trade. The deal went through on December 17, 1992, more than a month after Bush had already lost the presidential election to Democratic Arkansas governor Bill Clinton, who ran with Democratic Tennessee senator Al Gore. Both Bush and Clinton fended off third-party candidate Ross Perot, a Texas businessman and philanthropist who ran as an independent and managed to clinch nearly 19 percent of the vote.

After leaving a path of destruction through the Bahamas, Hurricane Andrew devastated South Florida as a Category 5 hurricane on August 24, 1992. A total of 65 people died and losses of more than $27 billion were assessed along Hurricane Andrew's path.

Riots broke out in Los Angeles when four local policemen were acquitted in the assault case of Rodney King, a taxi driver who had been on parole for robbery and was arrested a year earlier on charges of driving under the influence, following a high-speed chase through the streets of L.A. After the acquittals, riots spanned six days and resulted in 63 deaths, more than 2,300 injuries, 7,000 fires, and almost $1 billion in damages.

The 27th Amendment was added to the United States Constitution on May 5, 1992, following a 202-year ratification process. The amendment, forbidding senators and representatives from granting themselves pay raises, was initially proposed in 1789 but was pushed to the wayside as too few states voted for it.

Space Shuttle *Endeavour* charted its maiden voyage into space on May 7, 1992. *Endeavour* was the last vehicle built under the NASA Space Shuttle program and ventured on 25 flights. The Mall of America opened its doors in Bloomington, Minnesota, on August 11, 1992, to become the largest shopping mall in the United States at that time. Boasting 4,870,000 square feet and 530 stores, the Mall of America welcomes approximately 40 million visitors each year.

The Cartoon Network debuted on October 1, 1992, and aired all types of animated children's programming. Other channels featured primetime hits like *60 Minutes*, *Roseanne*, *Home Improvement*, *Murphy Brown*, *Coach*, *Cheers*, and *Full House*.

Top radio hits in 1992 were "I Will Always Love You" by Whitney Houston, "End of the Road" by Boyz II Men, "Tears in Heaven" by Eric Clapton, and "Smells Like Teen Spirit" by Nirvana. Moviegoers loved *Batman Returns*, *Lethal Weapon 3*, *Sister Act*, *Wayne's World*, *Home Alone 2: Lost in New York*, and *Aladdin*. This was the last year that both the Winter Olympiad and Summer Games were held in the same year; the U.S. scored 11 medals (five of them gold) at the Winter Olympics in Albertville, France, and 108 medals (37 golds) at the Summer Olympiad in Barcelona, Spain.

The average price for a new home in 1992 edged up to $144,000, while a 1992 Ford Escort hatchback could be bought at a base price of $8,355, representing one of the lowest prices for a new car from one of the "Big 3" domestic auto manufacturers at that time. The price of a first-class postage stamp remained at 29 cents, while a gallon of gas could be bought for $1.13. A gallon of milk was $2.78 and a dozen eggs were 93 cents. Silver tracked around $3.95 per ounce, marking among the lowest average prices for the precious metal during the history of the American Silver Eagle program to date.

On the Numismatic Scene in 1992

The grand occasion of the United States Mint bicentennial inspired the release of a new program offering dimes, quarters, and half dollars in 90 percent silver Proof format. The 1992 Silver Proof Sets and 1992 Silver Prestige Proof Sets were instant hits.

In 1992 Congress established the Citizens' Commemorative Coin Advisory Committee (CCCAC) with the objective of reducing the proliferation of commemorative coins. Congress charged the committee with making annual recommendations regarding commemorative coin themes.

In the wake of the Soviet Union's dissolution in 1991, many mass-market promoters were making big bucks selling late-date coins of the Soviet Union, including Uncirculated examples of the last issues representing the communist regime from 1991 and the newly minted 1992 Russian Federation coins, the first struck under a freely elected government.

The days of Wall Street investors stampeding the bourse floors of major coins shows were a memory and coin collectors had free reign of the marketplace. Between a slower-paced numismatic market, relatively unremarkable activity on the bullion side, and dust from the market shakeup of 1989–1990 having largely settled, many remember 1992 as a tranquil time in the coin hobby.

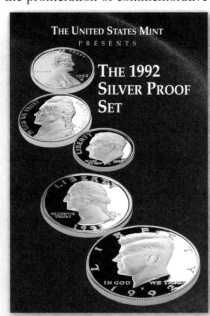

The 1992 U.S. Mint silver Proof sets splashed onto the numismatic scene and quickly found a large customer base.

1992, Bullion Strike

Mintage: 5,540,068

Minted at West Point and San Francisco with no mintmark

Mintages for the bullion Silver Eagle fell a drastic 26 percent from the previous year as investors backed off from buying, silver prices having dipped to some of the lowest prices in many years. Like many of the American Silver Eagles, the 1992 bullion strike is regarded by some as a tougher date. Its mintage of just over 5.5 million is a small fraction of the Silver Eagle's modern-day annual figures ranging beyond 15 million, a threshold so many collectors and investors have largely taken for granted with today's output for the series.

As par for the course, many certified 1992 American Silver Eagles exist in the grades of MS-66 to MS-68, with most grading MS-69 and much smaller populations still in MS-70. The record price for a 1992 Silver Eagle is $16,450, paid in September 2017 for an MS-70 example sold by Heritage Auctions.

1992, Bullion Strike

MARKET VALUES

	Raw	MS-69	MS-70
Value	$38	$48	$1,725

Note: "Raw" values are for average coins that are not professionally graded/slabbed.

CERTIFICATION DATA

	Total	<MS-69	MS-69	MS-70
# Certified	140,181	5,373	133,331	1,477
Percentage		3.83%	95.11%	1.05%

Note: Data compiled from NGC and PCGS reports, September 2022.

1992-S, Proof

Mintage: 498,654

Minted at San Francisco with S mintmark

This was the last year that regular-issue American Silver Eagle Proofs were minted in San Francisco, at least until 2011. The curtain call for the seven-year run of S-mint Proofs inspired barely an applause from collectors, with mintages below 500,000 for the first time in the Proof series. Examples in PF-69 are typical for this issue, while PF-70 coins demand significant premiums.

1992-S, Proof

MARKET VALUES

	Raw	PF-69	PF-70
Value	$85	$105	$500

Note: "Raw" values are for average coins in original Mint packaging, not slabbed.

CERTIFICATION DATA

	Total	<PF-69	PF-69	PF-70
# Certified	38,503	818	32,323	5,362
Percentage		2.12%	83.95%	13.93%

Note: Data compiled from NGC and PCGS reports, September 2022.

The Year 1993

Production of American Silver Eagle Proofs packed up and headed East for minting at the "mother mint" in Philadelphia. However, as mintage figures for the 1993-P Proofs would show, only relatively small numbers of collectors were eager at the time to purchase an example of this first-year Philadelphia coin. Conversely, the bullion Silver Eagles enjoyed a much-improved showing thanks to solidly positive movement in the bullion markets.

Current Events in 1993

President William J. Clinton was sworn in as the nation's 42nd president on January 20, 1993. Clinton would face many unprecedented challenges, with the one of the first being a devastating attack on the World Trade Center that occurred on February 26, 1993. Islamic fundamentalist terrorists packed a moving truck full of explosives and situated it in the multilevel underground parking garage, with the intention of bringing down the Twin Towers and killing tens of thousands of people. While detonation of the 1,336-pound bomb failed to topple the towers, it caused major damage to much of the parking garage and surrounding infrastructure, killing six and injuring 1,042.

On April 19 a massive conflagration engulfed the Branch Davidian compound in Waco, Texas, which became the site of a 51-day siege by the U.S. military, federal government, and Texas law enforcement when the religious group was suspected of stockpiling illegal weapons. In all, 86 died, including 25 children, two pregnant women, and David Koresh, the leader of the Branch Davidians.

A tsunami triggered after a 7.8-magnitude earthquake near Hokkaido, Japan, killed 230 on the Japanese island of Okushiri. War between the Eastern European nations of Bosnia and Herzegovina flared up, with ethnic fighting between Serbs, Croats, and Muslims sparked after the country of Yugoslavia was fractured.

Toy company Ty, Inc., released Beanie Babies, a line of small stuffed animals that became one of the first internet sensations and a major fad during the latter half of the 1990s. Many bought these plushies not as toys but as valuable collectibles, and some even bought them as investments, as a few proved quite rare and desirable. "Dreamlover" by Mariah Carey was one of the top songs on the radio, along with "Another Sad Love Song" by Toni Braxton, "(I Can't Help) Falling in Love With You" by UB40, and "I'd Do Anything for Love (But I Won't Do That)" by Meat Loaf. Top television shows were *Seinfeld*, *Law & Order*, *The X-Files*, *Full House*, *Star Trek: The Next Generation*, *The Simpsons*, and *Frasier*—a spinoff of *Cheers*, which ended with a major series finale event on May 20, 1993.

The year's blockbuster film was *Jurassic Park*. Other popular films of 1993 were *Mrs. Doubtfire*, *The Fugitive*, *Sleepless in Seattle*, *Indecent Proposal*, and *Schindler's List*.

Housing prices slipped in some parts of the United States in 1993, bringing the average price for a new home down to about $130,000. A new Buick Century sedan sold for $15,905, just a shade more than the $15,300 price tag on the trendy Mazda Miata convertible. A gallon of gas was around $1.11 and a gallon of milk was $2.86, with a dozen eggs fetching 87 cents and a loaf of bread 75 cents. The price of a first-class postage stamp remained 29 cents. The price of silver went to $4.31 an ounce, marking a notable uptick from the doldrums of 1993, when it regularly traded below $4.

On the Numismatic Scene in 1993

While 1992 marked the bicentennial of the 1792 founding of the U.S. Mint in Philadelphia, the year 1993 was the 200th anniversary of the first mass-produced federal U.S. coinage intended for widescale circulation. This extended the bicentennial jubilee into a second year at the Mint, which issued a special product called the Philadelphia Set, honoring the production of Proof Silver Eagles in Philadelphia as well as the 200th anniversary of striking the first official U.S. coins.

In 1993 Whitman Publishing released the first softcover (trade paperback) version of the *Guide Book of United States Coins*. Before that, since 1946, the popular "Red Book" had been issued in hardcover.

In other news, talk of reissuing a dollar coin was beginning to gain traction. This came as more and more Susan B. Anthony dollars, last struck in 1981, were being redistributed into circulation chiefly in the vending machine and mass transit circles. The American Numismatic Association Board of Governors formally supported a congressional bill proposing a golden-colored dollar coin, a concept that would go far on Capitol Hill in the coming years.

The 1993 United States Mint catalog offered a wide variety of popular numismatic products, including the 1993 Philadelphia Mint Bicentennial Set.

1993, Bullion Strike

Mintage: 6,763,762

Minted at West Point and San Francisco with no mintmark

Rising metals prices spurred speculators to dive back into the market, and they swarmed in big numbers around American Silver Eagles, which saw a tremendous spike in demand in 1993. Overall production totals were more than 6.7 million, marking a nearly 20 percent increase from the 1992 mintage. Most are found in the grades of MS-66 to MS-68, with decent quantities in MS-69 and a small number in MS-70.

PCGS certified many 1993 Silver Eagles that were retrieved from a World Trade Center vault, identified with a label declaring "WTC Ground Zero Recovery." Many 1993 Silver Eagles sport toning, though the great subjectivity behind attractive toning means the collector must decide which of these patinaed examples are worth pursuing.

There are a bevy of attractive 1993 Silver Eagles out there; the collector just has to seek them out.

The record price for a 1993 bullion Silver Eagle was achieved in January 2013 Heritage Auctions offerings, when a coin graded MS-70 hammered for $7,638.

1993, Bullion Strike

MARKET VALUES

	Raw	MS-69	MS-70
Value	$40	$50	$4,000

Note: "Raw" values are for average coins that are not professionally graded/slabbed.

CERTIFICATION DATA

	Total	<MS-69	MS-69	MS-70
# Certified	139,419	7,059	131,865	495
Percentage		5.06%	94.58%	0.36%

Note: Data compiled from NGC and PCGS reports, September 2022.

1993-P, Proof

Mintage: 405,913

Minted at Philadelphia with P mintmark

The inaugural year of Proof Silver Eagle production at the Philadelphia Mint was met with a lukewarm response,

seeing the lowest mintage up to that point. What may have seemed anomalous at the time would later show to be part of a larger trend of sluggish sales for the Proof offerings during the heart of the 1990s. Reasons for this are rather unclear, though they may be related to a rising number of other numismatic offerings by the U.S. Mint vying for the consumer's attention.

About 13,000 of the Proofs were included as part of the Philadelphia Set. Those seeking 1993-P Proof Silver Eagles will not be disappointed by the quality of available coins, most of which are stunning in PF-69. Of course, some people insist on PF-70 examples for their collections and will pay the substantial premiums required to get one.

1993-P, Proof

MARKET VALUES

	Raw	PF-69	PF-70
Value	$95	$130	$1,250

Note: "Raw" values are for average coins in original Mint packaging, not slabbed.

CERTIFICATION DATA

	Total	<PF-69	PF-69	PF-70
# Certified	40,568	1,701	34,595	4,272
Percentage		4.19%	85.28%	10.53%

Note: Data compiled from NGC and PCGS reports, September 2022.

1993 Philadelphia Mint Bicentennial Set

Mintage: 12,869

Minted at Philadelphia with P mintmark

The 1993 Philadelphia Mint Bicentennial Set effectively has a threefold purpose. In addition to celebrating the 200th anniversary of the U.S. Mint's earliest mass-produced coinage intended for circulation, the set also marks the first round of Proof Silver Eagles from the Philadelphia Mint; moreover, the set offers the *last* Gold Eagles from Philadelphia, which relinquished the $5, $10, and $25 gold Proofs in 1994 to the West Point Mint, where production of the $50 gold coins had occurred since their debut in 1986. Along with those four coins, the set, packaged in a special presentation case, includes a .76-ounce silver medal presenting a scene painted by John Ward Dunsmore, depicting First Lady Martha Washington's inspection of the first United States coins.

Release of the set was heralded by many inside the numismatic community and even beyond, with the Knight Ridder / Tribune media group running an article boldly headlined "Philadelphia Mint's 200 Years Are Honored." The widely published piece touted, "The U.S. Mint is offering a set of coins to mark the 200th anniversary of the first coins struck at the Philadelphia Mint. The Philadelphia Set, created for collectors, contains three fractional gold Eagle proofs, the silver Eagle proof, and a silver medal marking the mint's anniversary. All the proofs and medal bear the 'P' mint mark. The set will be sold only in 1993. It is the first year the Philadelphia Mint has struck the silver eagles, and the last year the Philadelphia Mint will strike fractional gold eagles. The Philadelphia Set sells for $499."

There are no hard numbers on how many of the Philadelphia Sets have been dismantled to obtain individual Proofs. However, collectors seeking the set in its original government packaging will be hard pressed to find a nice set for sale, especially those in which the Silver Eagle shows crisp black-white cameo contrast. Chemicals within the green cardboard and velvet construction of the original government packaging has lent heavy toning to the silver coins, some of which is quite attractive but might turn off those seeking only untoned examples. On the occasions when these original sets come up for sale, they enjoy fervent bidding.

1993 Philadelphia Mint Bicentennial Set
MARKET VALUES

	Raw	PF-69	PF-70
Value	$2,100	$2,600	

Note: "Raw" values are for average coins in original Mint packaging, not slabbed.

THE YEAR 1994

Increasing demand for bullion in India and political upheaval in Mexico led to a short-lived spike in silver prices during the early months of 1994. However, any major gains were largely erased as the year continued unfolding, and silver eventually settled back below $5 per ounce. Investors rushed toward American Silver Eagles when bullion looked sprightly in the first quarter of the year, but as metals activity calmed, demand for bullion Silver Eagles also subsided. Ultimately the 1994 Silver Eagle became the lowest-mintage bullion strike up to that point. The situation wasn't any better for the Proof strike, which also charted what was then an all-time low mintage for Silver Eagle Proofs.

Current Events in 1994

A deadly earthquake rocked the Los Angeles basin on January 17, 1994, with tremors reaching 6.7 in magnitude. The quake led to 57 deaths, more than 9,000 injuries, and over $25 billion in damage.

Later in the year, L.A. would become the setting for one of the highest-profile criminal cases in history. Former National Football League player O.J. Simpson became the prime suspect after his ex-wife Nicole Brown Simpson and her friend Ronald Goldman were found stabbed to death on June 12, 1994. Simpson was charged with the murders a few days later but did not turn himself in and evaded police in his white Ford Bronco, leading to a dramatic live-televised chase on the streets of L.A. Jury selection consumed the latter months of 1994, with the trial kicking off in January 1995.

Nelson Mandela was elected the first Black president of South Africa, bringing an end to the nation's decades-old system of racial segregation known as apartheid.

A four-year-old civil war in the African nation of Rwanda became a headline throughout the heart of 1994 when the local Hutu militia killed more than 500,000 individuals belonging to the minority Tutsi peoples. Political unrest in Haiti compelled thousands of Haitians to take makeshift boats across the waters of the Caribbean to the United States. Meanwhile, war in Bosnia continued.

Former President Richard M. Nixon died at the age of 81 on April 22, 1994. Hit television shows of 1994 were *Seinfeld*, *ER*, *Home Improvement*, *Friends*, and *Murder, She Wrote*. "The Sign" by Ace of Base, "The Power of Love" by Celine Dion, and "Hero" by Mariah Carey reaching the top of the charts. At the movies were *Forrest Gump*, *True Lies*, *The Mask*, *The Santa Clause*, *Dumb and Dumber*, and *The Lion King*.

The United States put forth a great showing at the 1994 Winter Olympic Games in Lillehammer, Norway, where American athletes scored 13 medals, including six golds.

New houses were selling for an average price of $154,500, while a 1994 Ford Ranger STX pickup truck with standard cab package went for $17,551. Gas was $1.11 a gallon and a gallon of milk was $2.88, with a dozen eggs and a loaf of bread selling for 87 cents and $1.59, respectively. First-class postage stamps were 29 cents. Overall, the U.S. economy was strengthening and the mid-1990s brought much financial success for many Americans. The average price of silver in 1994 was $5.29 per ounce.

On the Numismatic Scene in 1994

The U.S. Mint was busy churning out the most commemorative issues it had produced since the height of the classic commemorative program in the mid-1930s. With 21 coins across six distinct commemorative programs offered in U.S. Mint catalogs, many collectors were becoming overwhelmed with the options.

1994, Bullion Strike

Mintage: 4,227,319

Minted at West Point and San Francisco with no mintmark

Suppressed demand for the coin led to a relatively small overall output for this date. The 1994 Silver Eagle became the lowest-mintage issue for the series at the time, and to this day it remains the second-scarcest entry among the regular strikes.

Michael Garofalo comments, "The 1994 bullion Silver Eagle became the lowest mintage in this bullion series to date, with just under 4.3 million pieces. It was around this time that dealers and collectors began to notice white 'milk' spots that really affect the eye-appeal of the coins. Mint State-70 coins are very rare."

Collectors increasingly regard the 1994 bullion strike as a semi-key date and it's an absolute conditional rarity in MS-70, thanks to milk spotting and other surface imperfections. The record price for this date was set by an MS-70 coin that sold in November 2013 for $11,163.

1994, Bullion Strike

MARKET VALUES

	Raw	MS-69	MS-70
Value	$50	$85	$5,000

Note: "Raw" values are for average coins that are not professionally graded/slabbed.

CERTIFICATION DATA

	Total	<MS-69	MS-69	MS-70
# Certified	165,466	11,524	153,501	441
Percentage		6.96%	92.77%	0.27%

Note: Data compiled from NGC and PCGS reports, September 2022.

1994-P, Proof

Mintage: 372,168

Minted at Philadelphia with P mintmark

By the time the 1994-P Proofs had entered the marketplace, silver prices were ticking downward and older Proofs could be bought for less than the $23 issue price the U.S. Mint was charging for the 1994 issue. This kept mintages low—so low, in fact, that the 1994-P remains the scarcest of the regular-issue Silver Eagle Proofs offered for sale on an individual basis. Their relative scarcity has contributed to notable premiums over the secondary-market prices for many other similar Proofs.

Ranked 60th in *100 Greatest U.S. Modern Coins*, the 1994-P Proof is described by authors Scott Schechter and Jeff Garrett as an "issue that has emerged as a key date, often more difficult to locate than the 2006-W Reverse Proof issue, and therefore it can also be more expensive." While PF-69 examples are typical for the issue, "perfect" PF-70 examples command lofty prices.

1994-P, Proof
MARKET VALUES

	Raw	PF-69	PF-70
Value	$180	$195	$1,600

Note: "Raw" values are for average coins in original Mint packaging, not slabbed.

CERTIFICATION DATA

	Total	<PF-69	PF-69	PF-70
# Certified	37,144	1,786	31,269	4,089
Percentage		4.81%	84.18%	11.01%

Note: Data compiled from NGC and PCGS reports, September 2022.

THE YEAR 1995

A major doubled-die variety made national headlines in 1995, while numismatic publications were equally jubilant to share the news of a certain ultra-rarity coming down the pike for the American Silver Eagle series. The U.S. Mint was experiencing Olympic fever, kicking off a two-year commemorative coin campaign honoring the Summer Games to be held in Atlanta, Georgia, the following year, and buzz was swirling in certain Beltway circles about an ambitious commemorative program proposed in conjunction with the Washington quarter.

Current Events in 1995

The murder trial of former NFL player O.J. Simpson, charged with the deaths of ex-wife Nicole Brown Simpson and her friend Ronald Goldman, kicked off in January and carried on for most the year. On October 3, 1995, Simpson was found not guilty of the murders, a verdict that divided much of America along racial lines. In 2008 he was found guilty of lesser charges related to the incident and was sentenced to 33 years in prison. He was released in 2017.

On April 19, 1995, the Alfred P. Murrah Federal Building in downtown Oklahoma City was severely damaged by a 4,800-pound bomb, ripping away a third of the nine-story structure and killing 168 people, including 19 children at a daycare inside the building. The terrorist attack was homegrown and carried out by Timothy McVeigh, an extremist who witnessed the siege on the Branch Davidian complex in Waco, Texas, and identified with the group's anti-government beliefs. McVeigh was found guilty of the bombing in 1997 and sentenced to death. Terry Nichols, a friend of McVeigh's, was found an accomplice and sentenced to 161 consecutive life terms in prison.

A historic event unfolded in the sky as Space Shuttle *Atlantis* docked with the Russian Mir space station in orbit, marking a milestone moment few could have imagined during the tense Space Race between the United States and the Soviet Union.

The Bosnian wars drew to a close after involvement by the United Nations brought a peace agreement and ceasefire, while Syria engaged in peace talks with Israel and the United States placed economic sanctions against Iran. An Ebola virus outbreak in Central Africa killed 244 and Kobe, Japan, was rocked by a 7.3-magnitude earthquake that killed 6,433. On the Caribbean island of Montserrat, a previously dormant volcano erupted, sending two-thirds of the island's roughly 10,000 inhabitants to seek homes elsewhere. In the American Midwest, temperatures soared to more than 100 degrees Fahrenheit for five consecutive afternoons, with hundreds dying due to the excessive heat.

Major League Baseball ended a 232-day players' strike and basketball star Michael Jordan returned to the Chicago Bulls 17 months after announcing his retirement. Top television shows of the day were *ER*, *Seinfeld*, *Friends*, and *Home Improvement*. Coolio ruled the airwaves with "Gangsta's Paradise," while other hits included "Waterfalls" by TLC, "Fantasy" by Mariah Carey, "Have You Ever Really Loved a Woman?" by Bryan Adams, and "Kiss From a Rose" by Seal. *Batman Forever*, *Apollo 13*, *Toy Story*, *Pocahontas*, *Ace Ventura: When Nature Calls*, and *GoldenEye* were among top box-office draws.

The federal highway maximum speed limit of 55 miles per hour, instituted during the 1974 oil crisis, was repealed. Gas prices were $1.15 a gallon in 1995, while the average price of a new home ticked downward to about $135,000. Meanwhile, the price of a first-class postage stamp was up to 32 cents. A gallon of milk was $2.50 while a loaf of bread was $1.53 and a dozen eggs were 87 cents. A new Dodge Neon sedan was $19,908.22. The Dow Jones Industrial Average surpassed a new milestone threshold of 5,000 points in 1995. Silver prices posted an average closing price of $5.20 an ounce in 1995.

On the Numismatic Scene in 1995

Many in the numismatic realm recall 1995 with fondness, as rare-coin prices had stabilized and were showing signs of life again after the drastic losses following the market crash in late 1989 and 1990. In the spring the discovery of the 1995 doubled-die Lincoln cent was publicized. It was the first major doubled die discovered on a U.S. coin in nearly a dozen years, and its visibility to the naked eye on coins appearing in circulation excited the public. Some examples were trading for several hundred dollars apiece in the days following the discovery, but pricing came down as the variety was discovered to be more common than first thought.

The tenth anniversary of the American Eagle bullion program warranted a special Proof set issued by the U.S. Mint. This set included all four American Gold Eagle offerings in Proof as well as a special American Silver Eagle in Proof. The American Eagle 10th Anniversary Proof Set was the only method for purchasing the 1995-W Proof Silver Eagle, and with a price tag of $999 for the five-piece offering, it was beyond the financial reach of many collectors. Only 30,125 of the sets were sold, making the 1995-W Proof Silver Eagle a sought-after rarity from the get-go.

The Mint embarked on a zealous 32-coin commemorative program honoring the 1996 Atlanta Summer Olympics. Between the first round of Olympic coins and the programs honoring the Special Olympics World Games and Civil War Battlefield Preservation, a total of 24 different commemorative issues were released in 1995. Meanwhile, the Citizens Commemorative Coinage Advisory Committee (CCCAC) formally endorsed the proposed 50 State Quarters program

The euro was introduced in concept as the future currency for member nations of the European Union. The plan for a common currency was required by the Maastricht Treaty, which created the European Union in 1992.

1995, Bullion Strike

Mintage: 4,672,051

Minted at West Point and San Francisco with no mintmark

Silver prices moved up above $6 in May 1995, causing investors to stock more Silver Eagles in their portfolio. Yet, in the larger picture bullion had a quiet year and silver ended up losing about a dime per ounce when comparing average closing prices in 1995 versus 1994. That burst of activity in spring helped drive demand up for the 1995 bullion Silver Eagle, which saw an increase of about 10 percent over the previous year.

Decent examples are plentiful for collectors, who should be selective when choosing. The usual culprits of discoloration, dings, and milk spots are encountered on many 1995 bullion strikes, though there are many nice representatives for the year in MS-67, MS-68, and MS-69. The 1995 is difficult in MS-70, and premiums are strong. An example graded MS-70 tabbed $3,050 in a September 2017 David Lawrence Rare Coins auction.

1995, Bullion Strike

MARKET VALUES

	Raw	MS-69	MS-70
Value	$45	$65	$2,150

Note: "Raw" values are for average coins that are not professionally graded/slabbed.

CERTIFICATION DATA

	Total	<MS-69	MS-69	MS-70
# Certified	129,836	6,712	122,067	1,057
Percentage		5.17%	94.02%	0.81%

Note: Data compiled from NGC and PCGS reports, September 2022.

1995-W, Proof

Mintage: 30,125

Minted at West Point with W mintmark

If collectors ever needed reason to believe that the American Silver Eagle series has earned its numismatic stripes, it can be found with a study of the 1995-W Proof. Included only in the 1995 10th Anniversary American Eagle Proof Set, the 1995-W Proof was a bonus issue in a product that cost $999, which was an extraordinary price tag for even the most dedicated Silver Eagle collectors at the time. Although the set, housed in a vibrant red case, also included the 1995-W Proof strikes of the one-ounce, half-ounce, quarter-ounce,

and tenth-ounce gold coins, the nearly four-figure tab was viewed as excessive by some at a time when gold was averaging about $385.50 per ounce.

The tenth-anniversary Proof set had an authorized production limit of 45,000, but only 30,125 were sold. Today that tiny number can't possibly keep up with the incredible demand for the 1995-W Proof, which quickly rose in value during the late 1990s. Even when uncertified by a third-party grader, the coin sells today for well more than three times the entire original price of the five-coin Proof set. The 1995-W maintains its status as the series key, if no longer as the lowest mintage for the series, then certainly as the most sought after and expensive.

Recalls Troy Thoreson, "After the initial release of the 1986 Silver Eagle and steady decline in interest after the 1987 issue, the 1995-W Proof Silver Eagle was the turning point for the American Silver Eagles. At first the collector community was outraged with the U.S. Mint for offering such a premium on a special five-piece set, and it did take some time for the community to get over it. I thought the coin had a great chance at a low mintage and it would be the first with a W mintmark. This fueled my motivation to buy the sets. At the time, I was just out of college and didn't have much disposable income. Although it took several years for this coin to really start to appreciate, the buy obviously worked out."

Thoreson goes on, "I remember the first time the 1995-W Proof coin appeared in the dealer sheets of the day, at $70 or $75. I knew exactly how they came up with the number. I personally purchased seven sets from the mint at $1,000 each and was able to sell off the four gold coins at $930 each in four of the sets. That left me with a cost of $70 per coin. Soon after, the price of the coin did rise in the $600 range and then up from there. It was not difficult to calculate that with a mintage of only 30,125, this was clearly the key coin for the series. Even today I consider this coin the key to the set because of mishandling, and it is difficult to find perfect or even close to it. . . . Today the pricing for the coin is actually very complicated because of the mishandling or improper storage. Because of this, pricing can range from a few thousand to almost $20,000 for a select few perfect examples. Currently, most 1995-W Proof Silver Eagles can be found in the $4,000 to $7,000 range."

It would be remiss not to recall the some of the controversy this coin caused when it was issued. Many collectors were more than miffed that they could only obtain this coin at the time by spending $1,000 to buy the gold Proof set. As authors Scott Schechter and Jeff Garrett recall in *100 Greatest U.S. Modern Coins*, in which the 1995-W ranks fourth, "this offering was viewed as a ploy to convert collectors of silver to gold." Many U.S. Mint regular customers wrote letters of complaint, some vile, and droves stated they would boycott all future sales of Proof Silver Eagles.

U.S. Mint director Philip N. Diehl rebutted in January 1997, writing in a press release that "despite the controversy and criticism surrounding the issue of the 'W' mint mark Silver Proof Eagle and predictions in the numismatic community that customers would desert the coin wholesale, sales rebounded and rose 15 percent."

Those who could afford to bite the bullet and held their 1995-W Silver Eagles for at least a few years did extremely well for themselves. The 1995-W Proof Silver Eagle is permanently etched in the canon of the American Silver Eagle series and all modern U.S. coins as a rarity of significance, not to mention one of the lowest-mintage coins of the entire twentieth century. A PF-70 Deep Cameo coin summoned an outstanding $86,654.70 in a March 2013 GreatCollections auction.

1995-W, Proof

MARKET VALUES

	Raw	PF-69	PF-70
Value	$3,500	$4,700	$21,000

Note: "Raw" values are for average coins in original Mint packaging, not slabbed.

CERTIFICATION DATA

	Total	<PF-69	PF-69	PF-70
# Certified	11,551	1,610	8,715	1,226
Percentage		13.94%	75.45%	10.61%

Note: Data compiled from NGC and PCGS reports, September 2022.

1995-P, Proof

Mintage: 438,511

Minted at Philadelphia with P mintmark

The 1995-P Proof Silver Eagle performed better in sales than its 1994-P predecessor. However, even the 1995-P, with its unchanged $23 price tag during the much-promoted tenth anniversary of the series, fell far short of its smallish production maximum of 500,000. Perhaps it had something to do with some collectors feeling overwhelmed by the U.S. Mint's numerous other offerings, or maybe it was misdirected frustration that the real prize—the 1995-W Proof—sat behind a price barrier of nearly $1,000. Still, an output of nearly 440,000 coins was healthy, and the P-issue provided a far more affordable option than the 1995-W Proof.

In the years since the ascension of the 1995-W Silver Proof to royal "key" status, the 1995 date has been viewed as desirable by collectors. Even if the 1995-P plays second fiddle among Silver Eagle Proofs from that year, it still enjoys loftier premiums than other Proof Silver Eagles of similar or lower mintage from that era. PF-70 coins see particularly strong demand by collectors.

1995-P, Proof

MARKET VALUES

	Raw	PF-69	PF-70
Value	$85	$105	$700

Note: "Raw" values are for average coins in original Mint packaging, not slabbed.

CERTIFICATION DATA

	Total	<PF-69	PF-69	PF-70
# Certified	36,211	1,130	29,368	5,713
Percentage		3.12%	81.10%	15.78%

Note: Data compiled from NGC and PCGS reports, September 2022.

THE YEAR 1996

One year after the arrival of the 1995-W Proof American Silver Eagle emerged as the key to the entire series, the bullion Silver Eagles gained a key contender of their own. The U.S. Mint was also busy churning out the second year of commemorative coinage honoring the 1996 Summer Olympic Games in Atlanta.

Current Events in 1996

The XXVI Olympiad opened in Atlanta on the night of July 19, 1996, to become the first Summer Games held in the United States since the Los Angeles Olympics in 1984. Unfortunately, tragedy struck the Olympic Games on July 27, 1996, when a domestic terrorist detonated a pipe bomb at Atlanta's Centennial Park, killing one, injuring 111, and instigating a fatal heart attack in another victim. By the time the Games closed on August 4, 1996, the United States had won 101 medals, including 44 golds.

Mad cow disease ravaged herds of cattle in Great Britain and unnerved scores of beef-eaters around the world. Diana, princess of Wales, divorced Great Britain's Prince Charles after 15 years of marriage. A meningitis epidemic in West Africa led to 100,000 cases and more than 10,000 deaths.

Incumbent President Bill Clinton was reelected on November 5 after having fended off Republican Kansas senator Bob Dole and Reform Party contender Ross Perot. The digital video disc, or DVD, was released in late 1996.

On television, *ER*, *Seinfeld*, *Friends*, *Touched by an Angel*, and *Home Improvement* were among the primetime draws, while *Independence Day*, *Twister*, *Mission: Impossible*, *The Rock*, *The Birdcage*, *Ransom*, and *Jerry Maguire* packed movie theaters. "It's All Coming Back To Me Now" by Celine Dion, "Un-Break My Heart" by Toni Braxton, "Wannabe" by the Spice Girls, "I Believe I Can Fly" by R. Kelly, and "Fastlove" by George Michael were top radio hits.

The Dow Jones Industrial Average closed beyond 6,000 for the first time in 1996, a year when the typical new home sold for around $140,000 and a new Subaru Legacy

Wagon was $25,060. Gas cost $1.23 a gallon and milk went for $2.56 per gallon, with bread fetching $1.50 per loaf and eggs were $1.11 per dozen. Silver held more or less steady, with an average closing price of $5.20 per ounce.

On the Numismatic Scene in 1996

The big news of the year was the first coin to ever land $1 million or more at auction. This monumental moment happened in May 1996, when dealer Jay Parrino paid $1,485,000 for a 1913 Liberty Head nickel once owned by iconic collector Louis E. Eliasberg. This example of the ultra-rare nickel was offered by Bowers & Merena and was later graded by PCGS as PF-66—the finest of the coin's five examples.

Whitman Publishing issued a limited print run of 1,200 individually hand-numbered 50th-anniversary *Red Book*s in a maroon hardcover (reminiscent of the 1947-dated 1st edition). Some of these were given away as table favors at the American Numismatic Association's annual convention banquet that year.

The U.S. Mint continued with its second year of 1995–1996 Olympic commemorative coins. Few collectors even attempted to complete the entire run of nearly three dozen Olympic commemoratives honoring the 1996 Atlanta Games, and those who considered it could pay $2,261 to purchase the entire 32-coin set in a locking wooden presentation case. Few sold, and even fewer survive intact today.

While the U.S. Mint also issued commemoratives in 1996 recognizing national community service and the 150th anniversary of the Smithsonian Institution, some might say that—in hindsight—the most important news relating to the U.S. Mint were a few lines buried within the 1996 Commemorative Coin Act. Title III of the law required the secretary of the Treasury to study the feasibility of a commemorative coin program involving quarters that honor each of the 50 states. The secretary was also mandated to determine by August 1, 1997, if such a program was justified.

1996, Bullion Strike

Mintage: 3,603,386

Minted at West Point and San Francisco with no mintmark

It was a relatively humdrum year for silver investors, who saw the precious metal do little but bounce around the same figure it posted in 1995. Without much spurring investors to buy new Silver Eagles, the series saw little demand—an imperative for producing the made-to-order bullion coin. In all, barely more than 3.6 million were sold, a number constituting the smallest mintage ever recorded among regular-issue bullion coins in the series.

There are certainly smaller mintages for other entries in the Silver Eagle family, most notably among the Proofs and several of the other numismatic finishes that have since come along. Yet, the 1996 Silver Eagle is easily the key date for the bullion arm of the series and the scarcest issue that date-set collectors will encounter. "The

1996 is rare just by virtue of it being the lowest mintage of the [bullion] series," remarks Lee Minshull.

The coin ranked 78th in *100 Greatest U.S. Modern Coins*, with authors Scott Schechter and Jeff Garrett stating, "by the late 1990s, dealers were paying a few extra dollars per coin for 1996 Silver Eagles, irrespective of grade. Today it is not unusual for dealers to pay two to four times the prevailing rate for Silver Eagles [. . .] dated 1996!"

Troy Thoreson suggests analyzing the mintage numbers of the Uncirculated strikes of the standard American Silver Eagles to see what he calls the "trend line of popularity" with collectors. "1996 is also the lowest point of interest in the American Silver Eagle series," Thoreson says. "The 1996 Uncirculated example is the most difficult to find pristine, although I do have a slight prooflike example. Other mid-1990s-minted silver coins from around the world suffered this same lull. For the 1996 Silver Eagle, low mintage, mishandling, and storage resulting in tarnish, spots, and lack of luster are some of the reasons it is difficult to find pristine examples. It is important to note that a nicely toned Silver Eagle may be a good thing."

As is the case when buying any Silver Eagles of the era, collectors need to be wary of milk spots on the 1996 coins. "The 1996 bullion Silver Eagle had significant quality issues, as it, too, was plagued by milk spots," notes Michael Garofalo. "Only 3.6 million of these Uncirculated bullion coins were struck. MS-70 graded coins and problem-free ungraded issues can be difficult to find."

Taking the time to buy a spot-free coin is worth the effort. While MS-68 and MS-69 examples are plentiful and make wonderful additions to any Silver Eagle collection, the scarce MS-70 threshold is what so many collectors want. The record for this coin was realized with an MS-70 piece that hammered for $21,850 at a September 2009 Heritage Auctions sale.

1996, Bullion Strike

MARKET VALUES

	Raw	MS-69	MS-70
Value	$85	$120	$5,500

Note: "Raw" values are for average coins that are not professionally graded/slabbed.

CERTIFICATION DATA

	Total	<MS-69	MS-69	MS-70
# Certified	149,388	13,094	135,662	632
Percentage		8.77%	90.81%	0.42%

Note: Data compiled from NGC and PCGS reports, September 2022.

1996-P, Proof

Mintage: 500,000

Minted at Philadelphia with P mintmark

While the 1996 bullion Silver Eagle saw its lowest-ever mintage figure, the Proof strike accomplished a

different feat: hitting the maximum authorized production of 500,000 coins. That figure had been implemented as the mintage cap for Silver Eagle Proofs in 1990, but the limit had never been reached. The issue price remained at the same $23 rate in place since 1987 and may have begun looking ever-more economical for greater numbers of buyers. Mint director Philip Diehl stated in a May 13, 1997, press release that "the Proof Silver Eagle continues to the world leader in silver coins." He went on to say, "Its classic design and affordability make this coin a unique value, both artistically and for collectors." PF-69 examples represent the typical grade for this issue, with PF-70 examples scarcer and selling at notable premiums.

1996-P, Proof

MARKET VALUES

	Raw	PF-69	PF-70
Value	$85	$110	$600

Note: "Raw" values are for average coins in original Mint packaging, not slabbed.

CERTIFICATION DATA

	Total	<PF-69	PF-69	PF-70
# Certified	38,005	1,052	31,407	5,546
Percentage		2.77%	82.64%	14.59%

Note: Data compiled from NGC and PCGS reports, September 2022.

THE YEAR 1997

The family of American Eagle bullion coins were joined by the American Platinum Eagles in 1997. Meanwhile, Congress passed and President Bill Clinton signed a landmark bill that would forever change the U.S. collectible coinage scene.

Current Events in 1997

Princess Diana and her boyfriend, Egyptian film producer Dodi Fayed, were killed when their limousine, driven by Henri Paul, crashed in a Paris tunnel. In a sad twist of irony, Mother Teresa of Calcutta, with whom Princess Diana had become close friends during her many years of global philanthropy work, died at the age of 87 years, just a day before Princess Diana's funeral.

Dolly the sheep became the first mammal ever successfully cloned. The little ewe was born in July 1996, but the news of her birth was not publicly revealed until February 1997. In a win for artificial intelligence, IBM's chess-playing computer called Deep Blue defeated chess champ Garry Kasparov, becoming the first computer to beat the 34-year-old, who to that point had checkmated every human contender.

NASA's *Pathfinder* Mars rover touched down on the rocky red planet in July, after an eight-month voyage from planet Earth. Earthlings kept their eyes on the skies for Comet Hale-Bopp, which was discovered in 1995 and was visible to the naked eye for 18 months, peaking in brightness during April 1997.

The first book in the iconic *Harry Potter* series by author J.K. Rowling was released in Great Britain in June 1997 as *Harry Potter and the Philosopher's Stone*. Great Britain returned Hong Kong to Chinese rule, ending 156 years of British authority over what had been deemed a colony. A global warming conference in Kyoto, Japan, brought 150 nations to sign the Kyoto Protocol, which aimed to reduce greenhouse gas emissions and stem the rising tide of climate change. Avian flu gripped Hong Kong, where more than a million chickens were extinguished to help stop the spread of the deadly virus.

Microsoft, which was assessed at $261 billion, became the most valuable company in the world. The Dow Jones Industrial Average also made history in 1997 by charting its first closing above 7,000 points in February and 8,000 in July.

At 21 years old, golf phenom Eldrick "Tiger" Woods rose to the fore in 1997 after becoming the youngest person to win the Masters Tournament. Primetime hits included *Seinfeld*, *ER*, *Friends*, *Monday Night Football*, and *Touched by an Angel*. Top radio hits were "Tubthumping" by Chumbawumba, "I'll Be Missing You" by Sean Combs, "My Heart Will Go On" by Celine Dion, and "MMMBop" by Hanson. *Titanic*, *Men in Black*, *The Lost World: Jurassic Park*, *Liar Liar*, and *Good Will Hunting* were big hits on the silver screen.

New homes were selling for an average of $176,000, with a Chrysler Concorde setting back motorists $27,795. A gallon of gas was $1.23, milk was $3.22 a gallon, and a dozen eggs ran $1.17, with a first-class postage stamp snagging 32 cents. The average silver price for 1997 was $4.91.

On the Numismatic Scene in 1997

The American Platinum Eagle arrived as the third arm of the American Eagle bullion series. Authorized in 1996, the American Platinum Eagle is made from a .9995-fine composition and struck in four denominations that include a tenth-ounce $10 issue, quarter-ounce $25 issue, half-ounce $50 issue, and one-ounce $100 issue.

The first spiralbound softcover *Red Book* debuted with the 50th edition, published in 1997. (Whitman would next release the format in 1999, and has offered it annually since.)

The 50 States Commemorative Coin Program Act was signed into law by President Bill Clinton on December 1, 1997, authorizing the 50 State Quarters program that would begin in 1999. While the Treasury was reluctant to embark on the program, it received enthusiastic support from many on Capitol Hill and had a friend in influential Delaware governor Michael Castle, whose state became the first subject honored in the series.

Section four of the 50 States Commemorative Program Act is entitled United States $1 Coin Act of 1997, which provided for the creation of a new circulating dollar coin that "shall be golden in color, have a distinctive edge, [and] have tactile and visual features that make the denomination of the coin readily discernible." This law soon lent to the birth of the Sacagawea dollar, which debuted in 2000.

1997, Bullion Strike

Mintage: 4,295,004

Minted at West Point and San Francisco with no mintmark

With silver prices falling off their 1996 levels, speculator demand subsequently also weakened in 1997. This led to more tepid demand for the 1997 American Silver Eagle, the bullion issues of which ended the year by posting its third-lowest mintage of just less than 4.3 million. Some regard the 1997 Silver Eagle as a tough date, though premiums aren't generally all that much higher for this issue as compared to others from this period.

The 1997 bullion strike is readily available in grades up to MS-69, with MS-70 examples much scarcer and fetching drastically high premiums. An example graded MS-70 posted a record price of $6,462.50 in a September 2016 Heritage Auctions sale.

1997, Bullion Strike

MARKET VALUES

	Raw	MS-69	MS-70
Value	$40	$55	$1,500

Note: "Raw" values are for average coins that are not professionally graded/slabbed.

CERTIFICATION DATA

	Total	<MS-69	MS-69	MS-70
# Certified	124,639	6,652	116,888	1,099
Percentage		5.34%	93.78%	0.88%

Note: Data compiled from NGC and PCGS reports, September 2022.

1997-P, Proof

Mintage: 435,368

Minted at Philadelphia with P mintmark

Much like its bullion-finish counterpart, the 1997-P Proof strike notched what was the third-lowest mintage as of that time. Again, the bullion

market during much of the 1990s simply wasn't very active—something that many modern-day speculators, accustomed to marked daily, weekly, or monthly price swings, may find hard to comprehend. The issue price for the 1997-P Proof remained at the same $23, further evidence of the overall stability of the bullion markets during this period.

1997-P, Proof

MARKET VALUES

	Raw	PF-69	PF-70
Value	$85	$105	$675

Note: "Raw" values are for average coins in original Mint packaging, not slabbed.

CERTIFICATION DATA

	Total	<PF-69	PF-69	PF-70
# Certified	33,173	1,116	27,647	4,410
Percentage		3.36%	83.34%	13.29%

Note: Data compiled from NGC and PCGS reports, September 2022.

1997 Impressions of Liberty Set

Mintage: 5,000

Minted at Philadelphia with P mintmark

This limited-edition Proof set contains three coins and was produced to mark the first year of production for the platinum bullion series. This handsome set was sold in a handsome hardwood presentation case and includes one example of each of the one-ounce versions of the American Silver Eagle, American Gold Eagle, and American Platinum Eagle. The set also came with a certificate of authenticity signed and numbered by Mint director Philip Diehl, the first such numbered set offered by the U.S. Mint. Orders were limited to just one per household, and the set, priced at $1,499, sold out barely three weeks after its June 6, 1997, debut.

"The great response to this new coinage removes any doubt about numismatic platinum coinage and augurs well for the

launch of the bullion Platinum Eagle this fall," reported Diehl in a U.S. Mint press release.

1997, Impressions of Liberty Set
MARKET VALUES

	Raw	PF-69	PF-70
Value	$4,000	$4,400	

Note: "Raw" values are for average coins in original Mint packaging, not slabbed.

THE YEAR 1998

Bylaws of the Commemorative Coin Reform Act of 1996 took effect in 1998, limiting the number of commemorative coin programs to just two per year. Passage of the law was a clear response to complaints that the number of special issues being released each year was too great.

Current Events in 1998

Scandal rocked the Oval Office when President Bill Clinton was accused of having an affair with White House intern Monica Lewinsky. Congressional hearings aired on live television captivated the nation, and Clinton was impeached by the House on December 19, 1998, on charges of obstruction of justice and perjury to a grand jury.

Kosovo became a war zone as Serbs clashed with ethnic Albanians in what was then a province of the southeast European nation of Serbia. United States embassies in Kenya and Tanzania were bombed on August 7, 1998, in nearly simultaneous attacks that killed more than 200. A terrorist group known as al-Qaeda took responsibility for the attacks. The United States retaliated on August 20 by launching cruise missiles on suspected al-Qaeda bases in Afghanistan and Sudan.

Domestic terrorism was in the news with the sentencing of Ted Kaczynski, also known as "The Unabomber," who mailed or planted 16 bombs from 1978 through 1995 at various locations. His bombs killed three and injured 23 over the years, leading to eight consecutive life sentences without parole. Terry Nichols, an accomplice of Timothy McVeigh in the Oklahoma City bombing of the Alfred P. Murrah Federal Building was sentenced to life in prison without the possibility of a parole. Matthew Shepard was a 21-year-old college student attending the University of Wyoming when he was fatally beaten for being gay. His two assassins were charged with first-degree murder. The heinous attack brought greater awareness to hate crimes committed on the basis of sexual orientation.

Ohio senator John Glenn made headlines, 37 years after he became the first American to orbit the earth, by becoming the oldest person to venture into outer space at 77 years young. The Winter Olympics in Nagano, Japan, made the headlines with Americans claiming 13 medals (six golds), including the first gold for U.S. women's ice hockey and gold showings by alpine skiing's Picabo Street and figure skating's Tara Lipinski.

President Clinton presented the first balanced budget for the United States in three decades. Average prices for new homes climbed above $150,000 for the first time, reaching $152,500. The price for Toyota's new gasoline-electric hybrid Prius sedan was $19,995. The price of a gallon of gas edged downward to $1.08, while a gallon of milk registered $2.70 and a loaf of bread $1.58. The price of a first-class postage stamp ticked upward one cent to 33 cents. The Dow Jones Industrial Average closed above 9,000 points for the first time in April 1998. Silver had an average price of $5.55 per ounce.

On the Numismatic Scene in 1998

Following the passage of the $1 Coin Act of 1997, secretary of the Treasury Robert Rubin assembled a Dollar Coin Design Advisory Committee to select the subject for the new "golden" dollar slated for release in 2000. After 17 design concepts were submitted by members of the public, the committee recommended Sacagawea, a young Shoshone woman who served as a guide on the Lewis and Clark Expedition.

The Commemorative Coin Reform Act of 1996 went into effect in 1998, limiting the number commemorative coins that can be issued in any given year. The law, passed in response to growing controversy over the unwieldy number of commemoratives the U.S. Mint was making in the mid-1990s, helped curtail the recent runaway commemorative-coin production. While 1999 saw three commemorative programs (the Dolley Madison and Yellowstone silver dollars and the George Washington gold half eagle), most years saw two and some yielded just one.

The U.S. Mint's customer service team earned high marks by U.S. Democratic Maryland senator Paul S. Sarbanes, who presented a bronze Maryland Quality Award to Mint director Philip Diehl. He remarked, "This award is a testimony to the hard work and dedication of our staff at the Customer Care Center."

1998, Bullion Strike

Mintage: 4,847,549

Minted at West Point and San Francisco with no mintmark

Silver saw action in 1998, with a flurry of positive activity early in the year and closing about 65 cents higher than in 1997. This spurred seasoned speculators and lay investors alike into buying more Silver Eagles, which saw an uptick of 552,545 pieces over the 1997 mintage.

Like other 1990s Silver Eagles, the 1998 output is prone to nicks, ticks, and spotting. MS-68 and MS-69 examples are plentiful at nominal premiums, so there is no reason a buyer should have to settle for a subpar piece unless they are looking for the most affordable examples or are simply purchasing pieces for bullion investment aims.

The record price for a 1998 bullion Silver Eagle is $4,994, which was snagged by an MS-70 coin in an April 2013 Heritage Auctions event.

1998, Bullion Strike

MARKET VALUES

	Raw	MS-69	MS-70
Value	$38	$50	$1,900

Note: "Raw" values are for average coins that are not professionally graded/slabbed.

CERTIFICATION DATA

	Total	<MS-69	MS-69	MS-70
# Certified	139,734	5,464	133,341	929
Percentage		3.91%	95.42%	0.66%

Note: Data compiled from NGC and PCGS reports, September 2022.

1998-P, Proof

Mintage: 450,000

Minted at Philadelphia with P mintmark

All things must eventually come to an end, and in 1998 this meant the longstanding $23 issue price for Proof Silver

Eagles. After 11 years at that fixed price point, the Proof Silver Eagles were listed for $24, marking only the second price increase for the coin, which had been initially offered for $21 in 1986.

Along with the price hike came a drop-off in the maximum mintage cap, reduced from 500,000 to 450,000. Although there was a price increase, the 1998-P Proof Silver Eagles managed a sellout. This date is one of the most common among Proofs and, while selling at a marked premium in PF-70, trades for substantially lower prices than many of its same-grade Silver Eagle counterparts.

1998-P, Proof

MARKET VALUES

	Raw	PF-69	PF-70
Value	$85	$105	$300

Note: "Raw" values are for average coins in original Mint packaging, not slabbed.

CERTIFICATION DATA

	Total	<PF-69	PF-69	PF-70
# Certified	36,982	646	28,915	7,421
Percentage		1.75%	78.19%	20.07%

Note: Data compiled from NGC and PCGS reports, September 2022.

THE YEAR 1999

The 50 State Quarters program debuted on January 4, 1999; one new design came out about once every ten weeks, in the order each state entered the Union. The Susan B. Anthony dollar came out of retirement for one last year of production to fill a sudden demand for it, nearly 20 years after its discontinuation. In Europe, the euro was born.

Current Events in 1999

The Senate impeachment trial against President Bill Clinton began on January 7, 1999, the first such proceedings since 1868. Clinton, embroiled in a scandal arising from his affair with intern Monica Lewinsky, was tried on charges of perjury and obstruction of justice. However, the Senate failed to meet the two-thirds majority vote to convict him, and Clinton remained president through the end of his second term.

Columbine High School in Littleton, Colorado, became the site of one of the deadliest mass shootings in the nation's history when two students opened gunfire and ultimately killed 12 students and one teacher and injured 24 others, before killing themselves.

Category 4 Hurricane Floyd raked the eastern seaboard, killing more than 50. Oklahoma City, Oklahoma, was devastated with a massive F-5 tornado resulting in 36 fatalities, 583 injuries, and more than $1 billion in damage. Several major earthquakes struck in 1999, including a 5.9-magnitude earthquake that killed 143 in Athens, a 7.6-magnitude quake in Taiwan that killed 2,400, and an extreme 7.6-magnitude event in Turkey that killed more than 17,000. The mosquito-borne West Nile virus spread into various parts of the United States, posing risks of encephalitis and other potentially deadly maladies.

The Roth IRA was introduced in the Senate by Delaware senator William V. Roth Jr. in March. At the end of the year, the United States' unemployment rate dropped to 4 percent, its lowest since 1970.

SpongeBob SquarePants debuted on the Nickelodeon cable network on May 1, 1999. The quiz show *Who Wants to be a Millionaire?*, hosted by Regis Philbin, became a prime-time event.

Other top shows in 1999 included *ER*, *Friends*, *Frasier*, and *Everybody Loves Raymond*. "Baby One More Time" by Britney Spears, "Livin' La Vida Loca" by Ricky

Martin, "I Want it That Way" by The Backstreet Boys, and "Genie in a Bottle" by Christina Aguilera were top radio hits. At the movies were *Star Wars: Episode I—The Phantom Menace*, *The Sixth Sense*, and *The Matrix*.

The average price of a new house climbed to $161,000, while a 1999 Chrysler Sebring convertible cost $23,870. A gallon of gas was $1.17, and a gallon of milk was $2.84. Bread was $1.58 a loaf and bacon was priced at $2.55 a pound. A first-class postage stamp was 33 cents. The Dow Jones Industrial Average reached the lofty 10,000-point threshold on March 29, 1999, and closed above 11,000 for the first time just a few weeks later. The dot-com boom was about to go bust in the months ahead, and other socioeconomic challenges lay just beyond the horizon for a world whose population climbed past six billion. Silver was $5.22 an ounce.

On the Numismatic Scene in 1999

The first state to ratify the Constitution, Delaware, saw its day on the first of the 50 State Quarters program. The Delaware quarter hit pockets and purses on January 4, 1999, with the following state quarters released in the order each state joined the Union. Millions of Americans embarked on a treasure hunt to find each of the 50 State quarters.

During the height of the program, the U.S. Mint estimated approximately 147 million people were collecting the state quarters.

Susan B. Anthony dollars had found their way out of bank vaults and back into channels of commerce as the 1980s melted into the 1990s. Popular among the vending machine circuit and within mass transit systems, the "Susie B." proved useful despite being rebuffed by most of the public during the coin's initial 1979–1981 run. However, as more and more Susan B. Anthony dollars were entering circulation (again), fewer and fewer remained in government and bank supplies, with insufficient supplies on hand to tide the nation's coin supply through until 2000, when the new Sacagawea dollar was to debut.

Compounding matters was a sudden demand for hard money, the currency of choice for preppers, survivalists, and others who were worried about Y2K's effect on computers around the globe. The U.S. Mint struck more than 40 million new Susan B. Anthony dollars in 1999 to fulfill demands for dollar coins. Thankfully, Y2K came and went with virtually no computer glitches.

The famous 1804 Draped Bust dollar set a new world record when it sold for $4,140,000 in a Bowers & Merena auction. Known as "the King of American Coins," this 1804 dollar was graded by PF-68 and was presented in 1835 to the Sultan of Muscat as a diplomatic gift on behalf of the United States.

1999, Bullion Strike

Mintage: 7,408,640

Minted at West Point with no mintmark

Silver prices ticked downward slightly in 1999, helping spur a major buying boom for the bullion American Silver Eagle, which tracked its second-best year to that point. Some might say investors were buying on a dip, while others might explain the hike in demand by pointing to Y2K fears, which may have prompted some to stock up on physical metals lest people lose access to bank accounts. The fact that these were the last Silver Eagles of the twentieth century may have also helped drum up sales.

With the highest mintages for the series since 1987, the American Silver Eagles of 1999 are extremely common and usually trade for minimal premiums over spot. Collectors should be cautious of milk spots, which are frequently encountered. Plenty of near-flawless examples exist, and the coin is readily available up through MS-69. However, MS-70 examples are extremely rare. "Finding some dates, such as 1999, in pristine MS-70 condition can be a very daunting task," said Steve Feltner. "Locating these scarce coins can be a numismatic highlight for those who are patient enough to keep searching."

The record price for a 1999 Silver Eagle is a whopping $33,110, realized in a 2013 GreatCollections sale by a piece graded MS-70.

1999, Bullion Strike

MARKET VALUES

	Raw	MS-69	MS-70
Value	$42	$55	$14,500

Note: "Raw" values are for average coins that are not professionally graded/slabbed.

CERTIFICATION DATA

	Total	<MS-69	MS-69	MS-70
# Certified	124,254	7,679	116,122	453
Percentage		6.18%	93.46%	0.36%

Note: Data compiled from NGC and PCGS reports, September 2022.

1999-P, Proof

Mintage: 549,769

Minted at Philadelphia with P mintmark

The maximum authorized mintage for the 1999-P Proof Silver Eagle was increased to 550,000, though the issue price of $24 was carried

over from the previous year. Accounting for adjustments to orders, the coin was a sellout.

"As the last Proof Eagles to be issued in the 1900s, we anticipate very high demand for these coins," remarked Mint director Philip N. Diehl in a statement. The Mint sweetened the deal to those with orders of $150 by offering them a special Art Nouveau-style poster by Oren Sherman, depicting the iconic design of Miss Liberty made famous by designer Augustus Saint-Gaudens on the $20 gold double eagle.

The 1999 Proof Silver Eagle is common up through PF-70. While these "perfect-70" examples come with a premium, they aren't prohibitively expensive for set registry collectors and others who demand nothing less than the best. These coins are also gorgeous in PF-68 and PF-69, which are even more affordable still.

1999-P, Proof

MARKET VALUES

	Raw	PF-69	PF-70
Value	$85	$105	$400

Note: "Raw" values are for average coins in original Mint packaging, not slabbed.

CERTIFICATION DATA

	Total	<PF-69	PF-69	PF-70
# Certified	36,778	906	29,857	6,015
Percentage		2.46%	81.18%	16.35%

Note: Data compiled from NGC and PCGS reports, September 2022.

THE YEAR 2000

The year 2000 ushered in a wave of coin sets marking the passage of the second millennium and beginning of the third. One of the most popular U.S. Mint offerings was the 2000 United States Millennium Coinage and Currency Set.

Current Events in 2000

The 2000 U.S. presidential election became the most dramatic in modern history. Vying to become the nation's 43rd president were Democratic nominee and Vice President Al Gore running against Republican contender George W. Bush, who had served as the governor of Texas. On Election Day, November 7, electoral votes were registered in 49 states with a razor-thin lead in vote tallies in Florida favoring Bush, triggering an automatic recount. The recount process began a 36-day saga the likes of which were never seen before in a United States presidential election. When the case reached the U.S. Supreme Court, a 5-4 ruling stopped the manual recount and ultimately handed Bush and his running mate Dick Cheney the victory on December 13.

On October 12 the USS *Cole* Navy destroyer became the scene of a tragic terrorist attack when al-Qaeda bombers detonated a device on the ship, killing 17 Americans and injuring scores more.

Internet giant American Online purchased media company Time Warner in a $165 billion deal that marked a huge step in merging traditional music, film, and broadcasting with the growing world of digital networks. The leading television shows in 2000 were *Who Wants to be a Millionaire?*, *Survivor*, *Everybody Loves Raymond*, *Friends*, *ER*, and *Monday Night Football*, while the radio hit parade included "Breathe" by Faith Hill, "Say My Name" by Destiny's Child, and "What a Girl Wants" by Christina Aguilera. Top-grossing films in 2000 included *Mission Impossible II*, *What Women Want*, *Meet the Parents*, *Cast Away*, *Gladiator*, and *How the Grinch Stole Christmas*.

By many accounts, the 2000 Summer Olympics in Sydney, Australia, went down as the best Olympiad in modern history, with high ratings, relatively few hiccups, and many memorable moments. The U.S. placed first in the medal count, with 93 all around and 37 golds—fair dinkum!

While the dot-com bust saw internet and other tech stocks lose big on Wall Street, the U.S. economy overall marched along very well in 2000. A new house was $168,000, a new Honda Accord cost $15,350, and a first-class postage stamp was 33 cents. Milk was $2.78 per gallon, a loaf of bread was 92 cents, and a dozen eggs cost 96 cents. Silver clicked along at an average price of $4.95 per ounce.

On the Numismatic Scene in 2000

The U.S. Mint released the long-awaited 2000 Sacagawea dollar into circulation amid a large-scale promotion involving major private-sector retailers offering to both distribute and accept the new "golden" dollars. The new coins, bearing the likeness of Shoshone woman Sacagawea with her infant son, Jean Baptiste Charbonneau, in a papoose, caused much excitement early on with their distinctive golden color, but the public's enthusiasm for the coin soon wore off as a preference for paper money prevailed.

Anybody reading numismatic publications in 2000 had become accustomed to a multitude of advertisements from small dealers and mass promoters alike selling various iterations of products branded as "millennium sets," "20th century–21st century sets," and the like. They usually paired any variety of one coin minted either in 1900 or 1999 with its counterpart dated 2000. These sets were particularly popular as gifts.

The U.S. Mint offered its own version with The United States Millennium Coinage and Currency Set, containing a new (Series 1999) $1 Federal Reserve Note, 2000 Sacagawea dollar, and bullion-finish 2000 American Silver Eagle. The set was a quick sellout, with 75,000 units distributed at an issue price of $39 each.

2000, Bullion Strike

Mintage: 9,239,132

Minted at West Point with no mintmark

Excitement over coins dated with the new "2000" numerals, favorable prices for buying silver, and positivity about the economy helped push American Silver Eagle demand, with more than 9.2 million sold.

Examples in MS-68 and MS-69 are extremely common, but those in MS-70 are remarkably difficult, though the population has slowly grown over the years. The record price is held by an MS-70 example that realized $33,275 in a 2013 GreatCollections sale.

A number of 2000 American Silver Eagles were recovered from a vault buried deep inside the wreckage of the World Trade Center site and were encapsulated and labeled by PCGS as "WTC Ground Zero Recovery" coins.

2000, Bullion Strike

MARKET VALUES

	Raw	MS-69	MS-70
Value	$38	$47	$3,750

Note: "Raw" values are for average coins that are not professionally graded/slabbed.

CERTIFICATION DATA

	Total	<MS-69	MS-69	MS-70
# Certified	139,694	8,204	130,869	621
Percentage		5.87%	93.68%	0.44%

Note: Data compiled from NGC and PCGS reports, September 2022.

2000-P, Proof

Mintage: 600,000

Minted at Philadelphia with P mintmark

Production limits of 600,000 were set for the 2000-P Proof Silver Eagle, and every last one sold out at its $24 issue price. The coins were pitched as Y2K souvenirs by U.S. Mint acting director John P. Mitchell, who said, "The 2000 American Eagle gold and silver Proof coins are the perfect collector's items to commemorate the year 2000. Renowned classics of American design, the Proof Eagles rank among the most admired and sought-after coins in the world." Numerous examples are available at a small but significant premium for collectors seeking an example in a "perfect" grade of PF-70.

2000-P, Proof

MARKET VALUES

	Raw	PF-69	PF-70
Value	$85	$105	$400

Note: "Raw" values are for average coins in original Mint packaging, not slabbed.

CERTIFICATION DATA

	Total	<PF-69	PF-69	PF-70
# Certified	47,488	1,430	39,365	6,693
Percentage		3.01%	82.89%	14.09%

Note: Data compiled from NGC and PCGS reports, September 2022.

THE YEAR 2001

More and more Americans were collecting coins as the 50 State Quarters program went into its third year and the Sacagawea dollar, though failing to make inroads in commerce, continued making waves in the numismatic community. Many countries in Europe began phasing out their traditional currency systems as the European Union begin its final transition to the euro, the official denomination of EU member nations.

Current Events in 2001

In the days after President George W. Bush was inaugurated on January 20, 2001, many sociopolitical observers believed the landmark moments of the 43rd president's tenure would come with the passage of major tax cuts, a landmark education reform bill called "No Child Left Behind," and a controversial ban on federal funding for new embryonic stem cell research resources. But these significant domestic policy decisions faded into the background on the morning of September 11, 2001.

Four commercial airliners were hijacked by al-Qaeda terrorists. Two jets were flown into the upper floors of the World Trade Center Twin Tower skyscrapers in New York City and another into the Pentagon in Washington, D.C. The fourth plane, likely zeroing in on the U.S. Capitol Building in Washington, D.C., was overtaken by the passengers and driven into the ground in Shanksville, Pennsylvania, just minutes before hitting its intended target.

By noon eastern time, nearly 3,000 people had been killed, more than 6,000 were injured, and the World Trade Center had been destroyed before millions of eyes. President Bush and policymakers from both sides of the aisle joined together in a resolution to eliminate the al-Qaeda organization, remove the Taliban-led government in Afghanistan, and snuff out terrorist Osama bin Laden.

The 9/11 terror attacks heightened security protocols in many private and public venues across the United States. However, a rash of anthrax-laced letters began appearing in mailboxes around the nation, further testing nerves and prompting new procedures for how postal workers handled mail.

Apple released its popular iTunes platform, used for downloading and organizing music and video files. Russian space station Mir was deorbited, crashing safely into the Pacific Ocean. More than 180,000 gallons of oil threatened the pristine shores of the Galapagos Islands when an oil tanker ran aground near the Ecuadorian ecological preserve. Racing legend Dale Earnhardt died in the final lap of the Daytona 500 in Florida.

On television, *Everybody Loves Raymond*, *Will & Grace*, *Friends*, *The West Wing*, and *ER* drew big ratings, while *Harry Potter and the Sorcerer's Stone*, *The Lord of the Rings: The Fellowship of the Ring*, *Shrek*, *Rush Hour 2*, and *Monsters, Inc*, captivated crowds at the movies. "Hanging by a Moment" by Lifehouse, "Fallin'" by Alicia Keys, "All for You" by Janet Jackson, and "Drops of Jupiter (Tell Me)" by Train topped the radio charts.

The median price for a new home in 2001 was $175,200, with a new Toyota Corolla costing $12,793. A gallon of gas went for $1.46. A gallon of milk was $2.88, a loaf of bread was $1.58, and a dozen eggs was priced at 93 cents. Silver sank about 57 cents for the year to an average of $4.38 per ounce in 2001.

On the Numismatic Scene in 2001

The numismatic hobby was in terrific shape in 2001, with *Coin World* Editor Beth Deisher estimating two million Americans were active coin collectors, and many millions more collecting 50 State quarters and other coins on a more casual basis. Huge production runups at the U.S. Mint in recent years led to a glut of coinage and, subsequently, layoffs and other cutbacks at the Philadelphia Mint. Among the pileup in the vaults were nearly 200 million unused Sacagawea dollars, which had quickly proven to be a flop as a circulating coin.

If there was any successful coin program in 2001, it was the American Buffalo commemorative silver dollar. Bearing a faithful reproduction of the James E. Fraser design from the Buffalo nickels of 1913–1938, the American Buffalo dollar sold 500,000 units and helped inspire the creation of similar reprisals of classic coin designs in the future.

European currencies with familiar names, such as the Dutch guilder, French franc, German mark, Italian lira, Spanish peseta, and Greek drachma were officially being phased out in favor of the new euro, which became official legal tender on January 1, 2002.

2001, Bullion Strike

Mintage: 9,001,711

Minted at West Point with no mintmark

The 1990s may have been a period of anemic numbers for the American Silver Eagle, but the 2000s were about to make up for years of depressed mintages. Even though the 2001 bullion Silver Eagle was off by more than 230,000 pieces from its mintage in 2000, the lofty 9-million figure would serve as a low-end benchmark for the series over the next several years.

Though common, the 2001 Silver Eagle is tough in MS-70, and collectors should be wary of milk spotting and other minor detractions that can keep an example from ranking at the top of its league.

The record price for a 2001 Silver Eagle was $4,235, the amount hammered for a MS-70 coin at a June 2014 GreatCollections auction.

2001, Bullion Strike

MARKET VALUES

	Raw	MS-69	MS-70
Value	$38	$48	$825

Note: "Raw" values are for average coins that are not professionally graded/slabbed.

CERTIFICATION DATA

	Total	<MS-69	MS-69	MS-70
# Certified	172,443	7,819	163,079	1,545
Percentage		4.53%	94.57%	0.90%

Note: Data compiled from NGC and PCGS reports, September 2022.

2001-W, Proof

Mintage: 746,398

Minted at West Point with W mintmark

Proof Silver Eagle production was moved from Philadelphia to the West Point Mint in 2001. The Proofs saw an authorized production cap of 750,000, elevated from the previous year, and yet they still met that cap thanks to incredible demand for the new Proofs bearing a "W" mintmark, something still considered novel to many collectors at the time. Despite the presence of the nifty new "W" mintmarks, the Silver Eagle Proofs maintained their $24 issue price.

Mint director Jay W. Johnson explained the move in an April 6, 2001, press release, remarking the transition to W-mint Proofs was "part of the Mint's commitment to continuous improvement." He added, "We felt it was time to integrate and consolidate production of all the Proof American Eagle coins at one facility. The entire family of Eagles—gold, platinum, and silver—will now be manufactured at the West Point Mint, where we're renovating and expanding our production facilities."

Collectors should have little difficulty finding 2001-W Proofs in PF-69. Those seeking examples in the "perfect" grade of PF-70 will likely find this issue quite afford-able compared to the prices typically encountered for earlier pieces.

2001-W, Proof

MARKET VALUES

	Raw	PF-69	PF-70
Value	$85	$105	$200

Note: "Raw" values are for average coins in original Mint packaging, not slabbed.

CERTIFICATION DATA

	Total	<PF-69	PF-69	PF-70
# Certified	60,812	1,017	47,125	12,670
Percentage		1.67%	77.49%	20.83%

Note: Data compiled from NGC and PCGS reports, September 2022.

THE YEAR 2002

Numismatics was hitting its stride as the 50 State Quarter series entered its middle years. Increasing interest in rare coins helped establish new price records on the auction floor, meanwhile Europe entered a new day with the euro.

Current Events in 2002

The 9/11 terror attacks led to significant decreases in air travel in the months that followed, hitting many carriers in their pocketbooks.

In his first State of the Union speech, President George W. Bush focused on the challenges in fighting global terrorism and bolstering American security. In his famous "Axis of Evil" remarks, he pointedly declared, "either you are with us, or you are with the terrorists." The pursuit of Osama bin Laden continued in Afghanistan, where a multilateral war kicked off against the Taliban on October 7, 2001. Bush signed the No Child Left Behind Act in January 2002 and oversaw the formation of the Department of Homeland Security in November.

Sadly, terrorism continued. Two snipers killed ten people in Washington, D.C., and injured three in the culmination of a killing spree that crossed the nation and in total involved the murders of 17 and wounding of 10. In the Indonesian island of Bali, 202 people were killed and more than 200 injured in attacks on two nightclubs. Escalating violence between Israel and Palestinians led Palestinian leader Yasser Arafat to seclusion in his West Bank compound for months as rocket fire killed and maimed many in the region.

The nations of Switzerland and East Timor joined the United Nations. Former President Jimmy Carter was awarded the Nobel Peace Prize for his efforts in brokering a peace deal between Egypt and Israel in 1978 and his decades of humanitarian aid that followed.

In June, Fox premiered *American Idol*. *CSI: Crime Scene Investigation*, *Friends*, *ER*, and *Everybody Loves Raymond* drew large TV audiences while lines formed at movie theaters for *Spider-Man*, *The Lord of the Rings: The Two Towers*, *Star Wars: Episode II—Attack of the Clones*, *Harry Potter and the Chamber of Secrets*, and *My Big Fat Greek Wedding*. The 2002 Winter Olympics in Salt Lake City, Utah, marked the first gold medals for Black athletes in a Winter Games, with American Vonetta Flowers victorious in the bobsleigh and Canadian Jarome Iginla topping the competition in ice hockey; the United States earned 34 medals, 10 of which were gold.

Facing stiff competition from rival discount chains Walmart and Target, Kmart Corporation became the largest U.S. retailer to file for Chapter 11 bankruptcy protection.

The average price of a new home was $185,000, a 2002 Mazda Protégé was $16,455, and a gallon of gas cost $1.36. A gallon of milk was $2.72 and a loaf of bread cost $1.58, while a first-class postage stamp set letter-writers back by 37 cents. Silver averaged $4.61 an ounce in 2002.

On the Numismatic Scene in 2002

With estimates by the U.S. Mint that more than 139 million people had saved at least one of the 50 State quarters, numismatic author Q. David Bowers wrote, "Numismatics is expanding by leaps and bounds, with interest precipitated by television and shopping networks, Mint promotions, and more." Adding that inventory shortages were becoming commonplace among coin dealers, Bowers noted that quantity lots of large copper cents, formerly a commodity, were now typically seen only one at a time.

The sale of a 1933 Saint-Gaudens double eagle took the hobby by storm in 2002, particularly because this coin, once belonging to King Farouk of Egypt, had been declared illegal to own and had disappeared for four decades. The U.S. government agreed to monetize the coin, making it the only example of the 1933 double eagle legal for private ownership. When it crossed the auction block in a joint Stack's and Sotheby's sale, it garnered $7,590,020 to become the most valuable single coin ever sold at public auction at that time.

January 1, 2002, marked the formal launch of the euro as the official denomination of the European Union, which voted that year to add ten more nations to its bloc of twelve.

2002, Bullion Strike

Mintage: 10,539,026

Minted at West Point with no mintmark

Swelling demand for bullion pushed sales of the American Silver Eagle to its second-highest total to that point, with more than 10.5 million sold. Extremely common and beautifully struck, the 2002 bullion Silver Eagles are easy to locate in all the upper Mint States grades, including MS-70, where premiums are pronounced but not unaffordable for many collectors. Buyers should beware of milk spotting, which may become more prevalent on this issue over time.

The record price for a 2002 American Silver Eagle was hammered in a February 2013 Goldberg Auctioneers sale of an MS-70 coin, which sold for $3,105.

2002, Bullion Strike

MARKET VALUES

	Raw	MS-69	MS-70
Value	$38	$47	$250

Note: "Raw" values are for average coins that are not professionally graded/slabbed.

CERTIFICATION DATA

	Total	<MS-69	MS-69	MS-70
# Certified	216,732	6,417	202,426	7,889
Percentage		2.96%	93.40%	3.64%

Note: Data compiled from NGC and PCGS reports, September 2022.

2002-W, Proof

Mintage: 647,342

Minted at West Point
with W mintmark

When the U.S. Mint
released the 2002-W
Proof on June 5, it main-
tained the issue price of $24
in place since 1998. Sales were
robust, with higher figures for the 2002-W Proof than seen during the majority of the
preceding years. Nearly 650,000 were sold. However, that wasn't quite enough for the
U.S. Mint to declare a sellout, given the authorized maximum cap of 750,000 pieces.
Collectors seeking numismatic perfection will find PF-70 examples plentiful and relatively affordable, if nominally higher-priced than the more common PF-69.

2002-W, Proof

MARKET VALUES

	Raw	PF-69	PF-70
Value	$85	$105	$175

Note: "Raw" values are for average coins in
original Mint packaging, not slabbed.

CERTIFICATION DATA

	Total	<PF-69	PF-69	PF-70
# Certified	45,521	697	32,932	11,892
Percentage		1.53%	72.34%	26.12%

Note: Data compiled from NGC and PCGS reports,
September 2022.

THE YEAR 2003

As the 50 State Quarters program wrapped up its first half of a decade-long journey,
the U.S. Mint prepared for its next multi-year circulating coin series, this time involving nickels.

Current Events in 2003

More than a dozen years of safe flights and successful missions for NASA comes to a
tragic halt when Space Shuttle *Columbia* broke up minutes before it was supposed to
land at Cape Canaveral in Florida on February 1, 2003. The shuttle, carried its seven
crew members on a 16-day mission in space involving various science experiments.
NASA grounded its shuttle program for two years as officials regrouped on the near-
term safety of manned launches and long-term fate of the aging shuttle fleet.

China launched its first manned space mission when *Shenzhou 5* lifted off on October 15, 2003, becoming the third nation after the Soviet Union and the United States
to send humans into orbit.

Over unproven concerns that Iraq was harboring weapons of mass destruction, the
United States and United Kingdom began a massive military campaign in Iraq on
March 20 that opened with dramatic airstrikes and a ground invasion. Iraq President
Saddam Hussein was soon captured near the city of Tikrit.

The Human Genome Project completed sequencing on 99 percent of the human
genome, culminating a 13-year-long effort to map 20,000 gene pairs that compose the
framework of human DNA.

The Federal Trade Commission launched the National Do Not Call Registry in 2003 with the aim of reducing the number of unsolicited telemarketing calls.

A deadly tornado outbreak in early May dropped 393 tornadoes across 19 states in the Central and Eastern United States, the most twisters ever recorded during any single week in the nation. A massive earthquake in southeastern Iran killed more than 30,000. Some 15,000 perished during a deadly heat wave in France.

The Recording Industry Association of America sued internet users for violating copyright laws in trading songs, leading to many reforms in how music and other media were offered and shared online. The Apple iTunes music store debuted, and 10 million songs were downloaded within four months of its April 28, 2003, unveiling. *CSI: Crime Scene Investigation*, *American Idol*, *Friends*, *The Apprentice*, and *ER* were the top television hits of the day, while *The Lord of the Rings: The Return of the King*, *Finding Nemo*, *Pirates of the Caribbean: The Curse of the Black Pearl*, *Bruce Almighty*, and *The Matrix Reloaded* were major big-screen draws. On the radio were "In da Club" by 50 Cent, "Where is the Love?" by Black Eyed Peas, "Miss Independent" by Kelly Clarkson, and "Calling All Angels" by Train.

The cost of a new home in 2003 was $195,000, while a new Honda Civic LX sedan cost $16,010. A gallon of gas ran $1.83 and a gallon of milk was $2.76. A first-class postage stamp could be had for 37 cents, and the average price for an ounce of silver was $4.87. Overall, the economy trucked along well in 2003 despite hiccups during March, when the United States and United Kingdom embarked on their Iraq campaign.

On the Numismatic Scene in 2003

The upcoming bicentennial of the Lewis and Clark Expedition of 1804–1806 inspired Mint officials to seek a circulating commemorative coin program honoring the historic quest. The journey to survey land acquired in the 1803 Louisiana Purchase would be memorialized on a series of special designs to appear on the Jefferson nickel, anchored on the obverse by the president who oversaw the land purchase and the duo's subsequent geographical mission. The American 5-Cent Coin Design Continuity Act of 2003 was signed into law by President Bush on April 23 authorizing new designs for the nickel in 2004 and 2005, with the traditional Monticello visage to return in 2006.

In 2003 Congress disbanded the Citizens Commemorative Coin Advisory Committee and established the Citizens Coinage Advisory Committee to advise the secretary of the Treasury on themes and designs of all U.S. coins and medals. The CCAC has since served as an informed, experienced, and impartial resource to the Treasury Department and represents the interests of American citizens and collectors.

2003, Bullion Strike

Mintage: 8,495,008
Minted at West Point with no mintmark

Silver prices began climbing in 2003, and while silver's

average price for the year ticked in at $4.87, it neared $6 by the end of the calendar, representing a 26-cent hike in price from 2002. Despite this, Silver Eagle sales foundered toward the end of 2003 as the overall economy recovered well from its springtime sputter, persuading folks to put more money in stocks and bonds rather than silver. Still, the 2003 mintage was impressive as compared to the typical output during the 1990s.

Buyers should have little trouble locating decent examples of the 2003 bullion Silver Eagle in the upper echelons of the Mint State grading scale, though collectors need to keep an eye out for spotting, ticks, or other imperfections imparted by postmint mishandling. The record price for a 2003 American Silver Eagle is $1,523, fetched in a July 2011 GreatCollections auction by an MS-70 piece.

2003, Bullion Strike

MARKET VALUES

	Raw	MS-69	MS-70
Value	$38	$47	$275

Note: "Raw" values are for average coins that are not professionally graded/slabbed.

CERTIFICATION DATA

	Total	<MS-69	MS-69	MS-70
# Certified	176,275	6,341	163,731	6,203
Percentage		3.60%	92.88%	3.52%

Note: Data compiled from NGC and PCGS reports, September 2022.

2003-W, Proof

Mintage: 747,831

Minted at West Point with W mintmark

The 2003-W Proofs hit the sales circuit on April 2 with a price of $24. All told, nearly 748,000 were sold, just barely missing the authorized

production limit of 750,000. Increasing sales numbers for the 2003-W Proofs presaged a general buoyancy in sales figures for Proofs and other American Silver Eagles with numismatic finishes in the years ahead.

2003-W, Proof

MARKET VALUES

	Raw	PF-69	PF-70
Value	$85	$105	$140

Note: "Raw" values are for average coins in original Mint packaging, not slabbed.

CERTIFICATION DATA

	Total	<PF-69	PF-69	PF-70
# Certified	51,041	432	33,162	17,447
Percentage		0.85%	64.97%	34.18%

Note: Data compiled from NGC and PCGS reports, September 2022.

THE YEAR 2004

Westward Journey nickels debuted in 2004, beginning a special two-year circulating commemorative venture that honored Meriwether Lewis and William Clark's expedition to the Pacific Northwest. The 50 State Quarters series spawned two major varieties that enhanced interest in the special commemorative program halfway through the decade-long series. Silver prices began charting remarkably strong year-over-year gains in 2004.

Current Events in 2004

A 9.3-magnitude earthquake shook just offshore of Indonesia to become the world's strongest earthquake in 40 years. The underwater shockwave caused a devastating tsunami that deluged the coastlines of many Southeast Asian nations and killed more than 230,000 people, even as far away as South Africa.

President George W. Bush and Vice President Dick Cheney won the 2004 presidential election against Democratic Massachusetts senator John Kerry and his running mate, Democratic North Carolina senator John Edwards.

NASA's *Spirit* Mars rover was launched in June 2003 and arrived on the red planet in January 2004 to investigate if Mars could have ever supported life and analyzed rocks, minerals, and any evidence of water.

The European Union added ten new nations to its growing block of countries. The move brought several former Soviet republics into the Western economic trading zone. The United States Central Intelligence Agency declared there was no imminent threat of weapons of mass destruction in Iraq, the concern that precipitated the U.S.-led invasion in Iraq in 2003. Attacks against U.S. troops continued mounting, while in Spain suicide bombers killed 190 on commuter trains in Madrid.

Hurricane Charley killed at least 15 people on its path through Florida and caused nearly $17 billion in damage. Within weeks, Hurricanes Frances and Jeanne intersected the same path that Hurricane Charley took in Central Florida, further exacerbating devastation in that part of the state, while Hurricane Ivan slammed into Florida's panhandle region.

The 2004 Summer Olympics in Athens, Greece, proved successful for American swimmer Michael Phelps, who became the winningest athlete ever in a single Olympiad with six gold medals and a record eight medals total. In all, U.S. athletes won 101 total medals, including 36 golds. Major League Baseball's Boston Red Sox won their first World Series since 1918.

American Idol, CSI: Crime Scene Investigation, Desperate Housewives, Grey's Anatomy, and *Everybody Loves Raymond* were atop the primetime television charts while *Shrek 2, The Passion of the Christ, Harry Potter and the Prisoner of Azkaban,* and *The Incredibles* rocked the box office. Top radio hits were "Yeah!" by Usher featuring Lil Jon and Ludacris, "If I Ain't Got You" by Alicia Keys, "This Love" by Maroon 5, and "The Reason" by Hoobastank.

Harvard college students Mark Zuckerberg and Eduardo Saverin began a novel social networking website called Thefacebook in February 2004. The platform exploded under the name "Facebook" within months and boasts nearly 3 billion active users today.

For the first time, the median price of a new home crossed the $200,000 threshold. A 2004 Hyundai Sonata GLS sold for $18,799, and a gallon of gas went up to $1.88. The price of milk crept up to $3.21 a gallon, and a dozen eggs was $1.34. A first-class postage stamp was 37 cents. The price of silver averaged $6.66 per ounce.

On the Numismatic Scene in 2004

The Westward Journey nickel series launched in 2004 as a circulating tribute to the 200th anniversary of the Lewis and Clark Expedition. The original Jefferson nickel obverse by Felix Schlag remained the same, but the Monticello motif on the reverse was replaced during the first half of the year by the visage of an Indian Peace Medal, as adapted by Norman E. Nemeth, and in the latter months of 2004 by a design by Al Maletsky with a keelboat similar to the type used in Lewis and Clark's voyage west.

The 50 State Quarters program caused a different kind of stir in 2004 when not just one but two major varieties popped up on Denver Mint emissions of the Wisconsin state quarter. The varieties were first reported in December 2004 and involved the appearance of an extra high leaf on the corn stalk upon one iteration of the variety and on the other what looks like an extra low leaf on the stalk. Examples were selling for several hundred dollars in the days after news of the varieties spread. The varieties still fetch about $75 and up even in circulated grades.

In 2004 Whitman Publishing issued its first leather-bound Limited Edition of the *Guide Book of United States Coins* (58th edition, with a cover date of 2005), with a print run of 3,000 and an issue price of $69.95. These special editions would be issued annually, with diminishing print runs, through the 72nd (2018) edition.

Silver was on the move in 2004, mirroring a pattern also witnessed among other commodities such as food, oil, and chemicals. Rising demand from the emerging nations of Brazil, Russia, India, and China helped fuel these price increases, which hit silver with upswings in pricing not seen in years. Silver touched $8.29 in April 2004 before settling back to about $5.50 in May, but the metal's pricing trajectory was upward throughout much of the rest of the year.

2004, Bullion Strike

Mintage: 8,882,754

Minted at West Point with no mintmark

Rising silver prices engendered greater interest in the American Silver Eagle by investors and collectors, with the bullion coins notching a net increase in sales of 385,000 over the 2003 figures. Most were well struck and exhibit resplendent quality with typical grades of MS-67 to MS-69, though there are ample MS-70 pieces available at significant but not unapproachable premiums.

A rainbow-toned 2004 American Silver Eagle graded MS-68 claimed the record price for the date when it crossed the block for $587.50 at an October 2017 Legend Rare Coin Auctions event.

2004, Bullion Strike

MARKET VALUES

	Raw	MS-69	MS-70
Value	$39	$48	$200

Note: "Raw" values are for average coins that are not professionally graded/slabbed.

CERTIFICATION DATA

	Total	<MS-69	MS-69	MS-70
# Certified	176,475	5,619	162,818	8,038
Percentage		3.18%	92.26%	4.55%

Note: Data compiled from NGC and PCGS reports, September 2022.

2004-W, Proof

Mintage: 801,602

Minted at West Point with W mintmark

Demand for the 2004-W Proof was up from the previous year, but it wasn't enough to threaten the increased authorized maximum of 850,000. Perhaps this is because the U.S. Mint implemented its first price increase for the coin since 1998, with the Proof Silver Eagle issue price lurching upward from $24 to $27.95, a reflection of rising bullion prices and production costs. Though PF-70 examples take higher prices than the more common PF-68 and PF-69 pieces do, the 2004-W Proof is quite common even in the top grading echelon and is a relatively affordable coin regardless of grade.

2004-W, Proof

MARKET VALUES

	Raw	PF-69	PF-70
Value	$85	$105	$125

Note: "Raw" values are for average coins in original Mint packaging, not slabbed.

CERTIFICATION DATA

	Total	<PF-69	PF-69	PF-70
# Certified	53,063	364	33,087	19,612
Percentage		0.69%	62.35%	36.96%

Note: Data compiled from NGC and PCGS reports, September 2022.

THE YEAR 2005

A year after two major varieties were discovered on 2004-W Wisconsin state quarters, the 2005-P Minnesota state quarter went on to yield more than 50 varieties of doubled dies. Meanwhile, Congress approved a new multiyear commemorative program to take shape on the circulating "golden" dollar coin.

Current Events in 2005

Hurricane Katrina made landfall near New Orleans, Louisiana, on August 29, 2005, killing more than 1,800 people and causing $150 billion in damage in one of the worst natural disasters to ever affect the United States.

President George W. Bush, who was inaugurated to his second term on January 20, 2005, announced at the G8 summit that he did not support legally binding restrictions on carbon emissions. The Kyoto Protocol, aiming to reduce back on greenhouse gases, went into effect in 2005 without the support of the United States. Prisoners at U.S.-operated Guantanamo Bay Naval Base in Cuba went on hunger strike to declare their innocence and protest conditions at the terrorist detention camp.

Pope John Paul II died in Vatican City on April 2, 2005, at the age of 84. Pope Benedict XVI became the next Bishop of Rome. Prince Charles of Wales married Camilla Parker Bowles at Windsor Castle on April 9, 2005. A series of terrorist bombs went off in London on July 7, killing 52 people and injuring 784.

Riots near Paris, France, went on for three weeks in the wake of police brutality. Pakistan suffered a terrible 7.6-magnitude earthquake that killed more than 80,000 while a major 8.7-magnitude rattler rocked Sumatra, Indonesia, and killed more than 900. Hurricane Stan killed more than 1,620 people in Mexico and in other regions of Central America. A major ice storm clobbered the Eastern Seaboard in December, knocking out power to at least 1 million homes and businesses.

YouTube was founded in 2005 by Chad Hurley, Steve Chen, and Jawed Karim. The video-sharing website has since become one of the most successful media platforms in history. Hurricane Katrina and continued geopolitical disturbances in the Middle East caused gas prices to head northward during 2005 to an average of $2.30 a gallon.

NBC debuted a new mockumentary series called *The Office*, which would become one of the biggest hits of its time. Other primetime hits were *American Idol*, *CSI: Crime Scene Investigation*, *Desperate Housewives*, *Grey's Anatomy*, and *Dancing with the Stars*. At the movies were *Star Wars: Episode III—Revenge of the Sith*, *Harry Potter and the Goblet of Fire*, *War of the Worlds*, *Wedding Crashers*, and *The Chronicles of Narnia: The Lion, the Witch and the Wardrobe*. Madonna hit a top charter with "Hung Up," while other radio hits were "Don't Cha" by The Pussycat Dolls, "You're Beautiful" by Ray Blunt, "Bad Day" by Daniel Powter, and "We Belong Together" by Mariah Carey.

Loosened lending practices led to a spike in demand for homes, and this pushed the median price of a new home to new heights of about $230,000. The feverish market began tempering by the end of the year, triggering falling home prices and other economic problems in 2006. A 2005 Dodge Caravan SE went for $22,920, a gallon of milk was $3.20, a loaf of bread cost $1.58, and a first-class postage stamp rose to 39 cents. The price of silver climbed to an average of $8.82 an ounce.

On the Numismatic Scene in 2005

The Presidential $1 Coin Act of 2005 was signed into law by President Bush on December 22, 2005. The program began in 2007 and honored four presidents each year, with commanders-in-chief being recognized in the chronological order that they served in the White House and meeting eligibility for depiction on the coins at least two years after their death.

The Westward Journey nickel series entered its second year with a new obverse portrait of President Thomas Jefferson by Joe Fitzgerald and two reverse designs, one a side view of an American bison by Jamie Franki and the other a scenic coastline view of the Pacific Ocean, emblazoned with the words "Ocean in View! O! The Joy!"

A year after the Wisconsin quarter varieties garnered national press attention, the 2005-P Minnesota state quarters revealed no fewer than 50 different doubled dies, ranging from obscure to dramatic. Mostly involving the appearance of an extra spruce tree on the reverse, these doubled dies bewildered the numismatic community and are worth anywhere from a few dollars to more than $100, depending on the variety and condition.

The American Numismatic Association (ANA) saw its membership click above 32,000 in 2005, the same year it named its museum in Colorado Springs, Colorado, for former ANA president, executive director, and *The Numismatist* editor Edward C. Rochette. PCGS launched its "First Strike" program and NGC began its "Early Release" label designation soon after, both aimed at recognizing encapsulated coins submitted for certification within the first days of their initial distribution.

2005, Bullion Strike

Mintage: 8,891,025

Minted at West Point with no mintmark

The runup of silver bullion prices in 2005 led many investors to buy Silver Eagles in big numbers. Ultimately, the overall mintage for the bullion offering bested the previous year's tally by only a little more than 8,000, yet this represented a third consecutive year of increasing output.

Collectors should have little trouble buying pristine examples of the 2005 bullion Silver Eagle for sets, with most pieces grading MS-67 to MS-69 and multitudes reaching the "perfect" grade of MS-70. The record price for a 2005 American Silver Eagle was notched by an MS-70 coin that took $1,058 in a June 2013 Heritage Auctions offering.

2005, Bullion Strike

MARKET VALUES

	Raw	MS-69	MS-70
Value	$38	$48	$200

Note: "Raw" values are for average coins that are not professionally graded/slabbed.

CERTIFICATION DATA

	Total	<MS-69	MS-69	MS-70
# Certified	219,688	3,841	207,381	8,466
Percentage		1.75%	94.40%	3.85%

Note: Data compiled from NGC and PCGS reports, September 2022.

2005-W, Proof

Mintage: 816,663

Minted at West Point with W mintmark

The U.S. Mint began offering 2005 Proof American Silver Eagles on March 15, weeks earlier than the usual releases. Mintage caps were also eradicated for the normal Proof offerings, given continued rising demand for these numismatic issues. However, the issue price for the 2005-W Proof Silver Eagle remained at $27.95, the price implemented in 2004.

The 2005 Proof surpassed distribution figures of its 2004 predecessor by more than 15,000, marking the fourth consecutive year of upward trajectory in sales. The 2005-W Proof is readily available in grades up to PF-70.

2005-W, Proof

MARKET VALUES

	Raw	PF-69	PF-70
Value	$85	$105	$125

Note: "Raw" values are for average coins in original Mint packaging, not slabbed.

CERTIFICATION DATA

	Total	<PF-69	PF-69	PF-70
# Certified	62,448	284	39,399	22,765
Percentage		0.45%	63.09%	36.45%

Note: Data compiled from NGC and PCGS reports, September 2022.

The Year 2006

Two new formats of American Silver Eagle premiered in 2006, a year also marked by the return of the Monticello reverse on the nickel—albeit with a new obverse featuring a forward-looking Thomas Jefferson.

Current Events in 2006

Many overseas affairs led the headlines in 2006. European newspapers ran a controversial cartoon depicting the Prophet Muhammad, causing outrage among many in the Islamic community in Western Europe. United Nations inspectors were rebuffed by Iran, leading many to speculate whether the Persian nation was building nuclear weaponry. Meanwhile, North Korea made no effort to hide its intent on mounting a nuclear arsenal, detonating its first nuke on October 9, 2006. Former Iraq president Saddam Hussein was found guilty of crimes against humanity in an Iraqi tribunal. Hussein was sentenced to death on November 5 and executed on December 30.

An unthinkable mass murder occurred on October 2 at a little one-room schoolhouse in an Amish village in Lancaster County, Pennsylvania, when a man entered the class and shot ten girls, killing five.

A monstrous tsunami walloped the Indonesian island of Java and killed more than 660 people. Tropical Cyclone Larry made landfall in Far North Queensland, Australia, causing one indirect death and unleashing $1.1 billion in damage. The Land Down Under dealt with another form of extreme weather when temperatures of 112 degrees Fahrenheit baked the nation's largest city of Sydney. Heat waves also caused strife in Europe and the United States in 2006. In the Southern and Central U.S., a tornado outbreak unleashed 73 twisters that killed 12 people, injured 157, and caused $650 million in damage from April 6 to 8.

The 2006 Winter Olympics were held in Turin, Italy, hosting 2,600 athletes representing 80 nations. The United States won 25 medals, nine of them gold.

The biggest primetime television shows included *American Idol*, *Dancing with the Stars*, *CSI: Crime Scene Investigation*, *Grey's Anatomy*, and *House*. Top box-office draws were *Pirates of the Caribbean: Dead Man's Chest*, *Cars*, *X-Men: The Last Stand*, *The Da Vinci Code*, and *Superman Returns*. The charting radio hits included "Temperature" by Sean Paul, "Unwritten" by Natasha Bedingfield, "Crazy" by Gnarls Barkley, "Ridin" by Chamillionaire featuring Krayzie Bone, and "Be Without You" by Mary J. Blige.

The Dow Jones Industrial Average traipsed across the 12,000-point mark for the first time. The cost of a new home approached $250,000 in the middle of 2006. However, economic conditions soured during the late spring and into the summer months and by the end of the year home prices were beginning to stabilize. Foreclosures began mounting, particularly on homes financed by high-rate subprime mortgages. A new Nissan Altima cost $17,750, a gallon of gas went for $2.59, a gallon gas cost $3.23, and a dozen eggs were 98 cents. A first-class postage stamp was 41 cents. Silver averaged $11.54 per ounce.

On the Numismatic Scene in 2006

The American Silver Eagle series celebrated its 20th anniversary in 2006, with the U.S. Mint unveiling a Burnished strike and Reverse Proof issue for the first time.

These were produced at the West Point Mint like the more typical bullion and Proof issues. The new additions to the American Silver Eagle lineup would make frequent if irregular appearances in the U.S. Mint catalog in the years ahead.

The Jefferson nickel was issued under the Return to Monticello banner, with the elevational view of Thomas Jefferson's stately Virginia home back on the reverse, with a few minor enhancements. Jamie Franki was tapped to replace the original side-view portrait of Jefferson with one showing the third president looking forward, which acting Mint director David Lebryk dubbed, "a fitting tribute to [Jefferson's] vision."

John Mercanti, himself a visionary of the numismatic type, received a much-deserved promotion to chief engraver of the U.S. Mint in 2006. Not only did he design the reverse of the American Silver Eagle but also many other coins, including the reverses of several state quarters and a multitude of commemoratives. As *Coin World* noted in their June 12, 2006, issue, Mercanti was stepping into an increasingly taxing role. "The demands on the engraving staff today include projects that in the early stages of Mercanti's career would have been granted many months of preparation time, but now have deadlines just weeks after inception. The workload has nearly tripled over the past few years and is only expected to increase."

Whitman Publishing celebrated the 60th anniversary of the *Red Book* in 2006 with a 1947-dated "Tribute Edition"—a recreation of the book's 1st edition, released in November 1946. The books were issued in a mainstream hardcover format (with dust-jacket), and also in a limited edition of 500 leather-bound hardcovers.

2006, Bullion Strike

Mintage: 10,676,522

Minted at West Point with no mintmark

Rising metals prices coupled with significant promotion of the American Silver Eagle coins during their grand anniversary year helped bolster sales past 10 million for the second time since 2002—a feat perhaps unthinkable for the series during the lean years of the 1990s. The 2006-W bullion strikes are categorically immaculate, most grading MS-69 or better. Any examples encountered in rough shape are either the oddball exception or, more likely, caused by post-mint mishandling. Collectors wanting an MS-70 should have no trouble finding one, if at a relatively nominal premium.

The record price for a 2006-W Silver Eagle was realized by an MS-70 example that crossed the block at a September 2016 Heritage Auctions sale for $764.

2006, Bullion Strike

MARKET VALUES

	Raw	MS-69	MS-70
Value	$38	$48	$180

Note: "Raw" values are for average coins that are not professionally graded/slabbed.

CERTIFICATION DATA

	Total	<MS-69	MS-69	MS-70
# Certified	376,776	3,333	363,232	10,211
Percentage		0.88%	96.41%	2.71%

Note: Data compiled from NGC and PCGS reports, September 2022.

2006-W, Burnished

Mintage: 468,020

Minted at West Point with W mintmark

What the U.S. Mint terms "Uncirculated," collectors generally refer to as "Burnished" when it comes to American Silver Eagles with this satiny strike, boasting reflective surfaces and lettering against frosty fields. The "Burnished" reference is used by the U.S. Mint to describe the state of the planchets used to make these special Silver Eagles. The coins were released under the balloons and streamers trumpeting the 20th anniversary of the series and would become a fixture in the production lineup.

The 2006-W Burnished Silver Eagles were available in a special three-piece 20th anniversary set as well as on an individual basis, the latter going for $19.95—a price point about halfway between the prevailing price of a regular bullion coin at the time and a Proof. Sales were robust for this first-year offering, with more than 468,000 sold. Collectors may find the Burnished Silver Eagles nearly indistinguishable from their bullion-finish kin, with the glaring exception that these numismatic offerings carry a mintmark on the reverse, while the normal bullion pieces do not.

The 2006-W Burnished American Silver Eagle places 64th in the *100 Greatest U.S. Modern Coins* book, which remarks, "the coin market was hungry for the Uncirculated eagle with the W mintmark, and it felt like there were never enough. Individual pieces were trading for $50 even as they were still being sold by the Mint for $20." An MS-70 example commanded $2,300 at a November 2007 Heritage Auctions sale to claim the reigning price record for this issue.

2006-W, Burnished

MARKET VALUES

	Raw	MS-69	MS-70
Value	$75	$85	$265

Note: "Raw" values are for average coins in original Mint packaging, not slabbed.

CERTIFICATION DATA

	Total	<MS-69	MS-69	MS-70
# Certified	111,862	689	89,642	21,531
Percentage		0.62%	80.14%	19.25%

Note: Data compiled from NGC and PCGS reports, September 2022.

2006-W, Proof

Mintage: 1,092,477

Minted at West Point with W mintmark

The 2006-W Proof Silver Eagle did what no other Proof entry in the series had done since 1986: surpassed a sales total of 1 million. Some of these Proofs were included in the three-piece 20th anniversary set, which saw nearly 250,000 units sell. The U.S. Mint released the 2006-W Proof strikes on April 5 at an issue price of $27.95. While the majority grade PF-69, there are plenty to be had in the top tier of PF-70.

2006-W, Proof

MARKET VALUES

	Raw	PF-69	PF-70
Value	$85	$105	$125

Note: "Raw" values are for average coins in original Mint packaging, not slabbed.

CERTIFICATION DATA

	Total	<PF-69	PF-69	PF-70
# Certified	136,439	1,393	84,201	50,845
Percentage		1.02%	61.71%	37.27%

Note: Data compiled from NGC and PCGS reports, September 2022.

2006-P, Reverse Proof

Mintage: 248,875

Minted at Philadelphia with P mintmark

Regarded as much a novelty as a technical marvel, the 2006-P Reverse Proof American Silver Eagle became the first coin of its kind to ever roll out of the United States Mint. It was exclusively available in the three-piece 20th anniversary American Silver Eagle set released on August 30, 2006, and helped push sales of that special offering to a virtual sellout.

The U.S. Mint described the Reverse Proof as having "a unique finish which results in a frosted field, or background, and a brilliant, mirror-like finish on the raised elements of the coin, including the design and inscriptions." The 2006-P Reverse Proof ranked at 32nd in *100 Greatest U.S. Modern Coins*, noting "its look is so distinctive within the series that the Reverse Proof will always be a curious standout among Silver Eagles."

Later joined by other Reverse Proof Silver Eagles, this 2006-P issue is no longer as unique as it was during its first year of issue. But numismatic observer Eric Jordan posited in an August 21, 2012, *Numismatic News* article, that it maintains its individualism in Silver Eagle circles. "If collectors start working on sets of Reverse Proofs as a cost-effective way to get around buying an expensive 1995-W, then this 2006-P and by extension its Reverse Proof siblings may get a life of their own."

2006-P, Reverse Proof

MARKET VALUES

	Raw	PF-69	PF-70
Value	$165	$185	$325

Note: "Raw" values are for average coins in original Mint packaging, not slabbed.

CERTIFICATION DATA

	Total	<PF-69	PF-69	PF-70
# Certified	81,617	2,378	62,084	17,155
Percentage		2.91%	76.07%	21.02%

Note: Data compiled from NGC and PCGS reports, September 2022.

2006 American Eagle 20th Anniversary Silver Coin Set

Mintage: 248,875

Minted at West Point and Philadelphia with W and P mintmarks

Marking the 20th anniversary of the American Silver Eagle and issued for $100, this three-piece set of numismatic-finish Silver Eagles sold like hotcakes within about ten weeks of its August 30, 2006, release. It includes the standard Proof along with the two new kids on the block, the Uncirculated ("Burnished") and Reverse Proof. Production was limited to 250,000 sets with a household limit of ten sets. At one point in 2007 the set was selling for closer to $600, but prices have since settled down a bit.

"Silver Eagle Anniversary sets continue to make an impact," says Troy Thoreson. "The 2006 three-piece anniversary set had another huge impact. The introduction of this anniversary set the tone for many other special sets to be issued in the coming years. This set again took the interest in the Silver Eagle series to a new level."

2006 American Eagle 20th Anniversary Silver Coin Set
MARKET VALUES

	Raw	69	70
Value	$215	$300	$900

Note: "Raw" values are for average coins in original Mint packaging, not slabbed.

2006-W American Eagle 20th Anniversary Gold and Silver Coin Set

Mintage: 20,000

Minted at West Point with W mintmarks

This special two-coin offering honored the 20th anniversary of both the American Silver Eagle and the American Gold Eagle with its duo of one-ounce "Uncirculated" ("Burnished") issues from the West Point Mint, packaged together in a handsome black presentation case. The U.S. Mint offered this set for $850 with a production limit of 20,000, all of which sold in swift fashion.

2006-W American Eagle 20th Anniversary Gold and Silver Coin Set
MARKET VALUES

	Raw	MS-69	MS-70
Value	$2,200	$2,600	

Note: "Raw" values are for average coins in original Mint packaging, not slabbed.

THE YEAR 2007

The U.S. Mint ceremoniously released its new Presidential $1 coin series, which honors the nation's presidents in the order they served in the White House. The program moved along at a clip of four new designs a year, predicated on the requirement that each honored president had to have been deceased for at least two years before they appeared on the coins. During the latter months of the year, President George W. Bush signed into law a new dollar-coin program that would commence in 2009 and was designed to help further inspire the public to collect (and spend) the "golden" dollar.

Current Events in 2007

The Apple iPhone hit stores in June 2007, ushering in a new chapter of the digital revolution. NASA continued its exploration of Mars with the launch of *Phoenix* Mars lander in August.

The field of people running for president in 2008 grew to historic proportions for both Republicans and Democrats, although the candidates would winnow ahead of party primaries in early 2008.

On April 16, 2007, an undergraduate student of Virginia Tech in Blacksburg, Virginia, opened fire on campus, killing 32 and injuring 23. The Interstate 35 bridge over the Mississippi River in Minneapolis, Minnesota, collapsed during rush-hour traffic on August 1, 2007, killing 13 people and injuring 145. Brazil Flight 3054 went down, killing 199.

The town of Greensburg, Kansas, was destroyed when a tornado packing winds of 200 miles per hour tore through on May 4, 2007, killing 11 people. California wildfires burned more than 1.5 million acres and destroyed thousands of buildings. A massive blizzard froze Denver, Colorado, while a persistent drought in Australia caused widespread crop failures on the island continent. More than 10,000 perished in a Bangladesh cyclone.

Harry Potter and the Deathly Hallows became the final book in the best-selling series by author J.K. Rowling.

American Idol, Dancing with the Stars, NBC Sunday Night Football, Grey's Anatomy, and *House* were among the top primetime television shows. *Spider-Man 3, Shrek the Third, Transformers, Pirates of the Caribbean: At World's End,* and *Harry Potter and the*

Order of the Phoenix ranked best at the box office. The top hits on the radio included "Irreplaceable" by Beyoncé, "Umbrella" by Rihanna featuring Jay-Z, "The Sweet Escape" by Gwen Stefani featuring Akon, "Big Girls Don't Cry" by Fergie, and "Before He Cheats" by Carrie Underwood.

Annual home prices peaked around $250,000, then fell by as much as 15 percent across much of the country as the housing bubble burst amid a worsening economy and a record pace of foreclosures. A 2007 Ford Five-Hundred listed for $25,270, a gallon of gas was $2.80, and a gallon of milk cost $3.87. A first-class stamp remained 41 cents. The Dow Jones Industrial Average eclipsed 13,000 points in April and trounced 14,000 in July. Silver charted an average price of $13.32 per ounce.

On the Numismatic Scene in 2007

The Presidential $1 coin launched in January 2007 with much fanfare, with hopes that the new circulating commemorative program would encourage the public to use dollar coins in daily transactions. Media stirred around the series in the first months after some examples of the George Washington dollar were found without its edge lettering, a component not seen on circulating U.S. coinage since the $20 gold double eagle in the early 1930s. These so-called "Godless dollars," so termed because the national motto IN GOD WE TRUST was absent from its usual place on the edge of the dollar coins, became hot collector commodities worth hundreds of dollars for a time.

The Native American $1 Coin Act was signed into law by President Bush on September 20, 2007, authorizing the start of a dollar coin program depicting "images celebrating important contributions made by Indian tribes and individual Native Americans to the development of the United States and the history of the United States." Beginning in 2009, a new reverse design would be paired each year with the common Sacagawea obverse that premiered on the dollar coin in 2000.

At the August 2007 awards ceremony of the Numismatic Literary Guild (a society for writers, editors, and publishers), Whitman Publishing distributed 125 copies of the 2008-dated (61st) leather-bound Limited Edition *Red Book*. This small quantity of the much larger (but still relatively small) 3,000 print run was specially imprinted on the back covers. Collectors recognized the rarity, and a copy sold for $1,200 the following year; values have since stabilized around $650. Whitman's connection to the NLG goes back to 1968, when *Red Book* creator R.S. Yeoman was one of the guild's founding members.

2007, Bullion Strike

Mintage: 9,028,036

Minted at West Point with no mintmark

Production numbers for the 2007 bullion Silver Eagle were off by over a million as compared to the previous year's tally, but with a mintage of more than 9 million, this date is still more common than most that preceded it. The 2007 Silver Eagles are quite common and flaunt remarkable quality. Collectors wanting an MS-70 piece for their collections can find one with ease for a relatively small premium. A coin graded MS-70 and bearing a "First Strike" label claimed $1,821 in a May 2013 Heritage Auctions sale.

2007, Bullion Strike

MARKET VALUES

	Raw	MS-69	MS-70
Value	$38	$48	$125

Note: "Raw" values are for average coins that are not professionally graded/slabbed.

CERTIFICATION DATA

	Total	<MS-69	MS-69	MS-70
# Certified	178,618	1,496	166,566	10,556
Percentage		0.84%	93.25%	5.91%

Note: Data compiled from NGC and PCGS reports, September 2022.

2007-W, Burnished

Mintage: 621,333

Minted at West Point with W mintmark

Following the debut of the Burnished Silver Eagle in 2006, the U.S. Mint followed up with a second issue in 2007. They were sold directly to the public for $21.95 per coin, marking an increase of $2 from the previous year. They were also sold in the 2007 Annual Uncirculated Dollar Coin Set that included a 2007 Sacagawea dollar and the four 2007 Presidential dollars for a total of $31.95. Most 2007-W Burnished Silver Eagles cross the market in MS-69, though MS-70 examples can be had for a small premium.

2007-W, Burnished

MARKET VALUES

	Raw	MS-69	MS-70
Value	$45	$65	$90

Note: "Raw" values are for average coins in original Mint packaging, not slabbed.

CERTIFICATION DATA

	Total	<MS-69	MS-69	MS-70
# Certified	116,911	621	85,183	31,107
Percentage		0.53%	72.86%	26.61%

Note: Data compiled from NGC and PCGS reports, September 2022.

2007-W, Proof

Mintage: 821,759

Minted at West Point with W mintmark

The 2007-W Proof Silver Eagle was released on March 27 at an issue price of $29.95— $2 higher than in 2006. Though minted without maximum authorized limits, sales declined by over 270,000 from 2006, perhaps in part due to the higher sticker price. Certified coins are split almost evenly between PF-69 and PF-70, with the latter bringing only a small premium.

2007-W, Proof

MARKET VALUES

	Raw	PF-69	PF-70
Value	$85	$105	$120

Note: "Raw" values are for average coins in original Mint packaging, not slabbed.

CERTIFICATION DATA

	Total	<PF-69	PF-69	PF-70
# Certified	79,456	365	44,449	34,642
Percentage		0.46%	55.94%	43.60%

Note: Data compiled from NGC and PCGS reports, September 2022.

THE YEAR 2008

The last of the Lincoln Memorial cents rolled off the mint presses after a half century of production. Meanwhile, a worsening economic picture sent demand soaring for the American Silver Eagle, which smashed its previous all-time-record mintage by nearly double.

Current Events in 2008

A contentious presidential primary season saw infighting among Democrats and Republicans as each party sought to choose their nominee. Ultimately, an increasingly divided Republican party chose Arizona senator John McCain as their nominee and Alaska governor Sarah Palin as his running mate, while Democrats eschewed the establishment figure of tenured New York senator Hillary Clinton for relatively unknown first-term Illinois senator Barack Obama. The presidential race turned out throngs of voters across aisles to vote for Obama, who paired himself with genial Senate figure Joe Biden as his running mate and won 52.9 percent of the vote and 365 electoral votes.

In Switzerland the European Organization for Nuclear Research launched its Large Hadron Collider to begin testing particle theory.

As the U.S. economy continued collapsing, President George W. Bush approved a number of economic stimulus initiatives. Among the spending was a $150 billion tax cut aimed at working-class and middle-income households, while a $700 billion bailout was provided to the U.S. financial system. The Federal Reserve lowered interest rates to help curtail the recession and spur more spending.

Governor of Illinois Rod Blagojevich was arrested on federal corruption charges on the grounds of bribery as well as wire and mail fraud; the Illinois House of Representatives voted to impeach him. Cuban President Fidel Castro stepped down after nearly 50 years leading the island nation just south of Florida. A tropical cyclone struck Myanmar, killing more than 138,000, and a magnitude-7.9 earthquake killed more than 87,000 in the Chengdu region of China's Sichuan province.

The 2008 Summer Olympics in Beijing saw U.S. athletes win an overall 112 medals, including 36 golds. Despite a major writers' strike in Hollywood, primetime television offered a variety of hits like *American Idol*, *Dancing with the Stars*, *The Mentalist*, *CSI: Crime Scene Investigation*, and *60 Minutes*. Silver screen draws were *The Dark Knight*, *Iron Man*, *Indiana Jones and the Kingdom of the Crystal Skull*, *Hancock*, and *WALL-E*. Top songs were "So What" by Pink, "When I Grow Up" by The Pussycat Dolls, "Hot N Cold" by Katy Perry, "I'm Yours" by Jason Mraz, and "Closer" by Ne-Yo.

The median price of a new home fell to about $211,900 in 2008, while a new Toyota Prius went for $21,500. The price for a gallon of gas hit a record high in the summer of 2008 at $4.17 per gallon, while a gallon of milk was $3.80 and a loaf of bread reached $1.37. A first-class postage stamp cost 42 cents. Silver prices averaged $14.99 per ounce.

On the Numismatic Scene in 2008

The Lincoln Memorial cent breathed its last in 2008 as the design by Frank Gasparro was retired after a 50-year tenure. Also coming to an end was the 50 State Quarters program, which had helped spur a massive revival in interest for numismatics since it began in 1999. Few multiyear circulating commemoratives have come close to approaching the mainstream popularity of the 50 State Quarters series. A souring economy was beginning to hit the collectible coin market, though American Silver Eagles were enjoying record demand as more and more investors buttressed failing stock and bond portfolios with precious metals.

Whitman Publishing introduced a new format of *Red Book* in 2008—the spiralbound hardcover, giving collectors the durability of a hardcover and the convenience of a stay-flat spiral binding.

The popular United States Mint Gold Buffalo program expanded in 2008 to include fractional options of the one-ounce gold coins modeled after James Earle Fraser's iconic Buffalo nickel design.

2008, Bullion Strike

Mintage: 20,583,000

Minted at West Point with no mintmark

A new record mintage for the American Silver Eagle program was achieved in 2008 when more than 20.5 million bullion strikes rolled off West Point Mint presses. The record nearly doubled the previous high-water mark of 11,442,335 strikes from 1987. The outstanding demand for the Silver Eagle taxed the U.S. Mint, which at one point temporarily suspended orders before later rationing took effect, with Proof orders stopped so blanks could be rerouted to bullion production.

The tremendous supply of 2008 bullion Silver Eagles lends plenty of stock for collectors today, and quality isn't a problem for these beautifully struck coins. However, a significant but affordable premium applies for MS-70 examples, which represent a relatively small percentage of the certified population. The record price for a 2008 Silver Eagle was achieved by a piece labeled as a "First Strike" and graded MS-70, which took $298 at a February 2012 GreatCollections sale.

2008, Bullion Strike

MARKET VALUES	Raw	MS-69	MS-70
Value	$36	$45	$90

Note: "Raw" values are for average coins that are not professionally graded/slabbed.

CERTIFICATION DATA	Total	<MS-69	MS-69	MS-70
# Certified	524,163	60,594	435,986	27,583
Percentage		11.56%	83.18%	5.26%

Note: Data compiled from NGC and PCGS reports, September 2022.

2008-W, Burnished

Mintage: 533,757

Minted at West Point with W mintmark

The 2008-W Burnished Silver Eagle marked the third consecutive year of production

for this issue. Like its predecessors, the 2008-W hails from the West Point Mint, but it was issued at $25.95 per coin—up $4 from the previous year. No mintage limits were set, but total distribution was down by around 90,000 from the previous year. The coin was sold to individual collectors and also included in the 2008 U.S. Mint Annual Uncirculated Dollar Coin Set, which was priced at $37.95 and included satin-finish versions of the 2008 Sacagawea dollar and the four Presidential $1 coins.

2008-W, Burnished

MARKET VALUES	Raw	MS-69	MS-70
Value	$48	$65	$100

Note: "Raw" values are for average coins in original Mint packaging, not slabbed.

CERTIFICATION DATA	Total	<MS-69	MS-69	MS-70
# Certified	63,424	55	28,630	34,739
Percentage		0.09%	45.14%	54.77%

Note: Data compiled from NGC and PCGS reports, September 2022.

2008-W, Burnished, Reverse of 2007

Mintage: 47,000 estimated.

Minted at West Point with W mintmark

Discovered in mid-April 2008, this scarce piece has become the

most important variety of the entire American Silver Eagle series, with many collectors not considering their sets complete without it. The variety arose during the creation of a new hub amid the implementation of digital engraving—a huge step for the U.S. Mint at the time. The reverse of the Silver Eagle was seeing some small but noticeable design changes, including the font of the legends. The "U" of UNITED exhibits the most important diagnostic for this variety. From 1986 through 2007, the base of the "U" is smooth and rounded, while the new font that debuted in 2008 shows a descender, or spur, on the right side of the vowel.

This highly collectible variety is featured in *Cherrypickers' Guide to Die Varieties* and ranks 17th in *100 Greatest U.S. Modern Coins*, the latter noting, "The Mint responded quickly, acknowledging that during three production shifts for the 2008 coins, dies originally crafted for 2007-W Silver Eagle production were used inadvertently. Approximately 47,000 Silver Eagles had been struck with the reverse style of 2007. This type of variety is called a transitional because it is a hybrid that combines the styles of coins used in two consecutive years."

2008-W, Burnished, Reverse of 2007

MARKET VALUES

	Raw	MS-69	MS-70
Value	$450	$550	$1,400

Note: "Raw" values are for average coins in original Mint packaging, not slabbed.

CERTIFICATION DATA

	Total	<MS-69	MS-69	MS-70
# Certified	17,505	59	9,114	8,332
Percentage		0.34%	52.07%	47.60%

Note: Data compiled from NGC and PCGS reports, September 2022.

2008-W, Proof

Mintage: 700,979

Minted at West Point with W mintmark

The outstanding demand for Silver Eagles in 2008 caused many blanks originally appropriated for Proof coinage to be given over to the bullion strikes,

which took priority over collector coins. The U.S. Mint suspended sales of Proofs in August, by which point the Proof sales had already topped 700,000. That could be considered a lofty mid-year figure, even despite the fact the U.S. Mint had raised the issue price for the Proof to $31.95, up $2 from 2007.

The Proof Silver Eagles would not return until 2010, but there were plenty of 2008 Proofs to keep collectors busy for the time being. The 2008-W Proofs boast exceptional strike and surface quality, which is the norm for the West Point Silver Eagles, particularly Proof pieces. This ensures there are plenty of PF-70 examples for those who want them, and at modest premiums over PF-69 examples, buyers demanding only "perfect" pieces will often have few reservations about putting out a little more money to procure the best of the best.

2008-W, Proof

MARKET VALUES

	Raw	PF-69	PF-70
Value	$85	$105	$125

Note: "Raw" values are for average coins in original Mint packaging, not slabbed.

CERTIFICATION DATA

	Total	<PF-69	PF-69	PF-70
# Certified	69,006	343	35,911	32,752
Percentage		0.50%	52.04%	47.46%

Note: Data compiled from NGC and PCGS reports, September 2022.

The Year 2009

The Lincoln cent became the canvas for four commemorative reverse designs depicting Abraham Lincoln throughout his life. The U.S. Mint began a one-year circulating quarter initiative called the District of Columbia and U.S. Territories Quarters program, which served as an effective extension of the 50 State Quarters program. The Presidential $1 coins were slightly modified to ensure no more "Godless" dollars would emit from the Mint, and the Native American dollar series launched. Unprecedented demand for bullion-finish American Silver Eagles pushed the Mint to suspend all numismatic offerings for the program, leaving collectors without any Proof Silver Eagles for the first time since the series began in 1986.

Current Events in 2009

Barack Obama was inaugurated as the first African American president of the United States on January 20, 2009. Obama also became the nation's first commander-in-chief born in the 1960s and, at the age of 47, the fifth-youngest person sworn in as United States president. Obama was elected on a platform of "change," with the goal of implementing universal healthcare a major campaign promise. However, continued economic woes became the central focus for much of his first year in office.

Exacerbating the situation overseas was a dispute between Russia and Ukraine over $2.4 billion in debts, leading the Russians to cut off all gas supplies to the Ukrainians and interrupting the flow of oil into the rest of Europe.

The H1N1 pandemic, widely known as the "swine flu," swept the globe beginning in the spring of 2009, causing about 1 billion infections worldwide and at least 150,000 deaths.

NASA sent astronauts aboard a final Space Shuttle mission to the Hubble Telescope, which needed significant repairs. Shortly after takeoff from New York City's LaGuardia Airport, US Airways Flight 1549 was struck by a flock of Canada geese, causing the jet to lose engine power. Captain Chesley "Sully" Sullenberger and Jeffrey Skiles made the decision to glide the plane into the nearby Hudson River, an act that by all accounts saved all 155 onboard.

"King of Pop" Michael Jackson died on June 25, 2009, at the age of 50. Movie theaters lured millions with *Transformers: Revenge of the Fallen*, *Harry Potter and the Half-Blood Prince*, *Up*, *The Twilight Saga: New Moon*, and *Avatar*. On primetime television were *American Idol*, *Dancing with the Stars*, *NCIS*, *Sunday Night Football*, and *The Mentalist*. "Boom Boom Pow" by The Black Eyed Peas, "Poker Face" by Lady Gaga, "Love Story" by Taylor Swift, "Right Round" by Flo Rida, and "Single Ladies (Put a Ring on It)" by Beyoncé were all top songs.

The economy bottomed out during 2009 and began showing some glimmers of life by the end of the year. Median new-home prices hovered around $214,500 nationwide, while the price of a Daimler AG Smart Fortwo car was $12,500. A gallon of gas was $2.35, a gallon of milk came in at $3.11, a loaf of bread went for $1.58, and the price of a first-class postage stamp increased to 44 cents. An ounce of silver had an average price of $14.66.

On the Numismatic Scene in 2009

The enduring Lincoln cent fielded a run of four special, circulating reverse designs honoring the life of Abraham Lincoln, who was born 200 years earlier in 1809. The bicentennial cents featured motifs paying homage to Lincoln's birth and early childhood in a Kentucky log cabin, his formative years as a rail splitter who devoured books, his professional life in Illinois, and his presidency in Washington. Also in 2009, the U.S. Mint endeavored on another one-year commemorative program with the District of Columbia

The MMIX Ultra High Relief Gold Coin was a one-year offering that reinvents the legendary Augustus Saint-Gaudens design for the double eagle in the extremely high relief format that the artist envisioned but was impractical to produce in mass scale when the Saint-Gaudens double eagle debuted in 1907.

and U.S. Territories Quarters, which recognized Washington, D.C., Puerto Rico, Guam, American Samoa, U.S. Virgin Islands, and Northern Mariana Islands.

Also beginning in 2009 was the Native American dollar program, which repurposed the beleaguered Sacagawea dollar as the stage honoring "the important contributions made by Indian tribes and individual Native Americans to the development [and history] of the United States," as the authorizing legislation required. The obverse of the Sacagawea dollar remained largely the same, with the date and mintmark moved to the edge along with the legend E PLURIBUS UNUM. The reverse began seeing one new design each year.

The U.S. Mint also stayed busy with refining old designs, as was seen with the Presidential $1 coins. The series, debuting in 2007, had seen some unwanted publicity when a number of these coins were struck without their edge inscriptions, notably the national motto IN GOD WE TRUST. Some conspiracy theorists suggested it was a bold attempt to "remove God" from coins, when in fact it was a simple matter of the coins not receiving their incused edge lettering (which also included the date, mintmark, and legend E PLURIBUS UNUM) in a separate step of the minting process. The Consolidation Appropriations Act of 2008 required the relocation of IN GOD WE TRUST to either the obverse or reverse, with the former chosen as the new location for the motto beginning in 2009. The date, mintmark, and E PLURIBUS UNUM remained on the edge of the coin.

Whitman Publishing innovated with a new style of *Red Book* in 2009: the large-sized Journal Edition. This featured a three-ring binder, color-coded tabbed dividers, and removable pages. This was a one-year experiment. The company's leather-bound Limited Edition *Red Book* was reduced from 3,000 copies to 1,500 in 2009, with the 2010-dated 63rd edition.

In 2009 Whitman broke new ground with the *Professional Edition* of the *Red Book*, an 8.5 x 11–inch spiralbound, softcover, expanded version of the traditional best-seller. Longtime *Red Book* collector Frank J. Colletti, author of the *Guide Book of the Official Red Book of United States Coins,* called it "a truly innovative development in the sixty-year history of the *Red Book*" and "a new invaluable resource." The *Professional Edition,* published alongside the regular *Red Book* from 2009 to 2014, would in later years transform into the 1,504-page *Mega Red.*

2009, Bullion Strike

Mintage: 30,459,000

Minted at West Point with no mintmark

A cratering Wall Street and tumultuous U.S. economic scene led investors to precious metals, where they found the American Silver Eagle an appealing buy. This caused the Silver Eagle to once again trounce all-time mintage records, posting sales of more than 30 million in 2009—a number certainly unimaginable to observers in the 1980s or 1990s. The U.S. Mint struggled to procure enough blanks to meet the demand, rationing all Silver Eagle planchets for bullion strikes only and thus allocating none for Proofs or Uncirculated ("Burnished") coins.

Silver planchet supplies improved going into the late spring of 2009, and the U.S. Mint subsequently lifted distributor rationing on June 15. However, by the end of November the Mint temporarily suspended sales and then reinstituted rationing until demand for the bullion coins could again be met.

By the time all was said and done, there was no way the U.S. Mint was able to resume Proof and Burnished Silver Eagle strikes with a 2009 date. Of course, this leaves even the most advanced American Silver Eagle sets with just one coin representing the date: the 2009 bullion strike. Thankfully, the massive number of 2009 Silver Eagles in existence leave plenty of MS-70 examples, and these top-end coins can be had for affordable premiums. A 2009 American Silver Eagle graded MS-70 and bearing a "First Strike" label took $286 in a February 2012 GreatCollections sale.

2009, Bullion Strike

MARKET VALUES	Raw	MS-69	MS-70
Value	$36	$45	$90

Note: "Raw" values are for average coins that are not professionally graded/slabbed.

CERTIFICATION DATA	Total	<MS-69	MS-69	MS-70
# Certified	510,709	126,188	326,300	58,221
Percentage		24.71%	63.89%	11.40%

Note: Data compiled from NGC and PCGS reports, September 2022.

THE YEAR 2010

Even as demand for the American Silver Eagle continued growing since 2009, the U.S. Mint was able to procure enough supply of Silver Eagle blanks to resume offering numismatic strikes. Also keeping Mint officials busy was the new America the Beautiful Quarters series, which recognized national parks and landmarks from each of the 50 states, District of Columbia, and U.S. territories in the order that each attraction opened to the public. Meanwhile, a new permanent reverse design premiered on the Lincoln cent.

Current Events in 2010

The global economy continued on a sluggish note, with U.S. housing prices still in the doldrums and unemployment numbers remaining relatively high. Layoffs were happening in virtually every sector. One of the few bright spots for President Barack Obama on the domestic scene was the passage of the Affordable Care Act (ACA), which he signed into law on March 23, 2010.

The 163-story skyscraper known as Burj Khalifa opened in the United Arab Emirates to become the world's tallest building.

China launched *Chang'e 2* as its second moon probe, while the SpaceX commercial space flight program successfully launched its Dragon capsule into the heavens during a test mission aimed at eventually bringing cargo and crew into low-Earth orbit.

British Petroleum's Deepwater Horizon oil rig explosion in the Gulf of Mexico on April 20, 2010, killed 11 and became the largest marine oil spill in the history of the petroleum industry. In total, more than 210 million gallons of oil spurted from the damaged well into waters 5,000 feet deep off the coast of Louisiana.

A massive 7.0-magnitude earthquake devastated Haiti, while an 8.8-magnitude quake in Chile killed more than 500. Flooding in Pakistan submerged 20 percent of the nation, leaving millions homeless.

The 2010 Winter Olympics in Vancouver, Canada, welcomed more than 2,500 athletes representing 82 different countries, with the United States garnering 37 medals, nine of them gold. *American Idol*, *Dancing with the Stars*, *Sunday Night Football*, *The Mentalist*, and *Criminal Minds* were top television shows, while *Toy Story 3*, *Alice in Wonderland*, *Iron Man 2*, *The Twilight Saga: Eclipse*, and *Harry Potter and the Deathly Hallows: Part 1* were big box-office draws. "Tik Tok" by Kesha, "Need You Now" by Lady Antebellum, "Hey, Soul Sister" by Train, "California Gurls" by Katy Perry featuring Snoop Dogg, and "OMG" by Usher featuring will.i.am were big radio hits.

The median price for a new home languished at around $221,500, while the 2010 Nissan Versa sold for $14,350. A gallon of gas was $2.79 and a gallon of milk cost $3.26, while a loaf of bread was $1.41. A first-class postage stamp was 44 cents. The price for an ounce of silver trended upward to $20.19.

On the Numismatic Scene in 2010

As economic fallout from the Great Recession continued rippling throughout every corner of the nation, the coin market softened significantly. This did not stop trophy coins from claiming big prices, like one of the five known 1913 Liberty nickels that auctioned for $3,737,500. Yet, overall market activity was perceptibly slower in 2010, and this affected the broadest swath of the hobby.

The U.S. Mint kept collectors busy with the introduction of the America the Beautiful Quarters honoring national parks and landmarks around the United States, the District of Columbia, and U.S. territories. Alongside the circulating quarter program was a series of five-ounce bullion coins denominated at 25 cents and carrying designs identical to those seen on the quarter. The Lincoln cent donned a new shield reverse design by Lyndall Bass, emblematic of President Abraham Lincoln's preserving the United States as a single, united nation.

Whitman Publishing introduced an oversized version of the *Guide Book of United States Coins* in 2010, the 63rd edition. Since then, the Large Print Edition *Red Book* has been a popular annual format—as coin collectors get older and need reading glasses!

At the U.S. Mint, John Mercanti retired as chief engraver in late 2010. Born in Philadelphia, Mercanti received his artistic training at the Pennsylvania Academy of Fine Arts, the Philadelphia College of Art, and the Fleisher Art Memorial School. He joined the Mint in 1974 as a sculptor-engraver under the legendary Frank Gasparro, created a remarkable portfolio of coin and medal designs, and in 2006 was named chief engraver.

2010, Bullion Strike

Mintage: 34,764,500

Minted at West Point with no mintmark

In its efforts to keep pace with mounting demand in 2009, the United States Mint continued striking 2009-dated Silver Eagles right up through the end of the year. This left no lead time for the Mint to get a jump start on the production of 2010-dated Silver Eagles and thus pushed the release of the bullion coins back to January 19, nearly three weeks after the typical release date for the American Silver Eagle.

The U.S. Mint rationed Silver Eagles in allocations to its authorized distributors, with core focus going to the production of bullion strikes. As the year pressed into the summer with no Proofs or Burnished strikes, many were left to wonder if there would be a repeat of 2009—leaving the hobby sans numismatic strikes once more. The U.S. Mint began offering Proofs in the middle of the autumn, though the production of Burnished coins waited until 2011.

An abundance of 2010 bullion Silver Eagles leave plenty for collectors to pursue. They are widely available up through MS-70, where even the "perfect" coins sell for affordable premiums. A piece graded MS-70 and bearing a West Point label realized $154 in an October 2011 GreatCollections auction.

2010, Bullion Strike

MARKET VALUES	Raw	MS-69	MS-70
Value	$36	$45	$80

Note: "Raw" values are for average coins that are not professionally graded/slabbed.

CERTIFICATION DATA	Total	<MS-69	MS-69	MS-70
# Certified	906,571	3,158	779,410	124,003
Percentage		0.35%	85.97%	13.68%

Note: Data compiled from NGC and PCGS reports, September 2022.

2010-W, Proof

Mintage: 849,861

Minted at West Point with W mintmark

Collectors had to wait until October before learning if the U.S. Mint would produce a Proof Silver Eagle for 2010. Orders began rolling in on November 19 and shipping commenced on December 1. Pent-up demand for the Proof Silver Eagle carried this issue past the 700,000 mark within two weeks, with the total mintage nearly reaching 850,000 despite the issue price for the coin being set at $45.95, or an increase of $14 over the last Proof issued in 2008. Pieces grading PF-70 are both plentiful and affordable.

The Coin Modernization, Oversight, and Continuity Act of 2010 was signed into law by President Obama on December 14, 2010, and permitted the U.S. Mint to allocate blanks for Proofs and other collectible Silver Eagles even in cases wherein the demand for bullion-finish coins cannot be met. This all but assures there will never be a situation like 2009 again.

2010-W, Proof

MARKET VALUES

	Raw	PF-69	PF-70
Value	$85	$105	$125

Note: "Raw" values are for average coins in original Mint packaging, not slabbed.

CERTIFICATION DATA

	Total	<PF-69	PF-69	PF-70
# Certified	97,460	506	44,360	52,594
Percentage		0.52%	45.52%	53.96%

Note: Data compiled from NGC and PCGS reports, September 2022.

THE YEAR 2011

The 25th anniversary (or "silver" anniversary) of the American Eagle bullion program inspired the release of a special set of five Silver Eagles representing the various finishes offered by the United States Mint at that time.

Current Events in 2011

Terrorist mastermind and al-Qaeda leader Osama bin Laden was found and killed by U.S. Navy SEALs in Pakistan on May 2, 2011, following a manhunt that had lasted nearly a decade.

On March 11 a 9.0-magnitude earthquake off the shores of Japan instigated a tsunami with waves measuring more than 120 feet in height. The massive tremor and ensuing inundation from the sea led to meltdowns at the Fukushima Daiichi Nuclear Power Plant, becoming the worst nuclear disaster since the meltdown at the Chernobyl Nuclear Plant in 1986. The devastating earthquake left in its wake 16,000 deceased, 6,000 injured, and 3,000 missing.

Sociopolitical uprisings took place across the Middle East and saw tens of thousands of citizens speak out against their governments. Dubbed the "Arab Spring," these largely simultaneous protests were fueled at the grassroots level by social media.

Occupy Wall Street protests in the United States began in September and put a spotlight on income equality, leading to the phrase "We are the 99 percent."

Great Britain's Prince William and Kate Middleton wed on April 29. A car bomb blast in Oslo, Norway, killed eight people, two hours before a related mass shooting killed 69 more on the nearby island of Utoya. Democratic Arizona congressperson Gabrielle Giffords was shot in the head during a public appearance in which 18 others were shot, six of whom died, including a nine-year-old girl. Giffords survived but eventually resigned her congressional seat to focus on her recovery. A massive tornado in Joplin, Missouri, killed at least 158, injured more than 1,100 others, and caused $2.8 billion in damages.

Sunday Night Football, *NCIS*, *Dancing with the Stars*, *American Idol*, and *The Big Bang Theory* were top television hits. At the movies were *Harry Potter and the Deathly Hallows: Part 2*, *Transformers: Dark of the Moon*, *The Twilight Saga: Breaking Dawn Part 1*, *The Hangover Part II*, and *Pirates of the Caribbean: On Stranger Tides*. "Rolling in the Deep" by Adele, "The Edge of Glory" by Lady Gaga, "We Found Love" by Rihanna, "Look at Me Now" by Chris Brown, and "Paradise" by Coldplay were tops on the music charts.

As the economy began showing more steam, housing prices were bottoming out in many parts of the United States. The median price for a new home was about $224,300. The price for a gallon of gas had reached $3.53, while a gallon of milk was similarly priced at $3.57. A loaf of bread was $1.48, and a first-class postage stamp was 44 cents. Silver reached a multi-decade high of $49.50 per ounce on April 28, 2011, but the metal's overall average for the year was a nonetheless impressive $35.12 per ounce.

On the Numismatic Scene in 2011

Precious metals were hot buys in 2011. This drew investors toward the American Silver Eagle series, which charted its fourth consecutive all-time-record mintage for the bullion offerings. This led the U.S. Mint to expand production of its standard bullion strikings to San Francisco.

In July 2011 a landmark court case, involving a family that inherited ten of the extremely rare 1933 Saint-Gaudens double eagles, made headlines when a jury decided that the coins, which the United States had declared were illegal to own, were subject to seizure by the government. The case reached the U.S. Third Circuit Court of Appeals, which in 2016 upheld the lower court's ruling against the family, and was denied any hearing by the United States Supreme Court in 2017.

The leather-bound Limited Edition of the *Red Book* became even more collectible in 2011. This year its print run was cut by one-third, from 1,500 copies to 1,000. Whitman maintained its issue price at $69.95.

2011, Bullion Strike

Mintage: 40,020,000

Minted at West Point and San Francisco with no mintmark

Demand for the American Silver Eagle continued into 2011, which kicked off with sales for the bullion coin amounting to six million in January. U.S. Mint officials decided to supplement production with help from the San Francisco Mint and sought more suppliers of silver blanks to help meet increasing demand.

Collectors looking for ways to distinguish the West Point and San Francisco bullion Silver Eagles will fail to find any diagnostics, as coins from either facility look identical. However, new pieces still contained in "monster box" shipments with markings from the San Francisco Mint offer a telltale giveaway, and coins submitted to the major grading companies and still sealed in these cartons will be recognized as "San Francisco" coins.

The U.S. Mint released data revealing that 34,984,500 of the 2011 Silver Eagles were minted at the West Point Mint and 5,035,500 hailed from San Francisco. Some collectors will try obtaining one example of each, with the San Francisco coins tending to sell for slightly higher prices due to their relative scarcity. Either a (W) or (S) 2011 Silver Eagle is easily obtainable in grades up to MS-70. A piece graded MS-70 and coupled with an "Early Releases" label fetched $253 in a January 2012 Heritage Auctions sale.

2011, Bullion Strike

MARKET VALUES

	Raw	MS-69	MS-70
Value	$36	$45	$80

Note: "Raw" values are for average coins that are not professionally graded/slabbed.

CERTIFICATION DATA

	Total	<MS-69	MS-69	MS-70
# Certified	1,184,229	6,342	1,017,505	160,382
Percentage		0.54%	85.92%	13.54%

Note: Data compiled from NGC and PCGS reports, September 2022.

2011-W, Burnished

Mintage: 409,927

Minted at West Point with W mintmark

The United States finally returned to producing Uncirculated (or "Burnished") Silver Eagles for the first time since 2008. They were originally offered for sale on September 8, 2011, at $60.45, but as silver prices settled in the last months of the year, the U.S. Mint lowered the issue price in kind to $50.95. They were sold individually and as part of the five-piece 25th Anniversary Silver Eagle Set. Quantities are available in grades up to MS-70.

2011-W, Burnished

MARKET VALUES

	Raw	MS-69	MS-70
Value	$50	$65	$95

Note: "Raw" values are for average coins in original Mint packaging, not slabbed.

CERTIFICATION DATA

	Total	<MS-69	MS-69	MS-70
# Certified	37,495	97	17,137	20,261
Percentage		0.26%	45.70%	54.04%

Note: Data compiled from NGC and PCGS reports, September 2022.

2011-W, Proof

Mintage: 947,355

Minted at West Point with W mintmark

Demand was strong for the 2011-W Proof, which sold nearly 370,000 units in the first six days after release on June 30. The coin's issue price bounced from $59.95 in June to $68.45 in September, before falling back to $58.95. The coin was available both on an individual basis and in the 25th Anniversary Silver Eagle Set, which sold through its run of 100,000.

Coin World reporter Steve Roach observed in a September 19, 2011, article that the pricing fluctuations dictated by the U.S. Mint had ripple effects in the secondary marketplace. "For Proof American Eagle silver bullion coins, the Mint's price increase from the June 30 issue price of $59.95 to $68.45 on Aug. 29 sent secondary wholesale market prices for 1986 to 2011 Proof American Eagle silver coins soaring from $56 to $66 in just 48 hours," he said.

2011-W, Proof

MARKET VALUES

	Raw	PF-69	PF-70
Value	$85	$105	$125

Note: "Raw" values are for average coins in original Mint packaging, not slabbed.

CERTIFICATION DATA

	Total	<PF-69	PF-69	PF-70
# Certified	113,113	1,066	46,554	65,493
Percentage		0.94%	41.16%	57.90%

Note: Data compiled from NGC and PCGS reports, September 2022.

2011-P, Reverse Proof

Mintage: 99,882

Minted at Philadelphia with P mintmark

Another issue exclusively offered in the 25th Anniversary Silver Eagle Set was the 2011-P Reverse Proof, a coin whose distinctive frosted fields and mirrored devices and inscriptions helped drive the five-coin set to a sellout within hours of its October 27, 2011, release. "Hotly anticipated coins have a sales curve much like movie tickets," remarked market reporter Eric Jordan in *Coin World* on August 21. He went on to write, "Each succeeding week's sales are about half that of the previous week and between 60 and 75 percent of an unlimited annual sales run will up in the first four weeks."

The 2011-P Reverse Proof gained attention in *100 Greatest U.S. Modern Coins*, in which it ranked 18th. "Collectors could not resist the allure of the coins that were unique to this set, including the Reverse Proof," wrote coauthors Scott Schechter and Jeff Garrett. "With only 100,000 minted, the 2011-P Reverse Proof is by far the scarcest of all Reverse Proof Silver Eagles yet issued and is among the most highly sought-after of all recent U.S. Mint releases."

2011-P, Reverse Proof

MARKET VALUES

	Raw	PF-69	PF-70
Value	$255	$280	$500

Note: "Raw" values are for average coins in original Mint packaging, not slabbed.

CERTIFICATION DATA

	Total	<PF-69	PF-69	PF-70
# Certified	51,069	554	19,903	30,612
Percentage		1.08%	38.97%	59.94%

Note: Data compiled from NGC and PCGS reports, September 2022.

2011-S, Burnished

Mintage: 99,882

Minted at San Francisco with S mintmark

This limited-edition Silver Eagle was available exclusively in the 25th Anniversary Silver Eagle Set and helped push sales of that five-coin set to a sellout of 100,000 units within hours of release on October 27, 2011. All told, the final audited mintage for the coin was 99,882 pieces, making it among the scarcest of all Silver Eagles.

Reasons for why the Silver Eagle was struck at the San Francisco Mint are both symbolic and practical, with the first Silver Eagles having been struck at the San Francisco Mint, the facility that also produced the Proof coins from 1986 through 1992. Furthermore, the U.S. Mint had expanded production of the bullion strikes to assist the West Point Mint in making the standard coinage.

Lee Minshull highlights, "The 2011-S Burnished is the only S-mint Burnished issue in the series and was only available in the 25th anniversary set."

The 2011-S Burnished Silver Eagle was ranked 47th in *100 Greatest U.S. Modern Coins*, in which coauthors Scott Schechter and Jeff Garrett assert, "Wow! This was the coin that really got everyone talking!" In an August 21, 2012, *Numismatic News* article entitled "Silver Eagle: The Modern Morgan," writer Eric Jordan commented, "Sometimes a mintage listing is worth a thousand words and that is certainly the case with the 2011-S silver dollar."

2011-S, Burnished

MARKET VALUES

	Raw	MS-69	MS-70
Value	$225	$275	$350

Note: "Raw" values are for average coins in original Mint packaging, not slabbed.

CERTIFICATION DATA

	Total	<MS-69	MS-69	MS-70
# Certified	50,296	621	18,309	31,366
Percentage		1.23%	36.40%	62.36%

Note: Data compiled from NGC and PCGS reports, September 2022.

2011 25th Anniversary Silver Eagle Set

Mintage: 99,882

Minted at West Point, Philadelphia, and San Francisco with various mintmarks

The numismatic community was buzzing in August 2011 when the U.S. Mint dropped the news of a five-piece Silver Eagle set with a limited mintage of 100,000 and two exclusive coins. The 25th Anniversary Silver Eagle Set was released at noon Eastern Time on October 27, 2011, with an issue price of $299.95 and order limits of just five per household. U.S. Mint customer service lines were jammed, as was the Mint's website. Many were left disappointed and empty handed, having to shell out $500 or more to buy the set on the secondary market.

The set includes an array of five 2011-dated Silver Eagles: the bullion strike, produced at the San Francisco Mint; two Burnished coins, one each from the West Point and San Francisco mints; the Proof coin, minted at West Point; and the Reverse Proof, produced at the Philadelphia Mint. The 2011-S Burnished coin and the 2011-P Reverse Proof were only available through the set.

Collectors who want to certify coins from the anniversary set with PCGS or NGC need to submit the entire set in its original, mint-sealed shipping box.

2011 25th Anniversary Silver Eagle Set

MARKET VALUES

	Raw	69	70
Value	$630		

Note: "Raw" values are for average coins that are not professionally graded/slabbed.

CERTIFICATION DATA

	Total	<69	69	70
# Certified	104,003	1,127	32,842	70,034
Percentage		1.08%	31.58%	67.34%

Note: Data compiled from NGC and PCGS reports, September 2022.

THE YEAR 2012

The U.S. Mint embarked on a new limited-edition Proof set that brought together its various silver coins, including the American Silver Eagle.

Current Events in 2012

The presidential election cycle was in full swing, with incumbent President Barack Obama facing a strong challenge from Republican Utah senator and one-time Massachusetts governor Mitt Romney. However, while Romney performed well in the Deep South and Plains states, Obama carried the Northeast, Upper Midwest, Pacific Coast, and swing state of Florida to win reelection to the White House.

Hurricane Sandy raked the eastern United States, inflicting heavy damage on the New Jersey shore and New York City upon landfall on October 29. "Superstorm

Sandy," as it is often referenced, killed 233 people in eight nations from the Caribbean to Canada and caused $68.7 billion in damage.

Sandy Hook Elementary School in Newtown, Connecticut, was the scene of one of the grisliest massacres in modern history. On December 14, 2012, a 20-year-old gunman killed 26 people, most of them children. The tragedy brought about a national conversation on gun control and mental health not seen since the Columbine High School shooting more than a decade earlier.

Queen Elizabeth II of the United Kingdom celebrated her diamond jubilee to mark her 60th anniversary on the British throne.

Britons had even more reason to celebrate beginning July 27, the first day of the Summer Olympic Games in London. United States swimmer Michael Phelps earned four gold medals and two silvers, bringing him to 22 total medals and bestowing on him the coveted title of being the most decorated Olympian ever. Overall, American athletes led the medal table with 47 golds and 104 total medals at the 2012 Olympiad.

Award-winning singer Whitney Houston died on February 11, 2012, at the age of 48. Top tunes of 2012 were "Somebody That I Used to Know" by Gotye, "Call Me Maybe" by Carly Rae Jepsen, "Thrift Shop" by Macklemore and Ryan Lewis, "Diamonds" by Rihanna, and "Locked Out of Heaven" by Bruno Mars. The top shows on television were *NCIS*, *Sunday Night Football*, *The Big Bang Theory*, *Person of Interest*, and *Dancing with the Stars*. *The Avengers*, *The Hunger Games*, *Skyfall*, and *Brave* were top box-office draws.

While housing prices were still at relatively affordable levels in many parts of the nation, the median price for a new home began moving upward to about $242,100. A 2012 Dodge Challenger SXT coupe sold for $25,795, a gallon of gas was $3.62, a gallon of milk went for $3.49, and a loaf of bread cost $1.58. A first-class postage stamp rose in price by a penny to 45 cents. An ounce of silver averaged $31.15.

On the Numismatic Scene in 2012

In November 2012 the U.S. Mint unveiled its first Limited Edition Proof Set. Released on November 27, 2012, the eight-coin set boasted 2.338 ounces of silver and included the .999-fine silver 2012-W Proof American Silver Eagle and seven 90 percent silver coins: the 2012-S Proof Kennedy half dollar, the five 2012-S Proof America the Beautiful quarters, and a 2012-S Roosevelt dime. The set had a mintage limit of 50,000 and sold for $149.95, with initial ordering limits of two per household.

The year marked the end of the road for production of circulation-issue dollar coins, which had shown time and time again in modern history to be something the public did not seem to want. While the U.S. Mint stopped making dollar coins for circulation in 2012, production continued for the ongoing Presidential $1 coins and Native American dollars. More than a billion of the coins lay in government storage ready for use in the future.

For the 2012 Trustees' Award banquet of the American Numismatic Society in New York City, Whitman Publishing created 250 special copies of the 66th-edition hardcover *Red Book*. They included a bookplate honoring Trustees' Award recipient (and *Red Book* contributor) Roger Siboni.

2012, Bullion Strike

Mintage: 37,996,000

Minted at West Point and San Francisco with no mintmark

The 2012 bullion Silver Eagle burst out of the gate with a flurry of sales, led by a special promotional sale at the January 2012 Florida United Numismatists Show. However, sales figures slipped a bit as the year progressed, likely a factor of the marked drop in silver bullion prices in 2012 as compared to 2011.

All told, the West Point Mint produced 29,575,000 bullion strikes while the San Francisco Mint emitted 8,421,000. Examples hailing from the San Francisco Mint tend to enjoy slightly more robust prices than their more common West Point counterparts, but both formats are abundant across the upper tiers of the grading spectrum and can be had in MS-70 at premiums friendly for many budgets.

2012, Bullion Strike

MARKET VALUES

	Raw	MS-69	MS-70
Value	$36	$45	$80

Note: "Raw" values are for average coins that are not professionally graded/slabbed.

CERTIFICATION DATA

	Total	<MS-69	MS-69	MS-70
# Certified	597,826	7,461	399,667	190,698
Percentage		1.25%	66.85%	31.90%

Note: Data compiled from NGC and PCGS reports, September 2022.

2012-W, Burnished

Mintage: 226,120

Minted at West Point with W mintmark

The 2012-W Burnished Silver Eagle went on sale August 2, 2012, with an issue price of $45.95. The coin continued a newfound tradition of offering a burnished strike alongside the yearly offerings of regular Proofs and by this point had become a standard addition to advanced sets of American Silver Eagles.

2012-W, Burnished

MARKET VALUES

	Raw	MS-69	MS-70
Value	$60	$85	$140

Note: "Raw" values are for average coins in original Mint packaging, not slabbed.

CERTIFICATION DATA

	Total	<MS-69	MS-69	MS-70
# Certified	26,056	106	11,260	14,690
Percentage		0.41%	43.21%	56.38%

Note: Data compiled from NGC and PCGS reports, September 2022.

2012-W, Proof

Mintage: 869,386

Minted at West Point with W mintmark

The 2012-W Proof was released on April 12, 2012, and originally issued for $59.95, though the price dropped to $54.95 as silver bullion trends fell back over the next months. Absent an authorized maximum production cap, the 2012-W Proof enjoyed strong sales, particularly after the $5 cut in price. The issue enjoyed another boost when it was offered in the 2012 Limited Edition Silver Proof Sets. While sales were not as strong as they were for the 2011-W Proof, a tally of nearly 870,000 was nevertheless remarkable. Plenty of examples are available for collectors, with "perfect" PF-70 coins trading at affordable premiums.

2012-W, Proof

MARKET VALUES

	Raw	PF-69	PF-70
Value	$85	$105	$120

Note: "Raw" values are for average coins in original Mint packaging, not slabbed.

CERTIFICATION DATA

	Total	<PF-69	PF-69	PF-70
# Certified	52,548	153	22,137	30,258
Percentage		0.29%	42.13%	57.58%

Note: Data compiled from NGC and PCGS reports, September 2022.

2012-S, Proof

Mintage: 285,184

Minted at San Francisco with S mintmark

The 2012-S Proof was originally marketed as an exclusive item in the two-coin 2012-S San Francisco Proof Set, which also included the 2012-S Reverse Proof Silver Eagle. However, the public was made aware of changes to this sales plan in July when the U.S. Mint announced the 2012-S Proof Silver Eagle would also be available in the Making American History Coin and Currency Set, which paired the Proof Silver Eagle with a Series 2009 $5 Federal Reserve Note.

"Surprisingly, the U.S. Mint's recent announcement that it would be producing more Proof 2012-S American Eagle silver coins has not taken the pressure off of the 2012-S San Francisco Two-Coin Anniversary set," reported *Coin World* editor Steve Roach in an August 2012 market analysis.

The U.S. Mint, responding to a few grumbles in the numismatic community from customers who bought the two-coin San Francisco Proof Set thinking it was the only vehicle for the 2012-S Proof Silver Eagle, stated, "We provided customers a four-week window to order the set and indicated that we would mint to the demands that our customers expressed during that period. Sales totals reached more than 251,000 sets. . . . Actual product development for the [Making American History] set was under way prior to the American Eagle San Francisco Two-Coin Silver Proof Set on May 2. The United States Mint, in developing these products, was responding to customers who have indicated an attraction to products produced in San Francisco and having the 'S' mintmark. In retrospect, it may have been appropriate to announce our intentions to produce the coin and currency set earlier in the year or perhaps simultaneously with the two-coin set."

However, all is well that ends well for those who bought the 2012 San Francisco Anniversary Proof Set. While the 2012-S Proof did not wind up being an exclusive offer in that set, the 2012-S Reverse Proof it was packaged alongside was!

2012-S, Proof

MARKET VALUES

	Raw	PF-69	PF-70
Value	$85	$105	$165

Note: "Raw" values are for average coins in original Mint packaging, not slabbed.

CERTIFICATION DATA

	Total	<PF-69	PF-69	PF-70
# Certified	72,592	469	40,424	31,699
Percentage		0.65%	55.69%	43.67%

Note: Data compiled from NGC and PCGS reports, September 2022.

2012-S, Reverse Proof

Mintage: 224,981

Minted at San Francisco with S mintmark

The 2012-S Reverse Proof was an exclusive offer in the two-coin 2012 San Francisco Anniversary Proof Set, which also featured the 2012-S Proof—a coin that, much to the dismay of some collectors, later became available in the Making American History Coin and Currency Set. "The good news is there are no plans to sell more 2012-S Reverse Proof silver American Eagle coins," declared *Numismatic News* in an August 14, 2012, front-page item.

The 2012-S Reverse Proof ranks 87th in *100 Greatest U.S. Modern Coins*. As coauthors Scott Schechter and Jeff Garrett noted, "after processing of returns and order cancellations, net orders slid back to 224,998, pushing the rarity of this coin ahead of the 2006 Reverse Proof."

2012-S, Reverse Proof

MARKET VALUES

	Raw	PF-69	PF-70
Value	$125	$175	$250

Note: "Raw" values are for average coins in original Mint packaging, not slabbed.

CERTIFICATION DATA

	Total	<PF-69	PF-69	PF-70
# Certified	64,685	288	35,980	28,417
Percentage		0.45%	55.62%	43.93%

Note: Data compiled from NGC and PCGS reports, September 2022.

2012 American Eagle San Francisco Two-Coin Silver Proof Set

Mintage: 224,981

Minted at San Francisco with S mintmarks

Offered for a four-week window spanning from June 7 to July 5, the 2012 American Eagle San Francisco Two-Coin Silver Proof Set contains the 2012-S Proof Silver Eagle and 2012-S Reverse Proof Silver Eagle. With an issue price of $149.95, the two-coin Proof set saw robust sales of 224,981, with first-day sales totaling 85,000. Many of these purchases were made on the collectors' presumption that both S-mint Proof Silver Eagles were exclusively available in this set. However, the 2012-S Proof would later be offered in another two-piece set, dubbed the 2012 Making American History Coin and Currency Set.

2012 American Eagle San Francisco Two-Coin Silver Proof Set

MARKET VALUES

	Raw	PF-69	PF-70
Value	$220	$265	$350

Note: "Raw" values are for average coins in original Mint packaging, not slabbed.

CERTIFICATION DATA

	Total	<PF-69	PF-69	PF-70
# Certified	64,685	288	35,980	28,417
Percentage		0.45%	55.62%	43.93%

Note: Data compiled from NGC and PCGS reports, September 2022.

2012 Making American History Coin and Currency Set

Mintage: 56,857

Minted at San Francisco with S mintmark

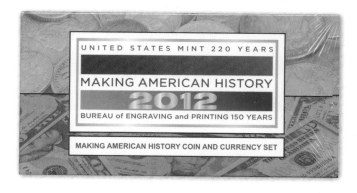

A few weeks after the last orders were taken for the 2012 American Eagle San Francisco Two-Coin Silver Proof Set, word came on July 26 of the 2012 Making American History Coin and Currency Set. This two-piece set honored the 220th anniversary of the U.S. Mint and 150th anniversary of the Bureau of Engraving and Printing, with both collaborating on this special set that paired a 2012-S Proof Silver Eagle with the (then-current) Series 2009 $5 Federal Reserve Note bearing the seal of the Federal Reserve Bank of San Francisco. Adding to the allure of this unique set is a special attribute of the $5 bill's serial number, each of which begins with "150." The set, which had a maximum authorized production of 100,000 units, was offered for $72.95 and debuted at the American Numismatic Association World's Fair of Money.

2012 Making American History Coin and Currency Set
MARKET VALUES

	Raw	PF-69	PF-70
Value	$95	$150	$195

Note: "Raw" values are for average coins in original Mint packaging, not slabbed.

THE YEAR 2013

As the economy continued recovering, the rare-coin market also saw some impressive gains, with one coin breaking all-time price records as the first to score an eight-figure hammer price at auction.

Current Events in 2013

President Barack Obama was inaugurated to his second term in the White House on January 20, 2013, amid a slowly recovering economy and a period of relative peace on the home front, even as the U.S.-led war in Afghanistan continued well into its second decade. The Dow Jones Industrial Average eventually surpassed the 15,000 mark and later in the year the threshold of 16,000, pointing to positive attitudes about the economy on Wall Street and, by proxy, elsewhere in the nation.

On April 15 two pressure-cooker bombs were detonated near the finish line of the Boston Marathon, killing three people and injuring 264. U.S. officials said that the National Security Agency illegally collected tens of thousands of personal emails from American citizens who had no links to suspected terrorists, causing many in the public to criticize the agency and grow skeptical about their privacy.

A shutdown of the U.S. government began on October 1, 2013, following failed efforts to approve funding for many agencies. Lawmakers on Capitol Hill moved to raise the debt ceiling in an eleventh-hour bipartisan deal that reopened the U.S. government and brought hundreds of thousands of federal workers back to their jobs.

A meteor exploded over Chelyabinsk, Russia, on February 15, injuring some 1,500 people and inflicting damage on thousands of buildings in the region. A garment factory in Dhaka, Bangladesh, collapsed, killing 1,134 people and injuring 2,500, becoming the deadliest unintended structural failure in modern history. A large EF-5 tornado ripped through Moore, Oklahoma, on May 20, killing 24 and causing $2 billion in damage that left the town in ruins.

Sunday Night Football, *NCIS*, *The Big Bang Theory*, *Dancing with the Stars*, and *The Blacklist* were top primetime television hits, while *The Hunger Games: Catching Fire*, *Iron Man 3*, *Frozen*, *Despicable Me 2*, and *Man of Steel* drummed up crowds at cinemas. Topping the charts in music were "Blurred Lines" by Robin Thicke featuring T.I. and Pharrell Williams, "Get Lucky" by Daft Punk, "Hold On, We're Going Home" by Drake, "Roar" by Katy Perry, and "Wrecking Ball" by Miley Cyrus.

Median prices on new homes climbed to $265,000, indicating that even the battered housing market had finally begun recovering after its foreclosure crisis. A 2013 Honda Fit four-door hatchback sold for $15,325, a gallon of gas ticked in at $3.53, a gallon of milk cost $3.46, and a loaf of bread was $1.58. A first-class postage stamp rose to 46 cents. Silver prices settled back to an average of $23.79 per ounce.

On the Numismatic Scene in 2013

An impressive example of the 1794 Flowing Hair dollar, which many theorize was the first silver dollar ever struck, sold for $10,016,875. The sale of this coin made headlines well beyond the numismatic community. It became the first individual coin to ever sell for eight figures in a public auction and put the hobby back in the public limelight.

Whitman Publishing introduced a 352-page magazine-sized softcover version of the *Red Book* in 2013. Called the *Essential Edition*, it was aimed at mainstream readers, featuring large print and focusing on the most popular federal coins. This format was published annually from 2013 to 2017. Whitman publisher Dennis Tucker described the new "bookazine": "As with the regular-edition *Red Book*, we promote the *Essential Edition* through mainstream bookstores like Barnes and Noble and Books-A-Million. Beyond that, it's also carried in Sam's Club—the eighth-largest retailer in the United States, serving 47 million members. We're excited to be able to offer this version of the *Red Book* to such a large audience, and to introduce the hobby to a new generation of collectors."

2013, Bullion Strike

Mintage: 49,875,000

Minted at West Point and San Francisco with no mintmark

The American Silver Eagle was a huge hit with investors, who saw silver kick the new year off at levels over $31 an ounce. An avalanche of orders in January caused the U.S. Mint to temporarily suspend orders in the middle of the month until a substantial reserve of inventory could be created. Sales resumed in late January, and that month ended up seeing the sale of 7,498,000 units, the highest single-month sales record for the Silver Eagle.

Overall, sales remained robust throughout the year and allowed the Silver Eagle to chart a new annual sales record—one that would not last long. The West Point Mint struck 36,775,000, while San Francisco produced 13,100,000. Coins submitted to PCGS and NGC in "monster boxes" received designation of a parenthetical West Point (W) or San Francisco (S) origin, depending on the markings visible on the sealed shipping cartons. Coins from either mint are easy to locate and relatively affordable in grades of MS-70.

2013, Bullion Strike

MARKET VALUES

	Raw	MS-69	MS-70
Value	$36	$45	$80

Note: "Raw" values are for average coins that are not professionally graded/slabbed.

CERTIFICATION DATA

	Total	<MS-69	MS-69	MS-70
# Certified	865,848	3,810	631,982	230,056
Percentage		0.44%	72.99%	26.57%

Note: Data compiled from NGC and PCGS reports, September 2022.

2013-W, Burnished

Mintage: 222,091

Minted at West Point with W mintmark

The 2013-W Burnished Silver Eagle was released on May 28, 2013, at an issue price of $48.95. The issue price was later lowered to $43.95, commensurate with falling silver prices in the latter months of 2013. The 2013-W Burnished Silver Eagle was sold individually and as part of the 2013 Annual Uncirculated Dollar Coin Set, which also included that year's Presidential $1 coins and Native American dollar.

2013-W, Burnished

MARKET VALUES

	Raw	MS-69	MS-70
Value	$65	$80	$125

Note: "Raw" values are for average coins in original Mint packaging, not slabbed.

CERTIFICATION DATA

	Total	<MS-69	MS-69	MS-70
# Certified	22,354	43	7,889	14,422
Percentage		0.19%	35.29%	64.52%

Note: Data compiled from NGC and PCGS reports, September 2022.

2013-W, Enhanced Uncirculated

Mintage: 235,689 estimated.

Minted at West Point with W mintmark

A new numismatic frontier was charted in 2013 with the debut of the Enhanced Uncirculated Silver Eagle, which boasts three distinct finishes. These include a brilliant-mirrored finish on the obverse date, blue field and red stripes of the American flag, the lines of Miss Liberty's dress, and various elements of the devices held by the eagle on the reverse; a light frosted finish on the obverse and reverse fields; and a heavy frosted finish on remaining design elements and the inscriptions.

In Troy Thoreson's view, the 2013-W Enhanced Uncirculated Silver Eagle is its own animal. "I guess someday there will be a type album available with the single hole for each

Silver Eagle format. One format will be the special edition 2013-W Enhanced Uncirculated Silver Eagle, which is still very affordable. I'd have to say this is currently the most underrated American Silver Eagle," Thoreson said. "Is it a Proof? Is it Uncirculated? It is an Enhanced Uncirculated example only offered in 2013. At first glance, I thought the coin was a Proof and I really didn't pay too much attention to it for years. Then after running across the coin many times, I started to fully appreciate its beauty. It is my favorite finish and may be unique for all of time. I say this because of the many factors used in its production that I doubt can be perfectly duplicated. According to U.S. Mint reports at the time, this was not the first time this finish application had been used on a U.S. coin. That being true, this was the first time this process was used on an American Silver Eagle, and it turned out fantastic. This coin will certainly appreciate over time as collectors come to realize how special it really is—it is kind of like a pattern coin."

While this Enhanced Uncirculated offering represented a first for the Silver Eagle program, a March 25, 2013, *Coin World* article by Paul Gilkes revealed that multiple finishes were used in striking the Uncirculated 2012-P Hawai'i Volcanoes National Park five-ounce silver bullion coins and .999-fine silver September 11 medals struck in 2011 and 2012.

The 2013-W Enhanced Uncirculated Silver Eagles were struck with remarkable precision and care, and most certified examples grade MS-70.

2013-W, Enhanced Uncirculated

MARKET VALUES

	Raw	MS-69	MS-70
Value	$145	$175	$250

Note: "Raw" values are for average coins in original Mint packaging, not slabbed.

CERTIFICATION DATA

	Total	<MS-69	MS-69	MS-70
# Certified	774	174	478	122
Percentage		22.48%	61.76%	15.76%

Note: Data compiled from NGC and PCGS reports, September 2022.

2013-W, Proof

Mintage: 934,812

Minted at West Point with W mintmark

The 2013-W Proofs hit the streets at high noon Eastern Time on January 24, 2013, with an issue price of $62.95. There were no household limits imposed and, as had become standard for the Silver Eagle Proofs at that point, no maximum authorized production limits. A whopping 258,860 coins flew out the door within five days of their release, and mounting pressures from the tremendous demand pushed the Mint to declare a sellout on November 11, 2013, as officials sought more planchets. An inaccurate sales report led the U.S. Mint to sell nearly 4,200 coins on February 20, 2014, to some 780 buyers whose orders were cancelled and had the opportunity to buy the remaining inventory on a "first-in, first-served" basis.

2013-W, Proof

MARKET VALUES

	Raw	PF-69	PF-70
Value	$85	$105	$125

Note: "Raw" values are for average coins in original Mint packaging, not slabbed.

CERTIFICATION DATA

	Total	<PF-69	PF-69	PF-70
# Certified	61,443	130	22,517	38,796
Percentage		0.21%	36.65%	63.14%

Note: Data compiled from NGC and PCGS reports, September 2022.

2013-W, Reverse Proof

Mintage: 235,689 estimated.

Minted at West Point with W mintmark

The 2013-W Reverse Proof was sold as part of a two-coin set struck at the West Point Mint to honor that facility's 75th anniversary. The set also included the distinctive 2013-W Enhanced Uncirculated Silver Eagle, a first-of-its-kind offering for the American Silver Eagle program.

2013-W, Reverse Proof

MARKET VALUES

	Raw	PF-69	PF-70
Value	$115	$140	$160

Note: "Raw" values are for average coins in original Mint packaging, not slabbed.

CERTIFICATION DATA

	Total	<PF-69	PF-69	PF-70
# Certified	91,749	110	35,867	55,772
Percentage		0.12%	39.09%	60.79%

Note: Data compiled from NGC and PCGS reports, September 2022.

2013 American Eagle West Point Two-Coin Silver Set

Mintage: 235,689

Minted at West Point with W mintmark

This handsome two-piece set included the 2013-W Enhanced Uncirculated Silver Eagle and 2013-W Reverse Proof Silver Eagle. Honoring the 75th anniversary of the West

Point Mint in New York, this two-coin set was issued for $139.95 during a four-week window between May 9 and June 6. to the final sales totaled 235,689 sets, one of the best-selling American Eagle anniversary sets up to that point.

2013 American Eagle West Point Two-Coin Silver Set

MARKET VALUES

	Raw	69	70
Value	$280	$345	$385

Note: "Raw" values are for average coins in original Mint packaging, not slabbed.

CERTIFICATION DATA

	Total	<69	69	70
# Certified	153,103	338	55,737	97,028
Percentage		0.22%	36.40%	63.37%

Note: Data compiled from NGC and PCGS reports, September 2022.

THE YEAR 2014

The Mint debuted new curved or domed coins commemorating the Baseball Hall of Fame. These coins, featuring a concave obverse and a convex reverse, were technological feats that made waves when first introduced. Also making headlines in 2014 was a special gold Kennedy half dollar marking the 50th anniversary of the popular series.

Talk of a new reverse design for the American Silver Eagle entered the public discourse.

Current Events in 2014

An Ebola outbreak in West Africa spread beginning in March 2014 and became an epidemic. Ebola, which kills about 50 percent of the people it infects, made it into the United States when a man arrived at a Dallas, Texas, hospital presenting serious symptoms of the virus. However, eight of the ten U.S. patients were successfully treated, and the epidemic was declared over by the World Health Organization on June 10, 2016.

While al-Qaeda had slowly eroded away from the forefront of terrorist activity in the West, the Islamic State of Iraq and Syria, an organization known as ISIS, became a much larger threat both in the Middle East and abroad. Malaysian Airlines Flight 370 vanished over the southern Indian Ocean with 239 people onboard. Conflict in Ukraine opened the door for Russia to annex a peninsula in eastern Ukraine known as Crimea, potentially providing a path for Moscow to build support among rebels and eventually occupy more of the former Soviet nation.

Nationwide protests erupted in November when a grand jury declined to indict a White police officer in the fatal shooting of unarmed Ferguson, Missouri, teenager Michael Brown. Another grand jury decision a few weeks later bypassed indictment of another White police officer in the death of Eric Garner, an unarmed Black man who died after a chokehold. Comedian Bill Cosby, who starred in popular television programs *I Spy*, *Fat Albert*, and *The Cosby Show*, was accused of sexual assault charges by some 60 women. *American Sniper*, *Guardians of the Galaxy*, *Captain America: The Winter Soldier*, and *The LEGO Movie* were top box-office hits in 2014. Popular on television were *Sunday Night Football*, *The Big Bang Theory*, *NCIS*, *Empire*, and *Dancing with the Stars*. Top songs were "Happy" by Pharrell Williams, "Dark Horse" by Katy Perry featuring Juicy J, "All of Me" by John Legend, "Fancy" by Iggy Azalea featuring Charli XCX, and "Counting Stars" by OneRepublic.

The 2014 Winter Olympics in Sochi, Russia, earned the dubious distinction of becoming the most expensive Games ever held, costing $51 billion—more than four times its initial $12 billion budget. Making up for the huge financial outlay was a massive global audience of 2.1 billion. American athletes took home 28 medals, nine of which were gold.

On July 3 the Dow Jones Industrial Average closed above 17,000 points for the first time and surpassed 18,000 on the closing bell December 23. The median price of a new home climbed to $283,775, while a Chevrolet Impala cost $27,535. A gallon of gas was $3.37, a gallon of milk cost $3.69, and a loaf of bread went for $1.58. A first-class postage stamp increased in price to 49 cents. An ounce of silver hovered at an average of $19.08.

On the Numismatic Scene in 2014

The U.S. Mint pushed its technological envelope in 2014 with the creation of three curved commemoratives honoring the 75th anniversary of the Baseball Hall of Fame. These coins feature a common motif with a catcher's mitt on the concave obverse and a baseball on the convex reverse. The clad half dollar, silver dollar, and gold half eagle were designed by Cassie McFarland and sculpted by Don Everhart.

Lines formed at the American Numismatic Association World's Fair of Money in Chicago in August 2014. Much of the flock waiting to get in were there to buy the first examples of the 2014 gold Kennedy half dollar, which had a limit of one per household and was being sold at the show by the U.S. Mint. Many among the crowd were paid by coin dealers to stand in line and buy one example of the coin and then flip it back to the dealer at a given price, plus a bonus for the purchaser's time and effort. The coin, containing three-quarters of an ounce of 24-karat gold, was released to commemorate the 50th anniversary of the Kennedy half dollar.

A special Central States Numismatic Society edition of the 68th-edition *Guide Book of United States Coins* was issued in 2014 to raise funds and recognition for the group. Only 500 copies were printed, making it a popular collectible among those who seek one of every *Red Book*.

During the March 11, 2014, meeting of the Citizens Coinage Advisory Committee (CCAC), Chairman Gary Marks raised the topic of changing the reverse of the American Silver Eagle. During the next CCAC meeting in April, a review of many possible new designs for the silver coin included one proposal for

The American Silver Eagle was a top item in the 2014 United States Mint customer catalog.

a side profile of an eagle in flight, clutching an olive branch in its talons. Many on the CCAC liked the floated proposals, and some hobby observers thought a new design specifically for the Burnished issues might spur more sales. However, the U.S. Mint declined to move forward at that time on changing the reverse.

2014, Bullion Strike

Mintage: 54,151,500

Minted at West Point and San Francisco with no mintmark

It was another banner year for the American Silver Eagle, which smashed all-time annual sales records in 2014 with an astounding year-end total of 54,151,000. This, despite the fact the U.S. Mint labored to produce sufficient planchet supplies to meet the incredible demand. While 2014 was a relatively quiet year for silver prices, buyers took advantage of the serene bullion scene to snap up silver while prices were at their lowest levels in a few years. As sales ramped up during the fourth quarter of 2014, the U.S. Mint had to place a short suspension on sales in early November, though orders resumed before Thanksgiving. The West Point Mint struck 46,920,500 examples and the San Francisco produced 7,231,000.

2014, Bullion Strike
MARKET VALUES

	Raw	MS-69	MS-70
Value	$36	$45	$80

Note: "Raw" values are for average coins that are not professionally graded/slabbed.

CERTIFICATION DATA

	Total	<MS-69	MS-69	MS-70
# Certified	687,799	15,323	391,214	281,262
Percentage		2.23%	56.88%	40.89%

Note: Data compiled from NGC and PCGS reports, September 2022.

2014-W, Burnished

Mintage: 253,169

Minted at West Point with W mintmark

The 2014-W Burnished Silver Eagle went on sale on April 10, 2014, at an issue price of $43.95. Individual examples of the coin sold out by December, but the coin could still be purchased into 2015 by way of the 2014 Annual Uncirculated Dollar Coin Set, which contained the 2014-W Burnished Silver Eagle, the four Presidential $1 coins, and the 2014 Native American dollar, and was priced at $44.95—not a bad deal at just a buck more than the price of a single 2014-W Burnished Silver Eagle!

2014-W, Burnished

MARKET VALUES

	Raw	MS-69	MS-70
Value	$55	$80	$100

Note: "Raw" values are for average coins in original Mint packaging, not slabbed.

CERTIFICATION DATA

	Total	<MS-69	MS-69	MS-70
# Certified	21,802	40	6,840	14,922
Percentage		0.18%	31.37%	68.44%

Note: Data compiled from NGC and PCGS reports, September 2022.

2014-W, Proof

Mintage: 944,770

Minted at West Point with W mintmark

The 2014-W Proof American Silver Eagle was released for sale on January 23 and was warmly received by collectors, who bought 446,773 during the first three months of 2014. While the bulk of sales were individual purchases, significant sums were distributed through the 2014 Congratulations Set and 2014 Limited Edition Silver Proof Set.

An interesting footnote on the sale of the 2014-W Proofs is that many were sold by the Mint in 2015. It's not uncommon that some product offerings linger on the Mint catalog for more than one year—occasionally even longer than two years. However, the 2014 Limited Edition Silver Proof Set was not even offered for sale until March 17, 2015. The set, which was issued for $139.95 and had a production limit of 50,000, saw this prolonged delay due to packaging issues that in part stemmed from improvements the Mint made following a spate of returns for the 2013 set.

2014-W, Proof

MARKET VALUES

	Raw	PF-69	PF-70
Value	$85	$105	$125

Note: "Raw" values are for average coins in original Mint packaging, not slabbed.

CERTIFICATION DATA

	Total	<PF-69	PF-69	PF-70
# Certified	75,143	324	26,227	48,592
Percentage		0.43%	34.90%	64.67%

Note: Data compiled from NGC and PCGS reports, September 2022.

THE YEAR 2015

Bullion prices softened significantly in 2015, giving investors a chance to stock up on silver and gold coins at some of the lowest prices, gram for gram, in several years. The sinking price of silver led to another year for strong sales of American Silver Eagles. In another corner of the numismatic world discussion was amplifying on the "penny," a coin that was becoming increasingly expensive to manufacture yet, if abolished, would create an automatic "inflation" of prices to the nearest nickel. What's more, a new nationwide poll in 2015 suggested a majority of Americans were in favor of keeping the Lincoln cent around.

Current Events in 2015

Two Islamic extremists claiming to represent a faction of al-Qaeda burst into the offices of satirical newspaper *Charlie Hebdo* in Paris and killed 12 and injured 11 on January 7. The attacks heightened concerns around Paris of similar future attacks—a fear realized months later when a series of coordinated terrorist attacks in Paris killed 130 and injured 416 at several sites during the evening of November 13.

On June 26, the United States Supreme Court made a landmark decision in the case of *Obergefell v. Hodges*, ruling 5-4 that the U.S. Constitution guaranteed same-sex couples full and equal marriage rights in all 50 states.

Ensuring the protection of basic human rights was a theme that played out in many ways in 2015, as fatal law-enforcement shootings of Black men Walter Scott and Freddie Gray continued a chorus of protests over police perceptions of Black males and, on a larger scale, how society views people of color.

In a shooting at Emanuel AME Church in Charleston, South Carolina, a 21-year-old White supremacist killed nine Black attendees. The heinous attack was one of several that included massacres at a college campus in Oregon, a military recruiting office in Tennessee, and a Planned Parenthood clinic in Colorado.

The derailment of an Amtrak commuter train in Philadelphia on May 12 killed eight and injured 200.

An extreme heatwave in the Pacific Northwest brought triple-digit temperatures and all-time record highs to dozens of towns and cities in Washington, Oregon, and Idaho. Record-low snowpacks in the West threatened not only freshwater supplies but also ski resort towns. Back East, record rainfall deluged South Carolina and a dozen winter storms buried New England in snow.

The median price for a new home was around $273,300, and the cost to purchase a new Toyota RAV4 was $23,680. A gallon of gas was $2.49, while a gallon of milk went for $3.42. A loaf of bread fetched $1.58 and a first-class postage stamp was 49 cents. Silver saw an average price of $15.68 per ounce.

On the Numismatic Scene in 2015

A perfect storm of economic events around the world led to softening bullion prices in 2015. China's economy was getting shaky, impacting the nation's stock market. Meanwhile, the U.S. dollar was gathering strength, and the Federal Reserve was looking to raise rates after years near zero in the wake of the Great Recession. Gold prices were on the verge of dipping below $1,050 for the first time since 2010, and silver was trading as low as $14.30 an ounce during the last weeks of the year. Investors looking to stuff their portfolios with precious metals did.

Talk of discontinuing the one-cent coin had been bubbling up from time to time since the mid-1970s and appeared again in 2015 as metal prices and production costs continued marching northward.

By 2015, continued hikes in metal prices and production expenditures led a gathering push to abolish the one-cent coin. Yet, a Harris Poll surveying 2,273 U.S. adults from July 15 through July 20, 2015, showed 51 percent of Americans were against eliminating the coin, down from 56 percent in 2008 but still a solid majority. At the time, the Harris Poll also showed 80 percent of Americans preferred the dollar bill over dollar coins.

In July 2015 at the Philadelphia Mint, Whitman Publishing numismatic director Q. David Bowers and publisher Dennis Tucker, along with professional numismatists John W. Dannreuther and David Sundman, made a startling discovery—previously unknown dies, hubs, and other working tools for a 1964-dated Morgan dollar. Their find indicated that the Mint had explored the possibility of making new silver dollars with the old design. (It would actually strike 1964-dated Peace dollars, in 1965, with the entire mintage then slated for melting.)

This was the year that Whitman unrolled its monumental 1,504-page *Deluxe Edition* of the *Red Book*, which would come to be known officially by its nickname, *Mega Red*.

2015, Bullion Strike

Mintage: 47,000,000

Minted at West Point and Philadelphia with no mintmark

The 2015 bullion Silver Eagle represents the first striking of the standard issue at the Philadelphia Mint, as confirmed by the U.S. Mint's deputy director of the office of corporate communications, Adam Stump, who reported 70,000 bullion Silver Eagles dated 2015 were produced at the Philadelphia Mint in late 2014 as a "process validation run." This was later updated to reveal that a larger but still miniscule number of bullion Silver Eagles were produced at the Philadelphia Mint bearing 2015 dates. Michael Garofalo remembers how the findings unfolded and what it meant for the numismatic community: "In an unusual turn of events, a Freedom of Information Act (FOIA) request was made to the United States Treasury, and it was discovered that a run of 2015 (P) Uncirculated bullion Silver Eagle coins were struck at the Philadelphia Mint. This was previously unknown information. A mere 79,500 bullion Silver Eagles were struck at the Philadelphia Mint, making this the lowest silver bullion issue of the series to date."

Lee Minshull remarks, "The 2015 Philly Mint coin is a really well-undervalued coin."

The vast majority of the 2015 Silver Eagles came from the West Point Mint, and the Philadelphia coins were integrated with the West Point emissions before distribution, making it all but impossible to differentiate the pieces. Therefore, third-party graders concluded early on that they would be unable to encapsulate any 2015 bullion Silver Eagles as "Philadelphia Mint" strikes without solid evidence that they were made there.

Nevertheless, sales of the 2015 bullion Silver Eagles were spectacular, if falling a little short of the overall 2014 mintage. In January 5,530,000 coins were sold—a number nearly tied in July, when 5,529,000 were sold despite a temporary suspension in sales from July 7 through July 27 so the U.S. Mint could replenish their inventory. The overall mintage of 47 million is impressive, given that minting duties almost solely fell on the shoulders of the West Point Mint; San Francisco struck none of the 2015-dated Silver Eagles and Philadelphia fewer than 80,000.

Those Philadelphia Mint strikes became a fixture in numismatic headlines for a time, in large part because that tiny run of Silver Eagles easily represents the smallest mintage of any bullion issue in the series. More details began emerging about this production of

2015 (P) Silver Eagles on March 20, 2017. The U.S. Mint clarified that—contrary to earlier implications that the Philadelphia-struck Silver Eagles were indifferently mixed into the larger West Point output—the Philadelphia issues were indeed identifiable by serial numbers and the color of bands used to secure 500-coin "monster boxes."

New knowledge in hand, third-party graders began certifying 2015 Silver Eagles from Philadelphia contained in monster boxes matching the criteria set forth by the U.S. Mint. Such pieces saw an immediate price increase of 1,000 to 2,000 percent given their relative scarceness, with MS-69 coins taking $450 to $500 and MS-70 examples fetching north of $5,000. The situation turned sour in May 2017 as the U.S. Mint issued yet another report on the 2015 Philadelphia Silver Eagles, stating inaccuracies in the March information. Among the most alarming of statements in the Mint's May statement was the correction of information that "resulted in a mistaken belief that some of these coins are rarities."

Further remarks on the situation came on June 30, 2017, when the U.S. Mint stated that some of the tracking numbers on boxes of 2015 American Silver Eagles that were denoted as Philadelphia emissions were applied to West Point boxes. All of the Philadelphia-struck bullion issues were manually packaged. The news ruffled many feathers in the industry. "Because of duplication of box tracking numbers at Philadelphia and West Point, as well as any mistakes in labelling or the possibility that labels on the boxes could have bene removed or altered at any point after shipping," Mint officials would "make no effort" to "verify the origin" of 2015 Silver Eagles.

In a June 19, 2017, editorial, *Coin World* Editor William T. Gibbs opined on the "deeper philosophical undercurrents" regarding the "merits of the modern slabbed coin market and the concepts of condition rarity and special slab labels." He noted the situation "disturb[ed] a lot of longtime numismatists," who were concerned about "the prices charged (and paid) for some coins that would be judged common if removed from the context of the label on their slab."

2015, Bullion Strike

MARKET VALUES

	Raw	MS-69	MS-70
Value	$36	$45	$85

Note: "Raw" values are for average coins that are not professionally graded/slabbed.

CERTIFICATION DATA

	Total	<MS-69	MS-69	MS-70
# Certified	364,162	47,656	148,043	168,463
Percentage		13.09%	40.65%	46.26%

Note: Data compiled from NGC and PCGS reports, September 2022.

2015-W, Burnished

Mintage: 201,188

Minted at West Point with W mintmark

The 2015-W Burnished (called "Uncirculated" by the U.S. Mint) Silver Eagle was offered for sale beginning March 26 at an initial issue price of $39.95. Its mintage of just over 200,000 pieces, while respectable, marked a significant decline of 20 percent over the output for the 2014-W Burnished Silver Eagle.

2015-W, Burnished

MARKET VALUES

	Raw	MS-69	MS-70
Value	$55	$80	$110

Note: "Raw" values are for average coins in original Mint packaging, not slabbed.

CERTIFICATION DATA

	Total	<MS-69	MS-69	MS-70
# Certified	26,913	25	7,444	19,444
Percentage		0.09%	27.66%	72.25%

Note: Data compiled from NGC and PCGS reports, September 2022.

2015-W, Proof

Mintage: 707,518

Minted at West Point with W mintmark

The 2015-W Proof Silver Eagles became the first product available from the United States Mint catalog that was dated for the new year. They were issued for $48.95 each and saw strong sales at the Florida United Numismatists Show in Orlando in January. A total mintage of more than 700,000 is historically robust for the Proof Silver Eagle, but the 2015-W Proof was later recognized as the higher end of a decline in sales that persisted for the rest of the decade.

2015-W, Proof

MARKET VALUES

	Raw	PF-69	PF-70
Value	$85	$105	$125

Note: "Raw" values are for average coins in original Mint packaging, not slabbed.

CERTIFICATION DATA

	Total	<PF-69	PF-69	PF-70
# Certified	78,432	123	18,276	60,033
Percentage		0.16%	23.30%	76.54%

Note: Data compiled from NGC and PCGS reports, September 2022.

THE YEAR 2016

The 30th anniversary of the American Eagle bullion-coin program was marked with the 2016-W Proof and Burnished strikes bearing a special 30TH ANNIVERSARY edge inscription.

Current Events in 2016

As par for the course during most presidential election cycles, the 2016 campaign saw a large and diverse crowd of contenders. Democrats fielded no fewer than 30 candidates appearing on at least one state primary ballot. Republicans saw about a dozen serious hopefuls. The Democrats eventually nominated former First Lady and New York senator Hillary Clinton, who ran alongside Virginia senator Tim Kaine and became the first female presidential nominee of a major political party in the United States. Topping the Republican ticket was businessman and reality television star Donald Trump, whose running mate was Indiana governor Mike Pence. A contentious election landed Trump in the White House on November 8, despite his having lost the popular vote by nearly 3 million votes.

Another headlining election had occurred in Great Britain, where the nation voted to exit the European Union in a movement portmanteaued as "Brexit."

A state of emergency was declared in Flint, Michigan, where the municipal water supply was causing a public health crisis due to corroded and aging pipes.

The worst mass shooting up to that point in modern United States history occurred at the Pulse nightclub in Orlando, Florida, where 49 people were killed. The lone gunman targeted the club's largely gay and lesbian clientele, instigating a new national conversation on expanding protection from hate crimes and tightening gun laws.

A global panic over mosquitoes emerged due to the discovery of the Zika virus, a disease that could cause birth defects such as an underdeveloped brain and small head. While Zika was spreading throughout many equatorial nations, transmissions were occurring in Florida and Texas.

The emergence of the Zika virus, which was widespread in Brazil, did not dissuade the 11,238 athletes competing in the 2016 Olympics in Rio de Janeiro. Americans took home 121 medals, including 46 golds.

Deaths of famous figures were sadly prominent in 2016, including David Bowie, Prince, Muhammad Ali, Gene Wilder, Zsa Zsa Gabor, Nancy Reagan, Arnold Palmer, and Fidel Castro.

Top television shows in 2016 were *The Big Bang Theory*, *NCIS*, *Sunday Night Football*, *This is Us*, and *Dancing with the Stars*. Top films were *Rogue One: A Star Wars Story*, *Finding Dory*, *Captain America: Civil War*, *The Secret Life of Pets*, and *The Jungle Book*. Hit songs were "One Dance" by Drake, "Work from Home" by Fifth Harmony, "Work" by Rihanna, and "Don't Let Me Down" by The Chainsmokers.

The Dow Jones Industrial Average saw its first close above 19,000 points. Median prices for new homes traipsed upward to $308,800, while a Scion iM sedan retailed for $18,460. A gallon of gas was $2.14, which marked the lowest annual average price of gas since 2004. Also dropping back was the price of a first-class postage stamp, which went down to 47 cents. A gallon of milk went for $3.20 and a loaf of bread cost $1.37. Silver was $17.14 an ounce.

On the Numismatic Scene in 2016

The 30th anniversary of the American Eagle program was recognized on numismatic versions of the Silver Eagle, which bore its first-ever edge lettering with the celebratory inscription 30TH ANNIVERSARY. This marked the first significant design change for the American Silver Eagle, not to mention the first time the coin had ever seen anything other than reeding on its edge.

2016, Bullion Strike

Mintage: 37,701,500

Minted at West Point, San Francisco, and Philadelphia with no mintmark

The American Silver Eagle had a strong sales showing during its major anniversary year, though orders occurred in fits and starts as silver prices moved from about $14 early in the year to more than $20 over the summer, before settling back to $16 during the later months of the year.

While the numismatic strikes bore the special 30TH ANNIVERSARY edge lettering, the bullion strikes were produced with the standard edge reeding. The U.S. Mint delegated the Philadelphia and San Francisco Mints to assist with production of bullion strikes to provide time for the West Point Mint to outfit its presses with the right equipment to impart the 30TH ANNIVERSARY edge inscriptions on the Proofs and Burnished coins.

The West Point Mint struck 31,900,000 Silver Eagles, while the Philadelphia and San Francisco facilities provided 1,151,500 and 4,650,000, respectively.

2016, Bullion Strike

MARKET VALUES

	Raw	MS-69	MS-70
Value	$36	$45	$85

Note: "Raw" values are for average coins that are not professionally graded/slabbed.

CERTIFICATION DATA

	Total	<MS-69	MS-69	MS-70
# Certified	671,525	59,646	244,594	367,285
Percentage		8.88%	36.42%	54.69%

Note: Data compiled from NGC and PCGS reports, September 2022.

2016-W, Burnished

Mintage: 216,501

Minted at West Point with W mintmark

Released on December 1, the 2016-W Burnished American Silver Eagles were a late entry in the U.S. Mint catalog for the year. Issued for $44.95, they came with no household ordering limits and enjoyed decent sales— higher than the 2015-W Burnished offering to say the least, thanks to the 30th anniversary of the series. In conjunction with the occasion, this issue dons special edge lettering stating 30TH ANNIVERSARY, the first Silver Eagle without edge reeding.

The 2016-W Burnished Silver Eagle was also included in the 2016 Uncirculated Dollar Coin Set, packaged with the 2016 Native American dollar and the three final planned entries for the Presidential $1 coin program, which that year rounded out the series with memorials to late former presidents Richard Nixon, Gerald Ford, and Ronald Reagan.

2016-W, Burnished

MARKET VALUES

	Raw	MS-69	MS-70
Value	$55	$80	$125

Note: "Raw" values are for average coins in original Mint packaging, not slabbed.

CERTIFICATION DATA

	Total	<MS-69	MS-69	MS-70
# Certified	35,524	71	10,102	25,351
Percentage		0.20%	28.44%	71.36%

Note: Data compiled from NGC and PCGS reports, September 2022.

2016-W, Proof

Mintage: 651,453

Minted at West Point with W mintmark

The 2016-W Proof Silver Eagle was a hot collectible with its 30TH ANNIVERSARY edge inscription, a feature signed into law in December 2015 by President Barack Obama as a provision of the Fixing America's Surface Transportation (FAST) Act. Applying the incused edge lettering to the coins was achieved with a three-segment collar that imparted the inscription at the same time the obverse and reverse dies struck the coin.

The Proofs were not released until September 16, later than the bulk of other Proof offerings in the series to date. As the U.S. Mint explained, this was to provide time for the West Point Mint to provide the "necessary tooling for the collar die that imparts the edge inscription" as well as "testing [that] took time to complete." The Proofs were issued individually at $53.95 and could be bought in the Congratulations Set and Limited Edition Silver Proof Set, which cost $54.95 and $139.95, respectively.

Another vehicle for purchasing the 2016-W Proof Silver Eagle was the Ronald Reagan Coins and Chronicles Set. Issued for $68.95, the set offered a 2016-S Reverse Proof Ronald Reagan Presidential dollar, a 1.5-inch bronze facsimile of the 2000 Congressional Gold Medal produced for Ronald and Nancy Reagan, an engraved presidential portrait produced by the Bureau of Engraving and Printing, and a Coin and Chronicles book profiling the life and times of President Reagan.

2016-W, Proof

MARKET VALUES

	Raw	PF-69	PF-70
Value	$85	$105	$125

Note: "Raw" values are for average coins in original Mint packaging, not slabbed.

CERTIFICATION DATA

	Total	<PF-69	PF-69	PF-70
# Certified	182,330	217	33,987	148,126
Percentage		0.12%	18.64%	81.24%

Note: Data compiled from NGC and PCGS reports, September 2022.

THE YEAR 2017

In honor of the U.S. Mint's 225th anniversary in 2017, Lincoln cent strikes from Philadelphia carried a "P" mintmark for the first time. The 2017-P Lincoln cents were distributed into regular circulation, where they caused quite a stir as non-collectors were unfamiliar with the mintmark, while many in the numismatic community saw it as a golden collectible opportunity.

Current Events in 2017

President Donald Trump was inaugurated on January 20, 2017, to begin a presidency marred by a series of controversies ranging from trenchant comments on social-media platform Twitter to the dismissal of media stories negative toward his administration as "fake news." However, Trump also accomplished stricter vaping regulations, building a 5G network protected from Chinese surveillance, faster approval by the Food and Drug Administration of generic drugs, and the appointment of highly effective Federal Reserve Chairman Jerome Powell.

On October 1, a gunman shooting from the 32nd-story window of a hotel killed 58 at an outdoor concert in Las Vegas, sadly exceeding the death toll of the Pulse nightclub shooting to become the largest mass shooting in modern U.S. history. A bombing at an Ariana Grande concert in Manchester, England, killed 22 and injured scores more. A number of terror attacks utilizing cars to plow into pedestrians and tourists on city sidewalks collectively killed dozens in New York City, London, and Barcelona.

A protest in Charlottesville, Virginia, by neo-Nazi groups objecting to the removal of a statue of Confederate General Robert E. Lee exploded into a conflagration when a clash with counter-protestors led to many injuries and the murder of peaceful protestor Heather Heyer. Meanwhile, protests of a different sort played out at NFL stadiums as players, coaches, and other sports officials knelt during the playing of the National Anthem to call attention to police brutality and unequal treatment of Black Americans.

North Korean leader Kim Jong-un tested a series of ballistic missiles capable of delivering nuclear weapons to the United States and other nations around the world. The world watched as Kim and Trump mocked each other on social media, leaving many concerned that a war of words could turn into a military conflict.

A solar eclipse drew millions to a narrow swath of land spanning from the Pacific shores near Portland, Oregon, to the Atlantic Ocean by Charleston, South Carolina, during the mid-morning to early afternoon hours of August 21, 2017. Viewers donned special protective eyewear to view the heavenly spectacle without burning their vision.

Top television hits were *The Big Bang Theory*, *NCIS*, *Sunday Night Football*, *This is Us*, and *The Good Doctor*. Hit films of 2017 included *Star Wars: Episode VIII—The Last Jedi*, *Beauty and the Beast*, *Wonder Woman*, *Jumanji: Welcome to the Jungle*, and *Guardians of the Galaxy Vol. 2*. Prevailing on the music charts were "Shape of You" by Ed Sheeran, "Despacito (Remix)" by Luis Fonsi and Daddy Yankee featuring Justin Bieber, "That's What I Like" by Bruno Mars, "Humble" by Kendrick Lamar, and "Something Just Like This" by The Chainsmokers and Coldplay.

It was a banner year for Wall Street, with the Dow Jones Industrial growing by nearly 25 percent. Not only was the threshold of 20,000 points passed, but it was left in the dust, placing the milestone of 25,000 within sight by the end of the year. The Dow fell just short of closing 2017 at that level. Median prices for new homes were around $321,000, and a 2017 Toyota Corolla XSE was $22,680. A gallon of gas was $2.41, a gallon of milk cost $3.35, and a loaf of bread cost $1.57. A first-class postage stamp went back to 49 cents. An ounce of silver averaged $17.04.

On the Numismatic Scene in 2017

The 225th anniversary of the U.S. Mint was a momentous occasion for the United States Mint, which recognized the founding of the nation's mint in Philadelphia by placing the "P" mint-mark on the Lincoln cent for the first time ever. The one-year-only gesture recognized the Philadelphia Mint, which was established in 1792.

This year, the back of the 71st-edition classic hardcover *Red Book* featured a gold-foil portrait of the first director of the United States Mint, David Rittenhouse.

The 2017 United States Mint Holiday Gift Guide, one of the last such direct-mail print offerings by the U.S. Mint, touted the American Silver Eagle as a wonderful gift idea.

2017, Bullion Strike

Mintage: 18,065,500 estimated.

Minted at West Point, San Francisco, and Philadelphia with no mintmark

Sales of the 2017 bullion American Silver Eagle started off strong, with the first going on sale January 9 and seeing a 35 percent increase on first-day orders over the 2016 Silver Eagle. After that, sales started falling off and never kept pace with the rush of demand seen in the previous year. Ultimately, the total mintage of just over 18 million was more than 50 percent lower than the 2016 total mintage of 37,701,500. Not all the 2017 output came from West Point, with 1,000,000 coming from Philadelphia and 3,000,000 hailing from San Francisco, and these were mixed in with the West Point emissions.

2017, Bullion Strike

MARKET VALUES

	Raw	MS-69	MS-70
Value	$36	$45	$85

Note: "Raw" values are for average coins that are not professionally graded/slabbed.

CERTIFICATION DATA

	Total	<MS-69	MS-69	MS-70
# Certified	620,269	20,047	211,394	388,828
Percentage		3.23%	34.08%	62.69%

Note: Data compiled from NGC and PCGS reports, September 2022.

2017-W, Burnished

Mintage: 176,739

Minted at West Point with W mintmark

The 2017-W Burnished American Silver Eagle went on sale June 29, 2017, for $44.95 and absent any household ordering limits or production caps. The 2017-W Burnished Silver Eagle was outfitted with a reeded edge, as customary for the coin except for 2016-W Burnished strikes, which bore the incused edge inscription 30TH ANNIVERSARY.

Sales of just over 176,739 for the 2017-W Burnished strike were off by some 40,000 as compared to the mintage of the 2016-W Burnished Silver Eagle. Lackluster sales may be attributed to the fact that Burnished strikes bear an almost-identical resemblance to the much more affordable bullion strikes, with the exception of a mintmark visible on the reverse.

2017-W, Burnished

MARKET VALUES

	Raw	MS-69	MS-70
Value	$65	$90	$110

Note: "Raw" values are for average coins in original Mint packaging, not slabbed.

CERTIFICATION DATA

	Total	<MS-69	MS-69	MS-70
# Certified	31,040	15	3,683	27,342
Percentage		0.05%	11.87%	88.09%

Note: Data compiled from NGC and PCGS reports, September 2022.

2017-W, Proof

Mintage: 440,596

Minted at West Point with W mintmark

The 2017-W Proof Silver Eagle was released on March 23, 2017, and issued for $53.95. The 2017-W Proof saw the restoration of the traditional reeded edge, replacing the single-year commemorative edge lettering on Proofs declaring the 30TH ANNIVERSARY of the American Silver Eagle.

Sales for the 2017-W Proof were brisk on opening day, with 226,173 units sold. All told, the distribution of 440,596 Proofs was solid but still a net loss when compared to the previous few years.

2017-W, Proof

MARKET VALUES

	Raw	PF-69	PF-70
Value	$85	$105	$125

Note: "Raw" values are for average coins in original Mint packaging, not slabbed.

CERTIFICATION DATA

	Total	<PF-69	PF-69	PF-70
# Certified	122,784	53	14,368	108,363
Percentage		0.04%	11.70%	88.25%

Note: Data compiled from NGC and PCGS reports, September 2022.

2017-S, Proof

Mintage: 123,799

Minted at San Francisco with S mintmark

The 2017-S Proof marked the first time since 2012 Silver Eagle that Proofs were minted in San Francisco, the facility where series Proofs were struck from 1986 through 1992. Unlike many other Silver Eagle Proof offerings, the 2017-S was not sold individually but rather came in two products: the 2017 Congratulations Set and 2017 Limited Edition Silver Proof Sets. The Congratulations Set went on sale April 4, 2017, for $54.95 and with a maximum authorized production of just 75,000, but no household ordering limit. The sets sold out in two minutes and were soon selling for $200 on the secondary market.

Many disgruntled collectors shelled out $139.95 to buy the Limited Edition Silver Proof Set, which had a maximum authorized production of 50,000 sets. This set just missed selling out, with a total of 48,906 sold as of March 2018. Prices eventually came down on the 2017-S Proof Silver Eagle, though they trade for more than $100 even in a grade of "only" PF-68. The majority of certified examples grade PF-70 and can be had for a premium.

2017-S, Proof

MARKET VALUES

	Raw	PF-69	PF-70
Value	$115	$150	$200

Note: "Raw" values are for average coins in original Mint packaging, not slabbed.

CERTIFICATION DATA

	Total	<PF-69	PF-69	PF-70
# Certified	77,124	55	23,394	53,675
Percentage		0.07%	30.33%	69.60%

Note: Data compiled from NGC and PCGS reports, September 2022.

THE YEAR 2018

The U.S. Mint broke new barriers of technology when it embarked on the 2018 Breast Cancer Awareness $5 half eagle, a pink-gold coin reminiscent of the hues associated with the advocacy for and support of breast cancer survivors.

Current Events in 2018

On February 14, 2018, a gunman broke into Marjory Stoneman Douglas High School in Parkland, Florida, and killed 17. The unresolved topics of gun control and school safety again entered the public conversation and led thousands to demonstrate at the March 24, 2018, rally "March for Our Lives."

Public outrage over Bill Cosby and the rape accusations against him as well as similar charges laid on former Hollywood film producer Harvey Weinstein in 2017 gave greater power to the #MeToo movement. Allegations of nonconsensual behavior hit many high-profile players in the entertainment industry and in politics. One of the biggest #MeToo moments of 2018 came when allegations against Supreme Court nominee Brett Kavanaugh entered his pre-confirmation hearings, though he was eventually sworn in as a justice.

In one of the most closely watched midterm election seasons in modern history, Democrats wrested control of the House from Republicans, the latter bolstering their majority in the Senate.

Terrible wildfires almost completely destroyed the city of Paradise, California, killing 85 people and burning more than 14,000 homes and businesses. It was the deadliest U.S. wildfire in a century and one of several that collectively consumed hundreds of thousands of acres in 2018. Hurricane Michael became the first Category 5 storm to hit the contiguous United States since Hurricane Andrew in 1992 and was responsible for killing more than 30 people and causing $25.5 billion in damage.

The 2018 PyeongChang Winter Olympics in South Korea hosted 2,922 athletes hailing from 93 countries. The United States brought home 23 medals, nine of which were gold.

Hot shows on television were *Sunday Night Football*, *This is Us*, *The Masked Singer*, *The Big Bang Theory*, and *Grey's Anatomy*. Top movies were *Black Panther*, *Avengers: Infinity War*, *Incredibles 2*, *Jurassic World: Fallen Kingdom*, and *Deadpool 2*. Popular songs were "I Like It" by J Balvin, "In My Feelings" by Drake, "This is America" by Donald Glover, "One Kiss" by Calvin Harris, and "High Horse" by Kacey Musgraves.

The Dow Jones Industrial had another stellar year of performance, closing above 25,000 points for the first time on January 4 before eclipsing 26,000 less than two weeks later. While no other major thresholds were surpassed for the rest of the year, the bulls were dominant in an economy that saw low unemployment and high consumer confidence. The median price for a new home was $323,100 and the cost for a Chevrolet Equinox was $23,580. A gallon of milk went for $3.25 and a loaf of bread was $1.29. A first-class postage stamp cost 50 cents. Meanwhile, the average price for an ounce of silver was $15.71.

On the Numismatic Scene in 2018

The U.S. Mint unveiled the 2018 Breast Cancer Awareness commemorative coins, which included a clad half dollar, silver dollar, and a pink-hued $5 gold half eagle. The gold coin was produced with a novel 85 percent gold, 14.8 percent copper, and 0.2 percent zinc alloy to create a pinkish hue harmonizing with the international color for breast cancer advocacy and support. This was a first for the U.S. Mint, which struck the coin at its West Point facility and issued the commemorative in Uncirculated for $421 and in Proof for $431.

The American Silver Eagle was clearly becoming an ever-larger target for counterfeiters. By 2018, the Industry Council on Tangible Assets (ICTA, an organization now known as the National Coin & Bullion Association) reported on a survey of 363 dealers declaring the Silver Eagle as "the counterfeit bullion coin most widely encountered by U.S. dealers." Astonishingly, 43.3 percent of respondents had encountered customers wanting to sell them bogus Silver Eagles, and more than 80 percent witnessed an increasing presence of counterfeit coins and bars over the previous five years.

The 72nd-edition *Red Book*, published in 2018, featured a gold-foil portrait of Kenneth Bressett, who was promoted this year to editor emeritus, with Jeff Garrett taking over as senior editor. Q. David Bowers continued in his role as the book's research editor. The 72nd edition also had a special ten-page chapter titled "Honoring Kenneth Bressett," with tributes penned by Garrett and Bowers, along with an illustrated history and Bressett's own reflections on nearly 60 years of working on the *Red Book*.

2018, Bullion Strike

Mintage: 15,700,000 estimated.

Minted at West Point with no mintmark

The American Silver Eagle started off 2018 with sluggish sales, which remained the case for most the year. If there were any bright spots, they could be found in a spike in sales in September, causing a short depletion of Silver Eagle inventory at the Mint. The final tally that rolled in for the 2018 bullion strikes showed suppressed demand, with more than 2,500,000 fewer sales than in 2017. The lower numbers are a factor of softer silver prices in 2018, which saw silver reach its highest price of $17.52 in January before trending downward for the rest of the year, and at one point dipping below $14 in November. A strong stock market also helped siphon some investors away from precious metals.

2018, Bullion Strike

MARKET VALUES

	Raw	MS-69	MS-70
Value	$36	$45	$85

Note: "Raw" values are for average coins that are not professionally graded/slabbed.

CERTIFICATION DATA

	Total	<MS-69	MS-69	MS-70
# Certified	374,805	10,526	129,049	235,230
Percentage		2.81%	34.43%	62.76%

Note: Data compiled from NGC and PCGS reports, September 2022.

2018-W, Burnished

Mintage: 138,947

Minted at West Point with W mintmark

The U.S. Mint offered the 2018-W Burnished beginning on May 24, 2018, at a price of $46.95, marking an increase of $2 from 2017. The pace of sales for the 2018 Burnished Silver Eagle was sedate, and the coin remained for sale on the U.S. Mint website well into 2019, with sales still not breaching 140,000 by late May 2019.

2018-W, Burnished

MARKET VALUES

	Raw	MS-69	MS-70
Value	$65	$90	$110

Note: "Raw" values are for average coins in original Mint packaging, not slabbed.

CERTIFICATION DATA

	Total	<MS-69	MS-69	MS-70
# Certified	20,672	3	3,926	16,743
Percentage		0.01%	18.99%	80.99%

Note: Data compiled from NGC and PCGS reports, September 2022.

2018-W, Proof

Mintage: 411,513

Minted at West Point with W mintmark

The 2018-W Proof was released on January 4, 2018, with an issue price of $55.95, which was $2 higher than the previous year. There were no household ordering limits and sales of individual coins had reached 226,506 by February 5. The 2018-W Proofs were also available in the Congratulations Set and 210-coin bulk packs, the latter offered to approved bulk purchasers.

2018-W, Proof

MARKET VALUES

	Raw	PF-69	PF-70
Value	$85	$105	$125

Note: "Raw" values are for average coins in original Mint packaging, not slabbed.

CERTIFICATION DATA

	Total	<PF-69	PF-69	PF-70
# Certified	102,209	82	14,420	87,707
Percentage		0.08%	14.11%	85.81%

Note: Data compiled from NGC and PCGS reports, September 2022.

2018-S, Proof

Mintage: 208,265

Minted at San Francisco with S mintmark

The San Francisco Mint produced Proof Silver Eagles for the second year in a row. Proofs were released on August 14 for an issue price of $55.95 and could be bought individually or as part of the 2018 Limited Edition Silver Proof Set, which hit the streets on October 18 for $144.95.

2018-S, Proof

MARKET VALUES

	Raw	PF-69	PF-70
Value	$115	$130	$135

Note: "Raw" values are for average coins in original Mint packaging, not slabbed.

CERTIFICATION DATA

	Total	<PF-69	PF-69	PF-70
# Certified	66,063	18	7,431	58,614
Percentage		0.03%	11.25%	88.72%

Note: Data compiled from NGC and PCGS reports, September 2022.

THE YEAR 2019

In a major shift, the U.S. Mint increased the purity of collectible silver from the historic 90 percent silver standard to .999 fine, bringing many of the most popular collector options, such as silver Proof Washington quarters and commemorative silver dollars, in line with the fineness of popular bullion coins like the American Silver Eagle and five-ounce silver America the Beautiful quarters.

Current Events in 2019

United States Special Counsel Robert Mueller wrapped up a two-year investigation into allegations that President Donald Trump colluded with the Russians during the 2016 presidential election. The 448-page Mueller Report presented findings that Mueller could not conclude whether Trump had committed a crime and stated the investigation was not a "witch hunt," as some claimed it was.

Oval Office drama unfolded in grand fashion later in the year, when a whistleblower revealed Trump had called Ukrainian President Volodymyr Zelenskyy asking him to dig up dirt on former Vice President and 2020 presidential contender Joe Biden and his son Hunter Biden, the latter a board member of a Ukrainian energy company. Making matters stickier were speculations that Trump withheld $400 million in aid to the Ukrainians on the condition of receiving information on the Bidens. This led to the formal impeachment inquiry that began in Congress in November 2019, with the House of Representatives approving articles of impeachment on December 18, 2019. This made Trump only the third U.S. president to be impeached, after Andrew Johnson and Bill Clinton.

Another scandal hitting the news in 2019 involved well-connected and wealthy parents cheating on their children's college admission applications to help them get into elite universities.

On March 15 a gunman killed 51 at a mosque in Christchurch, New Zealand.

Notre-Dame cathedral in Paris, France, was nearly destroyed by a fire on April 15 during renovation work. The inferno incinerated the 850-year-old church's iconic spire and virtually all of its wooden roof.

Massive wildfires in South America destroyed 2,240,000 acres of the Amazon rainforest. Ethiopian Airlines Flight 302 crashed on March 10 and killed 157, with the tragedy marking the second occurrence of a Boeing 737 MAX 8 aircraft going down in less than six months. All Boeing 737 MAX planes were grounded until the problem, a design flaw, could be fixed.

Top television shows were *Sunday Night Football*, *NCIS*, *FBI*, *Blue Bloods*, and *Chicago Fire*. "Old Town Road" by Lil Nas X, "Bad Guy" by Billie Eilish, "Sucker" by the Jonas Brothers, "7 Rings" by Ariana Grande, and "Dancing with a Stranger" by Lewis Capaldi were hit songs. Major box office hits were *Avengers: Endgame*, *The Lion King*, *Toy Story 4*, *Frozen II*, and *Captain Marvel*.

The median price for a new house was $323,100. A new Hyundai Elantra Eco Sedan was $21,050, and a gallon of gas was $2.50. A gallon of milk was $3.41, a loaf of bread cost $1.45, and a first-class postage stamp leapt up by a nickel to 55 cents. The average price of silver per ounce was $16.21.

The Dow Jones Industrial Average was on a roll in 2019, eventually surpassing 28,000 points before the year was out. It seemed to many as though nothing could stop the economic boom. Little did most Americans know during the latter months of 2019 that a novel strain of virus known as SARS-CoV-2 was beginning to circulate in the city of Wuhan, China, and was on track to change the world as we knew it.

On the Numismatic Scene in 2019

The U.S. Mint all but abandoned the practice of minting silver coins from a .900-fine composition, first established in the United States during the 1830s, and switched to .999-fine silver purity for its collectible silver coins. The move was authorized under the Fixing America's Surface Transportation (FAST) Act signed into law by President Barack Obama in December 2015.

Several coins were affected by this shift, including silver Proof Roosevelt dimes, Washington quarters, and Kennedy half dollars, as well as commemorative silver dollars. The higher-purity planchets were certain to attract a new breed of collector and even entice more precious-metals investors to spend extra money on virtually pure silver Proofs. However, .999-fine silver coins have a long history at the United States Mint tracing back decades and have been in use for American Silver Eagles since their launch in 1986.

The West Point Mint began issuing America the Beautiful Quarters for circulation bearing the "W" mintmark. This initiative grabbed national headlines as these coins became the first with the West Point mintmark to be intentionally distributed into normal channels of commerce. Making this release even more special was the limited mintage of just two million coins for each of the five designs issued for the program in 2019, with none of the five 2019-W quarters being offered in coin sets or sold by the U.S. Mint. As the quarters began turning up in pocket change, many sold for $20 or even more apiece.

The Chicago Coin Club marked its 100th anniversary with a special edition of the *Red Book*—a limited edition of only 250 copies with a customized hardcover.

In February 2019 Joseph Menna, an artist with more than three decades of classical training and professional experience, became the 14th chief engraver of the United States Mint. Menna had joined the Mint in 2005 as its first full-time digitally skilled artist, after working as a sculptor and instructor at the Johnson Atelier Fine Art Foundry in New Jersey and in other artistic venues.

2019, Bullion Strike

Mintage: 14,863,500 estimated.

Minted at West Point with no mintmark

Sales of the 2019 bullion Silver Eagle were strong during the first half of the year, safely outpacing the 2018 emission. The U.S. Mint even ran dry on supply of the Silver Eagle in late February, suspending sales of the coin until April 1. However, by the back half of the year the sales slowed down, and when all was said and done the final output was lower than the anemic figure of 15,700,000 for the 2018 Silver Eagle.

In the context of history, the seemingly dismal mintages of 2018 and 2019 were still miles beyond production totals from any time before 2008—a point that should not be forgotten in a world where bullion coins move faster than ever. At any rate, the situation of lower mintages for the Silver Eagle would soon turn with the unforeseen fate of the world in the early 2020s.

2019, Bullion Strike

MARKET VALUES

	Raw	MS-69	MS-70
Value	$36	$45	$85

Note: "Raw" values are for average coins that are not professionally graded/slabbed.

CERTIFICATION DATA

	Total	<MS-69	MS-69	MS-70
# Certified	373,994	2,086	124,975	246,933
Percentage		0.56%	33.42%	66.03%

Note: Data compiled from NGC and PCGS reports, September 2022.

2019-W, Burnished

Mintage: 141,030 estimated.

Minted at West Point with W mintmark

The 2019-W Burnished American Silver Eagle was released on May 29, 2019, for $46.95, the same price as the previous year's issue. There was no authorized maximum mintage and no household ordering limit for this issue, which saw sales only slightly better than the 2018-W Burnished Silver Eagle.

2019-W, Burnished

MARKET VALUES

	Raw	MS-69	MS-70
Value	$70	$95	$125

Note: "Raw" values are for average coins in original Mint packaging, not slabbed.

CERTIFICATION DATA

	Total	<MS-69	MS-69	MS-70
# Certified	21,002	27	4,378	16,597
Percentage		0.13%	20.85%	79.03%

Note: Data compiled from NGC and PCGS reports, September 2022.

2019-W, Proof

Mintage: 407,804 estimated.

Minted at West Point with W mintmark

The 2019-W Proof was released on January 10, 2019, and issued at $55.95 as an individual product option. It could also be purchased in the Congratulations Set for $56.95 or in a 40-coin bulk lot sold exclusively to approved members of the U.S. Mint Numismatic Bulk Purchase Program.

2019-W, Proof

MARKET VALUES

	Raw	PF-69	PF-70
Value	$85	$105	$125

Note: "Raw" values are for average coins in original Mint packaging, not slabbed.

CERTIFICATION DATA

	Total	<PF-69	PF-69	PF-70
# Certified	90,099	74	14,138	75,887
Percentage		0.08%	15.69%	84.23%

Note: Data compiled from NGC and PCGS reports, September 2022.

2019-W, Enhanced Reverse Proof

Mintage: 99,675 estimated.

Minted at West Point with W mintmark

Issued as part of the historic Pride of Two Nations set, the 2019-W Enhanced Reverse Proof became available to the public on July 3, 2019, and was coupled with a Canadian $5 silver Maple Leaf, at a price of $139.95 for U.S. customers. All told, the U.S. Mint approved striking up to 110,000 of the 2019-W Enhanced Reverse Proofs, with 100,000 allocated for sets offered in the U.S. and 10,000 for those offered in Canada, which also boasted a population roughly one-tenth that of the United States.

2019-W, Enhanced Reverse Proof

MARKET VALUES

	Raw	PF-69	PF-70
Value	$150	$170	$220

Note: "Raw" values are for average coins in original Mint packaging, not slabbed.

CERTIFICATION DATA

	Total	<PF-69	PF-69	PF-70
# Certified	44,043	32	5,581	38,430
Percentage		0.07%	12.67%	87.26%

Note: Data compiled from NGC and PCGS reports, September 2022.

2019-S, Proof

Mintage: 200,696 estimated.

Minted at San Francisco with S mintmark

The 2019-S Proof Silver Eagle was first offered for sale on August 6, 2019, and was issued for $55.95. The coin was produced absent any household ordering limits or authorized mintage maximums. The 2019-S Proof Silver Eagle was sold both individually and as part of the 2019 Limited Edition Silver Proof Set, the latter released in October at an issue price of $149.95 and becoming the first such set in which all coins were .999-fine silver.

2019-S, Proof

MARKET VALUES

	Raw	PF-69	PF-70
Value	$115	$130	$135

Note: "Raw" values are for average coins in original Mint packaging, not slabbed.

CERTIFICATION DATA

	Total	<PF-69	PF-69	PF-70
# Certified	44,683	68	5,959	38,656
Percentage		0.15%	13.34%	86.51%

Note: Data compiled from NGC and PCGS reports, September 2022.

2019-S, Enhanced Reverse Proof

Mintage: **29,909** estimated.

Minted at San Francisco with S mintmark

Pandemonium ensued when the U.S. Mint released the 2019-S Enhanced Reverse Proof Silver Eagle on November 14, 2019. The coin was issued for $65.95 and had a household ordering limit of one. Making this offering even more special was a total authorized mintage of just 30,000. A small number of these coins were offered by the Mint at the Whitman Coin and Collectibles Baltimore Expo, with certificates of authenticity autographed at the show by Mint director David Ryder.

Noting the significance of this coin, Michael Garofalo obverses, "The 2019 Enhanced Reverse Proof Silver Eagle, struck at the San Francisco Mint, not only has an Enhanced Reverse Proof finish, but it also boasts of a mintage of only 29,909 coins, which makes it even a lower mintage than the 1995-W Proof coin."

The Silver Eagles sold out within 20 minutes, leaving thousands of customers dismayed and disappointed. The U.S. Mint had to fend off bots and cyberattacks, many aiming to bypass the household ordering limit and make bulk purchases. One of the most frustrating outcomes was customers adding the Silver Eagle to an order only to find it no longer available upon checkout. U.S. Mint spokesperson stated in a press release that "items are not automatically made unavailable to others when they are placed in a customer's cart. Instead, inventory is decremented once billing information is entered and verified."

As *Coin World* Managing Editor William T. Gibbs provided in an editor's letter, some dealers legally circumvented the household ordering limit by "publicly offering individuals a profit of $150 for any coin they might purchase." Many were able to sell their coins on the secondary market for extraordinary sums beyond the original issue price, with some selling for more than $2,000. One example coupled with a certificate of authenticity numbered "#16" and hand-signed by Ryder sold on eBay for an impressive $14,001.

2019-S, Enhanced Reverse Proof

MARKET VALUES

	Raw	PF-69	PF-70
Value	$1,250	$1,400	$2,500

Note: "Raw" values are for average coins in original Mint packaging, not slabbed.

CERTIFICATION DATA

	Total	<PF-69	PF-69	PF-70
# Certified	21,041	84	6,164	14,793
Percentage		0.40%	29.30%	70.31%

Note: Data compiled from NGC and PCGS reports, September 2022.

2019 Pride of Two Nations Set

Mintage: 99,675 U.S. sets; 10,000 Canadian sets

Minted at West Point with W mintmark (American Silver Eagle) and Ottawa (Maple Leaf)

This historic two-coin set, the first Mint product issued jointly by the United States Mint and Royal Canadian Mint, went on sale July 3, 2019. Both mints sold the set, with 100,000 allocated for United States customers and 10,000 reserved for Canadians. The U.S. Mint issued the set for $139.95, while the Canadian version sold for $189.95 in Canadian dollars, a price difference largely accounting for the relative value of the set as measured by the exchange rate between the two nations.

The set was unveiled in a grand ceremony at the Philadelphia Mint with U.S. Mint director David Ryder and Royal Canadian Mint president and chief officer Marie Lemay on hand to sign certificates of authenticity. Both were also part of a joint event at the American Numismatic Association's World's Fair of Money. The Pride of Two Nations Set was marked unavailable within a week of its release on the U.S. Mint website, with the Royal Canadian Mint also indicating a quick sellout.

There are some packaging differences between the sets. The U.S. iteration is packaged in a blue presentation case situating the American Silver Eagle on the left and Maple Leaf on the right. Canada's set reverses the arrangement, with the Maple leaf on the left and American Silver Eagle on the right. Packaging graphics and literature were also different between the two kinds of sets.

2019, Pride of Two Nations Set
MARKET VALUES

	Raw	PF-69	PF-70
Value	$195	$235	$300

Note: "Raw" values are for average coins in original Mint packaging, not slabbed.

THE YEAR 2020

A global pandemic shut down economies around the world and drove investors to the traditional "safe haven" investment of precious metals.

Current Events in 2020

The most tumultuous year in recent history started with a rash of flu-like illnesses spreading through China and crossing borders to become the deadliest global pandemic since the 1918 Spanish Flu. COVID-19 was on a lethal path that traversed the globe in a matter of weeks. Nations around the world enforced a variety of rules intended to slow the spread of the disease, including mask-wearing mandates, quarantines, and shutdowns of non-essential businesses. After intensive global research efforts, the first vaccines were administered to the public by December.

A rancorous 2020 presidential election campaign unfolded as the pandemic precluded the typical stump speeches and townhall rallies. Incumbent President Donald Trump and prevailing Democratic contender Joe Biden spent much of the late spring and early summer making their cases to the American public by virtual events hosted online or broadcast on television. By the fall, in-person events were being held again, many requiring attendees to wear masks and physically distance themselves from others. President Trump caught COVID-19 during the height of the campaign in early October. Longtime Delaware senator and two-term vice president Joe Biden won the election with running mate Kamala Harris, who became the nation's first female vice president as well as the first person of color in that role.

The matter of race entered the American conversation in a way not seen since the height of the civil rights era in the 1960s when George Floyd, a Black man in Minneapolis, was murdered by White police officer Derek Chauvin on May 25, 2020, during an arrest for allegedly passing a counterfeit $20 bill. Protests broke out around the nation over the following days, most generally peaceful but some quite destructive, with calls for changes to policing tactics.

Hurricane Laura was a powerful storm that ravaged the Caribbean and made landfall in Louisiana with Category 4 winds killing 81 and causing some $20 billion in damage along its path.

The 2020 Summer Olympics slated for Tokyo, Japan, were postponed until 2021 due to the pandemic.

The Dow Jones Industrial Average climbed past 29,000 points in January 2020, but as the pandemic hit many recent gains evaporated as investors sold stock and moved into other areas of speculation. The market eventually recovered its losses and tracked above 30,000 by the end of the year. Despite the pandemic, the housing market was on fire as many Americans adjusted to life working from home. The median price for a new home lurched north to $334,900. Gas prices dropped below $2 a gallon at one point in 2020 as the pandemic kept people off the roads, but Americans eventually got moving again and a gallon of gas averaged $2.17 for the year. Milk was $4.12 and a loaf of bread went for $1.40. A first-class stamp remained at 55 cents. An ounce of silver traded for $20.55.

On the Numismatic Scene in 2020

The COVID-19 pandemic interrupted operations at the U.S. Mint, like most other business functions around the country. This, coupled with supply-chain shortages and an increased demand for American Silver Eagles and other coinage, only compounded a challenging scenario at the mint. The West Point Mint suspended operations from March 28 through March 31 after an employee tested positive for COVID, and it again paused production from April 15 through April 21. Executive orders in California closed the San Francisco Mint from March 18 through May 4.

A national coin shortage unfolded in the spring as consumers were using plastic cards or payment apps rather than spending coins to complete transactions. The situation eased a bit going into the latter months of the year but never fully let up as millions of Americans avoided touching coins and currency out of fear of contracting COVID. Others simply preferred not carrying cash around anymore—a big hindrance to keeping coins circulating regardless of how many the U.S. Mint strikes.

The Citizens Coinage Advisory Committee began a long stretch of meeting telephonically and online, instead of at Mint headquarters in Washington, in response to the pandemic.

The Philippine Collectors Forum issued a special edition of the 74th-edition *Red Book* this year, honoring the 1920–2020 centennial of the opening of the Mint of the Philippine Islands, in Manila. Of the 250 books printed, several dozen were destroyed in shipping, resulting in only 212 copies being available for collectors. These quickly sold out at $25 apiece, raising money for the PCF's numismatic educational programs. Today they sell for closer to $100, or more.

The Mint reactivated its Presidential $1 coin program for the addition of a dollar coin honoring President George H.W. Bush, who had died in 2018 and became eligible for recognition in the series given that two years had passed since his death. Coins memorializing President Bush were offered in Uncirculated sets, Proof sets, and other Mint products.

2020, Bullion Strike

Mintage: 30,089,500 estimated.

Minted at West Point, San Francisco, and Philadelphia with no mintmark

Investors were skittish about long-term prospects once COVID-19 began shutting down businesses and sending the public into crisis mode. As usual during tough economic times, speculators turned to silver and other precious metals. Many were buying American Silver Eagles on the cheap in mid-March, when silver traded around $12 per ounce—the lowest price in more than a decade. However, silver prices began climbing as the year went on and reached $28.88 by September 1. Incidentally, gold prices hit a record high of $2,067 per ounce in August.

Due to temporary closures of the West Point and San Francisco Mints, the Philadelphia Mint took over production of Silver Eagles from April 8 through April 20. During that time, the Philadelphia Mint struck 240,000 "emergency run" Silver Eagles, which immediately hit the secondary market as "Emergency" Silver Eagles that were selling for huge premiums over standard American Silver Eagles.

Outstanding demand for Silver Eagles pushed mintages to a multi-year high of more than 31 million, reversing a long decline in sales for the bullion strike.

2020, Bullion Strike

MARKET VALUES

	Raw	MS-69	MS-70
Value	$38	$45	$83

Note: "Raw" values are for average coins that are not professionally graded/slabbed.

CERTIFICATION DATA

	Total	<MS-69	MS-69	MS-70
# Certified	927,187	21,005	361,018	545,164
Percentage		2.27%	38.94%	58.80%

Note: Data compiled from NGC and PCGS reports, September 2022.

2020-W, Burnished

Mintage: 154,861 estimated.

Minted at West Point with W mintmark

The 2020-W Burnished (or "Uncirculated" in U.S. Mint jargon) Silver Eagle was released on July 8, 2020, at a price of $54, with this increasing to $67 on October 13 along with price hikes for other American Silver Eagle offerings. The coin was available without any household ordering limits and or maximum authorized mintage.

2020-W, Burnished

MARKET VALUES

	Raw	MS-69	MS-70
Value	$70	$95	$150

Note: "Raw" values are for average coins in original Mint packaging, not slabbed.

CERTIFICATION DATA

	Total	<MS-69	MS-69	MS-70
# Certified	31,278	32	7,675	23,571
Percentage		0.10%	24.54%	75.36%

Note: Data compiled from NGC and PCGS reports, September 2022.

2020-W, Proof

Mintage: 405,553 estimated.

Minted at West Point with W mintmark

The 2020-W Proof American Silver Eagle was issued January 9, 2020, at a price of $64.50, up $8.55 from 2019. The price increased later in the year to $73 due to pressure from rising silver prices, increasing costs, and more challenging production and logistics issues. The 2020-W Proof Silver Eagle was also available in the 2020 Congratulations Set, which was released on January 9 and sold for $65.50.

2020-W, Proof

MARKET VALUES			
	Raw	PF-69	PF-70
Value	$85	$105	$125

Note: "Raw" values are for average coins in original Mint packaging, not slabbed.

CERTIFICATION DATA				
	Total	<PF-69	PF-69	PF-70
# Certified	108,134	85	16,964	91,085
Percentage		0.08%	15.69%	84.23%

Note: Data compiled from NGC and PCGS reports, September 2022.

2020-W, End of World War II 75th Anniversary, with Privy Mark, Proof

Mintage: 74,709 estimated.

Minted at West Point with W mintmark

The United States Mint honored the 75th anniversary of the Allied victory in World War II with a privy mark, a special feature not normally seen on U.S. coins. The "V75" privy mark is situated within an incused cartouche in the shape of the Rainbow Pool as seen from above the World War II Memorial in Washington, D.C.

The V75 privy mark was struck on 75,000 Proof 2020-W Silver Eagles and was seen on other coins minted that year, including a limited number of one-ounce American Gold Eagle $50 coins and on all five different 2020-W America the Beautiful quarters, each of which saw a mintage of two million. The 2020-W Silver Eagles with V75 privy mark went on sale November 5 at a price of $83, well above the $69.50 originally billed for the coin. Regardless of the last-minute price hike, the coin sold virtually all of its stock within a few weeks.

Observes Lee Minshull on this special release, "I really love the 2020-W V75, which boasts the first privy mark of the series."

"These coins were in great demand and brought the United States Mint's website to its knees when they were sold to the public," recalls Michael Garofalo. "Although the mintage was 75,000 coins, all were quickly absorbed in the marketplace and many collectors were disappointed in not being able to either order one through the Mint or buy one in the secondary market."

2020-W, End of World War II 75th Anniversary, with Privy Mark, Proof

MARKET VALUES			
	Raw	PF-69	PF-70
Value	$325	$375	$600

Note: "Raw" values are for average coins in original Mint packaging, not slabbed.

CERTIFICATION DATA				
	Total	<PF-69	PF-69	PF-70
# Certified	37,925	349	11,069	26,507
Percentage		0.92%	29.19%	69.89%

Note: Data compiled from NGC and PCGS reports, September 2022.

2020-S, Proof

Mintage: 258,904 estimated.

Minted at San Francisco with S mintmark

Following closure-related delays, supply issues, and other extenuating circumstances, the 2020-S Proof Silver Eagle was released on October 13, 2020, with an issue price of $73—markedly higher than the $63.25 originally announced for the coin. Along with individual sales, the 2020-S Proof was available in the 2020 Limited Edition Silver Proof Set, which went on sale December 10, 2020, at a dramatically increased price of $201.

2020-S, Proof

MARKET VALUES

	Raw	PF-69	PF-70
Value	$95	$115	$140

Note: "Raw" values are for average coins in original Mint packaging, not slabbed.

CERTIFICATION DATA

	Total	<PF-69	PF-69	PF-70
# Certified	94,857	80	16,777	78,000
Percentage		0.08%	17.69%	82.23%

Note: Data compiled from NGC and PCGS reports, September 2022.

THE YEAR 2021

A long-awaited change in the reverse design of the American Silver Eagle occurred during the middle of the year, with the original 1986 John Mercanti motif of a modern heraldic eagle replaced by a side view of an eagle approaching its landing, as depicted by Emily S. Damstra. The new design was also accompanied by other changes to the coin, including obverse enhancements and a new security feature on the edge of the coin.

Current Events in 2021

Millions lined up each day for COVID-19 vaccines as the world cautiously waited for a return to normalcy. However, new strains of the COVID-19 virus led to more waves of infections throughout the rest of the year. Various government health agencies rolled out booster vaccines to help quell the cases and mitigate symptoms in those who still contracted the virus.

What should have been a period of peaceful transition of power between outgoing President Donald Trump and President-elect Joe Biden became a firestorm that shocked the world. On January 6, protesters gathering in Washington, D.C., to rally against the November 2020 election results invaded the U.S. Capitol Building, causing lawmakers in session to seek emergency shelter as hundreds flooded the building and damaged offices, artwork, and other property, with four dead. The insurrection was the first time the Capitol Building had been breached by attackers since the War of 1812.

In June a 12-story condominium tower in Surfside, Florida, crashed down during the middle of the night, killing 98 residents. The building had been plagued for years by various structural issues, giving rise to concerns about the safety of other aging shoreside high-rises.

An unusual tornado outbreak in December spawned a twister that ripped through Mayfield, Kentucky, and killed 57 people.

The United States pulled the last troops out of Afghanistan in August, bringing an end to a war that lasted a generation and killed more than 2,400 United States military personnel. However, the withdrawal led to a quick takeover of the country by the Taliban, leaving many to fear for the safety of Afghan citizens under the control of an extremist regime.

After their postponement in August 2020, the Summer Olympics opened in Tokyo on July 23 under tight COVID-related restrictions. The Summer Games, which held the unique distinction of being the first since 1900 not held during a leap year, saw Americans rank in the lead with 113 medals, 39 of them gold.

Sunday Night Football, *NCIS*, *The Voice*, *911*, and *Grey's Anatomy* were among the most-watched primetime television shows. At the movies were *Spider-Man: No Way Home*, *Shang-Chi and the Legend of the Ten Rings*, *Venom: Let There Be Carnage*, *Black Widow*, and *F9: The Fast Saga*. The tops songs included "Butter" by BTS, "Kiss Me More" by Doja Cat, "Peaches" by Justin Bieber featuring Giveon and Daniel Caesar, "Montero (Call Me By Your Name)" by Lil Nas X, and "Easy on Me" by Adele.

While the economy was dogged by millions of unfilled job openings and a parade of unloaded freighters waiting outside ports, Wall Street tracked a year of phenomenal growth, with the Dow Jones Industrial Average closing above 36,000 points for the first time in early November. Signs of trouble started appearing toward the end of the year as inflation began touching multi-decade highs, causing consumers to pull back on spending. Still, median prices for new homes soared to $393,900. A 2021 Ford Bronco went for $28,500, a gallon of gas was $2.93, a gallon of milk cost $3.66, and a loaf of bread was priced at $1.59. A first-class postage stamp was 58 cents. The average price of silver was $25.44 per ounce.

On the Numismatic Scene in 2021

A new reverse design debuted on the American Silver Eagle for the first time since its launch in 1986. Among the changes was a new eagle motif by Emily S. Damstra replacing the original design by John Mercanti, as well as the implementation of new security features, such as a notch of missing edge reeding on the new coin. The new American Silver Eagles, dubbed the "Type II" design, were released in the middle of the year alongside new reverse designs for the American Gold Eagle.

The combination of economic stimulus payments and more time at home during the pandemic invited many into the world of collectibles, with numismatics enjoying a shot in the arm like few could have dreamt as recently as 2019. The coin market was on fire, with prices strong across much of the marketplace. The lone privately owned 1933 Saint-Gaudens double eagle was offered for sale by Sotheby's in June 2021, where the ultra-rarity realized $18,872,250 and became the most valuable coin ever sold at public auction.

Attentions turned to late-date Kennedy half dollars, which had been appearing with greater frequency in rolls acquired from banks, despite the coin not having been made for circulation since 2001. Higher-than-normal mintages for 2021-P and 2021-D

Kennedy halves piqued further curiosity. Inquisitive hobby observers learned the Federal Reserve had ordered 2021 Kennedy half dollars for circulation, spurring many to wonder if it was part of a coordinated effort to infuse the nation's channels of commerce with more curiosities in the same vein of 2017-P Lincoln cents, 2019-W quarters, and 2020-W quarters with privy marks.

Continued coin shortages plagued businesses around the country, leaving many merchants to encourage exact-change transactions and some even offering small discounts on goods and services if paid in coin. The U.S. Mint did its part to allay the ongoing coin shortage issues by striking a cumulative 14.4 billion cents, nickels, dimes, quarters, half dollars, and dollars.

The *Red Book* was in its 75th year in 2021, having evolved from a simple listing of two or three different grades of coins to a detailed catalog with pricing in nearly a dozen grades. The 1st edition had included prices for about 3,400 different coins; the 75th had nearly 8,000, with some 32,000 retail valuations. To mark the diamond anniversary, the classic red hardcover version had special silver-foil lettering and an emblem on the back cover. At the annual American Numismatic Association convention, Whitman Publishing released Kenneth Bressett's *A Penny Saved: R.S. Yeoman and His Remarkable Red Book*, a combined history of the *Red Book*, biography of its creator (Richard S. Yeo, known professionally as R.S. Yeoman), and memoirs of Bressett himself.

2021, Heraldic Eagle Reverse, Bullion Strike (Type I)

Mintage: 13,106,500

Minted at West Point with no mintmark

Continued demand for precious-metal coinage brought strong sales for the 2021 American Silver Eagle, which saw more than 28 million minted during the course of the year despite planchet supply issues. Strong demand for the bullion issues in 2021 was driven by the mid-year design change as well as robust investor activity during the uncertain economic picture stemming from the second year of the COVID-19 pandemic. This issue marked the last of the bullion-strike Type I American Silver Eagles with John Mercanti's heraldic eagle design. The final Type I Silver Eagle, struck by David Ryder, was sold by Stack's Bowers Galleries in September 2022 for $85,000.

2021, Heraldic Eagle Reverse (Type I), Bullion Strike

MARKET VALUES

	Raw	MS-69	MS-70
Value	$35	$45	$65

Note: "Raw" values are for average coins that are not professionally graded/slabbed.

CERTIFICATION DATA

	Total	<MS-69	MS-69	MS-70
# Certified	994,960	7,775	310,147	677,038
Percentage		0.78%	31.17%	68.05%

Note: Data compiled from NGC and PCGS reports, September 2022.

2021-W, Heraldic Eagle Reverse (Type I), Proof

Mintage: 415,855 estimated.

Minted at West Point with W mintmark

This Type I American Eagle Proof was struck at the West Point Mint and sold to the public for $73. Naturally, demand was high for this issue, the last of its kind for the Mercanti design.

2021-W, Heraldic Eagle Reverse (Type I), Proof

MARKET VALUES

	Raw	PF-69	PF-70
Value	$145	$165	$195

Note: "Raw" values are for average coins in original Mint packaging, not slabbed.

CERTIFICATION DATA

	Total	<PF-69	PF-69	PF-70
# Certified	169,572	141	24,991	144,440
Percentage		0.08%	14.74%	85.18%

Note: Data compiled from NGC and PCGS reports, September 2022.

2021-W, Heraldic Eagle Reverse (Type I), Reverse Proof

Mintage: 124,823 estimated.

Minted at West Point with W mintmark

Reverse Proofs have proven popular for the U.S. Mint, and the 2021 Silver Eagles were no exception. This Reverse Proof, the only one produced in 2021 with the Type I design, was released as part of the 2021 American Eagle One Ounce Silver Reverse Proof Two-Coin Set Designer Edition, which also included a San Francisco Reverse Proof donning the Type II motif.

2021-W, Heraldic Eagle Reverse (Type I), Reverse Proof

MARKET VALUES

	Raw	PF-69	PF-70
Value	$160	$195	$240

Note: "Raw" values are for average coins in original Mint packaging, not slabbed.

CERTIFICATION DATA

	Total	<PF-69	PF-69	PF-70
# Certified	20,710	46	3,615	17,049
Percentage		0.22%	17.46%	82.32%

Note: Data compiled from NGC and PCGS reports, September 2022.

2021, Flying Eagle Reverse (Type II), Bullion Strike

Mintage: 14,768,500

Minted at San Francisco and West Point with no mintmark

The U.S. Mint began striking the Type II American Silver Eagles with Emily S. Damstra's flying eagle design on April 10, 2021. Mintage figures were strong on examples bearing the new motif, which attracted major sales by collectors and investors as well as mass marketers, who ordered both varieties of Silver Eagle in large numbers from the U.S. Mint's Authorized Purchasers for sale as promotional items. The first Type II Silver Eagle, struck by David Ryder in a special ceremony, realized $80,000 in a September 2022 Stack's Bowers Galleries auction.

2021, Flying Eagle Reverse (Type II), Bullion Strike

MARKET VALUES

	Raw	MS-69	MS-70
Value	$40	$45	$85

Note: "Raw" values are for average coins that are not professionally graded/slabbed.

CERTIFICATION DATA

	Total	<MS-69	MS-69	MS-70
# Certified	748,466	6,068	202,695	539,703
Percentage		0.81%	27.08%	72.11%

Note: Data compiled from NGC and PCGS reports, September 2022.

2021-W, Flying Eagle Reverse (Type II), Burnished

Mintage: 187,294 estimated.

Minted at West Point with W mintmark

The 2021-W Burnished (or "Uncirculated," using the U.S. Mint's parlance) Silver Eagle was minted at West Point. It marks the first time the Type II reverse was seen in this matte format. It was issued for $67.

2021-W, Flying Eagle Reverse (Type II), Burnished

MARKET VALUES

	Raw	MS-69	MS-70
Value	$75	$95	$125

Note: "Raw" values are for average coins in original Mint packaging, not slabbed.

CERTIFICATION DATA

	Total	<MS-69	MS-69	MS-70
# Certified	22,022	28	2,374	19,620
Percentage		0.13%	10.78%	89.09%

Note: Data compiled from NGC and PCGS reports, September 2022.

2021-W, Flying Eagle Reverse (Type II), Proof

Mintage: 385,253 estimated.

Minted at West Point with W mintmark

As the first Type II Proof hailing from the West Point Mint, this coin became an instant hit with collectors. It was sold for an issue price of $73. The San Francisco Mint also struck the Type II in a regular Proof finish, giving collectors two options on obtaining the new design in this format.

2021-W, Flying Eagle Reverse (Type II), Proof

MARKET VALUES

	Raw	PF-69	PF-70
Value	$130	$150	$190

Note: "Raw" values are for average coins in original Mint packaging, not slabbed.

CERTIFICATION DATA

	Total	<PF-69	PF-69	PF-70
# Certified	142,793	117	16,658	126,018
Percentage		0.08%	11.67%	88.25%

Note: Data compiled from NGC and PCGS reports, September 2022.

2021-S, Flying Eagle Reverse (Type II), Proof

Mintage: 273,871 estimated.

Minted at San Francisco with S mintmark

The 2021-S Proof American Silver Eagle marks the gorgeous debut of the Type II design as rendered by the San Francisco Mint in this traditional Proof finish. It was offered at an issue price of $73. Along with the West Point Proofs carrying the Type II design, collectors could pursue two iterations of the new design in the popular Proof finish.

2021-S, Flying Eagle Reverse (Type II), Proof

MARKET VALUES

	Raw	PF-69	PF-70
Value	$145	$165	$195

Note: "Raw" values are for average coins in original Mint packaging, not slabbed.

CERTIFICATION DATA

	Total	<PF-69	PF-69	PF-70
# Certified	106,767	112	15,791	90,864
Percentage		0.10%	14.79%	85.10%

Note: Data compiled from NGC and PCGS reports, September 2022.

2021-S, Flying Eagle Reverse (Type II), Reverse Proof

Mintage: 124,823 estimated.

Minted at San Francisco with S mintmark

One half of the 2021 American Eagle One Ounce Silver Reverse Proof Two-Coin Set Designer Edition, this San Francisco Reverse Proof was the first example of the Type II Silver Eagle design in Reverse Proof and was paired with a West Point Reverse Proof sporting the last such iteration of the Type I motif.

2021-S, Flying Eagle Reverse (Type II), Reverse Proof

MARKET VALUES

	Raw	PF-69	PF-70
Value	$160	$195	$240

Note: "Raw" values are for average coins in original Mint packaging, not slabbed.

2021 American Eagle One-Ounce Silver Reverse Proof Two-Coin Set Designer Edition

Mintage: 124,823 estimated.

Minted at San Francisco and West Point with S and W mintmarks

Fielding the last Reverse Proof of the Type I era and the first of the Type II, the 2021 American Eagle One-Ounce Silver Reverse Proof Two-Coin Set Designer Edition was no slouch in sales. However, it did keep collectors on their toes as they anticipated a release date of August 24, which was pushed back to September 13, with the usual frenzied pace of online orders coming in right as the clock struck noon Eastern. The set, which spawned two low-mintage issues, sold for $175 and was soon trading for much more on the secondary market.

**2021 American Eagle One-Ounce Silver Reverse Proof
Two-Coin Set Designer Edition**
MARKET VALUES

	Raw	PF-69	PF-70
Value	$310	$380	$450

Note: "Raw" values are for average coins in
original Mint packaging, not slabbed.

THE YEAR 2022

The American Silver Eagle bearing Emily S. Damstra's reverse design, as rendered by Michael Gaudioso, saw its first full year of production. Demand for this coin was strong, with the bullion strikes, Proofs, and Burnished coins all posting respectable sales figures. American Silver Eagles drove a lot of the business in 2022, in part influenced by the popularity of the new designs but also driven by continued uncertainty in the greater state of the economy.

Current Events in 2022

Inflation in the United States reached its worst levels since the early 1980s, causing the Federal Reserve to raise interest rates in an attempt to stem the inflationary trend.

Geopolitical tensions were also grating on the nerves of the public, with President Vladimir Putin of Russia leading an invasion of neighboring Ukraine beginning on February 24. The conflict, essentially unprovoked by the standards of the free world, made defiant Ukrainian President Volodymyr Zelenskyy a hero in his own nation and a figure of hope around the world as he rallied his country against Russian troops.

The COVID-19 pandemic continued spreading around the world but began evolving into a weaker strain that, while still potentially deadly, was causing generally milder symptoms than was seen in cases of the virus during 2020 and 2021.

On May 24 an 18-year-old gunman killed 19 children and two teachers at an elementary school in Uvalde, Texas. Just ten days earlier, on May 14, another 18-year-old gunned down shoppers at a grocery store in Buffalo, New York, killing 10 and injuring three.

A China Eastern Airlines Boeing 737-800 crashed into a mountain near Guangzhou, killing all 132 aboard. A tornado tore through the town of Gaylord, Michigan, killing 2 and injuring 44, on May 20.

Top Gun: Maverick became one of the top movies of 2022, while "Boyfriend" by Dove Cameron and "As It Was" by Harry Styles topped the music charts. Primetime network TV drew big crowds with *Ghosts*, *Young Sheldon*, *NCIS*, and *This is Us*, and Netflix drummed up robust viewership of its own with the second season of *Bridgerton* and fourth season of *Stranger Things* drawing millions.

The 2022 Winter Olympic Games in Beijing, China, saw Finland win its first gold medal in ice hockey, while American snowboarding icon Shaun White retired after a successful career that landed him three Olympic gold medals. COVID-19 restrictions meant small, invite-only audiences for the Olympic events.

Queen Elizabeth II died in September, just a few months after celebrating her 70th anniversary on the throne. Her son, Charles, became the new ruler of Great Britain.

On the Numismatic Scene in 2022

While it was the 230th anniversary of the United States Mint, it was business as usual for minting operations, which churned out billions upon billions of coins. The American Silver Eagle program marched along with vigor as 2022 marked the first full calendar year during which the Type II design appeared on coins.

2022, Bullion Strike

Mintage: To be announced.

Minting locations to be announced

Production of the 2022 bullion strike started the year off strong, with 5,001,000 examples rolling off presses in January alone. Nearly 11 million bullion strikes were produced during the first six months of 2022.

2022, Bullion Strike

MARKET VALUES

	Raw	MS-69	MS-70
Value	$40	$45	$85

Note: "Raw" values are for average coins that are not professionally graded/slabbed.

CERTIFICATION DATA

	Total	<MS-69	MS-69	MS-70
# Certified	436,774	650	136,001	300,123
Percentage		0.15%	31.14%	68.71%

Note: Data compiled from NGC and PCGS reports, September 2022.

2022-W, Burnished

Mintage: To be announced.

Minted at West Point with W mintmark

The line of Burnished ("Uncirculated," in the terminology of the U.S. Mint) grew by one more in 2022 with this West Point effort. Issued for $67, this coin boasted an advertised product limit of 160,000.

2022-W, Burnished

MARKET VALUES

	Raw	MS-69	MS-70
Value	$75	$95	$125

Note: "Raw" values are for average coins in original Mint packaging, not slabbed.

CERTIFICATION DATA

	Total	<MS-69	MS-69	MS-70
# Certified	19,167	1	1,504	17,662
Percentage		0.01%	7.85%	92.15%

Note: Data compiled from NGC and PCGS reports, September 2022.

2022-W, Proof

Mintage: To be announced.

Minted at West Point with W mintmark

An ever-popular offering for the American Silver Eagle line, this emission from the West Point Mint was issued for $73.

2022-W, Proof

MARKET VALUES

	Raw	PF-69	PF-70
Value	$95	$110	$130

Note: "Raw" values are for average coins in original Mint packaging, not slabbed.

CERTIFICATION DATA

	Total	<PF-69	PF-69	PF-70
# Certified	122,569	21	10,788	111,760
Percentage		0.02%	8.80%	91.18%

Note: Data compiled from NGC and PCGS reports, September 2022.

2022-S, Proof

Mintage: To be announced.

Minted at San Francisco with S mintmark

This San Francisco issue joined its West Point sister in summer 2022, selling for $73 with an advertised product limit of 200,000.

2022-S, Proof

MARKET VALUES

	Raw	PF-69	PF-70
Value	$95	$115	$140

Note: "Raw" values are for average coins in original Mint packaging, not slabbed.

CERTIFICATION DATA

	Total	<PF-69	PF-69	PF-70
# Certified	24,997	3	1,870	23,134
Percentage		0.01%	7.48%	92.55%

Note: Data compiled from NGC and PCGS reports, September 2022.

APPENDIX

Can You Retire on Your Coins?

How Some Specialists Include Gold and Silver Coins in an IRA

by Joshua McMorrow-Hernandez

This article originally appeared in the April 2019 issue
of COINage *and is reprinted here with permission.*

It sounds like such a simple and fun concept: Buy some American Eagle gold and silver bullion coins, and place them in your IRA (Individual Retirement Arrangement). The advertisements urging you to do this are enticing. But despite the flashy ads and the shine of the metals themselves, the legal requirements and accounting rules are complicated.

Please seek the professional advice of a lawyer and accountant before attempting to include coins in an IRA. As I am not a lawyer or accountant, and while the information and advice in this article neither constitutes nor substitutes legal or accounting advice, it is nevertheless an educational primer into the complex world of precious metals and IRAs. And it's a world no less confusing now than it has been over the past several decades, as emerging tax laws open—or in some cases close—opportunities for merging coins into tax-deferred retirement plans.

Despite an oft-confusing set of rules, the opportunity for merging precious metals into a government-approved retirement plan has some benefits. Bullion-backed IRAs certainly have appeal among investors who worry about throwing their money into stocks and bonds, which took a rollercoaster ride in late 2018 amid domestic and international geopolitical upheaval.

IRAs have been around since 1974, when they were introduced with the enactment of the Employee Retirement Income Security Act (ERISA). These tax-sheltered accounts seem may seem simple in principle, but they come with an ever-evolving set of rules that keep investors, financial planners, and tax attorneys on their toes.

In the early days, IRAs were limited to individuals who were not covered by employee-based retirement plans, such as pensions. They are offered by financial institutions to provide workers with a retirement savings account that allows them to reduce their taxable income by the amount of their contributions.

The rules of the IRA game were different in the early years. From the mid-1970s through 1981, maximum yearly contributions were only $1,500 or 15% of one's annual income—whichever was less. But for a time, these investors also had greater choice with the types of assets they could roll into an IRA. In 1979, the U.S. Labor Department loosened some ERISA regulations, opening IRA doors for non-income producing assets, such as artwork, diamonds, stamps, and collectible coins among these.

A major game changer came barely two years later, on August 13, 1981, with the passage of the Economic Recovery Tax Act (ERTA) endorsed by President Ronald Reagan as part of his massive tax overhaul. The sweeping changes opened up IRAs to all working taxpayers under the age of 70-1/2, with maximum contributions increasing to $2,000 per year as of 1982, and $250 yearly on behalf of a nonworking spouse. But there were some drawbacks with those ERTA-related changes, with the most notable of these for numismatists being the exclusion of collectible coins.

Congress permitted investors to roll American Eagle silver and gold coins into IRAs with the introduction of the United States bullion-coin program in 1986. For many years, these were the only coins one could include in their IRA plans. More changes came with the Taxpayer Relief Act of 1997, which opened doors for many other types of bullion coins to be rolled into IRAs, including investment-grade precious-metal coins from other nations around the world. These include silver, gold, platinum, and palladium versions of British Britannias and Lunar series pieces, Chinese Pandas, Canadian Maple Leafs, Austrian Philharmonics, Mexican Libertads, Australian Koalas, and other popular bullion coins from around the world.

Since their debut in 2008, United States Gold Buffalo coins have also been included among IRA-safe products. Additionally, certain silver, gold, platinum, and palladium bars and rounds produced by NYMEX (New York Mercantile Exchange) or COMEX (Commodity Exchange, Inc.) -approved refineries or national government mints with a fineness of at least 0.995 purity are also permitted. Most precious metals bars are at least 0.999 fine, surpassing that government-stipulated minimum purity threshold for precious metals products in IRAs. That purity threshold obviously excludes a variety of bullion-related products that are popular sellers, including silver dollars, 90% silver Proof sets, and pre-1965 90% silver coins in any quantity.

However, the rules aren't always clear cut. In some regards, the policies regarding IRAs and precious metals can even seem downright arbitrary and inconsistent. For example, American Gold Eagles, which have a gold purity of 0.9167 fineness, are permitted in IRAs. Yet, South African Krugerrands, which also boast 0.9167 purity and have been among the world's most popular gold bullion coins since their inception in 1967, are not. This major exception marks one of many areas where some investors often seek loopholes and, in some cases, eventually find themselves in legal hot water with the government.

For many, the "safe" investment route isn't lined with paper and promises. Rather, it's precious metals that frequently proves more alluring. Silver and gold have an attractive track record, especially as compared to stocks and other investments vehicles during times of trade wars, stock market plunges, and energy crises. But gold and silver are not sure winners.

Both silver and gold are significantly lower in price from their most recent highs in 2011, with silver having peaked at $48 per ounce in April of that year and gold topping $1,800 a few months later in August. As of press time, silver stands at about $16 per ounce and gold hovers around $1,320. And these figures represent relatively performance over the past few years and certainly down markedly from their feverish levels of nearly a decade ago.

Yes, paper investments in failed companies such as Texas energy company Enron Corporation are now worthless, while others—like the once-mighty Sears-Roebuck nationwide department store chain—hang on by proverbial threads as mediocre penny stocks. But, overall, stocks have performed well over the past few years. Even with its recent troubles, the Dow Jones Industrial Average market index is way up since 2011, when the average closing level was nearly 12,000. As of press time, that figure hangs around 24,500.

The above point-counterpoint illustration of recent stock trajectory versus bullion performance is not a case against investing in precious metals, but rather a market scenario that should be considered with prudence when deciding a retirement investment strategy. And prudence is one of the key ingredients for successful long-term outcomes when choosing how to build your bullion IRA and determining how far to push the envelope with not just the types of precious metal products you place in your IRA, but also how and where you hold them (more on that shortly).

Anyone who wishes to enroll precious-metals coins into an IRA needs to study up on the topic or risk losing his or her proverbial shirt to Uncle Sam. Here are three of the most common mistakes: depositing coins that aren't permitted in an IRA program; attempting to roll over bullion coins that have been purchased outside of an IRA program (i.e. trying to place coins that were purchased before the IRA was initiated); and attempting to store IRA-enrolled precious-metals coins at home or in a personal vault.

As of press time, February 2019, the government allows each individual under the age of 50 to contribute as much as $5,500 per year into his or her IRA. [The limit has since been raised to $6,000.] Those who will be over the age 50 by the end of a given year may deposit as much as $6,500 annually [now $7,000] beginning that year. While one can theoretically throw all of that annual allotment into precious metals, a host of financial advisors suggest diversifying retirement account assets to prevent or mitigate losses should one type of investment, such as stocks, bonds, or—yes—precious metals, suffer substantial losses. In other words, you've probably already heard some of the best financial advice you'll get anywhere: Avoid putting all of your proverbial eggs into one basket.

Every financial advisor may offer you different specific advice on what share of an investment should go into precious metals, depending on your long-range goals, age, and investment desires. But many leading experts pitch a figure of about 10%. So if one contributes about $5,000 to his or her IRA in a particular year and invests 10% of that figure into precious metals, that works out to $500 per year allocated for IRA-related bullion investments. Of course, that does not leave much room for buying gold when it trades at $1,320 per ounce. And this is exactly where those investors with a zealously speculative spirit for buying precious metals need to exercise a degree of prudence and patience.

Many believe they can skirt this law by rolling over their existing, pre-IRA bullion holdings into their retirement accounts. But not so fast! The only precious metals you currently own that may rolled into a new IRA plan are those that are already deposited in an existing IRA. In other words, you may not deposit IRA-approved precious-metals coins, such as American Silver Eagles, from your personal vault or bank safety deposit box into your new IRA. Only those pieces which you may already hold in another IRA can be rolled over into your new plan. Even then, only an IRS-approved custodian can physically and logistically handle that task for you.

And then comes the question of which coins can and can't be deposited into an IRA. The list I provided to you of American Eagle products and other .995-fine or better coins, bars, and rounds from the United States and various world mints serves as a good rule of thumb on what you *can* include in your IRA. With this knowledge, you can avoid scams from predatory companies falsely claiming Liberty Walking half dollars, Morgan dollars, Saint-Gaudens $20 gold double eagles, and other popular collectible coins are tax-safe and legitimate IRA assets. Perhaps they were in 1980. But they certainly aren't today. Fall for a bullion IRA scam like that and you'll be the one footing the tax bill.

Another precious-metals IRA trap to avoid? One suggesting you can keep your bullion assets at home. Some companies claim you can do this with crafty legal finagling. Unfortunately, these "home storage" bullion IRA plans often lead to Uncle Sam knocking on their owners' doors. That's because IRA regulations generally require those tax-deferred precious-metal holdings to be physically stored with an approved, independent custodian.

This means you can't keep your IRA precious metals in your own vault, bank deposit box, or another type of personal safe. They must be located in an IRA-regulated offsite depository. One of the most popular, Delaware Depository, is preferred by many investors. Based in the northeastern city of Wilmington, Delaware, Delaware Depository is close to major access routes but geographically far from places such as New York City and Washington, D.C., which are prime targets for events that could threaten the assets stored within the facility.

In the cases of most self-directed IRAs, choosing an approved depository is up to the individual investor. Of utmost concern is making sure the depository has received positive ratings from the Better Business Bureau. This is an absolute must, and investors should choose a company that has received an A+ rating from the Better Business Bureau and has a solid track record of customer satisfaction and problem resolution. Some factors to consider before selecting a depository include deciding between segregated storage or unsegregated storage. In segregated storage, your precious metals products are stored separately from those held by others, and those exact pieces are returned to you upon withdrawal, whereas in unsegregated storage types of precious metals together as opposed to separating them. So, if you place a 2010 tenth-ounce Gold Eagle in an unsegregated depository, you'll get a 2010 tenth-ounce Gold Eagle back, but it may not be the one you deposited.

Other considerations in choosing a depository include facility insurance coverage and annual storage fees. These are important factors to weigh, because they affect not just level of protection you receive, but also how much you may pay per year to keep your precious metals in said depository. Additionally, precious metals IRAs may incur annual audit fees possibly ranging from $100 to $150 per year.

The process of buying precious metals and having them stored in a depository is relatively simple, though requires some paperwork. The IRA owner requests his or her custodian, such as the bank, credit union, trust company, or another IRS-licensed and -regulated entity to make the purchase of precious metal assets and then directs those assets be sent to a specific depository. In many cases, bullion dealers and brokers can facilitate such transactions.

For many investors, having an independent custodian purchase precious metal coins and then submit them to a depository is a practical solution that evokes little emotion in the account owner. However, there are many in the numismatic community who may be intrigued by the idea of rolling precious metals into a tax-deferred retirement account, but simply can't stomach the idea of neither personally handling their valuable gold and silver coins nor keeping them unseen in some faraway vault. Half the fun for self-proclaimed bullion "stackers" is watching their treasure trove grow in physical size and worth. And many of these individuals simply can't fathom the idea of letting their personal stacks out of sight. For them, the physical arrangements of a bullion IRA are a major deal breaker, period.

It's in part due to those individuals that so-called "home delivery," "home-storage," or "self-storage" IRAs have a market. However, these tempting "home-storage" offers come with several pitfalls, not the least of which is possible taxation of all assets held within—a highly counterproductive penalty. Some of the more legally "creative" self-storage proposals require setting up a Limited Liability Corporation (LLC) custodial entity for the account owner, and as the IRA owner also owns the LLC, he or she would, in essence, become his or her own custodian and be able to physically keep the gold or silver wherever he or she wishes. If not done correctly, such an arrangement could trigger a tax event, and other legal liabilities could also follow. It's certainly not a game for the feeble or faint of heart.

In a recent report from the state government of Texas on the matter, Attorney General Ken Paxton warned gold consumers that home storage of precious metals IRAs are a myth. He went on to say: "Be wary of home storage IRA plans, as these have not been thoroughly tested with the U.S. Treasury or IRS. Stick with reputable independent custodians."

The Texas attorney general and his department outlined several key risks with home-storage IRAs, including the prevalence of scammers who prey on those who wish to physically buy or hold their own precious metals.

Should an IRS audit reveal a taxpayer storing his or her precious metals IRA assets at home, the penalties could be steep, including the owner paying federal income tax on all of the assets and a possible 10% penalty if the consumer is under the age of 59-1/2. Consequently, taxpayers placing gold and silver coins in IRAs must use an established custodian or financial institution that specializes in holding precious metals for IRAs in compliance with the IRS requirements.

During his over 40 years as a prominent New York City coin attorney, David L. Ganz, author of *Planning Your Rare Coin Retirement* (Bonus Books, 1998), has advised many individuals and institutions on numismatic legal nuances. He says there are many gray areas when it comes to the unique and complex issues concerning precious metals IRAs. "I don't think that anybody is providing home delivery services to try and scam anybody. I think that they are creating, in some respects, confusion as to what is and is not allowed."

Ganz believes one step investors can take in protecting themselves from penalties is to receive written guarantees, both on the types of precious metals material stored in an IRA as well as how or where it is deposited. "If you can get someone that offers a guarantee, and that something is includable or not includable, it's always better than having a situation where the guarantee is the product itself. But none of that says that it's actually good, it just says it's capable of being put into the IRA."

Still, Ganz says the very topic of what's permissible or not permissible in an IRA has inspired colorful debate among he and his colleagues. "I think the best way to describe it is there are some gold and silver coins are permitted explicitly by law. Some are specifically excluded, and then there's a muddy area where the experts just don't agree because the language is not specific enough to be clear."

He goes on, "I'm not one to say that they're wrong, but I know that late Diane Piret [of Industry Council for Tangible Assets, now the National Coin & Bullion Association] and I had many long arguments on this point, and she didn't persuade me, and I didn't persuade her. You can put [collectible] coins in IRAs under the tax law until the passage of [clause] 314-B of the 1981 Revenue Act—that's your starting point. But the thing is, 314-B took away the rights that an individual had to put coins in general into their IRAs. That doesn't make it any clearer, it just gives bolsterance to the opinions that circulate."

Ganz suggests much of the confusion over what coins really can and can't go into an IRA, or if those assets could remain in the personal possession of an account owner, would be cleared up if someone simply took the matter up with the IRS in a courtroom. The subsequent ruling would ultimately set some type of precedent for other investors and what they could or couldn't do with their bullion IRAs.

"Actually trying [the matter] as a case before the IRS—nobody has done that yet," Ganz says. "There have been some people who have thought about it but haven't yet because the filing fee is about $25,000. I don't think anyone is willing, at least at this time, to be the person who pays the 25 grand and then basically give away the intellectual property that is associated with it."

Until then, several questions linger such as whether or not American Silver Eagles with Proof, Burnished, or other special numismatic finishes are acceptable for inclusion in an IRA. Most interpretations of the IRA rules say they are, but there are occasions where the numismatic nature of these special-finish bullion coins give investors pause. "I have an opinion that they are includable," Ganz concludes of Proof, Burnished, and other semi-numismatic bullion coins. "And there are others who have an opinion that they are not." At this time, the consensus is Proof American Eagles in *original holders* are acceptable, but those certified by major grading companies such as the Professional Coin Grading Service (PCGS) or Numismatic Guaranty Corporation [now known as Numismatic Guaranty Company] (NGC) are not.

Complicating the problem even more is determining set prices for IRA-held coins and how much over spot they are worth. This could affect everything from accurate asset reporting to potentially pushing certain bullion coins into "collectible" territory if their market value significantly exceeds their intrinsic spot value. "One of the problems with IRA bullion is you have to give an annual report to the Treasury report as to what the worth of the package is, and the prices are all over the board. There is no particular guide that the government uses to evaluate prices."

Determining how much your precious metals assets are worth may prove challenging, especially if there are no guidelines set forth by the IRS or other government agencies. Perhaps one place to start is with the dealer wholesale prices as listed in *Monthly Greysheet*, which has been distributed by CDN Publishing since 1963.

While there may not be a clear set of rules as to what type of premium over spot constitutes a coin being a numismatic collectible rather than a bullion item, it still pays to know the market values for IRA-worthy bullion coins. This can help you avoid overpaying for coins and give you a clearer sense on the true market value of your IRA bullion assets both for auditing purposes and for strategizing liquidation scenarios.

With silver at about $16 per ounce as of press time, *Greysheet* shows bullion-quality late-date one-ounce American Silver Eagles trading in wholesale circles for about $17.83 apiece. Meanwhile those same pieces fetch about $21 each in the retail sector according to the CPG retail guide. Meanwhile, Proof Silver Eagles go for about $38 each in wholesale trades while they sell for $45 in retail settings. For its part, gold takes $1,320 per ounce as of late January, and a one-ounce American Gold Eagle goes for $1,334 in dealer-to-dealer transactions, while they notch about $1,670 in retail trades. Proof one-ounce Gold Eagles snag $1,329 apiece in the dealer circle while they take $1,660 in the retail arena.

Understanding spreads between spot and market prices not only maximizes your ability to better strategize the inclusion of precious metals in your IRA, but it may also help you dodge tax-related pitfalls. Donald Kagin of Kagin's numismatic services in Tiburon, California, says investors need to be careful trying to deposit bullion products that have numismatic-like price premiums. "Presumably, if premiums rise causing certain coins to be valued above 15% over melt value by price guides, then they may be deemed unacceptable."

That essentially means placing rare Proof eagles, such as the coveted 1995-W American Silver Eagle (a $3,000+ coin according to *Greysheet*), in an IRA could trigger some undesirable consequences from Uncle Sam. So, too, might his discovery of slabbed Eagles in your IRA, and most certainly those with the numismatically "perfect" grades of MS-70 or Proof-70.

Ultimately, the best strategy for determining what coins to place in an IRA—and how to hold those assets, comes down to playing it safe. Why run the risk of facing stressful audits, expensive tax penalties, and unnecessary paperwork? Remember, one of the benefits of investing in an IRA is the opportunity to accumulate tax-sheltered funds for your future plans. Of course, this means playing by Uncle Sam's rules. That's not what everyone reading this article wants to see. But, if you optimize your precious-metals IRA within legally conservative guidelines then the light at the end of the tunnel will be bright.

APPENDIX B

Protecting Your Coins Against the Elements

by Joshua McMorrow-Hernandez

*This is a condensed version of an article that originally appeared in the
February-March 2020 issue of* COINage *and is reprinted here with permission.*

Storms, winds, floods, and fires are nothing new—humankind has coped with such natural disasters for millions of years. Numismatists are increasingly finding themselves and their coin collections at the mercy of Mother Nature.

A major threat to folks who live in the Midwest and Plains states are tornadoes. About 1,000 tornadoes touch down every year in a region of the United States known as Tornado Alley, encompassing the states of Oklahoma, Kansas, the Texas Panhandle, Nebraska, eastern South Dakota, and eastern Colorado.

In Tornado Alley, climate change brings an increased risk of more frequent and particularly more violent tornadoes. It's a threat that former APMEX Director of Numismatics Michael Garofalo knows all too well. "As someone who lives in Oklahoma, we tend to always be 'weather aware,'" says the New England transplant. "I keep my coins and numismatic treasures in several bank boxes in multiple locations. In that way, if anything happens at one bank, I'm still protected."

He also says insurance on the assets he keeps at each bank is quite reasonable. "You sleep better at night knowing your collection is secure and insured!"

He remarks that most bank safe deposit boxes aren't insured by the bank, but you can purchase discounted coin collection insurance as a member of the American Numismatic Association or through an insurance agent. "A rider to your homeowner's policy protecting a coin collection that is stored in as bank vault should not be very expensive," says Garofalo.

"Keep copies of your purchase invoices and take photographs of your more expensive coins or currency. It is an insurance policy that you might never want to use, but you can rest more comfortably knowing you have it."

In addition to robust insurance policies, Garofalo and his family also have a tornado shelter in their home and own a hand-crank weather radio, which he says can be a "lifesaver." He goes on to say that, "whether you believe in climate change or not, it is important to safeguard what you own. Weather is nothing if not unpredictable and it can change in a minute. Keeping good records and having photographs of valuables is very important should the worst weather happen to you."

As tornadoes terrorize collectors in the Midwest and Plains, numismatists closer to the Pacific are paying more attention to the fires raging with greater fury in the West. And while fires aren't necessarily a form of weather, their frequency and intensity are directly related to weather patterns.

Drought conditions help create kindling ground for fires, which may start with a lightning bolt, a downed electrical wire, an unattended campfire, or a careless toss of a lit cigarette. Sometimes, and more nefariously, arson is the cause. Summer is the dry season for much of California, and fires are most intense in autumn, when conditions there are at their driest. Dry vegetation fuels fires and strong winds fan the flames, with the Santa Ana winds of southern California capable of carrying embers for many miles.

Unfortunately, climate change is expected to bring hotter, drier conditions to much of the American Southwest, and researchers are already seeing the results of this. Since the year 2000, an average of 72,400 fires have blazed 7 million acres each year—and that's about double the number of acres set alight by wildfire during the 1990s.

In California, wildfire records are being eclipsed almost each year. And as more urban development converts formerly virgin forests into new, densely populated communities, people are putting themselves ever more on the brink of danger. Unfortunately, many have already lost their lives to California's wildfires, as was the case with the devastating Camp Fire that killed 86 people and decimated the northeastern Sacramento Valley city of Paradise in November 2018. Virtually all of the town's 26,800 residents were displaced—most permanently.

Many of the people who had homes in Paradise were coin collectors, including Joe Best. He began collecting coins when he was a child in the 1950s and '60s, following in his dad's numismatic footsteps. Like many collectors, he focused on building a family and career in his middle years, but his coin collection remained a constant throughout that busy time in his life. He has also passed his love of numismatics onto his son and grandson. Best has clearly experienced many joys in his life, but also many sorrows. The worst, he said came on the morning of November 8, 2018.

"I woke up to a red glow," he describes in a blog post published in March 2019 on the Professional Coin Grading Service (PCGS) website. "The red glow was a fire way off in the distance that we've seen so many times. Not a big, red flag—yet. The next thing I knew is this fire was not like any other fire in the state of California, where I have lived since I was born in 1951. It was moving extremely fast," he writes.

He heard explosions all around him as propane tanks blew up from the heat of the fast-approaching fire. "We escaped with our lives along with our animals so for that right there I thank God in heaven." He left with armfuls of irreplaceable photo albums and a few coin albums, but his main collection was left in a 1942 jeweler's safe in the house, which soon was reduced to ashes by the fire.

Saving Coins from Natural Disasters

While some of Best's coins were unfortunately destroyed, many survived and were conserved by PCGS. "The challenge with these coins comes from how unique every situation is and the need to improvise and adapt our procedures to handle each individual case. They all arrive in varying degrees of distress, often involving raw and holdered coins from both PCGS and other third-party services," explains PCGS Senior Director of Marketing Heather Boyd, who personally handled many of Best's coins and helped oversee the efforts to save hundreds of collectible coins recovered from the Camp Fire and other fires around the country via PCGS Restoration.

While PCGS Restoration helps conserve coins that have been impacted from a variety of natural disasters, cases like Best's are familiar to the PCGS team. "Fire is definitely the number one natural disaster for which we receive submissions," Boyd adds.

She also says that while much of California faces regular threats from wildfires, the company's headquarters near Irvine is not likely to be impacted by wildfires. "Even so, we follow strict fire safety code. Coins in our custody are also 100% insured."

PCGS Vice President of Operations David Rosenberg notes the most difficult part of the task is removing coins from melted holders. "While encapsulated coins fair significantly better than raw coins and often experience very little ill effects from fires so long as the coins remained covered, the process of removing the disfigured slabs is time consuming and requires great care."

Rosenberg says the process of conserving a coin begins by carefully removing the coin from its holder and then undergoes the company's standard process of evaluating the coin for restoration, namely determining if the coin is a good candidate for restoration. "Most coins encapsulated in a PCGS holder fare extremely well and experience little to no grade change, it is undoubtedly the safest way to store your collection," he says. "Our holders are made of an inert plastic which means, even if it melts, it does not release chemicals that negatively impact the coin."

The composition of the holder is important, as many chemicals can impart adverse effects on coins when exposed to high heat. "The number-one way a collector can ensure the safety of their collection is to have it graded and encapsulated by a reputable third-party grading company that has put the time and effort into researching a holder that will stand the test of time and the environment," remarks Rosenberg.

Back in Florida, David Camire at Numismatic Conservation Service (NCS), a subsidiary of Numismatic Guaranty Company (NGC), sees coins affected by a plethora of disasters, including those involving water. "People generally focus on hurricanes as a wind event, but much of the damage is a result of flooding," explains the NCS president. "NCS can conserve coins that have been affected by floods. The prospects for NCS's conservation depend on the length of exposure and the type of water—fresh water, salt water, or sewage," he adds.

"In addition, whether the coins were raw or holdered matters, since coins in NGC holders generally fare much better than raw coins." Camire notes that every case is different but, at the very least, NCS can stop further damage to the coins. Ultimately, Camire says coins and moisture shouldn't mix. Yet, water is associated with many of the natural disasters that are becoming more frequent and sever due to climate change, including hurricanes, tropical storms, and greater amounts of localized seasonal rainfall and humidity.

"Collectors should be aware of potential risks based on where they live," Camire says. "Along the Gulf and Atlantic coasts, hurricanes pose a risk." Meanwhile, heat and humidity affect large swaths of the nation. "Hobbyists need to make sure their coins are in an environment controlled for temperature and humidity." He says attics, basements, and garages are not recommended, nor are storage facilities. "Even certain bank vaults may not necessarily be ideal. Collectors should ask specific questions about the temperature range and humidity, including after hours."

Collectors who submit their coins to NCS or parent company NGC need not worry about their coins when they've arrived at the firm's offices for processing and evaluation. Although NGC's headquarters are in Florida, a state many mistakenly believe is geologically flat and entirely located at or just above sea level, the company's around-the-clock climate-controlled offices are located 25 feet above sea level and more than nine miles inland. "It is not in a flood zone or in any of Sarasota County's hurricane evacuation zones," Camire explains. "Nevertheless, the building is rated to withstand a major hurricane."

Numismatic expert Scott Travers is not only a longtime coin collector, but he's also a lifelong Republican. Yet, despite the common assumption that individuals aligning with conservative viewpoints generally eschew climate-change matters, the popular numismatic personality admits he is worried about the increasing climate threats. "I'm concerned about the impacts climate change may have on my coin collection," he says.

Travers, who wrote *The Coin Collector's Survival Manual, Revised Seventh Edition*, looks at the matter from the standpoint of both preventing coins from succumbing to tragedy and resolving damages should they unfortunately occur. "Whether manmade or natural, the need to be prepared for catastrophes such as hurricanes, floods, tornadoes, and fires is of supreme importance," he says.

"Of course, simple survival is the principal priority," he reiterates, "but beyond safeguarding your person, anyone who collects rare coins or has gold or silver bullion as a form of 'insurance' should give careful consideration to how those coins or bullion would be safeguarded or accessed in an emergency—and how he or she would be protected against serious financial loss in the event these assets were lost, damaged, or destroyed."

In the context of potentially more frequent and intense natural disasters, the first matters one needs to consider is insurance, which due to numerous devastating hurricanes, fires, and floods, is often more difficult than ever to obtain these days. "In obtaining insurance, you should be absolutely certain that your policy does not exclude coverage for floods or other natural disasters," Travers notes. "As a matter of course, many home insurance policies contain exclusions for natural disasters. In New York City, for example, some of the largest insurance companies routinely exclude coverage for earthquakes, and you have to specifically request that coverage and pay extra to obtain it—perhaps a couple of hundred dollars per year on an average policy or $25 to $50 on a smaller policy."

In the face of the insurance industry's drastic responses to an increasing number of expensive disasters, Travers tells those who have inclusive "all-risk" policies to be extra watchful for substantial premium increases upon policy renewal or reinsurance. "Customers holding such insurance could well encounter higher premiums because the reinsurers would either raise their fees substantially or decline to accept the risk altogether."

And don't expect the Federal Emergency Management Agency (FEMA) to kick in the funds to replace your coin collection. As numismatic expert, author, and attorney David Ganz warns, federal insurance plans are covering less today, and those whose coin collections are damaged or destroyed by fire or flooding episodes (even floods that originate due to hurricanes or other media-headlining disasters) will generally not see a dime for such damages.

"For major collections, I recommend choosing Lloyd's of London," Ganz suggests, referring to the British-based company accustomed to insuring major rarities and other novelties. "It's the kind of place where you go to get legs insured," he explains. "For more modest collections of perhaps $2,500 or so, it's possible to get those insured by home insurance companies." The American Numismatic Association (ANA) can also help put collectors in touch with insurance agencies that cover coin collections.

Planning for the Present, Preparing for the Future

Collectors who live in areas at increased risk of floods, fires, tornadoes, or other natural disasters need to reexamine not just their coin storage and protection methods but also their insurance policies. Those who don't have fire or flood coverage should be extra judicious in choosing a plan that provides protection from these and other excluded disasters—the sooner, the better.

This is also the opportunity to beef up the immediate protection of coin collections. That could mean buying new, inert holders and albums with fewer harmful chemicals that, when heated or exposed to moisture, may pose increased risks to coins. Perhaps it's time to submit raw coins for encapsulation by reputable third-party coin certification firms so they are encased within safe, secure holders.

And whether threatened by a flood, fire, or hurricane, a coin collection stands a better chance of survival when it's protected by a top-quality vault. If seeking insurance for their collections, collectors may have to buy a vault, and it will likely need to be approved by Underwriters Laboratories (UL) or abide by other guidelines set forth by the insurance agency.

Vaults and safes are typically classified by their overall strength and fire rating. Internal temperature tolerance is just as important as external temperature resistance. A vault that withstands outer temperatures of 2,000 degrees Fahrenheit but keeps the internal temperature below 500 degrees won't adequately protect coin slabs that could melt at 350 or 400 degrees. However, a vault rated 125 UL will keep the internal temperature below 125 degrees—much safer temperatures for coins and holders contained within. And the more protection offered by the vault, the better insurance coverage one could receive and for lower premiums, too.

Climate change may be a new reality, but it need not take the joy out of coin collecting. By accepting the situation and adapting to the new and increasing risks we face from natural disasters of all kinds, numismatists can continue enjoying the hobby they love while preparing for—and hopefully preventing—the worst. And that's something everyone can get behind.

APPENDIX
C

Keeping Track of Your Coins Can Be Taxing

★

by Joshua McMorrow-Hernandez
This article originally appeared in the April-May 2020
issue of COINage *and is reprinted here with permission.*

Surely you keep your coins safe in an album, folder, or display case. Perhaps your numismatic books are organized neatly on a shelf in your study. And you might even dedicate a special spot for storing your numismatic supplies and accessories. But how well do you keep records of the valuables you have in your collection?

Is managing your numismatic collection on paper, a computer program, or smartphone app something you do at all? Have a thorough list of your numismatic assets in case a natural disaster or other emergency strikes? Know what to show Uncle Sam in case he (or his well-dressed associates) comes knocking on your door for answers about the bullion coins you claim for tax deferment in your Individual Retirement Account? Are you aware of the stipulations—and loopholes—concerning collectibles and retirement accounts? And, as much as you may not want to think about this, do you have all your affairs sorted so your heirs know what to do with your collection—or even where to *find* it?

Yes, these questions may be heavy and many, but they're designed to get you thinking about keeping your numismatic house organized on paper. And these probably aren't the questions you signed up to answer when you began collecting coins—or selling coins, if you're a part-time coin dealer or numismatist who has liquidated coins for personal reasons. Yet for better or perhaps worse, we're no longer in an era when a simple handshake is good enough to seal a numismatic deal, or in a time when financial matters can be sorted merely in one's own mind, or when taxing authorities turn a blind eye to profits made on a coin sold for the purpose of upgrading a collection—or for simply paying the rent.

The truly vast and diverse topic of numismatic-related documentation is worthy of many books individually dedicated to various facets of this ever-evolving topic. But it's introduced here to familiarize you with the subject and to hopefully prompt an evaluation of what you can do to get—or keep—your numismatic financial house in order.

Records are Your Friend

Robert Fligel knows finance, and he loves numismatics. He began collecting coins when he was a kid, organizing his finds in blue Whitman folders. His love for money evolved from collecting it in the form of coinage. Graduating from the University of North Carolina in 1972 with a bachelor's degree in accounting, he practiced as a Certified Public Accountant for many years before parlaying his love for money into recruiting and staffing efforts for CPA firms. He later founded RF Precious Metals, LLC to assist collectors and investors with asset protection and to help facilitate the purchase or sale of rare coins and bullion portfolios.

He tells collectors and investors that the best way to protect themselves—and their assets—is to keep clear record of them. "I believe folks should be very upfront with insurance companies, taxing agents, and others about their collections," he says. "What people do behind closed doors is nobody's business, but if you get on the wrong side of the law, government, or Internal Revenue Service, it would be torturous."

Fligel says IRS audits these days are often less dramatic than what some people may recall from an earlier era or may have seen on a television show or in a movie. "If you ever get audited, and the percentage of those who do is very low these days, more often than not it's a correspondence audit," he explains. "The IRS is no longer really doing desk audits, where an IRS associate comes to an office to see records. Most times these days they request clarification on certain documentation, and if you can't furnish a receipt, they'll send you a bill for that tax amount."

But that doesn't mean you can't get in hot water—very quickly—if you don't have records and receipts to back up your financial dealings. "There's something called the Taxpayer Compliance Measurement Program [TCMP], in which taxpayers are randomly selected to help the IRS gather statistics." And these audits are thorough. "If you're selected for one of these audits, you have to document *everything* on your tax return. Every income. Every expense. Every cent," he notes. "Even people who keep good records don't keep *everything*," he adds. "It's probably a little easier these days as banks keep track of everything but gathering all of these documents can be difficult."

Keeping invoices, receipts, disbursements, and a chronological record of all transactions is the way to go. Thankfully, there is a plethora of computer programs and smartphone apps that help make swift work of keeping these records organized and readily accessible. "Whether you're aggressive or unaggressive about keeping records, it's important. Whether you have a paper ledger, an online program, an Excel spreadsheet, or an accountant do it for you, just keep a good record."

"Who Gets Daddy's Coins?"

Sadly, that's a question that is asked every day and often without a definitive answer. "I think there's a huge percentage of people who do not have wills for a variety of reasons," Fligel says. "Maybe these folks don't want to face their mortality or take the time to set up a will. But, regarding coins, it's even more important to face this serious human-nature issue."

Fligel relates a story he once read about one particularly eccentric coin collector who had valuable coins hidden in his house in different places, and his heirs weren't even aware of them. "The next thing you know, things get thrown away, the coins end up at the flea market or in the dump, and nobody knew about them except the collector. . . . In similar scenarios, the collector passes away and the collectibles are hidden somewhere until the new homeowners get a nice surprise while cleaning the house or remodeling it," he says. "And hopefully they went to a reputable coin dealer."

The bottom line here? If you don't want your collectibles to end up in the garbage, be sold for pennies on the dollar at a flea market, or land in the hands of a total stranger, plan ahead and make sure your valuables are accounted for in a legal will. "You can't make anybody do anything, and I'm the exact opposite—I'm an over-planner—but if you're doing something that's worthwhile such as collecting coins and there's value to it, and you want your heirs to get your items, whether they're coins, paintings, silverware, or other heirlooms, you *have to* document it."

Documenting all of your valuables doesn't have to be as daunting as it may sound. "Whether you do it through technology or in a notebook with a pen and paper, there are many avenues for keeping track of what you own and where it's stored so that your heirs will have knowledge of the assets you own and wish to share," Fligel says.

The goal with creating such directives is preventing the loss of your assets to a government agency, having them end up in the wrong hands, or touching off a family feud. "Your loved ones need to know who is going to get your stuff. Otherwise it will be a free-for-all with fights over who gets Daddy's coins."

He suggests using an estate-planning checklist to ensure each and every potential issue is addressed. Another important consideration is to have a black book of individuals who should be contacted when the times comes for your assets to be parceled out. It helps your heirs even more if you list out professional individuals, attorneys and accountants, and collectibles firms you trust in handling the sale of these items, should such transactions be in the cards.

"Have an attorney or financial professional assist you in this," he advises. And divulge *all* the details. "Don't forget to provide login credentials such as usernames and passwords for your accounts," he notes. "If your loved ones—or even the agents helping you carry out your wishes—don't know your passwords, they can't get in." And be sure to (discreetly) share any information on where you may be hiding your valuables. "It's not unwise to hide your coins, cash, or other valuables in secret places," says the New York financial planner, who recommends storing numismatic items in safety deposit boxes maintained in the name of a limited liability company (LLC) or a trust. "But your heirs need to know where the assets and related documents are when the time comes."

At the end of the day, an ounce of planning now is worth a pound of needless courtroom probate circuses in the future. "If you spent your whole life saving money, sending the kids to college, and being a good person, are you going to chuck all of that just because you're dead?" Fligel asks. "Keep it simple for them! You hear so many stories about surviving spouses being lost in a financial and logistic nightmare and paying thousands of dollars for an accountant to recreate records that may exist somewhere—but nobody knows where," he laments. "Don't be selfish! Make it easy for your heirs. Don't leave a giant mess for them."

Retiring on Coins

Coins have been permitted in IRAs since the tax-deferred retirement plans debuted in 1974. But the *types* of coins allowed in these accounts have changed over the years. Before 1982, numismatists could roll their collectible coins into IRAs, using vintage coinage as part of a tax-deferred savings account redeemable for funds upon retirement. But legislation that was passed in the early 1980s changed this part of the IRA code, banning numismatic coins (and other types of collectibles) from inclusion in these retirement accounts. Despite the repeal of collectibles from IRAs, bullion coins are still permitted.

"I think everybody should have 5% to 10% of their asset allocation—maybe even more—in precious metals or rare coins," Fligel advises. "It's a good hedge against inflation and what I see as instability in the financial system. But learn how to do it the *right* way—know what to buy, how to buy it, who to buy it from, how to evaluate dealers, and all the other nuances."

Then there's understanding what you can and can't put into your IRA. For example, American Eagle bullion coins are allowed in these plans, while pre-1933 United States gold coins aren't. What's more, much to the chagrin of collectors and investors who like to have physical possession of their gold and silver, IRAs require that all tangible assets must be managed by a custodian and kept in an off-site depository.

"Do you have a custodian? Do you have a depository?" asks Fligel. "These are all important matters. And if you mess it up, it's a serious thing. Tax penalties and loss of the tax-deferred aspect of the IRA converting to taxable status are just some of the immediate risks." In these cases, having a financial advisor and very clear records of what you own and where it is stored (if you've rolled your qualified bullion coinage into your IRA the right way) can save your back. "Penalties and all that stuff are real. And it's really best to have an advisor help set you on the right path."

Wayfair Unfair?

Speaking of taxes, there are many coin dealers—full-time, part-time, and vest pocket— who are just learning about an emerging set of tax regulations concerning interstate sales. And the impacts are both wide reaching and confusing. The new state-level tax codes resulted from a United States Supreme Court decision from a case the justices there heard that involves American online retailer Wayfair and the state of South Dakota. The story? South Dakota officials felt they were missing out on a huge share of revenue from profits made by remote company Wayfair on the sale of goods to customers in the Mount Rushmore State. The ruling? That states can require businesses without a physical presence in a given state and with more than 200 transactions or $100,000 of in-state sales to pay sales taxes on transactions conducted in that state. What's happened since the decision in *South Dakota v. Wayfair* in 2018 is that various states have enacted a hodgepodge of tax rules regarding online businesses and interstate sales. And everyone is trying to figure out what the rules are today, how they apply, if they apply to them, and how to manage and facilitate these tax payments.

Many of these regulations are inconsistent between one state and the next and are little understood by retailers, particularly small business owners. That is, until the tax man comes to collect fees and fines due to interstate transactions that did not result in the remittance of tax monies to the correct authorities. And, yet again, having a clear record of all sales is the coin dealer's best move.

Working under the table to keep these interstate transactions off the books? Not a very good idea. You *will* get caught, if not now then eventually. But what this new set of tax regulations means in the long run for coin dealers, or the coin collectors who end up paying higher prices for numismatic goods and services because of the new taxes, is still largely unknown.

"The impact of *Wayfair v. South Dakota* is still not the felt by the average person and may not be for years," says former United States Republican (and former Democrat) congressperson Jimmy Hayes. Once representing Louisiana's Seventh District in the United States House of Representatives and now serving as executive director of the Industry Council for Tangible Assets (ICTA) [since renamed the National Coin & Bullion Association], Hayes is helping collectors and dealers navigate the rough waters caused by the new and ever-evolving tax codes.

"When the effects of the *Wayfair* decision fully come to the fore, like a storm in the Gulf of Mexico, it will hit hard," he warns. "What we're going to do at ICTA is continue concentrating on enlarging, expanding, and returning the various tax exemptions that exist in almost 40 states." In the meantime, Hayes hopes to put greater focus on the Marketplace Fairness Act of 2013, pending legislation that garnered much bipartisan support but has yet to became law. It allows states to enforce their own tax-collection laws in a streamlined, consistent manner for online businesses not qualifying for certain small-business tax exemptions and conducting business in states other than their own.

"Prior to the [*South Dakota v. Wayfair*] Supreme Court decision, we had been trying to improve the Marketplace Fairness Act, which passed in the Senate but had a lot of practical problems," Hayes recalls. "But compared to the Wayfair complications, The Marketplace Fairness Act was a walk in the park. Because when you don't have parameters and don't have an outline, you've got a different challenge." He said that, in the wake of Wayfair, it all comes down to "not just how much money the states can make off taxes, but how big can they make the regulations?"

Hayes is concerned about the other litigation precedents that may come forth now from each state, such as whether they will further enforce restrictions on business licenses, begin assessing taxes on services that aren't presently taxed in the United States (such as ATM transaction fees), or launching other overarching means of pulling in taxes, fees, and fines. "There are a lot of unanticipated consequences going on here with the Wayfair decision," he says. "And there will be impacts on IRAs—sales and income tax on the items sold into IRAs. And then commodities . . ."

"Unfortunately, too few people will be talking about this with candidates," he says. "This is not a Democratic or Republican problem, but rather one which affects individuals and businesses across the spectrum."

Hayes says it's difficult to predict how much of an impact the new fees and taxes have on the hobby now or might in the future. "We see eBay charging more, and a lot of people see this and think 'oh, it's an eBay thing.' Except it's really not. New fees and higher surcharges there are, in part, due to the new assessments since the Wayfair decision. It's hard to judge how this will affect prices—you can't necessarily quantify how much the sales tax issue affects prices when you factor in bullion price changes, numismatic premiums, etc. There are just too many factors. But I assure you that the collecting value has gone down because taxes have gone up—even if the sheer collectible value itself has gone up."

For now, it's best to keep close documentation of what you're buying and selling, whether local or out of state. Now is certainly *not* the time to withhold paying your taxes on a stand of personal principle. Keep things out in the open for Uncle Sam and pay the tax bills you owe. But do stay aware of this ever-evolving area of tax code and check out the information on ICTA's website (http://www.ictaonline.org/) for the latest information on any new tax regulations and how they could affect you.

Storing and Accessing Records

Submitting coins for certification and encapsulation by a third-party grading firm is something done thousands of times each day. In many cases, individual collectors make these submissions directly to the grading companies, and in other situations coins will be submitted by coin dealers on the behalf of a collector(s). In either scenario, thorough paperwork once again can prove invaluable—even for those individuals who loathe filling out forms.

Regardless of the path one takes to submit a coin for grading and encapsulation, records are involved. Direct submissions to a grading firm require completing lengthy contract-like forms with information about you, the coin(s) submitted, and the submission service(s) desired, along with many other pertinent details. If you opt to submit your coin for grading via a coin dealer, there *should* be even more paperwork involved.

"As for keeping records, it's just common sense," opines John Albanese, who cofounded the Professional Coin Grading Service (PCGS) in 1986, established Numismatic Guaranty Corporation [since renamed Numismatic Guaranty Company] (NGC) in 1987, and began Certified Acceptance Corporation (CAC) in 2007. "I mean, sure, a lot of things are done in this industry on a handshake—they trust me, and I trust them. But if you've got a six-figure coin, I insist on signing for it."

He says you have no choice but to create records when you submit coins to the grading services, but he says there is something else he likes to keep with his submission documents. "I like to have photographs, too, for backup. If you're sending a coin to the grading service, rather than just submitting the coin and its accompanying form, it's a good idea to take a photo of the coin with even just your smartphone and scan the records, that way you know what the coin looks like, and you have the records on hand, too."

Albanese insists that, with modern mobile technology, taking photos of coins and forms is a cinch. "I'm not a photographer, but these days with smartphones it's pretty simple. You just take a photo of the coin when you send it in raw and when the coin is returned you take another photograph." And a couple clicks on the phone may save you from major headaches later.

There are many benefits to taking before-and-after photographs of coins being submitted for grading and holding onto records reflecting these transactions. "If you're to send the coin to another service for crossover, you have a photo file of it." And, he adds, while you should keep records concerning your submissions, crackouts, and crossovers, you should return old labels from cracked-out holders to their issuing companies. "Let's say you submit the coin to PCGS and they return the other grading service's sticker to you, I recommend you send that other sticker into the coin's original grading service to take it off their pop [population] report."

This helps both the coin's former grading service keep better records of how many examples of a particular coin are found within its holders. It also helps you, too. "I advise to send the sticker to the grading service to get it off the record, not just for their record but also for the market value of the coin, because if the coin is not taken off the pop report it shows up twice and may devalue the coin." Albanese recommends that those who wish to keep a record of the crossed-over coin's original label take a picture of it or make a photocopy.

Keeping tight records of any coins that leave your possession is wise, such as in the case of consignment. Bad things can unfortunately (but only rarely) happen to coins when you leave them in the custody of others, even with the largest of coin dealers and other professional numismatic firms. "If collectors are giving their coins to a dealer for consignment or submission to a grading company, the dealer shouldn't just receive the coin and then you go on your merry way. Dealers should sign for it and have a packing list, along with a serial number and info from the grading service," explains Albanese. "If it's a raw coin, I'd have the form filled out on the spot. Let's say you take 10 coins to a grading service, fill the forms out on the spot and then you have a receipt. It's very important to have a paper trail."

When coins are in the custody of a coin dealer, that dealer carries the responsibility of having the coins covered on his or her policy in the event of damage or total loss, such as a fire or burglary. Most reputable dealers who regularly handle consignments or grading submissions for customers have to maintain insurance coverage for multiples of the value of their own inventory.

Albanese tells dealers that even such good intentions can trigger questioning by the IRS. "I know one guy who was approached by the IRS, with them saying 'I know you've got only a half million in inventory, but you're taking out $2 million in insurance. What's up with that?' But the dealer explained that he needed to have multiples of coverage on his insurance policy to cover coins that were consigned to him, and he was able to prove to the IRS that he wasn't cheating." In that case once again, meticulous records saved the day.

"It's very important to have records for insurance claims, or for any type of coins changing hands, or any other time coins are in someone else's custody," he adds. "Even when you submit a coin to a grading service, you're going to have a receipt or something showing proof through signatures, transfers of the coin in the mail, or anything else showing that your coin left your hands and is in the custody of the post office, the grading service, or whatever."

Ultimately, in cases like these posed by Albanese, the paper trail helps determine responsibility in recovering your losses if something tragic happens to your coins while they're out of your hands. "I say it doesn't matter if you trust me. I could get hit by a truck or there could be a burglary. And I need to prove I had your coin. If not, you're not getting your insurance money."

Keeping it Personal

Whether or not you ever get audited by Uncle Sam, need to file an insurance claim, or dabble in bullion-based retirement investments, keeping a personal log of the coins you own, what you paid for them, where they're located, and how much they're worth now is simply the mark of a good collector. And there are so many more ways than ever before to embark on creating a paper trail, literal or virtual, for your numismatic holdings.

Yes, paper and pen don't need batteries, never need charging or updating, and won't leave you stranded when there's no Wi-Fi. But give digital technology a chance. It's easy and intuitive to use, provides an efficient path for completing numerous files of records, and can be securely stored in the digital "cloud," making it accessible to you and those confidentially entrusted to your information from virtually anywhere.

There's also a peace of mind in knowing that someplace there exists an itemized rundown of your coins and numismatic assets, what you paid for them, what they would cost to replace, and where you can find them. Ledgers like these have multiple benefits, including helping you see what holes you have in your collection and giving you a glimpse of what you may have multiples of and can sell to buy other items you really want for your collection.

Besides, many numismatists love looking back at what they paid for a coin 20, 30, even 50 years ago. As records age, they gain an importance not just as financial documents but also as historic archives. Such paperwork may one day help piece together a picture on what the coin market was like at a particular time and place in the past. Talk about leaving a legacy . . .

Healthy Record-Keeping Advice from the Doctor

Donald H. Kagin, Ph.D., has been collecting coins, cataloging pieces, and working in numismatics for more than 60 years. And during his decades in the industry he has learned the great value in memorializing his inventory and transactions in the form of records.

"Probably the primary reason to keep records is ultimately related to taxes," he says. "When it's time to sell—presumably at a profit—having those cost records will be critical. But, secondly, if you are pursuing a collection you want to keep track of what you have or need so you can be prepared to use that information at shows, auctions, or anywhere else you are to acquire material."

Kagin notes that records of what's in your collection can help form the basis of numismatic wish lists that will help you acquire what's presently *not* on the ledger. "Share those records with your preferred dealers to allow them to help you source hard-to-find dates."

For those who plan to build bullion-based individual retirement accounts (IRAs), Kagin says one of the key things to jot down and keep in safe storage are cost records. "You also need to be able to prove that your coins qualify for inclusion in your IRA. Records of what you bought can help prove that your assets are in compliance within the scope of the tax-deferred account."

Kagin also recommends taking photographs of coins submitted to custodians, such as pieces submitted to an offsite depository for IRA-related storage or sent to a third-party grading service. Photos also help when making claims on an insurance policy. And when it comes to obtaining numismatic insurance? "Get replacement-cost insurance, not insurance based on *your* cost, and in very few years you should get an updated independent replacement appraisal. Keep that formal appraisal with your coins."

The level of detail you include in these records may vary depending on what assets you're documenting and what your purposes are for doing so. "But make sure you get (at least) annual reports, appraisals, and that, if you want, you can have access to your coins in a timely fashion."

There are plenty of methods for keeping all of these records straight, including apps and programs. "Some are more sophisticated than others depending on the complexity of the material and how much information you want to carry above and beyond what's on the certification tag and what you paid, when, and from whom," remarks Kagin. "You should go online and find the appropriate program that works for you."

BIBLIOGRAPHY

CHAPTER 1

"1918 Pittman Act: Boondoggle or Necessary Morgan Dollar Massacre?" Gainesville Coins, October 8, 2013. Accessed August 21, 2021. https://www.gainesvillecoins.com/blog/1918-pittman-act-boondoggle-or-necessary-morgan-dollar-massacre.

A bill to provide for the disposal of silver from the National Defense Stockpile through the issuance of silver coins. S.2598. 97th Congress, 1982. https://www.congress.gov/bill/97th-congress/senate-bill/2598.

"Big U.S. Silver Sale Is Likely as Congress Reconciles Budget." *Wall Street Journal*, June 15, 1981.

Bressett, Kenneth. *Milestone Coins*. Atlanta, GA: Whitman Publishing, 2007.

Close, Elke. "Numismatics: Silver Turtles from Aegina." *Hellenistic History*, October 19, 2020. Accessed August 14, 2021. https://www.hellenistichistory.com/2020/08/17/coin-of-the-week/.

Dawson, Sam. "Market Silver Price Equals Treasury Level." *The Journal Times* (Racine, WI), September 10, 1963.

"Eisenhower Coin Blocked in House; Critics Want Silver." *The New York Times*, October 7, 1969. Accessed August 26, 2021. https://www.nytimes.com/1969/10/07/archives/eisenhower-coin-blocked-in-house-critics-want-silver.html.

Irvy, Bob. "Hunt brothers' silver stockpile the last of its kind." *The Seattle Times*, November 8, 2014. Accessed June 30, 2022. https://www.seattletimes.com/business/hunt-brothersrsquo-silver-stockpile-the-last-of-its-kind/.

Johnson, Lyndon. "Special Message to the Congress Proposing Changes in the Coinage System." June 3, 1965. American Presidency Project. Archived from the original on April 13, 2016. Accessed August 24, 2021. https://web.archive.org/web/20160413215004/http://www.presidency.ucsb.edu/ws/?pid=27015#.

Lange, David W. *History of the United States Mint and its Coinage*. Atlanta, GA: Whitman Publishing, 2006.

Lenzer, Robert. "Bunker Hunt: Disarming Tycoon." *The Boston Globe*, March 27, 1980.

Lowenstein, Roger. "U.S. Plan to Sell Silver from Its Stockpile Depresses Metal's Price 11%; Gold Drops." *Wall Street Journal*, September 18, 1981.

Marotta, Michael E. "The Bicentennial Coinage of 1976." *The Numismatist* (May 2001): 501-503, 541-542. Colorado Springs, CO: The American Numismatic Association.

Martin, David A. "1853: The End of Bimetallism in the United States." *The Journal of Economic History* 33, no. 4 (December 1973). Cambridge, UK: Cambridge University Press. Accessed August 17, 2021, via JSTOR: https://www.jstor.org/stable/2116788.

"National Security Silver Disposal Act of 1983, S. 269, 98th Cong., 1st sess." *Congressional Record 129, pt. 1:1050.*

Øydegaard, Floyd D.P. "Spanish Milled Dollar." Columbia Gazette. Accessed August 15, 2021. http://www.columbiagazette.com/smd.html.

Pollack, Norman. *The Populist Response to Industrial America*, 142. Cambridge, MA: Harvard University Press, 1976.

"Possible Silver Stockpile Sale Seen as Bullish for Market in Long Run." *Wall Street Journal*, September 10, 1976.

"Silver Prices—100-Year Historical Chart." Macrotrends. Accessed August 29, 2021. https://www.macrotrends.net/1470/historical-silver-prices-100-year-chart.

"Silver Price History 1960–1965." The Silver Institute. Accessed August 24, 2021. https://www.silverinstitute.org/silverprice/1960-1965/.

Sumner, W.G. "The Spanish Dollar and the Colonial Shilling." *The American Historical Review* 3, no. 4 (July 1898): 607-619. Oxford, UK: Oxford University Press. Accessed via JSTOR, August 15, 2021. https://www.jstor.org/stable/1834139?seq=1#metadata_info_tab_contents.

Tschoegl, Adrian E. "Maria Theresa's Thaler: A Case of International Money." *Eastern Economic Journal* 27, no. 4 (2001): 445–464.

Unger, Irwin. *The Greenback Era: A Social and Political History of American Finance 1865–1879.* Princeton, NJ: Princeton University Press, 1964.

"United States 1986 American Silver Eagle Bullion Coin." *CoinWeek*, July 2, 2021. Accessed January 1, 2022. https://coinweek.com/bullion-report/united-states-1986-american-silver-eagle-bullion-coin/.

"U.S. Mint History: The Crime of 1873." Washington, D.C.: The United States Mint Office of Corporate Communications, March 22, 2017. Accessed August 17, 2021. https://www.usmint.gov/news/inside-the-mint/mint-history-crime-of-1873.

"Unresolved Issues Concerning The Disposal Of Stockpile Silver." Washington, D.C.: U.S. General Accounting Office, 1982.

Westminster, Charlotte. "The History of the British Crown Coin." Westminster Collection, February 12, 2016. Accessed August 15, 2021. https://blog.westminstercollection.com/2016/02/12/the-history-of-the-british-crown-coin/?ewai=QOn_dbF05UU1.

CHAPTER 2

"1964-D Peace Dollar." Peace Dollars—My Coin Guides. Accessed September 25, 2021. https://peacedollars.com/1964-peace-dollar/.

"1964-D Peace Dollar." Professional Coin Grading Service. Accessed September 25, 2021. https://www.pcgs.com/top100/coin1.

Breen, Walter. *Walter Breen's Complete Encyclopedia of U.S. and Colonial Coins.* New York, NY: Doubleday, 1988.

Duncan, Kathleen. "The History of the Trade Dollar." *CoinWeek*, May 31, 2012.

Morgan, Charles. "When Dealing with Eisenhower Dollars, Grade is Everything." *CoinWeek*, August 10, 2021. Accessed September 25, 2021. https://coinweek.com/us-coins/when-dealing-with-eisenhower-dollars-grade-is-everything/.

Nasaw, Daniel. "Why the US keeps minting coins people hate and won't use." BBC, November 3, 2010. Accessed September 27, 2021. https://www.bbc.com/news/world-us-canada- 10783019

Reiter, Ed. "Gasparro's Greatest Challenge." *Coins* 26, no. 2 (February 1979): 116–117. Iola, WI: Krause Publications.

Chapter 3

"AIDS Crisis Timeline." *History*, July 13, 2017. Accessed November 23, 2021. https://www.history.com/topics/1980s/hiv-aids-crisis-timeline.

Crutsinger, Martin. "New Silver Dollars Snatched Up Quickly; Mint's Initial Supply Sold Out Within Hours." *Desert Sun*, November 25, 1986.

Devins, Richard M., Jr., Carol Boyd Leon, and Debbie L. Sprinkle. "Employment and Unemployment in 1984: A Second Year of Strong Growth in Jobs." Washington, D.C.: United States Bureau of Labor Statistics, 1984.

Edwards, Chris. "Reagan's Budget Legacy." The Cato Institute, June 8, 2004. Accessed November 19, 2021. https://www.cato.org/commentary/reagans-budget-legacy.

Frey, William. "The nation is diversifying even faster than predicted, according to new census data." Brookings Institute, July 1, 2020. Accessed June 30, 2022. https://www.brookings.edu/research/new-census-data-shows-the-nation-is-diversifying-even-faster-than-predicted/panic.

The HIV/AIDS Epidemic in the United States: The Basics. Kaiser Family Foundation, June 7, 2021. Accessed November 23, 2021. https://www.kff.org/hivaids/fact-sheet/the-hivaids-epidemic-in-the-united-states-the-basics/.

Houston, Jack. "Why Air Travel is So Cheap." *Business Insider*, November 8, 2019. Accessed November 23, 2021. https://www.businessinsider.com/why-air-travel-is-so-cheap-2019-11.

"Iran Releases American Hostages as Reagan Takes Office." The Learning Network, January 20, 2012. Accessed November 12, 2021. https://learning.blogs.nytimes.com/2012/01/20/jan-20-1981-iran-releases-american-hostages-as-reagan-takes-office/.

"Just Say No." *History*, May 31, 2017. Accessed November 23, 2021. https://www.history.com/topics/1980s/just-say-no.

Kamarck, Elaine. "Are You Better Off Than You Were 4 Years Ago?" WBUR, Harvard Kennedy School, September 11, 2012. Accessed November 12, 2021. https://www.hks.harvard.edu/publications/are-you-better-you-were-4-years-ago.

McCarthy, Niall. "Then & Now: The Decline Of Christianity In the U.S." Statista, October 17, 2019. Accessed June 30, 2022. https://www.statista.com/chart/19692/share-of-the-us-population-identifying-as-christian/.

"Mint Swamped with American Eagle Silver Dollar Orders." Associated Press, November 24, 1986.

Palmer, Gary. "Collectors' Opinions Collected." *San Pedro News Pilot*, March 11, 1973.

Pringle, Kenneth G. "The Culprits of the 1987 Market Crash Remain a Mystery. What Lessons Can We Draw From It Now?" Barron's, October 13, 2021. Accessed December 2, 2021. https://www.barrons.com/articles/the-culprits-of-the-1987-market-crash-remain-a-mystery-what-lessons-can-we-draw-from-it-now-51634112900.

Public Law 107-201. "Support of American Silver Eagle Bullion Program Act." Washington, D.C.: United States Congress, 2002. https://congress.gov/107/plaws/publ201/PLAW-107publ201.pdf.

Ranii, David. "Why Rare Coins Belong in Your Portfolio." *The Pittsburgh Press*, August 8, 1989.

"Recession of 1981–1982." Federal Reserve History. Accessed November 19, 2021. https://www.federalreservehistory.org/essays/recession-of-1981-82.

Reiter, Ed. "Numismatics—Debut of the American Gold Bullion Coins." *The New York Times*, September 21, 1986.

Rensberger, Boyce. "AIDS Cases in 1985 Exceed Total of All Previous Years." *Washington Post*, January 17, 1986. Accessed November 23, 2021. https://www.washingtonpost.com/archive/politics/1986/01/17/aids-cases-in-1985-exceed-total-of-all-previous-years/38c933d7-260c-414b-80f7-0dd282415cc6/.

Smith, Cathy. "Finns, Veterans Join Together to Honor Soldiers of Wars Past." *Fort Lauderdale News*, November 11, 1980.

Thomas, Lauren and Lauren Hirsch. "Here are 5 Things Sears Got Wrong That Sped its Fall." CNBC, October 11, 2018. Accessed June 23, 2022. https://www.cnbc.com/2018/10/11/here-are-5-things-sears-got-wrong-that-sped-its-fall.html.

United States Census Bureau Statistics, 1980.

United States Department of Veteran Affairs Statistics, 1980.

Valinsky, Jordan. "About 100 Sears Hometown Stores are Closing." CNN, May 31, 2022. Accessed June 30, 2022. https://www.cnn.com/2022/05/31/business/sears-hometown-closures/ index.html.

Chapter 4

1916 Annual Report of the Director of the Mint. Washington, D.C.: United States Treasury Department, 1916.

1986 Annual Report of the Director of the United States Mint. Washington, D.C.: United States Treasury Department, 1986.

1987 Annual Report of the Director of the United States Mint. Washington, D.C.: United States Treasury Department, 1987.

"Adolph A. Weinman." Smithsonian American Art Museum. Accessed June 12, 2022. https://americanart.si.edu/artist/adolph-weinman-5300.

"About the Adolph A. Weinman Papers." Smithsonian Archives of the Art. Accessed June 30, 2022 via Wayback Machine Internet Archive. https://web.archive.org/web/20081201123601/https://www.aaa.si.edu/collectionsonline/weinadol/overview.htm.

"As You Like It." *The Meriden Daily Journal*, January 4, 1917. Accessed June 5, 2022.

"Augustus Saint-Gaudens." Theodore Roosevelt Center. Accessed May 22, 2022. https://www.theodo1rerooseveltcenter.org/Learn-About-TR/TR-Encyclopedia/Culture%20and%20Society/Augustus%20Saint%20Gaudens#:~:text=Saint%2D Gaudens%20was%20in%20failing,his%20death%20in%20August%201907.

"Becoming an Authorized Purchaser." United States Mint. April 26, 2022. Accessed July 31, 2022. https://www.usmint.gov/news/consumer-alerts/business-guidelines/authorized-purchaser-program

Breen, Walter. *Walter Breen's Complete Encyclopedia of U.S. and Colonial Coins.* New York, NY: Doubleday, 1988.

Bowers, Q. David. *A Guide Book of the United States Mint.* Pelham, AL: Whitman Publishing, 2016.

Boyle, Brendan. "Krugerrand Production Halted." United Press International, November 13, 1985. Accessed June 20, 2022. https://www.upi.com/Archives/1985/11/13/Krugerrand-production-halted/5695500706000/.

Bullion Shark. "An Overlooked Modern Rarity? Burnished Silver Eagles." *CoinWeek*, April 9, 2019. Accessed June 27, 2022. https://coinweek.com/modern-coins/an-overlooked-modern-rarity-burnished-silver-eagles/.

Burdette, Roger W. *Renaissance of American Coinage 1916–1921.* Sterling, VA: Seneca Mill Press, 2005.

"Coinage Act of April 2, 1792." Washington, D.C.: The United States Mint. Accessed June 25, 2022. https://www.usmint.gov/learn/history/historical-documents/coinage-act-of-april-2-1792.

Fox, Bruce. "History of the Series." *The Complete Guide to Walking Liberty Half Dollars.* Virginia Beach, VA: DLRC Press, 1993. Archived from the original on August 1, 2014. Accessed June 5, 2022.

Fuljenz, Mike. "The Family of Eagles: From Beaumont to United States Bullion Coinage." Association of Mature American Citizens, March 20, 2015. Accessed June 20, 2022. https://amac.us/family-eagles-beaumont-united-states-bullion-coinage/.

Garside, M. "Mine Production of Silver Worldwide from 2005 to 2021." Statista, March 14, 2022.

Accessed July 6, 2022. https://www.statista.com/statistics/253293/silver-production-volume-worldwide/.

Gibbs, William T. "Breaking news: No 2022 Morgan or Peace dollars." *Coin World*, March 14, 2022. Accessed June 28, 2022. https://www.coinworld.com/news/us-coins/breaking-news-no-2022-morgan-or-peace-dollars?fbclid=IwAR0-4BzR8dnhXnLNpCbJupjmOsdE0JvUMEpaH3LlHJKqH0rw2ByfYRRB4ZQ.

"How Is Silver Mined?" APMEX. Accessed July 6, 2022. https://www.apmex.com/education/science/how-is-silver-mined.

"Iran Hostage Crisis." *History*, June 1, 2010. Accessed June 20, 2022. https://www.history.com/topics/middle-east/iran-hostage-crisis.

"Legislation to Allow for New Coins." Washington, D.C.: The United States Mint. Accessed May 30, 2022. https://www.usmint.gov/learn/history/historical-documents/legislation-to-allow-new-coin-designs.

McAdoo, William G. *Report of the Secretary of the Treasury on the State of the Finances, 1916.* Washington, D.C.: U.S. Government Printing Office, 1917.

McPike, Sharon. "U.S. Mint Police: A Call to Serve." Washington, D.C.: The United States Mint, May 15, 2017. Accessed June 27, 2022. https://www.usmint.gov/news/inside-the-mint/us-mint-police-a-call-to-serve.

Mercanti, John. *American Silver Eagles: A Guide to the U.S. Bullion Coin Program*, 4th ed. Pelham, AL: Whitman Publishing, 2022.

"Oscar Roty." Musee d'Orsay. Accessed June 4, 2022. https://www.musee-orsay.fr/en/artworks/la-semeuse-55299.

"Public Law 99-185." Washington, D.C.: United States Congress, 1985. https://www.govinfo.gov/content/pkg/STATUTE-99/pdf/STATUTE-99-Pg1177.pdf.

Reiter, Ed. "Debut of the American Gold Bullion Coins." *The New York Times*, September 21, 1986. Accessed June 18, 2022. https://www.nytimes.com/1986/09/21/arts/numismatics-debut-of-the-american-gold-bullion-coins.html.

Reiter, Ed. "Old Designs for the New Coins." *The New York Times*, April 27, 1986. Accessed June 20, 2022. https://www.nytimes.com/1986/04/27/arts/numismatics-old-designs-for-the-new-coins.html.

Reiter, Ed. "The Silver Bullion." *The New York Times*, December 14, 1986. Accessed June 20, 2022. https://www.nytimes.com/1986/12/14/arts/numismatics-the-silver-bullion.html.

Reiter, Ed. "The Weinman Legacy—Part 1." Professional Coin Grading Service, January 31, 2000. Accessed June 5, 2022. https://www.pcgs.com/news/the-weinman-legacy-part-1.

Saint-Gaudens National Historical Park. "Augustus Saint-Gaudens, Theodore Roosevelt, and the Coin." National Park Service, October 19, 2021.

Accessed May 22, 2022. https://www.nps.gov/articles/000/a-living-thing-and-typical-of-progress-augustus-saint-gaudens-theodore-roosevelt-and-the-coins.htm#_edn6.

"Saint-Gaudens, Weinman Designs on Bullion Coins?" *Coin World*, April 23, 1986.

Secter, Bob. "Reagan Bans Imports of S. Africa Krugerrand." *Los Angeles Times*, October 2, 1985. Accessed June 18, 2022. https://www.latimes.com/archives/la-xpm-1985-10-02-mn-16058-story.html.

"Silver Processed & Uses." The Natural Sapphire Company. Accessed July 6, 2022. https://www.thenaturalsapphirecompany.com/education/precious-metal-mining-refining-techniques/silver-mining-refining/.

"State of Emergency—1985." South African History Online. Accessed June 18, 2022. https://www.sahistory.org.za/article/state-emergency-1985.

Taxay, Don. *The U.S. Mint and Coinage*. London, UK: Arco Publishing, 1966.

"The New Coins." *The Allentown Leader*, February 17, 1917.

"The Renaissance of U.S. Coinage." American Numismatic Association. Accessed May 22, 2022. https://www.money.org/money-museum/virtual-exhibits/hom/case27.

"The Saltus Medal Award." American Numismatic Society. Accessed June 12, 2022. https://numismatics.org/saltuswinners/.

Tebben, Gerald. "100 years of the Walking Liberty Half Dollar." *Coin World*, October 13, 2016. Accessed May 30, 2022. https://www.coinworld.com/news/us-coins/walking-liberty-half-dollar-history-adolph-weinman-centennial.html.

"Treasury Makes it Official, Confirms Details of Bullion Coin Designs." *Coin World*, July 9, 1986.

Tucker, Dennis. *American Gold and Silver*. Pelham, AL: Whitman Publishing, 2016.

"United States Mint Selects 27 Artists for Artistic Infusion Program." Washington, D.C.: The United States Mint. July 17, 2019. Accessed June 18, 2022. https://www.usmint.gov/news/press-releases/united-states-mint-selects-27-artists-for-artistic-infusion-program.

Vermeule, Cornelius. *Numismatic Art in America*. Cambridge, MA: The Belknap Press of Harvard University Press, 1971.

"Walking Liberty Half Dollar." U.S. Commission of Fine Arts. Accessed June 5, 2022. https://www.cfa.gov/about-cfa/design-topics/coins-medals/walking-liberty-half-dollar.

Walsh, Kevin. *Forgotten New York: The Ultimate Urban Explorer's Guide to All Five Boroughs*. New York, NY: Collins, 2006.

CHAPTER 5

"2008-W Silver Eagle Reverse of 2007 Variety." Silver Eagle Guide. Accessed February 1, 2022. https://silvereagleguide.com/2008-w-silver-eagle-reverse-of-2007/.

Bentley, Alden. "12 Tonnes of Gold Buried Under Tower Debris." *The Vancouver Sun*, September 14, 2001.

Bullion Shark. "A New Modern Rarity: 2020 (P) American Silver Eagles." *CoinWeek*. May 8, 2020. Accessed February 4, 2022. https://coinweek.com/bullion-report/a-new-modern-rarity-2020-p-american-silver-eagles/.

Chatfield, Laura E. "9/11: 4th Plane was Headed for the Capitol." United Press International, September 12, 2002. Accessed February 2, 2022. https://www.upi.com/Defense-News/2002/09/12/911-4th-plane-was-headed-for-the-Capitol/69531031880092/.

"First Strike." Professional Coin Grading Service. Accessed January 27, 2022. https://www.pcgs.com/firststrike.

"'First Strike' or 'First Release' Designations." Washington, D.C.: The United States Mint, June 29, 2016. Accessed January 28, 2022. https://www.usmint.gov/news/consumer-alerts/consumer/first-strike-designations.

Folger, Jean. "Self-Directed IRAs (SDIRA)." Investopedia, December 21, 2021. Accessed February 21, 2022. https://www.investopedia.com/terms/s/self-directed-ira.asp.

Gilkes, Paul. "Mint FOIA Response Confirms Origins of American Eagles." *Coin World*, October 16, 2020. Accessed January 19, 2022. https://www.coinworld.com/news/us-coins/mint-foia-response-confirms-origins-of-american-eagles.

Gilkes, Paul. "Spotting on Silver American Eagles Remains a Challenge." *Coin World*, December 5, 2012. Accessed February 27, 2022. https://www.coinworld.com/news/precious-metals/spotting-on-silver-american-eagles-remains-a-.html.

Gilkes, Paul. "U.S. Mint Closes Two Facilities Amid Coronavirus Crisis." *Coin World*, April 3, 2020. Accessed January 31, 2022. https://www.coinworld.com/news/precious-metals/us-mint-closes-two-facilities-amid-coronavirus-crisis.

Gilkes, Paul. "Will Some American Eagle Silver Coins Have Low Mintages in 2021?" *Coin World*, February 5, 2021. Accessed January 31, 2022. https://www.coinworld.com/news/us-coins/will-some-american-eagle-silver-coins-have-low-mintages-in-2021.

"Historical IRA Contribution Limit." DQYDJ. Accessed February 16, 2022. https://dqydj.com/historical-ira-contribution-limit/.

"Initial Release Designation." Independent Coin Graders. Accessed January 28, 2022. http://www.icgcoin.com/initial-release-designation/.

Kelly, Mike. "Some Ghouls Don't Wait for Halloween." *The Record* (Hackensack, NJ), October 30, 2001.

Marotta, Michael. "Aaron Feldman: 'Buy the Book Before the Coin.'" Necessary Facts, April 8, 2018.

Accessed February 22, 2022. https://necessaryfacts. blogspot.com/2018/04/aaron-feldmanbuy-book-before-you-buy.html.

"Milk Spots on Coins May Be Removable." *Numismatic News*, June 25, 2018. Accessed February 27, 2022. https://www.numismaticnews.net/collecting-101/milk-spots-on-silver-coins-may-be-removable.

"NGC Releases Designations." Numismatic Guaranty Company. Accessed January 27, 2022. https://www.ngccoin.com/coin-grading/designations/.

"NGC to Certify San Francisco Mint Silver Eagles." Numismatic Guaranty Company, June 7, 2011. Accessed February 2, 2022. https://www.ngccoin.com/news/article/2192/San-Francisco-Silver-Eagles/.

"PCGS Policy for Spotting of Modern Silver Coins." Professional Coin Grading Service. Accessed February 27, 2022. https://www.pcgs.com/silver-coins-spot-policy.

Piret, Diane. "The ABCs of Precious Metals IRAs." *The Coin Dealer Newsletter*, February 12, 2010.

"Precious Metals Buried Under Debris." CNN, September 22, 2001. Accessed February 2, 2022. https://www.cnn.com/2001/US/09/22/rec.buried.treasure/index.html.

Rosen, Rob. "Collecting Sports Autographs." Professional Sports Authenticator, June 2, 2010. Accessed February 2, 2022. https://www.psacard.com/articles/articleview/6245/collecting-sports-autographs.

"Roth, William Victor, Jr." Biographical Directory of the United States Congress. https://bioguide.congress.gov/search/bio/R000460.

"Senate Version Permits Use of U.S. Bullion Coins in IRAs." *Coin World*, July 9, 1986.

"Senator William Roth Scorecard." League of Conservative Voters. Accessed February 20, 2022. https://scorecard.lcv.org/moc/william-v-roth.

"September 11 Attacks." History. Accessed February 2, 2022. https://www.history.com/topics/21st-century/9-11-attacks.

Stewart, Jackie. "Roth IRA Basics: 11 Things You Must Know." Kiplinger, November 22, 2021. Accessed February 17, 2022. https://www.kiplinger.com/retirement/retirement-plans/roth-iras.

"Tax Court Explicitly Bans Gold and Silver Coin Home Storage IRA Accounts." National Coin & Bullion Association. Accessed June 26, 2022. https://www.ictaonline.org/tax-court-explicitly-bans-gold-and-silver-coin-home-storage-ira-accounts.

"The Prohibition on Home Storage of Bullion Held in an IRA." Industry Council for Tangible Assets, 2018.

"Today Marks 42nd Anniversary of WTC Dedication." 9/11 Memorial & Museum, April 4, 2015. Accessed February 2, 2022. https://www.911memorial.org/connect/blog/today-marks-42nd-anniversary-wtc-dedication.

"What Types of Investments Can You Use in an IRA?" IRA Basics, April 6, 2011. Accessed February 16, 2022. https://www.ira-basics.com/what-types-of-investments-can-you-use-in-an-ira/.

White, Larry. "What Are 'Emergency' Silver Eagles?" Silver Doctors, March 16, 2021. Accessed January 30, 2022. https://www.silverdoctors.com/silver/silver-news/what-are-emergency-silver-eagles/.

"White Spots on Modern Silver Coins." Numismatic Guaranty Company. Accessed February 27, 2022. https://www.ngccoin.com/submit/coins-we-grade/white-spots/.

"William J. Roth, Jr. Biography." Delaware Historical Society. Accessed via Internet Archive Wayback Machine on February 17, 2022. http://web.archive.org/web/20160821053512/https://dehistory.org/research-collections/senator-william-v-roth-collection/roth-biography.

Chapter 6

Bisognani, Jim. "Will the 2019-S Enhanced Reverse Proof Silver Eagle Beat the 1995-W?" *CoinWeek*, November 25, 2019. Accessed March 11, 2022. https://coinweek.com/bullion-report/jim-bisognani-will-the-2019-s-enhanced-reverse-proof-silver-eagle-beat-the-1995-w/.

Bowers, Q. David. *A Guide Book of Lincoln Cents.* Atlanta, GA: Whitman Publishing, 2008.

Bulfinch, Chris. "The Key Date Type I American Silver Eagles." *CoinWeek*, May 14, 2021. Accessed March 11, 2022. https://coinweek.com/bullion-report/the-key-date-type-i-american-silver-eagles/.

Diehl, Philip. "Guest Commentary." *Coin World*, June 26, 1995.

Fivaz, Bill and J.T. Stanton. *Cherrypickers' Guide to Rare Die Varieties of United States Coins.* Atlanta, GA: Whitman Publishing, 2012.

Gilkes, Paul. "American Eagle struck on .900 fine planchet." *Coin World*, November 5, 2013. Accessed June 28, 2022. https://www.coinworld.com/news/precious-metals/2013/11/american-eagle-struck-on-900-fine-planchet.html.

Golino, Louis. "U.S. Mint Announces October Release of 25th Anniversary Silver Eagle Set." *CoinWeek*, August 20, 2011. Accessed March 12, 2022. https://coinweek.com/bullion-report/u-s-mint-announces-october-release-of-25th-anniversary-silver-eagle-set/.

Guth, Ron. "1909-S VDB 1C, RD (Regular Strike)." Professional Coin Grading Service CoinFacts. Accessed March 3, 2022. https://www.pcgs.com/coinfacts/coin/1909-s-vdb-1c-rd/2428.

Guth, Ron. "1995-W $1 Silver Eagle, DCAM (Proof)." Professional Coin Grading Service CoinFacts. Accessed March 3, 2022. https://www.pcgs.comcoinfacts/coin/1995-w-1-silver-eagle-dcam/9887.

Hall, David. "1909-S VDB 1C, RD (Regular Strike)." Professional Coin Grading Service CoinFacts. Accessed March 3, 2022. https://www.pcgs.com/coinfacts/coin/1909-s-vdb-1c-rd/2428.

Hernandez, Jaime. "1995-W $1 Silver Eagle DCAM (Proof). Professional Coin Grading Service Coin-Facts. Accessed March 3, 2022. https://www.pcgs.com/coinfacts/coin/1995-w-1-silver-eagle-dcam/9887.

Highfill, John. *The Comprehensive U.S. Silver Dollar Encyclopedia, Volume II*. Broken Arrow, OK: Highfill Press, Inc., 2017.

McAllister, Bill. "Mint Hopes Eagles Fly." *The Washington Post*, April 14, 1995.

Mercanti, John M. *American Silver Eagles: A Guide to the U.S. Bullion Coin Program*, 3rd ed. Pelham, AL: Whitman Publishing, 2018.

"Silver Prices—100-Year Historical Chart." Macrotrends. Accessed March 9, 2022. https://www.macrotrends.net/1470/historical-silver-prices-100-year-chart.

Sullivan, Jon. "Check your 1998 American Eagles: Guest Commentary." *Coin World*, October 25, 2015. Accessed June 28, 2022. https://www.coinworld.com/news/precious-metals/check-your-1998-american-eagles-they-might-be-on-wrong-planchet.html.

Unser, Darrin Lee. "2020-W American Eagle Coins Carry 'V75' Privy Mark for End of WWII." Coin-News.Net, November 5, 2020. Accessed March 12, 2022. https://www.coinnews.net/2020/11/05/2020-w-american-eagle-coins-carry-v75-privy-mark-for-end-of-wwii/.

Wiles, James. "1992-S $1 ASE DDR-001, PR-1-R-II-C." Variety Vista. Accessed March 12, 2022. http://varietyvista.com/1992SDDR001%20ASE%20dollar.htm.

Wiles, James. "2011 $1 ASE DDO-001, 1-O-VI." Variety Vista. Accessed March 12, 2022. http://varietyvista.com/2011PDDO001%20ASE%20dollar.htm.

CHAPTER 7

Bradley, Debbie. "CCAC Picks New Eagle." *Numismatic News*, April 11, 2014. Accessed June 28, 2022. https://www.numismaticnews.net/archive/ccac-picks-new-eagle.

"Bullion DNA." Royal Canadian Mint. https://www.mint.ca/en-us/bullion/bullion-dna.

Gilkes, Paul. "Anti-counterfeiting panel at Mint numismatic forum." *Coin World*, October 26, 2018. Accessed June 28, 2022. https://www.coinworld.com/news/precious-metals/anti-counterfeiting-panel-at-mint-numismatic-forum.html.

Gilkes, Paul. "CCAC considering silver Eagle bullion coin reverse design change." *Coin World*, March 28, 2014. Accessed June 28, 2022. https://www.coinworld.com/news/precious-metals/ccac-considering-silver-eagle-bullion-coin-reverse-design-change.html.

Gilkes, Paul. "Different American Eagle reverse designs favored by CCAC." *Coin World*, June 26, 2020. Accessed June 28, 2022. https://www.coinworld.com/news/us-coins/different-american-eagle-reverse-designs-favored-by-ccac.

Gilkes, Paul. "U.S. Mint to redesign gold and silver American Eagles, implement security devices." *Coin World*, October 11, 2019. Accessed June 28, 2022. https://www.coinworld.com/news/precious-metals/u-s-mint-to-redesign-gold-and-silver-american-eagles-implement-security-devices.

Golino, Louis. "The Coin Analyst: CCAC Recommends Bold Choice for New Silver Eagle Reverse, More Traditional One for Gold Eagle." *CoinWeek*, June 30, 2020. Accessed June 29, 2022. https://coinweek.com/bullion-report/bullion-coins-specialty-categories/the-coin-analyst-ccac-recommends-bold-choice-for-new-silver-eagle-reverse-more-traditional-one-for-gold-eagle/.

McAllister, Bill and Paul Gilkes. "CCAC pushes for new American Eagle reverse." *Coin World*, March 13, 2014. Accessed June 28, 2022. https://www.coinworld.com/news/precious-metals/ccac-pushes-for-new-american-eagle-reverse.html.

"United States Citizens Coinage Advisory Committee Meeting Transcript." Washington, D.C.: United States Government, March 11, 2014.

"United States Citizens Coinage Advisory Committee Meeting Transcript." Washington, D.C.: United States Government, April 8, 2014.

"United States Citizens Coinage Advisory Committee Meeting Transcript." Washington, D.C.: United States Government, June 23, 2020.

CHAPTER 8

"2008-W Silver Eagle Reverse of 2007 Variety." Silver Eagle Guide. Accessed February 1, 2022. https://silvereagleguide.com/2008-w-silver-eagle-reverse-of-2007/.

Bisognani, Jim. "Will the 2019-S Enhanced Reverse Proof Silver Eagle Beat the 1995-W?" *CoinWeek*, November 25, 2019. Accessed March 11, 2022. https://coinweek.com/bullion-report/jim-bisognani-will-the-2019-s-enhanced-reverse-proof-silver-eagle-beat-the-1995-w/.

Breen, Walter. *Walter Breen's Complete Encyclopedia of U.S. and Colonial Coins*. New York, NY: Doubleday, 1988.

Bulfinch, Chris. "The Key Date Type I American Silver Eagles." *CoinWeek*, May 14, 2021. Accessed March 11, 2022. https://coinweek.com/bullion-report/the-key-date-type-i-american-silver-eagles/.

Chatfield, Laura E. "9/11: 4th Plane was Headed for the Capitol." United Press International, September 12, 2002. Accessed February 2, 2022. https://www.upi.com/Defense-News/2002/09/12/911-4th-plane-was-headed-for-the-Capitol/69531031880092/.

Crutsinger, Martin. "New Silver Dollars Snatched Up Quickly; Mint's Initial Supply Sold Out Within Hours." *Desert Sun*, November 25, 1986.

Diehl, Philip. "Guest Commentary." *Coin World*, June 26, 1995.

Fivaz, Bill and J.T. Stanton. *Cherrypickers' Guide to Rare Die Varieties of United States Coins*. Atlanta, GA: Whitman Publishing, 2012.

Gibbs, William T. "Breaking news: No 2022 Morgan or Peace dollars." *Coin World*, March 14, 2022. Accessed June 28, 2022. https://www.coinworld.com/news/us-coins/breaking-news-no-2022-morgan-or-peace-dollars?fbclid=IwAR0-4BzR8dnhXnLNpCbJupjmOsdE0JvUMEpaH3LlHJKqH0rw2ByfYRRB4ZQ.

Gilkes, Paul. "American Eagle Struck on .900 Fine Planchet." *Coin World*, November 5, 2013. Accessed June 28, 2022. https://www.coinworld.com/news/precious-metals/2013/11/american-eagle-struck-on-900-fine-planchet.html.

Gilkes, Paul. "Mint FOIA Response Confirms Origins of American Eagles." *Coin World*, October 16, 2020. Accessed January 19, 2022. https://www.coinworld.com/news/us-coins/mint-foia-response-confirms-origins-of-american-eagles.

Gilkes, Paul. "Spotting on Silver American Eagles Remains a Challenge." *Coin World*, December 5, 2012. Accessed February 27, 2022. https://www.coinworld.com/news/precious-metals/spotting-on-silver-american-eagles-remains-a-.html.

Gilkes, Paul. "U.S. Mint Closes Two Facilities Amid Coronavirus Crisis." *Coin World*, April 3, 2020. Accessed January 31, 2022. https://www.coinworld.com/news/precious-metals/us-mint-closes-two-facilities-amid-coronavirus-crisis.

Gilkes, Paul. "Will Some American Eagle Silver Coins Have Low Mintages in 2021?" *Coin World*, February 5, 2021. Accessed January 31, 2022. https://www.coinworld.com/news/us-coins/will-some-american-eagle-silver-coins-have-low-mintages-in-2021.

Golino, Louis. "U.S. Mint Announces October Release of 25th Anniversary Silver Eagle Set." *CoinWeek*, August 20, 2011. Accessed March 12, 2022. https://coinweek.com/bullion-report/u-s-mint-announces-october-release-of-25th-anniversary-silver-eagle-set/.

Guth, Ron. "1909-S VDB 1C, RD (Regular Strike)." Professional Coin Grading Service CoinFacts. Accessed March 3, 2022. https://www.pcgs.com/coinfacts/coin/1909-s-vdb-1c-rd/2428.

Guth, Ron. "1995-W $1 Silver Eagle, DCAM (Proof)." Professional Coin Grading Service CoinFacts. Accessed March 3, 2022. https://www.pcgs.com/coinfacts/coin/1995-w-1-silver-eagle-dcam/9887.

Hernandez, Jaime. "1995-W $1 Silver Eagle DCAM (Proof)." Professional Coin Grading Service CoinFacts. Accessed March 3, 2022. https://www.pcgs.com/coinfacts/coin/1995-w-1-silver-eagle-dcam/9887.

Mercanti, John. *American Silver Eagles: A Guide to the U.S. Bullion Coin Program*, 4th ed. Pelham, AL: Whitman Publishing, 2022.

Reiter, Ed. "Debut of the American Gold Bullion Coins." *The New York Times*, September 21, 1986. Accessed June 18, 2022. https://www.nytimes.com/1986/09/21/arts/numismatics-debut-of-the-american-gold-bullion-coins.html.

Reiter, Ed. "Old Designs for the New Coins." *The New York Times*, April 27, 1986. Accessed June 20, 2022. https://www.nytimes.com/1986/04/27/arts/numismatics-old-designs-for-the-new-coins.html.

Reiter, Ed. "The Silver Bullion." *The New York Times*, December 14, 1986. Accessed June 20, 2022. https://www.nytimes.com/1986/12/14/arts/numismatics-the-silver-bullion.html.

Reiter, Ed. "The Weinman Legacy—Part 1." Professional Coin Grading Service, January 31, 2000. Accessed June 5, 2022. https://www.pcgs.com/news/the-weinman-legacy-part-1.

"September 11 Attacks." *History*. Accessed February 2, 2022. https://www.history.com/topics/21st-century/9-11-attacks.

"Silver Prices—100-Year Historical Chart." Macrotrends. Accessed March 9, 2022. https://www.macrotrends.net/1470/historical-silver-prices-100-year-chart.

Tebben, Gerald. "100 years of the Walking Liberty Half Dollar." *Coin World*, October 13, 2016. Accessed May 30, 2022. https://www.coinworld.com/news/us-coins/walking-liberty-half-dollar-history-adolph-weinman-centennial.html.

"Today Marks 42nd Anniversary of WTC Dedication." 9/11 Memorial & Museum, April 4, 2015. Accessed February 2, 2022. https://www.911memorial.org/connect/blog/today-marks-42nd-anniversary-wtc-dedication.

"Treasury Makes it Official, Confirms Details of Bullion Coin Designs." *Coin World*, July 9, 1986.

Tucker, Dennis. *American Gold and Silver*. Pelham, AL: Whitman Publishing, 2016.

"United States 1986 American Silver Eagle Bullion Coin." *CoinWeek* IQ, July 2, 2021. Accessed November 8, 2021. https://coinweek.com/bullion-report/united-states-1986-american-silver-eagle-bullion-coin/.

Unser, Darrin Lee. "2020-W American Eagle Coins Carry 'V75' Privy Mark for End of WWII." CoinNews.Net, November 5, 2020. Accessed March 12, 2022. https://www.coinnews.net/2020/11/05/2020-w-american-eagle-coins-carry-v75-privy-mark-for-end-of-wwii/.

White, Larry. "What Are 'Emergency' Silver Eagles?" Silver Doctors, March 16, 2021. Accessed January 30, 2022. https://www.silverdoctors.com/silver/silver-news/what-are-emergency-silver-eagles/.

Wolin, Neal. "Reducing the Surplus Dollar Coin Inventory, Saving Taxpayer Dollars." *Treasury Notes Blog*, December 13, 2011. Accessed September 27, 2021. https://www.treasury.gov/connect/blog/Pages/Reducing-the-Surplus-Dollar-Coin-Inventory-Saving-Taxpayer-Dollars.aspx.

About the Author

Joshua McMorrow-Hernandez is an author and journalist who has written hundreds of numismatic articles for various publications, including *COINage*, *The Numismatist*, *Numismatic News*, *CoinWeek*, *Professional Coin Grading Service Rare Coin Market Report*, *The Greysheet*, *The Centinel*, *Philadelphia Magazine*, *The Providence Journal*, *Tampa Bay Times*, and TheFunTimesGuide.com. In addition to authoring *Images of America: The United States Mint in Philadelphia*, he is also the editor-in-chief of *FUNTopics* for the Florida United Numismatists and is an editorial and writing consultant. He has won multiple Numismatic Literary Guild awards. A coin collector since 1992, he loves taking road trips, gardening, music, and meteorology.

Dedication

To my wife, my parents, my sister, and all my loved ones who have always stood by me. Thank you, and I love you.

Credits and Acknowledgments

This book was made possible thanks to the incredible assistance and research provided by so many numismatic experts, researchers, and editors, including Ronnie Abbazio, Janell Armstrong, Leonard Augsburger, Andrew Bowers, Q. David Bowers, Heather Boyd, John Brush, Roger Burdette, David Camire, Randy Campbell, David Crenshaw, Emily S. Damstra, Doug Davis, Beth Deisher, Matthew DiBiase, Mitch Ernst, John Feigenbaum, Steve Feltner, Mark Ferguson, Miley Frost, Mike Fuljenz, David L. Ganz, Michael Garofalo, Jeff Garrett, Michael Gaudioso, Dr. Robert Goler, Dave Harper, Ed Howard, Akio Lis, Todd Martin, Everett Millman, Lee Minshull, Patrick Ian Perez, Tom Power, David Ryder, Maurice Rosen, Jon Sullivan, Cheryl Taylor, Troy Thoreson, Scott Travers, Michael White, James Wiles, Joe Yaffe, Jack Young, and the Whitman Publishing team.

Image Credits

Unless otherwise noted below, images are from the Whitman Publishing archives or the personal archives of the author. Images are credited by page number. Where multiple images are depicted on a page, they are numbered left to right, top to bottom. The obverse and reverse of a coin are considered a single image. ANA = American Numismatic Association. CCAC = Citizens Coinage Advisory Committee. HA = Heritage Auctions. LOC = Library of Congress. NGC = Numismatic Guaranty Company. PCGS = Professional Coin Grading Service. SBG = Stack's Bowers Galleries. USM = U.S. Mint.

Cover: Images from NGC, PCGS, and USM.

Chapter 1: Pg 2.1–2.3, SBG. Pg 3.1, SBG. Pg 3.2–3.4, public domain. Pg 4.1, SBG. Pg 4.2, LOC. Pg 5.1, HA. Pg. 5.3, HA. Pg 5.4–5.5, SBG. Pg 6.1, HA. Pg 6.2, LOC. Pg 7.1, public domain. Pg 8.1, public domain. Pg 9.1, SBG. Pg 9.2–3, LOC. Pg 10.1, HA. Pg 11.1, SBG. Pg 11.2, public domain. Pg 11.3, SBG. Pg 11.4, NGC. Pg 11.5, public domain. Pg 11.6, HA. Pg 11.7, SBG. Pg 12.2, public domain. Pg 13.1, HA. Pg 16.1, LOC. Pg 16.2, public domain. Pg 17.1, Newspapers.com. Pg 18.1, Ronald Reagan Presidential Library.

Chapter 2: Pg 20.2, SBG. Pg 21.1–3, SBG. Pg 22.1, SBG. Pg 23.1, HA. Pg 24.2, Stack's. Pg 25.1, SBG. Pg 27.1, Q. David Bowers. Pg 27.2, public domain. Pg 28.1, Q. David Bowers. Pg 30.1–2, HA. Pg 31.1, Q. David Bowers. Pg 31.2, USM. Pg 32.1, Mariusz Szczygiel / Shutterstock. Pg 33.1, knelson20 / Shutterstock.

Chapter 3: Pg 36.1, USM. Pg 37.1, Keith Tarrier / Shutterstock. Pg 37.2–3, public domain. Pg 38.1, public domain. Pg 40.1, public domain. Pg 41.1, Newspapers.com. Pg 42.1, public domain. Pg 42.2, Hugo Robledo / Shutterstock. Pg 42.3, Peter Gudella / Shutterstock. Pg 42.4, RobertCop93 / Shutterstock. Pg 43.1, Vicki L. Miller / Shutterstock. Pg 43.2, public domain. Pg 44.1, PCGS. Pg 44.2, NGC. Pg 45.1, Mark Ferguson. Pg 47.1, ANA. Pg 49.4, USM. Pg 50.1, SBG. Pg 55.1, Mike Garofalo. Pg 61.1, knelson20 / Shutterstock.

Chapter 4: Pg 62.1, SBG. Pg 63.1, LOC. Pg 64.1–2, SBG. Pg 64.4, SBG. Pg 64.5, HA. Pg 65.2, HA. Pg 66.2, Tom Mulvaney. Pg 68.1, HA. Pg 68.2, Roi.dagobert / Wikimedia Commons. Pg 69.1, Q. David Bowers. Pg 72.1, SBG. Pg 72.2, Q. David Bowers. Pg 72.3, Frederic C. Chalfant / Wikimedia Commons. Pg 73.1, Q. David Bowers. Pg 73.2, USM. Pg 73.3, SBG. Pg 73.4, American Institute of Architects Archives. Pg 77.1, HA. Pg 79.1, ANA. Pg 82.1, Miley Frost. Pg 83.1, Miley Frost. Pg 86.1–3, SBG. Pg 86.4–5, HA. Pg 87.1, HA. Pg 87.2–3, SBG. Pg 87.4–5, HA. Pg 88.4, USM. Pg 89.2, USM. Pg 91.1, ANA. Pg 91.2, *Coin World* / Amos Media. Pg 93.1, Red ivory / Shutterstock. Pg 94.1–2, Sunshine Minting. Pg 97.1, National Archives. Pg 100.1, Historical Society of Pennsylvania. Pg 100.2, U.S. Mint / Wikimedia Commons. Pg 101.1–2,

USM. Pg 104.4, NGC. Pg 105.2, PCGS. Pg 106.1, HA. Pg 106.3, HA. Pg 107.1, USM. Pg 107.2, Stack's. Pg 108.1–5, USM. Pg 109.1, Q. David Bowers. Pg 110.1, blvdone / Shutterstock. Pg 111.1, public domain.

Chapter 5: Pg 113.1, Sergey Ryzhov / Shutterstock. Pg 114.2, NGC. Pg 117.1, NGC. Pg 117.2–3, USM. Pg 119.1, Miroslav Hlavko / Shutterstock. Pg 120.1, HA. Pg 121.1–2, HA. Pg 123.1, Troy Thoreson. Pg 124.1, HA. Pg 124.2, Mike Garofalo / APMEX. Pg 125.1, HA. Pg 127.1, HA. Pg 130.1–2, HA. Pg 134.1, Ayman Noureldin / Shutterstock. Pg 135.1, Vintage Tone / Shutterstock. Pg 135.2, NGC. Pg 135.3, USM. Pg 136.1, Maurice Rosen. Pg 138.1, Maxx-Studio / Shutterstock. Pg 139.1, JanS / Shutterstock. Pg 154.1, HA. Pg 155.1–2, HA. Pg 156.1–2, HA. Pg 158.1, Beth Deisher. Pg 159.1, Anti-Counterfeiting Educational Foundation. Pg 160.1–3, Jack Young. Pg 161.1–4, Jack Young. Pg 161.5, HA.

Chapter 6: Page 163.1, NGC. Page 164.1, HA. Pg 165.2, HA. Pg 167.1, PCGS. Pg 169.1–3, Variety Vista. Pg 169.4–6, HA. Pg 170.1–3, Variety Vista. Pg 171.1–2, Jon Sullivan. Pg 172.1–2, Jon Sullivan. Pg 173.1–2, Jon Sullivan.

Chapter 7: Pg 174.1, CCAC. Pg 175.1, USM. Pg 176.1–10, CCAC. Pg 177.1–6, CCAC. Pg 178.1, Heidi Wastweet. Pg 179.1, CCAC. Pg 180.1, CCAC. Pg 181.1, Pg 181.2, Gary Marks. Pg 183.1, CCAC. Pg 184.1, Lawrence Brown. Pg 188.1–10, CCAC. Pg 189.1–10, CCAC. Pg 190.1–10, CCAC. Pg 191.1–9, CCAC. Pg 193.1, Emily S. Damstra. Pg 194.1, Emily S. Damstra. Pg 196.1, CCAC. Pg 197.1, Emily S. Damstra. Pg 199.1–3, Emily S. Damstra. Pg 200.1–12, USM. Page 201.1–5, USM. Pg 202.1, Michael Gaudioso. Pg 203.1, USM. Pg 204.1, Michael Gaudioso. Pg 205.1–2, USM. Pg 206.1–6, USM. Pg 206.7, APMEX. Pg 206.8, USM.

Chapter 8: Pg 210.1, HA. Pg 217.1–2, NGC. Pg 220.1, NGC. Pg 228.1, NGC. Pg 231.1, NGC. Pg 233.2, NGC. Pg 237.1, NGC. Pg 240.1, NGC. Pg 241.1, NGC. Pg 241.2, APMEX. Pg 247.1, NGC. Pg 253.1, NGC. Pg 257.1, NGC. Pg 259.1–2, NGC. Pg 261.1, NGC. Pg 262.1, NGC. Pg 263.1, NGC. Pg 264.1, NGC. Pg 266.1, NGC. Pg 267.1, NGC. Pg 269.2, NGC. Pg 271.1, NGC. Pg 272.2, NGC. Pg 273.1, NGC. Pg 276.1, NGC. Pg 279.2, NGC. Pg 280.1, NGC. Pg 281.1, NGC. Pg 284.1, NGC. Pg 291.1, NGC. Pg 297.1, APMEX. Pg 306.1, PCGS. Pg 308.1, NGC. Pg 311.1, NGC. Pg 312.1, NGC. Pg 312.2, APMEX. Pg 313.1, USM. Pg 315.2, NGC. Pg 316.1, NGC. Pg 316.2, USM. Pg 317.1, NGC. Pg 319.1–2, NGC. Pg 320.1–2, USM. Pg 322.1, USM. Pg 323.1, PCGS. Pg 323.2, USM. Pg 324.1, PCGS. Pg 324.2, USM. Pg 325.1, USM. Pg 326.1, USM. Pg 328.1, NGC. Pg 329.1–2, USM. Pg 330.1–2, USM. Pg 331.1, USM. Pg 333.1, USM. Pg 334.1–2, USM. Pg 335.1–2, USM. Pg 336.1–2, USM. Pg 337.1, USM. Pg 337.2, APMEX. Pg 339.1–2, USM. Pg 340.1–2, USM.

INDEX

8 reales, 2, 3, 19, 20, 97
Albanese, John, 45, 358–359, 360
American Arts Commemorative
  Gold Medallions, 74–75
American Gold Eagles, vi, 36, 48,
  52, 62, 63, 76, 77, 79, 80, 81,
  82, 91, 92, 106, 116, 127, 140,
  144, 145, 146, 159, 163, 187,
  192, 195, 215, 219, 235, 239,
  241, 244, 249, 257, 259, 268,
  274–275, 330, 332, 342, 344,
  347
  Family of Eagles design, 76–77,
    82–83, 184–185, 192, 195
American Numismatic Association,
  iv, v, 26, 44, 78, 131, 148–149,
  150, 209, 213, 219, 227, 233,
  298, 304, 326, 333, 348, 352
  Numismatic Hall of Fame, v
American Numismatic Information
  Exchange, 46
American Numismatic Society, 65,
  71, 73, 149, 293
American Palladium Eagles, 72, 73,
  92, 108, 116, 145, 146
American Platinum Eagles, vi, 92,
  106, 116, 127, 145, 146, 185,
  246, 247, 249, 259
American Silver Eagles
  2014 design change discussions,
    175–182, 303, 304–305
  2021 design change discussion,
    182–192, 331
  collecting methods, 112–131
  finishes, iv, ix, x, 57, 102–105,
    117, 119, 129, 134, 135, 154,
    208, 244, 264, 274, 287,
    300–301, 346. See also bullion
    strikes, Burnished strikes,
    Enhanced Reverse Proof
    strikes, Enhanced Uncircu-
    lated strikes, Proof strikes, and
    Reverse Proof strikes
  flying eagle (Type II) design,
    125, 192, 195–199, 204, 206,
    207, 331, 332, 334, 335–337,
    339–340
  heraldic eagle (Type I) design, x,
    34, 61, 85, 119, 125, 174, 180,
    185, 192, 196, 206, 207, 208,
    331, 333–334. See also Chapter
    8 individual coin listings
  initial release, 46, 48–50, 52–54,
    55–57, 79–82, 90–92, 211,
    213–214, 241
  Mint sets, 57, 163, 165, 213,
    225, 233, 234, 235–236,

239–240, 241–242, 249, 255,
  256, 272, 273, 274–275, 277,
  280, 287, 289, 290–291, 292,
  293, 295–296, 297–298, 300,
  302–303, 305, 306, 312, 313,
  317, 320, 323, 324, 326, 329,
  331, 334, 337–338
  notched edge, 206, 331, 332
  novelty coins, 58, 128, 153
  reverse font change (2008), 102,
    160, 169, 280–281. See also
    varieties, 2008, Reverse of
    2007
ANACS, 14, 44, 122, 131, 149
ancient coins, 1–2
Andrew McNulty et al. v. Commissioner of Internal Revenue, 147
Anti-Counterfeiting Task Force
  and Education Foundation,
  150, 159
Antonucci, Steve, 101
APMEX, 59, 348
Authorized Purchasers, 36, 52, 55,
  90, 92–93, 117, 129, 151, 212,
  213, 214, 220, 286, 335
Baker, James, III, 79, 80, 82, 84, 90,
  91, 211
Balan, Paul C., 180–182
Bank Holding Act of 1970, 13
Barber, Charles E., 23, 65–67, 68,
  69
Barber, William, 24
Better Business Bureau, 148, 149,
  150, 344
Biden, Joe, 278, 321, 327, 331
Black Monday (1987), 45, 215
Bland-Allison Act, 7–8, 25
Blue Book, 44
Bowers & Merena, v, 244, 253
Bowers, Andrew, 135
Bowers, Q. David, iv–v, 261, 308,
  319
Breen, Walter, 69
Brenner, Victor David, 63, 65, 72,
  164
Bressett, Ken, 47, 125, 319, 333
Britannia (British bullion coin), 62,
  215, 342
Brown, Lawrence, 184
Brown, Michael, 79–82
Bugeja, Michael, 177
bullion coin programs, iv, vi, ix, x,
  5, 6, 17–18, 35, 48, 51, 52, 54,
  55–57, 58, 60, 61, 74, 76–78,
  90–92, 106–109, 112, 137,
  144, 157, 174, 175, 179, 180,
  182, 185, 187, 191, 208, 211,

212, 215, 239, 246, 247, 287,
  310, 321, 341, 342, 356
  75th Anniversary of the End of
    World War II gold coins,
    108–109
  400th Anniversary of the
    Mayflower gold coins, 108
  America the Beautiful silver
    bullion, 107–108, 286, 301,
    321
  American Buffalo .9999-Fine
    gold bullion coins, 106, 279,
    342
  American Liberty High Relief
    gold coins, 108, 181, 182, 185
  First Spouse $10 gold bullion
    coins, 106–107
  MMIX Ultra High Relief gold
    coins, 107, 283
Bullion DNA, 183–184
bullion market, U.S., 7, 8, 9, 10, 11,
  13, 14–15, 16, 26, 32, 35, 38,
  46, 47, 48, 57, 59, 61, 90–92,
  93, 115–116, 122, 124,
  126–127, 128, 129–130,
  134–135, 137, 139–142, 144,
  145–148, 151–154, 166, 217,
  222, 225, 228, 229, 230, 232,
  236, 240, 248, 253–254, 266,
  267, 269, 272, 284, 294, 295,
  305, 306, 307, 319, 328, 333,
  342, 343, 347, 351, 354, 358,
  360
bullion strikes, x, 50, 51, 52, 57, 61,
  99, 103, 104, 112, 115–116,
  117, 118, 119, 123, 124, 131,
  136–137, 152–153, 162, 163,
  164–166, 167, 168, 170, 172,
  207, 208, 209, 212, 213–214,
  217, 220, 222–223, 225–226,
  228, 231, 232, 233–234, 236,
  237, 240, 243, 244–245,
  247–248, 251, 253–254,
  256–257, 259, 261, 263–264,
  266, 269, 271, 272, 276–277,
  279–280, 281, 282, 284, 286,
  287, 288–289, 291, 292, 294,
  299–300, 305, 308–309,
  311–312, 315, 316, 319,
  322–323, 328–329, 333, 335,
  338, 339, 346
Burdette, Roger, 66, 67, 68
Burnished strikes, x, 104, 112, 116,
  117, 119, 153, 168, 169, 207,
  270, 272, 274, 275, 277,
  280–281, 284, 286, 289, 291,
  292, 294, 300, 305–306,

309–310, 312–313, 316, 319–320, 323, 329, 335, 338, 339, 346

Bush, George H.W., 218–219, 221, 227, 229, 328

Bush, George W., 30, 31, 255, 257, 258, 260, 263, 265, 267, 268, 275, 276, 278

Camire, David, 170, 350–351

Campbell, Randy, 158

Carter, Jimmy, 27, 37, 38, 39, 260

CDN Publishing, 131, 151–152, 347

Central States Numismatic Society, 46, 304

cents, 3, 63, 97, 261, 306, 307, 333
  Indian Head, 47
  Lincoln, iv, ix, 30, 47, 48, 63, 64, 65, 134, 145, 164, 207, 219, 239, 278, 279, 282, 283, 285, 286, 306, 313, 315, 333

certified coins, vii, 29, 44, 45, 46, 59, 113–114, 120, 121, 122, 123, 124, 125, 127, 129, 131, 149, 150, 154, 157, 158, 164, 170, 208, 212, 213, 214, 216, 217, 219, 222, 223, 231, 233, 256, 268, 277, 279, 301, 308, 309, 317, 346, 347, 350, 352, 358. See also Chapter 8 certification data charts

Citizens Coinage Advisory Committee, vi, 78, 100, 174, 175–191, 192, 197–198, 263, 304–305, 328

Citizens Commemorative Coinage Advisory Committee, 78, 230, 240, 263

Clinton, Bill, 30, 229, 232, 243, 246, 247, 250, 252, 321

Coin Box, 47

Coin Modernization, Oversight, and Continuity Act of 2010, 287

Coin World, 79, 83, 164, 170, 171, 182, 212, 213, 222, 258, 271, 290, 295, 301, 309, 325

COINage, 213, 341, 348, 353

Coinage Act of 1792, 6, 19, 97–98

Coinage Act of 1853, 6

Coinage Act of 1873, 7

Coinage Act of 1965, 11, 24, 27

Coinage Act of 1969, 12–13

COMEX, 15, 126, 342

Commemorative Coin Reform Act of 1996, 244, 250–251

commemorative coins, 13, 18, 19, 31, 40, 46, 47, 48, 72, 76, 79–80, 157, 165, 170, 175,

180, 187, 198, 200, 212, 216, 224, 229, 230, 237, 238, 240, 243, 244, 247, 250, 258, 263, 264, 267, 271, 276, 279, 282, 283, 304, 317, 318, 321, 322

Commission of Fine Arts, 26, 63, 65, 67, 72, 78, 84, 180, 187, 192, 197, 198

CONECA, 149

Congressional Gold Medals, 198, 200, 203, 205, 313

counterfeit coins and holders, 127, 139, 148, 154, 158–161, 174, 175, 180, 182, 318

COVID-19 pandemic, 45, 96–97, 100, 109–111, 122–123, 326–328, 331–333, 338

cull coins, viii, ix, 58, 153

Damstra, Emily S., x, 118, 119, 125, 192, 193–201, 203, 207, 331, 332, 335, 338

Dannreuther, John W., 308

David Lawrence Rare Coins, 151, 240

Davis, Doug, 159

de Francisci, Anthony, 9, 26, 63, 72

Diehl, Philip, 30, 163–164, 242, 246, 249, 251, 254

dimes, 6, 7, 9, 11–12, 23, 65, 66, 70, 108, 139, 178, 230, 333
  Liberty Head (Barber), 65, 68
  Mercury, 47, 63, 64, 65, 69, 72, 109, 164
  Roosevelt, 11, 207, 293, 322

Defense National Stockpile Center, 16, 17, 18, 35, 60, 61, 81, 96

Delaware Depository, 148, 344

dollars, 3–4, 19–34, 233, 293, 307, 333
  2021 centennial Morgan, 109, 111
  2021 centennial Peace, 109, 111
  Draped Bust, 21, 145, 253
  Eisenhower, 12–13, 27–28
  Flowing Hair, 4, 19–20, 299
  Gobrecht, 22–23
  "golden," 30–31, 200–201, 233, 247, 250, 253, 256, 257, 258, 267, 268, 275, 276, 277, 280, 282, 283, 293, 300, 305, 312, 313, 328
  Liberty Seated, 23, 24, 33, 34, 60
  Morgan, v, viii, 4, 5, 9, 19, 25, 32, 33–34, 35, 46, 48, 50, 59–60, 81, 118, 120, 224, 291, 308, 344

Peace, ix, 4, 5, 9, 19, 23, 26–27, 34, 35, 46, 63, 64, 81, 109, 111, 120, 157, 308
  silver dollars, vii, 4, 5, 7, 8, 9, 10, 12, 13, 19–34, 35, 36, 46, 48–50, 76, 81, 109, 111, 118, 120, 150, 165, 170, 185, 200, 201, 216, 251, 258, 291, 299, 304, 308, 318, 321, 322, 342
  Susan B. Anthony, 13, 28–29, 30, 32, 48, 233, 252, 253
  trade, 4, 7, 24–25, 82

double eagles, 44, 63, 64, 67, 74, 78, 83, 261, 276
  1907 Ultra High Relief, 107
  Saint-Gaudens, 44, 63, 64, 67, 79, 83, 150, 254, 261, 283, 288, 332, 344

Dow Jones Industrial Average, 215, 227, 243, 246, 250, 253, 270, 276, 298, 304, 311, 314, 318, 321, 327, 332, 343

eagles (coin denomination), 44, 63, 64, 78, 98, 164, 219
  Indian Head, 63, 64

Economic Recovery Tax Act of 1981, 39, 40, 143, 144

edge lettering, 31, 107, 119, 276, 283, 310, 311, 312, 313, 316

encapsulated coins, See certified coins

Enhanced Reverse Proof strikes, vii, x, 102, 105, 112, 116, 117, 119, 135, 153, 162, 166–167, 168, 324, 325

Enhanced Uncirculated strikes, 105, 112, 119, 168, 300–301, 302

error coins, 102, 117, 149, 153, 162, 170–173

Errorscope, 149

Everhart, Don, 179, 181, 304

Executive Order 6102, 9

exonumia, 58

Federal Reserve, 9, 42, 109, 278, 298, 307, 314, 333, 338

Federal Reserve Notes, 256, 295, 298

Feigenbaum, John, 151

Feltner, Steve, 113, 157, 158, 254

Fillmore, Millard, 6

Florida United Numismatists, 55–56, 136, 137, 158, 294, 310

flying eagle (Type II) design, 125, 192, 195–199, 204, 206, 207, 331, 332, 334, 335–337, 339–340

Ford, Gerald, 15, 37, 312

Fore, Henrietta Holsman, 101

Fraser, James Earl, 63, 65, 72, 106, 258, 279
Fraser, Laura Gardin, 72
Free Silver movement, 7–8
Frost (Busiek), Miley, 77, 82–83, 184, 192, 195
Gainesville Coins, 59, 134
Ganz, David L., 146, 345–346, 351–352
Garofalo, Michael, 14–15, 46, 55–57, 59, 126, 237, 245, 308, 325, 330, 348
Garrett, Jeff, 112, 115, 116, 128, 130, 134, 162, 167, 214, 238, 242, 245, 291, 296, 319
Gasparro, Frank, 27, 28, 279, 286
Gaudioso, Michael, 125, 201–205, 207, 338
Gibbs, William T., 309, 325
Gilkes, Paul, 182, 301
Gill, Sam, 184
Gobrecht, Christian, 22–23
Gold Bullion Coin Act of 1985, 55, 76, 77, 83
Gold Certificates, 9
gold rush, 6
Gold Standard Act of 1900, 8
Goldberg Auctioneers, 262
grading, x, 44, 47, 118, 129–131, 154, 157, 208–211
grading services, 14, 44–45, 59, 112, 114, 116, 120, 121, 123, 124, 125, 127, 129, 131, 149–150, 212–213, 216, 219, 289, 346, 350, 358–359. See also ANACS, ICG, PCGS, and NGC
GreatCollections, 217, 220, 242, 254, 256, 259, 264, 279, 284, 286
Greysheet, The, 46, 56, 57, 131, 146, 151, 347
half dimes, 6, 7
half dollars, x, 6, 7, 9, 11–12, 13, 23, 34, 40, 48, 51, 59, 62, 65, 66, 67, 68, 69, 70–71, 72, 76, 78, 83, 139, 165, 230, 304, 318, 333
  Kennedy, 11–12, 109, 216, 293, 303, 304, 322, 332, 333
  Liberty Head (Barber), 65, 68
  Liberty Seated, 6
  Liberty Walking, vii, x, 46, 63, 64, 66, 67, 68, 69, 70, 71, 72, 73, 84, 86, 109, 224, 344
half eagles, 22, 76, 78, 165, 216, 251, 304, 317, 318
  Classic Head, 22
  Indian Head, 63, 64

Hamilton, Alexander, 3, 4, 97
Harding, Warren G., 78
Harper, Dave, 76, 77
heraldic eagle (Type I) design, x, 34, 61, 85, 119, 125, 174, 180, 185, 192, 196, 206, 207, 208, 331, 333–334. See also Chapter 8 individual coin listings
Heritage Auctions, 221, 223, 226, 228, 231, 234, 245, 248, 251, 269, 271, 272, 277, 289
hoarding, 9, 10, 11, 14, 121, 128–129, 138
Hunt brothers, 13, 14–15, 16, 38
Independent Coin Graders, 122, 149, 158
Individual Retirement Accounts (IRAs), 54, 112, 137, 143–148, 252, 341–347, 353, 356, 357, 360
Industry Council for Tangible Assets, 145, 150, 318, 357, 358
insurance, 344, 348, 350, 351–352, 359–360
investment, v, vi–vii, ix, x, 6, 10, 15, 17, 32, 33, 34, 35, 36, 45–48, 50–54, 55, 59, 60, 75, 90, 112–113, 115, 116, 122–123, 130, 131, 133, 134–148, 151–154, 158–159, 162, 163, 166, 208, 212, 214, 215, 216, 218, 219, 221, 222, 223, 224–225, 229, 230, 231, 232, 236, 240, 244, 251, 254, 266, 269, 279, 284, 288, 299, 306, 307, 319, 322, 326, 327, 328, 333, 335, 341–347, 354, 356, 360
silver "stackers," v, 11, 35, 112, 133, 137–139, 145, 153, 154, 162, 345
Jansen, Erik, 175, 178
Janvier reducing lathe, 85, 89, 101, 102, 169, 203
Jefferson, Thomas, 3, 4, 97, 268, 270, 271
Johnson Matthey, 95
Jordan, Eric, 273, 290, 291
Kagin, Don, 78, 79, 347, 360
key dates, vi, x, 23, 25, 27, 115, 116, 117, 120, 151, 152, 153, 162–167, 237, 238, 243
  1995-W, vii, x, 60, 117, 118, 135, 136, 153, 162–164, 166, 167, 241–242, 243
  1996, bullion, x, 115, 153, 162, 164–166, 244–245

2019-S Enhanced Reverse Proof, x, 117, 153, 162, 166–167, 325
"Godless" dollars, 31, 276, 282
Kneass, William, 22
Kotlowski, Dean, 185
Krugerrands, 5, 15, 48, 74, 75, 76, 77, 79, 80, 145, 215, 342
labels, 113, 118, 120, 121–129, 149, 154, 309, 359
  autographed, 121, 125–126
  Early Release, 114, 121–122, 167, 268, 289
  Emergency Issue, 122–123, 124, 328
  First Strike, 121–122, 123, 167, 268, 277, 279, 284
  hoard, 128–129
  Initial Release, 122
  parenthetical mintmark, 124–125, 299, 286
  World Trade Center salvage, 126–129, 217, 223, 228, 233, 256
Legend Rare Coin Auctions, 151, 266
Libertad (Mexican bullion coin), 5, 35, 62, 75, 215, 218, 342
Liberty Coin Act, x, 18, 41, 55, 76, 78, 211
Liberty Walking design, vii, x, 34, 51, 52, 59, 62–71, 78–79, 81, 83, 85, 86, 109, 180, 206. See also half dollars, Liberty Walking
London Bullion Market Association, 93
Long Beach Expo, 46, 222
MacNeil, Hermon A., 63, 65
Maple Leaf (Canadian bullion coin), 6, 15, 75, 157, 182, 183, 215, 218, 220, 324, 326, 342
Marks, Gary, 178, 179, 180–182, 304
McClure, James, 16–18, 35, 81, 82
McCollum, Ellen, 110
Mercanti, John M., vi, x, 34, 61, 78, 79, 85, 88, 101–103, 118, 125, 126, 180, 185, 192, 204, 205, 207, 271, 286, 331, 332, 333, 334
Menna, Joseph, 101, 186, 205, 322
milk spots, 118, 154–158, 166, 210, 223, 237, 240, 245, 254, 259, 261
Millman, Everett, 59, 134, 144–145, 208
Minshull, Lee, 60, 126, 128, 135, 245, 291, 308, 330

Mint, U.S., 4, 5, 6, 7, 8, 9, 12, 13, 19, 22, 23, 26, 27, 29, 30, 31, 36, 40, 48, 50, 51, 52–54, 55–57, 58, 61, 62, 63, 65, 66, 69, 70, 74, 75, 76, 77, 78–79, 80–82, 83, 85, 90–92, 93, 94, 95–96, 97–99, 100–102, 103, 104, 105, 106–110, 111, 116, 117, 118, 119, 122–123, 124, 125–126, 128, 129, 132, 135, 143, 144, 146, 151, 152, 154–157, 158, 163–168, 169, 172–173, 175, 177, 179–180, 181–183, 184, 186, 187, 191–192, 194–195, 198, 201–205, 206, 211, 212, 213, 214, 216, 219, 223, 225, 226, 227, 228, 229, 230, 233, 234, 235, 237, 238, 239, 240, 241, 242, 243, 244, 246, 249, 251, 253, 254, 255, 256, 257, 258, 259, 261, 262, 263, 267, 269, 270, 271, 272, 273, 275, 277, 278, 279, 281, 282, 283, 284, 285, 286, 287, 288, 289, 290, 291, 292, 293, 295, 296, 297, 299, 301, 303, 304, 305, 306, 308, 309, 310, 312, 313, 315, 317, 318, 319, 321, 322, 323, 324, 325, 326, 327, 328, 329, 330, 333, 334, 335, 339
    Annual Report, 69–70, 90–92, 100
    Artistic Infusion Program, 78, 180, 183, 194, 195, 197
    Charlotte, 98
    Carson City, 23, 24, 25, 98
    Dahlonega, 98
    Denver, 9, 13, 23, 25, 26, 27, 28, 29, 30, 66, 67, 98, 99, 100, 102, 107, 117, 266
    Mint Police, 99–100
    New Orleans, 98
    Philadelphia, 9, 13, 22, 25, 26, 27, 29, 67, 98, 99, 117, 123, 163, 204, 229, 232, 233, 234, 235–236, 238, 242, 245, 248, 249, 251, 254, 257, 258, 259, 273, 274, 290, 292, 308–309, 311–312, 313, 315, 326, 328
    San Francisco, 9, 13, 25, 26, 27, 29, 36, 42, 81, 82, 90, 92, 98, 99, 117, 123, 124–125, 163, 168, 211, 213, 214, 27, 219, 220, 222, 223, 224, 226, 228, 231, 233, 237, 240, 244, 247, 251, 288–289, 291, 292, 294, 295, 296, 297, 298, 299, 305, 308, 311, 312, 315, 317, 320,
324, 325, 327, 328, 331, 334, 335, 336, 338, 340
    technology changes, 85, 100–103, 104, 105, 107, 119, 169, 304, 317
    West Point, 74, 90, 92, 95, 98, 99, 100, 108, 109, 110, 117, 123, 124, 155, 163, 168, 219, 220, 222, 225, 228, 231, 233, 235, 237, 240, 241, 244, 247, 251, 253, 256, 259, 261, 262, 263, 264, 266, 267, 269, 271, 272, 274, 25, 276, 277, 279, 280, 281, 284, 286, 287, 288, 289, 290, 291, 292, 294, 295, 299, 300, 301, 302–303, 305, 306, 308–309, 310, 311–312, 313, 315, 316, 318, 319, 320, 322, 323, 324, 326, 327, 328, 329, 330, 333, 334, 335, 336, 337, 339, 340
mintmarks, 29, 34, 57, 98, 99, 101, 104, 117, 123, 124–125, 168, 169, 172. See also Chapter 8 coin listings
"monster" boxes, 117, 123, 124–125, 128–129, 157, 289, 299, 309
Moran, Michael, 184, 187
Morgan, George T., 4, 5, 7, 25, 26, 65
Moy, Ed, 126
National Coin & Bullion Association, 147, 150, 318, 346, 357
National Silver Dollar Roundtable, 150
nickels, ix, 178, 262, 333
    Buffalo, 47, 63, 64, 65, 106, 258, 279
    Jefferson, 207, 263, 270, 271
    Liberty Head, 244, 285
    Westward Journey, 264, 265–266, 268
Nixon, Richard, 8, 13, 27, 37, 41, 236, 312
novelty coins, 58, 128, 153
Numismatic Conservation Service, 350
Numismatic Guaranty Company, 14, 25, 44–45, 114, 118, 121–122, 123, 124, 125, 128, 131, 150, 157, 158, 170, 208, 216, 268, 292, 299, 346, 350–351, 358. See also Chapter 8 coin certification data
Numismatic Literary Guild, v, 276
Numismatic News, 76, 213, 222, 273, 291, 296
Numismatist, The, 148, 149, 213, 268
NYMEX, 342
Obama, Barack, 278, 282, 285, 287, 292, 298, 313, 322
Olson, Michael, 177
Panda (Chinese bullion coin), 5–6, 35, 215, 342
Panic of 1873, 7
Perez, Patrick Ian, 131, 151–152
Philharmonic (Austrian bullion coin), 62, 215
Pittman Act, 8–9, 25, 26
planchet creation process, 93–94, 95–97, 98–99, 111
Pope, Donna, 36, 48, 54, 56, 78, 79–80, 91
Power, Tom, 95–97
Pratt, Bela Lyon, 63
privy marks, 135, 161, 168–169, 330, 333
Professional Coin Grading Service, 14, 20, 21, 25, 29, 44–45, 46, 113, 118, 121, 123, 125, 127, 128, 130, 131, 150, 157, 164, 170, 208, 212, 213, 216, 217, 223, 228, 231, 244, 256, 268, 292, 299, 346, 349–350, 358, 359. See also Chapter 8 coin certification data
Professional Numismatists Guild, v, 150, 159
Proof strikes, iv, vi, vii, ix, x, 13, 21, 23, 24, 25, 26, 27, 28, 29, 34, 36, 50, 52, 54, 57, 60, 208, 209–210, 212, 214–215, 216, 217–218, 220–221, 223, 226, 228–229, 230, 231, 232, 233, 234, 235, 236, 238239–240, 241–243, 245–246, 248, 249, 251–252, 254–255, 257, 259–260, 262, 264, 266, 269, 270–271, 272–273, 274, 277–278, 281, 284, 286, 287, 290–291, 292, 293, 294, 295–296, 297, 298, 301–302, 306, 310, 312, 313, 316–317, 320, 322, 323–325, 329–331, 334, 336–338, 340, 342, 346, 347
quarter eagles, 22, 78
    Classic Head, 22
    Indian Head, 63, 64
quarters, 6, 7, 9, 11, 23, 29, 107, 111, 139, 175, 178, 230, 333
    50 States and Territories, 240, 244, 247, 252, 253, 257, 258, 260, 261, 262, 264, 266, 267, 268, 271, 279, 282, 283

America the Beautiful, vi, 107, 179, 198, 199, 200, 285, 286, 293, 321, 322, 330

American Women, 198, 199, 201

Bicentennial, 13, 230, 233

Liberty Head (Barber) quarter, 65, 68, 164

Standing Liberty, 63, 65, 109, 164

Washington, 11, 207, 219, 238, 321, 322

Washington Crossing the Delaware, 205

raw coins, *See* uncertified coins

Reagan, Nancy, 42, 44, 311

Reagan, Ronald, x, 16–18, 38–41, 43, 44, 48, 50, 55, 74, 76, 77, 143, 212, 215, 218, 312, 313, 342

Red Book, vi, 44, 82, 109, 112, 125, 151, 152, 233, 244, 247, 266, 271, 276, 279, 283–284, 286, 288, 293, 299, 304, 308, 315, 319, 322, 328, 333

registry sets, x, 25, 59, 60, 113, 114, 117, 118, 121, 130, 131, 208, 214, 218, 254

Reiter, Ed, 48, 68, 76, 77, 79, 84, 213

Renaissance of American Coinage, 63–64, 68

retirement, 33, 141–148, 341–347, 353, 356, 359, 360. *See also* Individual Retirement Accounts (IRAs)

Reverse Proof strikes, 102, 104, 105, 112, 116, 119, 135, 153, 168, 238, 270, 273, 274, 290–291, 292, 295, 296, 297, 302, 313, 324, 334, 337

Rittenhouse, David, 4, 20, 315

Roosevelt, Franklin D., 9

Roosevelt, Theodore, 63

Rosen, Maurice, 136

Rosenberg, David, 350

Royal Canadian Mint, 15, 57, 157, 182–183, 193–195, 326

Ryder, David, 110–111, 125, 126, 182, 191–192, 206, 325, 326, 333, 335

Saint-Gaudens, Augustus, 62–63, 65, 67, 71, 79, 83, 84, 107, 184, 254, 283

Salmon, Robin, 184, 187

savings-and-loan crisis, 215, 221

Scarinci, Donald, 178, 179, 183, 186, 187

Schechter, Scott, 162, 213–214, 238, 242, 245, 291, 296

set-building, 114–119. *See also* American Silver Eagles, collecting methods

date sets, x, 115–116, 131, 244

inclusive series sets, 115, 116–118

type sets, viii, 24, 25, 115, 118–119, 132, 225

Sherman Silver Purchase Act, 8

Silver Certificates, ix, 8, 10

silver mining, 7, 8, 9, 10, 16, 17, 25, 26, 81, 82, 93–94

Silver Purchase Act of 1934, 26–27

Silver Thursday (1980), 14

slabbed coins, *See* certified coins

Sotheby's, 261, 332

South Dakota v. Wayfair, 356–358

Sower, 67–68

Spaleck machine, 104

spot prices, x, 6, 25, 109, 112, 115, 116, 151, 152–153, 347

Stack's Bowers Galleries, v, 20, 21, 135, 151, 261, 333, 335

Statue of Liberty-Ellis Island Commemorative Coin Act, *See* Liberty Coin Act

Stevens-Sollman, Jeanne, 178, 185–187

storage, coin, 113, 114, 116, 131–133, 138, 140, 142, 144–145, 146, 147, 223, 242, 245, 344–345, 350, 351, 352, 360. *See also* Whitman folders

Sullivan, Jon, 171

Sundman, David, 308

Sunshine Minting, 94–97

Support of American Eagle Silver Bullion Program Act, 61

Taft, William Howard, 64

talers, 2–3

Tax Equity and Fiscal Responsibility Act of 1982, 40

Thoreson, Troy, 124, 152, 241–242, 245, 274, 300–301

three-cent coins, 7

Together, A New Beginning, 76, 82–83. *See also,* American Gold Eagles, Family of Eagles design

toned coins, 115, 120, 136, 223, 225, 228, 233, 236, 245, 266

Travers, Scott, 130–131, 136–137, 140, 144, 154, 214, 351

Treasury, U.S., 7, 10, 11, 25, 28, 29, 30, 61, 62, 65, 75, 76, 77, 78, 79–81, 83, 84, 96, 100, 111, 144, 180, 181, 182, 211, 244, 247, 250, 53, 308, 345, 347

Trump, Donald, 31, 11, 182, 310, 314, 321, 327, 351

two-cent coins, 7

Tucker, Dennis, vi, vi 100, 184–187, 299, 308

type sets, viii, 24, 25, 115, 118–119, 132, 225

uncertified coins, vii, 59, 112, 113–114, 116, 117, 1233, 124, 129, 136, 140, 158, 164, 241, 350, 352, 359

Union Soldiers and Sailors, 68–69, 71, 72

United States Dollar Coin Act of 1997, 30, 247, 250

Uram, Thomas, 179, 183, 186, 187

varieties, x, 22, 25, 28, 29, 34, 47, 59, 102, 116, 117, 118, 119, 129, 149, 153, 162, 164, 169–170, 238, 239, 264, 266, 267, 268, 280, 281

1992-S, Doubled Die Reverse, 169

2008-W Burnished, Reverse of 2007, x, 102, 117, 119, 153, 169, 280–281

2011 Bullion, Doubled Die Obverse, 170

Vermeule, Cornelius, III, 71–72

Washington, D.C., 39, 40, 62, 71, 77, 81, 83, 99, 100, 126, 169, 182, 192, 258, 260, 283, 330, 331, 334

Washington, George, 3, 4, 13, 30, 40, 48, 62, 87, 175, 179, 251, 276

Wastweet, Heidi, 178

Weinman, Adolph A., x, 34, 51, 59, 62, 63, 65–67, 68–69, 70, 71–73, 78, 79, 83, 84, 85, 108, 109, 178, 180, 181, 184, 198, 204, 206

Weinman, Robert, 68, 69, 72, 84

Whitman folders, ix, 14, 44, 47, 115, 120, 131, 354

world coins, ix, 2–3, 5–6, 7, 15, 19, 20, 24, 35, 48, 62, 97, 127, 149, 157, 193, 215, 240, 252, 257, 258, 260, 261

Young, Jack, 160–161